Chapters of Opera

Henry Edward Krehbiel

Alpha Editions

This edition published in 2021

ISBN : 9789354849961

Design and Setting By
Alpha Editions
www.alphaedis.com
Email – info@alphaedis.com

As per information held with us this book is in Public Domain. This book is a reproduction of an important historical work. Alpha Editions uses the best technology to reproduce historical work in the same manner it was first published to preserve its original nature. Any marks or number seen are left intentionally to preserve its true form.

PREFACE

The making of this book was prompted by the fact that with the season 1907-08 the Metropolitan Opera House in New York completed an existence of twenty-five years. Through all this period at public representations I have occupied stall D-15 on the ground floor as reviewer of musical affairs for The New York Tribune newspaper. I have, therefore, been a witness of the vicissitudes through which the institution has passed in a quarter-century, and a chronicler of all significant musical things which were done within its walls. I have seen the failure of the artistic policy to promote which the magnificent theater was built; the revolution accomplished by the stockholders under the leadership of Leopold Damrosch; the progress of a German régime, which did much to develop tastes and create ideals which, till its coming, were little-known quantities in American art and life; the overthrow of that régime in obedience to the command of fashion; the subsequent dawn and development of the liberal and comprehensive policy which marked the climax of the career of Maurice Grau as an operatic director, I have witnessed since then, many of the fruits of wise endeavor and astute management frittered away by managerial incapacity and greed, and fad and fashion come to rule again, where for a brief, but eventful period, serious artistic interest and endeavor had been dominant.

The institution will enter upon a new régime with the season 1908-09. The time, therefore, seemed fitting for a review of the twenty-five years that are past. The incidents of this period are fixed; they may be variously viewed, but they cannot be changed. They belong to history, and to a presentation of that history I have devoted most of the pages which follow. I have been actuated in my work by deep seriousness of purpose, and have tried to avoid everything which could not make for intellectual profit, or, at least, amiable and illuminative entertainment.

The chapters which precede the more or less detailed history of the Metropolitan Opera House (I-VII) were written for the sake of the light which they shed on existing institutions and conditions, and to illustrate the development of existing taste, appreciation, and interest touching the lyrical drama. To the same end much consideration has been paid to significant doings outside the Metropolitan Opera House since it has been the chief domicile of grand opera in New York. Especial attention has been given for obvious reasons to the two seasons of opera at Mr. Hammerstein's Manhattan Opera House.

H. E. KREHBIEL.

Blue Hill, Maine, the Summer of 1908.

AUTHOR'S NOTE TO THIRD EDITION

For the purposes of a new and popular edition of this book, the publishers asked the author to continue his historical narrative, his record of performances, and his critical survey of the operas produced at the two chief operatic institutions of New York, from the beginning of the season 1908-1909 down to the close of the season 1910-1911. This invitation the author felt compelled to decline for several reasons, one of which (quite sufficient in itself), was that he had already undertaken a work of great magnitude which would occupy all his working hours during the period between the close of the last season and the publication of this edition.

Thereupon the publishers, who seemed to place a high valuation on the historical element in the book, suggested that the record of performances at least be brought up to date even if the criticism of new operas and the discussion of the other incidents of the season—such as the dissensions between the directors of the Metropolitan Opera House, the rivalry between them and the director of the Manhattan, the quarrels with artists, the successes achieved by some operas and the failure suffered by others—be postponed for the present at least for want of time on the part of the author to carry on the work on the scale of the original edition.

It was finally agreed that the author should supply the record for the period intervening between the appearance of the first edition of "Chapters of Opera" and the present publication by revised excerpts from the annual summaries of the activities of the seasons in question published by him in the New York Tribune, of which newspaper he has had the honor of being the musical critic for thirty years past. For the privilege of using this material the author is deeply beholden to the Tribune Association and the editor, Hart Lyman, Esq. The record may be found in the Appendices after the last chapter.

H. E. KREHBIEL.

Blue Hill, Maine, Summer of 1911.

CHAPTER I
INTRODUCTION OF OPERA IN NEW YORK

Considering the present state of Italian opera in New York City (I am writing in the year of our Lord 1908), it seems more than a little strange that its entire history should come within the memories of persons still living. It was only two years ago that an ancient factotum at the Metropolitan Opera House died who, for a score of years before he began service at that establishment, had been in various posts at the Academy of Music. Of Mr. Arment a kindly necrologist said that he had seen the Crowd gather in front of the Park Theater in 1825, when the new form of entertainment effected an entrance in the New World. I knew the little old gentleman for a quarter of a century or more, but though he was familiar with my interest in matters historical touching the opera in New York, he never volunteered information of things further back than the consulship of Mapleson at the Academy. Moreover, I was unable to reconcile the story of his recollection of the episode of 1825 with the circumstances of his early life. Yet the tale may have been true, or the opera company that had attracted his boyish attention been one that came within the first decade after Italian opera had its introduction.

Concerning another's recollections, I have not the slightest doubt. Within the last year Mrs. Julia Ward Howe, entertaining some of her relatives and friends with an account of social doings in New York in her childhood, recalled the fact that she had been taken as a tiny miss to hear some of the performances of the Garcia Troupe, and, if I mistake not, had had Lorenzo da Ponte, the librettist of Mozart's "Nozze di Figaro" and "Don Giovanni" pointed out to her by her brother. This brother was Samuel Ward, who enjoyed the friendship of the old poet, and published recollections of him not long after his death, in The New York Mirror. For a score of years I have enjoyed the gentle companionship at the opera of two sisters whose mother was an Italian pupil of Da Ponte's, and when, a few years ago, Professor Marchesan, of the University of Treviso, Italy, appealed to me for material to be used in the biography of Da Ponte, which he was writing, I was able, through my gracious and gentle operatic neighbors, to provide him with a number of occasional poems written, in the manner of a century ago, to their mother, in whom Da Ponte had awakened a love for the Italian language and literature. This, together with some of my own labors in uncovering the American history of Mozart's collaborator, has made me feel sometimes as if I, too, had dwelt for a brief space in that Arcadia of which I purpose to gossip in this chapter, and a few others which are to follow it.

There may be other memories going back as far as Mrs. Howe's, but I very much doubt if there is another as lively as hers on any question connected with social life in New York fourscore years ago. Italian opera was quite as aristocratic when it made its American bow as it is now, and decidedly more exclusive. It is natural that memories of it should linger in Mrs. Howe's mind for the reason that the family to which she belonged moved in the circles to which the new form of entertainment made appeal. A memory of the incident which must have been even livelier than that of Mrs. Howe's, however, perished in 1906, when Manuel Garcia died in London, in his one hundred and first year, for he could say of the first American season of Italian opera what Æneas said of the siege of Troy, "All of which I saw, and some of which I was." Manuel Garcia was a son of the Manuel del Popolo Vicente Garcia, who brought the institution to our shores; he was a brother of our first prima donna, she who then was only the Signorina Garcia, but within a lustrum afterward was the great Malibran; and he sang in the first performance, on November 29, 1825, and probably in all the performances given between that date and August of the next year, when the elder Garcia departed, leaving the Signorina, as Mme. Malibran, aged but eighteen, to develop her powers in local theaters and as a chorister in Grace Church. Of this and other related things presently.

In the sometimes faulty and incomplete records of the American stage to which writers on musical history have hitherto been forced to repair, 1750 is set down as the natal year for English ballad opera in America. It is thought that it was in that year that "The Beggar's Opera" found its way to New York, after having, in all probability, been given by the same company of comedians in Philadelphia in the middle of the year preceding. But it is as little likely that these were the first performances of ballad operas on this side of the Atlantic as that the people of New York were oblivious of the nature of operatic music of the Italian type until Garcia's troupe came with Rossini's "Barber of Seville," in 1825. There are traces of ballad operas in America in the early decades of the eighteenth century, and there can exist no doubt at all that French and Italian operas were given in some form, perhaps, as a rule, in the adapted form which prevailed in the London theaters until far into the nineteenth century, before the year 1800, in the towns and cities of the Eastern seaboard, which were in most active communication with Great Britain, I quote from an article on the history of opera in the United States, written by me for the second edition of "Grove's Dictionary of Music and Musicians":

Among French works Rousseau's "Pygmalion" and "Devin du Village," Dalayrac's "Nina" and "L'Amant Statue," Monsigny's "Déserteur," Grétry's "Zémire et Azor," "Fausse Magie" and "Richard Coeur de Lion" and others, were known in Charleston, Baltimore, Philadelphia, and New York in the last decade of the eighteenth century. There were traces, too, of Pergolese's "Serva padrona," and it seems more than likely that an "opera in three acts," the text adapted by Colman, entitled "The Spanish Barber; or, The Futile Precaution," played in Baltimore, Philadelphia, and New York, in 1794, was Paisiello's "Barbiere di Siviglia." From 1820 to about 1845 more than a score of the Italian, French, and German operas, which made up the staple of foreign repertories, were frequently performed by English singers. The earliest of these singers were members of the dramatic companies who introduced theatrical plays in the colonies. They went from London to Philadelphia, New York, Williamsburg (Va.), and Charleston (S. C.), but eventually established their strongest and most enduring foothold in New York.

Accepting the 1750 date as the earliest of unmistakable records for a performance of "The Beggar's Opera" in New York, the original home of opera here was the Nassau Street Theater—the first of two known by that name. It was a two-storied house, with high gables. Six wax lights were in front of the stage, and from the ceiling dangled a "barrel hoop," pierced by half a dozen nails on which were spiked as many candles. It is not necessary to take the descriptions of these early playhouses as baldly literal, nor as indicative of something like barbarism. The "barrel hoop" chandelier of the old theater in Nassau street was doubtless only a primitive form of the chandeliers which kept their vogue for nearly a century after the first comedians sang and acted at the Nassau Street Theater. Illuminating gas did not reach New York till 1823, and "a thousand candles" was put forth as an attractive feature at a concert in the American metropolis as late as 1845. "The Beggar's Opera" was only twenty years old when the comedians sent to the colonies by William Hallam, under the management of his brother, Lewis, produced it, yet the historic Covent Garden Theater, in which it first saw the stage lights (candles they were, too), would scarcely stand comparison with the most modest of the metropolitan theaters nowadays. Its audience-room was only fifty-four or fifty-five feet deep; there were no footlights, the stage being illuminated by four hoops of candles, over which a crown hung from the borders. The orchestra held only fifteen or twenty musicians, though it was in this house that Handel produced his operas and oratorios; the boxes "were flat in front and had twisted double branches for candles fastened to the plaster. There were pedestals on each side of the boards, with elaborately-painted figures of Tragedy and Comedy thereon." Hallam's actors went first to Williamsburg, Va., but were persuaded to change their home to New York in the summer of 1753, among other things by the promise that they would find a "very fine 'Playhouse Building'" here. Nevertheless, when Lewis Hallam came he found the fine playhouse unsatisfactory, and may be said to have inaugurated the habit or custom, or whatever it may be called, followed by so many managers since, of beginning his enterprise by erecting a new theater. The old one in Nassau Street was torn down, and a new one built on its site. It was promised that it should be "very fine, large, and commodious," and it was built between June and September, 1753; how fine, large, and commodious it was may, therefore, be imagined. A year later, the German Calvinists, wanting a place of worship, bought the theater, and New York was without a playhouse until a new one on Cruger's Wharf was built by David Douglass, who had married Lewis Hallam's widow, Hallam having died in Jamaica, in 1755. This was abandoned in turn, and Mr. Douglass built a second theater, this time in Chapel Street. It cost $1,625, and can scarcely have been either very roomy or very ornate. Such as it was, however, it was the home of the drama in all its forms, save possibly the ballad opera, until about 1765, and was the center around which a storm raged which culminated in a riot that wrecked it.

The successor of this unhappy institution was the John Street Theater, which was opened toward the close of the year 1767. There seems to have been a period of about fifteen years during which the musical drama was absent from the amusement lists, but this house echoed, like its earliest predecessors, to the strains of the ballad opera which "made Gay rich and Rich gay." "The Beggar's Opera" was preceded, however, by "Love in a Village," for which Dr. Arne wrote and compiled the music; and Bickerstaff's "Maid of the Mill" was also in the repertory. In 1774 it was officially recommended that all places of amusement be closed. Then followed the troublous times of the Revolution, and it was not until twelve years afterward—that is, till 1786—that English Opera resumed its sway. "Love in a Village" was revived, and it was followed by "Inkle and Yarico," an arrangement of Shakespeare's "Tempest," with Purcell's music, "No Song, No Supper," "Macbeth," with Locke's music, McNally's comic opera "Robin Hood," and other works of the same character; in fact, it may safely be said that few, if any, English operas, either with original music or music adapted from the ballad tunes of England, were heard in London without being speedily brought to New York and performed here. In the John Street Theater, too, they were listened to by George Washington, and the leader of the orchestra, a German named Pfeil, whose name was variously spelled Fyle, File, Files, and so on, produced that "President's March," the tune of which was destined to become associated with "Hail Columbia," to the words of which it was adapted by Joseph Hopkinson, of Philadelphia. On January 29, 1798, a new playhouse was opened. This was the Park Theater. A musical piece entitled "The Purse, or American Tar," was on the program of the opening performance, and for more than a score of years the Park Theater played an important rôle in local operatic history. For a long term English operas of both types held the stage, along with the drama in all its forms, but in 1819 an English adaptation of Rossini's "Barber of Seville"—the opera which opened the Italian régime six years later—was heard on its stage, and two years after that Henry Rowley Bishop's arrangement of Mozart's "Marriage of Figaro." At the close of the season of 1820 the Park Theater was destroyed by fire, to the great loss of its owners, one of whom was John Jacob Astor. On its site was erected the new Park Theater, which was the original home of Italian opera, performed in its original tongue, and in the Italian manner, though only a small minority of the performers were Italians by birth.

Garcia was a Spaniard, born in Seville. Richard Grant White, writing in The Century Magazine for March, 1882, calls him a "Spanish Hebrew," on what authority I am unable to guess. Not only was Manuel Garcia, the elder, a chorister in the Cathedral of Seville at the age of six, but it seems as likely as not that he came of a family of Spanish church musicians who had made their mark for more than fifty years before the father of Malibran was born. But it is a habit with some writers to find Hebrew blood in nearly all persons of genius.

The new Park Theater was looked upon as a magnificent playhouse in its day, and it is a pity that Mr. White, writing about it when it was a quarter of a century old, should have helped to spread the erroneous notion that it was quite unworthy of so elegant a form of entertainment as Garcia brought into it. It remained a fashionable house through all its career or at least for a long time after it gave refuge to the Italian muse, though it may not have been able to hold one of its candles to the first house built especially to house that muse eight years later. The barrel hoop of the first New York theater gave way to "three chandeliers and patent oil lamps, the chandeliers having thirty-five lights each." Mr. White's description of this house after it had seen about a quarter of a century's service is certainly uninviting. Its boxes were like pens for beasts. "Across them were stretched benches consisting of a mere board covered with faded red moreen, a narrower board, shoulder high, being stretched behind to serve for a back. But one seat on each of the three or four benches was without even this luxury, in order that the seat itself might be raised upon its hinges for people to pass in. These sybaritic inclosures were kept under lock and key by a fee-expecting creature, who was always half drunk, except when he was wholly drunk. The pit, which has in our modern theater become the parterre (or, as it is often strangely called, the parquet), the most desirable part of the house, was in the Park Theater hardly superior to that in which the Jacquerie of old stood upon the bare ground (par terre), and thus gave the place its French name. The floor was dirty and broken into holes; the seats were bare, backless benches. Women were never seen in the pit, and, although the excellence of the position (the best in the house) and the cheapness of admission (half a dollar) took gentlemen there, few went there who could afford to study comfort and luxury in their amusements. The place was pervaded with evil smells; and, not uncommonly, in the midst of a performance, rats ran out of the holes in the floor and across into the orchestra. This delectable place was approached by a long, underground passage, with bare, whitewashed walls, dimly lighted, except at a sort of booth, at which vile fluids and viler solids were sold. As to the house itself, it was the dingy abode of dreariness. The gallery was occupied by howling roughs, who might have taken lessons in behavior from the negroes who occupied a part of this tier, which was railed off for their particular use."

This was the first home of Italian opera, strictly speaking. It had long housed opera in the vernacular, and remained to serve as the fortress of the English forces when the first battles were fought between the champions of the foreign exotic and the entertainment which had been so long established as to call itself native. Its career came to an end in 1848, when, like its predecessor and successor, it went up in flames and smoke.

Presently I shall tell about the houses which have been built in New York especially for operatic uses, but before then some attention ought to be given to several other old theaters which had connection with opera in one or another of its phases. One of these was the New York Theater, afterward called the Bowery, and known by that name till a comparatively recent date. The walls of this theater echoed first to the voice of Malibran, when put forth in the vernacular of the country of which fate seemed, for a time, to have decreed that she should remain a resident. This was immediately after the first season of Italian opera at the Park Theater. The New York Theater was then new, having been built in 1826. Malibran had begun the study of English in London before coming to New York with her father; and she continued her studies with a new energy and a new purpose after the departure of her father to Mexico had left her apparently stranded in New York with a bankrupt and good-for-nothing husband to support. She made her first essay in English opera with "The Devil's Bridge," and followed it up with "Love in a Village." English operas, whether of the ballad order or with original music, were constructed in principle on the lines of the German Singspiel and French opéra comique, all the dialogue being spoken; and Malibran's experience at the theater and Grace Church, coupled with her great social popularity, must have made a pretty good Englishwoman of her. "It is rather startling," says Mr. White, in the article already alluded to, "to think of the greatest prima donna, not only of her day, but of modern times—the most fascinating woman upon the stage in the first half of the nineteenth century—as singing the soprano parts of psalm tunes and chants in a small town then less known to the people of London and Paris and Vienna than Jeddo is now. Grace Church may well be pardoned for pride in a musical service upon the early years of which fell such a crown of glory, and which has since then been guided by taste not always unworthy of such a beginning." Malibran's performances at the New York Theater were successful and a source of profit, both to the manager and M. Malibran, to whom, it is said, a portion of the receipts were sent every night.

Three other theaters which were identified with opera more or less came into the field later, and by their names, at least, testified to the continued popularity which a famous English institution had won a century before, and which endured until that name could be applied to the places that bore it only on the "lucus a non lucendo" principle. These were the theaters of Richmond Hill, Niblo's, and Castle Garden. The Ranelagh Gardens, which John Jones opened in New York, in June, 1765, and the Vauxhall Gardens, opened by Mr. Samuel Francis, in June, 1769, were planned more or less after their English prototypes. Out-of-doors concerts were their chief musical features, fireworks their spectacular, while the serving of refreshments was relied on as the principal source of profit. Richmond Hill had in its palmy days been the villa home of Aaron Burr, and its fortunes followed the descending scale like those of its once illustrious master. Its site was the neighborhood of what is now the intersection of Varick and Charlton streets. After passing out of Burr's hands, but before his death, the park had become Richmond Hill Gardens, and the mansion the Richmond Hill Theater, both of somewhat shady reputation, which was temporarily rehabilitated by the response which the fashionable elements of the city's population made to an appeal made by a season of Italian opera, given in 1832. The relics of Niblo's Garden have disappeared as completely as those of Richmond Hill, but its site is still fresh in the memory of those whose theatrical experiences go back a quarter of a century. They must be old, however, who can recall enough verdure in the vicinity of Broadway and Prince Street to justify the name maintained by the theater to which for many years entrance was gained through a corridor of the Metropolitan Hotel. Three-quarters of a century ago Niblo's Garden was a reality. William Niblo, who built it and managed it with consummate cleverness, had been a successful coffee-house keeper downtown. Its theater opened refreshingly on one side into the garden (as the Terrace Garden Theater, at Third Avenue and Fifty-eighth Street does to-day), where one could eat a dish of ice cream or sip a sherry cobbler in luxurious shade, if such were his prompting, while play or pantomime went merrily on within. Writing of it in 1855 Max Maretzek, who, as manager of the Astor Place Opera House, had suffered from the rivalry of Niblo and his theater, said:

The Metropolitan Hotel, Niblo's Theater, stores and other buildings occupy the locality. Of the former garden nothing remains save the ice cream and drinking saloons attached to the theater. These take up literally as much room in the building as its stage does, and prove that its proprietor has not altogether overlooked the earlier vocation which laid the foundation of his fortune. The name by which he calls it has never changed. It was Niblo's Garden when loving couples ate their creams or drank their cobblers under the shadow of the trees. It is Niblo's Garden now, when it is turned into a simple theater and hedged in with houses. Nay, in the very bills which are circulated in the interior of the building during the performances you may find, or might shortly since have found, such an announcement as the following, appearing in large letters:

"Between the second and third acts"—or, possibly, it may run thus when opera is not in the ascendant—"after the conclusion of the first piece an intermission of twenty minutes takes place, for a promenade in the garden."

You will, I feel certain, admit that this is a marvelously delicate way of intimating to a gentleman who may feel "dry" (it is the right word, is it not?) that he will find the time to slake his thirst.

When he returns and his lady inquires where he has been he may reply, if he wills it:

"Promenading in the garden."

It is not plain from Mr. White's account whether or not his memory reached back to the veritable garden of Mr. Niblo, but his recollections of the theater were not jaundiced like those of Mr. Maretzek, but altogether amiable. Speaking of the performances of the Shireff, Seguin, and Wilson company of English opera singers, who came to New York in 1838, he says:

Miss Shireff afterward appeared at Niblo's Garden, which was on the corner of Broadway and Prince Street, where the Metropolitan Hotel now stands. Here she performed in Auber's "Masked Ball" and other light operas (all, of course, in English), singing in a theater that was open on one side to the air; for Niblo's was a great place of summer entertainment. It was a great New York "institution" in its day—perhaps the greatest and most beneficent one of its sort that New York has ever known. It may be safely said that most of the elder generation of New Yorkers now living [this was written in 1881] have had at Niblo's Garden the greatest pleasure they have ever enjoyed in public. There were careless fun and easy jollity; there whole families would go at a moment's warning to hear this or that singer, but most of all, year after year, to see the Ravels—a family of pantomimists and dancers upon earth and air, who have given innocent, thoughtless, side-shaking, brain-clearing pleasure to more Americans than ever relaxed their sad, silent faces for any other performers. The price of admission here was fifty cents, no seats reserved; "first come, first served."

Last of all there was Castle Garden. Children of to-day can remember when it was still the immigrants' depot, which it had been for half a century. Tradition says that it was built to protect New York City from foreign invasion, not to harbor it; but as a fortress it must have suffered disarmament quite early in the nineteenth century. It is now an aquarium, and as such has returned to its secondary use, which was that of a place of entertainment. In 1830 and about that day it was a restaurant, but for the sale only of ice cream, lemonade, and cakes. You paid a shilling to go in— this to restrict the patronage to people of the right sort—and your ticket was redeemable on the inside in the innocent fluids and harmless solids aforementioned. A wooden bridge, flanked by floating bathhouses, connected the castle with the garden—i.e., Battery Park. North and east, in lower Broadway and Greenwich Street, were fashionable residences, whose occupants enjoyed the promenade under the trees, which was the proper enjoyment of the day, as much as their more numerous, but less fortunate fellow citizens. There balloons went up by day, and rockets and bombs by night, and there, too, the brave militia went on parade. To Mr. White we owe the preservation of a poetical description written by Frederick Cozzens in an imitation of Spenser's "Sir Clod His Undoinge":

   With placket lined, with joyous heart he hies
 To where the Battery's Alleys, cool and greene,
 Amid disparted Rivers daintie lies
 With Fortresse brown and spacious Bridge betweene
 Two Baths, which there like panniers huge are seen:
 In shadie paths fair Dames and Maides there be
 With stalking Lovers basking in their eene,
 And solitary ones who scan the sea,
 Or list to vesper chimes of slumberous Trinity.

The operas performed in the first season of Italian opera in America by the Garcia troupe in the Park Theater 1825-1826, were "Il Barbiere di Siviglia," "Tancredi," "Il Turco in Italia," "La Cenerentola," and "Semiramide" by Rossini; "Don Giovanni" by Mozart; "L'Amante astuto" and "La Figlia del Aria" by Garcia.

CHAPTER II
EARLY THEATERS, MANAGERS, AND SINGERS

The first opera house built in New York City opened its doors on November 18, 1833, and was the home of Italian Opera for two seasons; the second, built eleven years later, endured in the service for which it was designed four years; the third, which marked as big an advance on its immediate predecessor in comfort and elegance as the first had marked on the ramshackle Park Theater described by Richard Grant White, was the Astor Place Opera House, built in 1847, and the nominal home of the precious exotic five years.

The Astor Place Opera House in its external appearance is familiar enough to the memory of even young New Yorkers, though, unlike its successor, the Academy of Music, at Fourteenth Street and Irving Place, it did not long permit its tarnished glories to form the surroundings of the spoken drama after the opera's departure. The Academy of Music weathered the operatic tempests of almost an entire generation, counting from its opening night, in 1854, to the last night on which Colonel J. H. Mapleson was its lessee, in 1886, and omitting the expiring gasps which the Italian entertainment made under Signor Angelo, in October, 1886, under Italo Campanini, in April, 1888, and the final short spasm under the doughty Colonel in 1896. The first Italian Opera House (that was its name) became the National Theater; the second, which was known as Palmo's Opera House, when turned over to the spoken drama, became Burton's Theater; the Astor Place Opera House became the Mercantile Library. The Academy of Music is still known by that name, though it is given over chiefly to melodrama, and the educational purpose which existed in the minds of its creators was only a passing dream. The Metropolitan Opera House has housed twenty-three regular seasons of opera, though it has been in existence for twenty-five seasons. Once the sequence of subscription seasons was interrupted by the damage done to the theater by fire; once by the policy of its lessees, Abbey & Grau, who thought that the public appetite for opera might be whetted by enforced abstention. The Manhattan Opera House is too young to enter into this study of opera houses, their genesis, growth, and decay, and the houses which Mr. Oscar Hammerstein built before it in Harlem and in West Thirty-Fourth Street, near Sixth Avenue, lived too brief a time in operatic service to deserve more than mention.

I am at a loss for data from which to evolve a rule, as I should like to do, governing the length of an opera house's existence in its original estate as the home of grand opera.

The conditions which produce the need are too variable and also too vague to be brought under the operation of any kind of law. At present the growth of wealth, the increase in population, and with that increase the rapid multiplication of persons desirous and able to enjoy the privileges of social display would seem to be determining factors, with the mounting costliness of the luxury as a deterrent. The last illustration of the operation of the creative impulse based on the growth of wealth and social ambition is found in the building of the Metropolitan Opera House, Mr. Hammerstein's enterprise being purely individual and speculative. The movement which produced the Metropolitan Opera House marked the decay of the old Knickerbocker régime, and its amalgamation with the newer order of society of a quarter of a century ago. This social decay, if so it can be called without offense, began—if Abram C. Dayton ("Last Days of Knickerbocker Life in New York") is correct—about 1840, and culminated with the Vanderbilt ball, in 1882, to which nearly all the leaders of the old Knickerbocker aristocracy accepted invitations. "During the third quarter of the nineteenth century," said The Sun's reviewer of Mr. Dayton's book, "sagacious and far-sighted Knickerbockers began to realize that as a caste they no longer possessed sufficient money to sustain social ascendency, and that it behooved them to effect an intimate alliance with the nouveaux riches." To this may be added that when there were but two decades of the century left it was made plain that the Academy of Music could by no possibility accommodate the two classes of society, old and new, which had for a number of years been steadily approaching each other.

There was an insufficiency of desirable boxes, and holders of seats of fashion were unwilling to surrender them to the newcomers. So the Metropolitan Opera House was built in 1883, and the vigor of the social opposition, coupled with popular appreciation of the new spirit, which came in with the German régime, gave the deathblow to the Academy, whose loss to fashion was long deplored by the admirers of its fine acoustic qualities and its effective architectural arrangements for the purposes of display.

The period is not so remote that we cannot trace the influences of fashion and society in the rise of the first Italian Opera House, if not in its fall. The Park Theater was still a fashionable playhouse when Garcia gave his season of Italian opera in it in 1825-26, but within a decade thereafter the conditions so graphically described by Mr. White, combined with new ambitions, which seem to have been inspired to a large extent by Lorenzo

Da Ponte, prompted a wish for a new theater: one specially adapted to opera. The new entertainment was recognized as a luxury, and it was no more than fitting that it be luxuriously and elegantly housed. It will be necessary to account for the potent influence of Da Ponte, who was only a superannuated poet and teacher of Italian language and literature, and this I hope to do presently; for the time being it is sufficient to say that it was he who persuaded the rich and cultured citizens of New York to build the Italian Opera House, which stood at the intersection of Church and Leonard streets. The coming of Garcia had filled Da Ponte, then already seventy-six years old, with dreams of a recrudescence of such activities as had been his in connection with Italian Opera in Vienna and London. He made haste to identify himself in an advisory capacity with the enterprise, persuaded Garcia to include "Don Giovanni" in his list of operas, although this necessitated the engagement of a singer not a member of the company, and had already brought his niece, who was a singer, from Italy, and the Italian composer Filippo Trajetta, from Philadelphia, when his dream of a permanent opera, for which he should write librettos, his friend compose music, and his niece sing, was dispelled by Garcia's departure for Mexico, and his subsequent return to Europe. For the next five years Da Ponte seems to have kept the waters of the operatic pool stirred, for there is general recognition in the records of the fact that to him was due the conception of the second experiment, although its execution was left to another, who was neither an American nor an Italian, but a Frenchman named Montressor. Like Garcia, he was his own tenor, which fact must have eased him of some of the vexations of management, though it added to its labors. We are told that Montressor succeeded in making himself personally popular. He had an agreeable voice, a tolerable style, and was favorably compared with Garcia, though this goes for little, inasmuch as Garcia was past his prime when he came here. Among his singers were Signorina Pedrotti, who created a great stir (though, I fancy, this was largely because of her beauty and the fact that the public, remembering the Signorina Garcia, wanted somebody to worship) and a basso named Fornasari.

Signorina Pedrotti effected her entrance on October 17, in a new opera, Mercadante's "Elisa e Claudio," which made the hit of the season, largely because of the infatuation of the public for the new singer. Mr. White gives us a description of her (from hearsay and the records) in his article published in The Century Magazine, of March, 1882:

Not much has been said of her, for she had sung only in Lisbon and in Bologna, and had little reputation. But she took musical New York off its feet again. She had a fine mezzo-soprano voice, of sympathetic quality; and although she was far from being a perfectly finished vocalist, she had an impressive dramatic style and a presence and a manner that enabled her to take possession of the stage. She was a handsome woman—tall, nobly formed, with brilliant eyes and a face full of expression. She carried the town by storm.

Like Malibran, and many another singer since, Fornasari made a fine reputation here, and was afterward "discovered" in Europe, where he rose to fame. He seems to have been of the tribe of lady-killers, of whom every opera company has boasted at least one ever since opera became a fashion—which is only another way of saying ever since it was invented. But Fornasari had a noble voice, besides his mere physical attractions. Mr. White, who saw him long years afterward, when he chanced to be passing through New York on his way to Europe, describes him: He was very tall; his head looked like that of a youthful Jove; dark hair in flaky curls, an open, blazing eye; a nose just heroically curved; lips strong, yet beautifully bowed; sweet and persuasive (one would think that White got his description from some woman—what man ever before or since was praised by a man for having a Cupid's bow mouth?), and withal a large and easy grace of manner.

Montressor's season opened on October 6, 1832, at the Richmond Hill Theater, which became respectable for the nonce, and collapsed after thirty-five representations. The receipts for the season were $25,603—let us say about half as much as a week's receipts at the Metropolitan Opera House to-day. The operas given were Rossini's "Cenerentola," "L'Italiana in Algeri"; Bellini's "Il Pirata," and Mercadante's "Elisa e Claudio," the last winning the largest measure of popularity. The chief good accomplished was the bringing to New York from Europe of several excellent orchestral players, who, after the failure of the enterprise, settled here, to the good of instrumental music and the next undertaking.

Why men embark in operatic management, or, rather, why they continue in it after they have failed, has always been an enigma. Once, pointing my argument with excerpts from the story of all the managers in London, from Handel's day down to the present, I tried to prove that the desire to manage an opera company was a form of disease, finding admirable support for my contention in the confession and conduct of that English manager who got himself into Fleet Prison, and thence philosophically urged not only that it served him right (since no man insane enough to want to be an operatic impresario ought to be allowed at large), but also that a jail was the only proper headquarters for a manager, since there, at least, he was secure from the importunities of singers and dancers. Lorenzo Da Ponte was, obviously, of the stuff of which impresarios are made. Montressor's failure, for which he was in a degree responsible (and which he discussed in two pamphlets which I found twenty years ago in the library of the New York Historical

Society), persuaded him that the city's greatest need was an Italian opera house. His powers of persuasion must have been great, for he succeeded in bringing a body of citizens together who set the example which has been followed several times since, and built the Italian Opera House at Church and Leonard streets, on very much the same social and economic lines as prevail at the Metropolitan Opera House to-day. European models and European taste prevailed in the structure and its adornments. It was the first theater in the United States which boasted a tier composed exclusively of boxes. This was the second balcony. The parterre was entered from the first balcony, a circumstance which redeemed it from its old plebeian association as "the pit," in which it would have been indecorous for ladies to sit. The seats in the parterre were mahogany chairs upholstered in blue damask. The seats in the first balcony were mahogany sofas similarly upholstered. The box fronts had a white ground, with emblematic medallions, and octagonal panels of crimson, blue, and gold. Blue silk curtains were caught up with gilt cord and tassels. There was a chandelier of great splendor, which threw its light into a dome enriched with pictures of the Muses, painted, like all the rest of the interior, as well as the scenery, by artists specially brought over for the purpose from Europe. The floors were carpeted. The price of the boxes was $6,000 each, and subscribers might own them for a single performance (evidently by arrangement with the owners) or the season. Apropos of this, Mr. White tells a characteristic story:

It was told of a man who had suddenly risen to what was then great wealth, that, having taken a lady to the opera, he was met by the disappointing assurance that there were no seats to be had.

"What, nowhere?"

"Nowhere, sir; every seat in the house is taken, except, indeed, one of the private boxes that was not subscribed for."

"I'll have that."

"Impossible, sir. The boxes can only be occupied by subscribers and owners."

"What is the price of your box?"

"Six thousand dollars, sir."

"I'll take it."

And drawing out his pocketbook he filled up a check for six thousand dollars and escorted his lady to her seat to the surprise and, indeed, to the consternation of the elegant circle, which saw itself completed in this unexpected manner.

The new house, which, with the ground, had cost $150,000, was opened on November 18, 1833, under the joint management of the Chevalier Rivafinoli and Da Ponte, with Rossini's "La Gazza ladra," but two months before that date there was a drawing for boxes, concerning which and some of the details of the opening performance an extract from the diary of Mr. Philip Hone, once mayor of the city, presents a much livelier picture than I could draw:

(From the diary of Philip Hone, Esq.)

September 15, 1833. The drawing for boxes at the Italian Opera House took place this morning. My associates, Mr. Schermerhorn and General Jones, are out of town, and I attended and drew No. 8, with which I am well satisfied. The other boxes will be occupied by the following gentlemen: Gerard H. Coster, G. C. Howland, Rufus Prime, Mr. Panon, Robert Ray, J. F. Moulton, James J. Jones, D. Lynch, E. Townsend, John C. Cruger, O. Mauran, Charles H. Hall, J. G. Pierson and S. B. Ruggles.

November 18, 1833. The long expected opening of the opera house took place this evening with the opera "La Gazza ladra"; all new performers except Signor Marozzi, who belonged to the old company. The prima donna soprano is Signorina Fanti. The opera, they say, went off well for a first performance; but to me it was tiresome, and the audience was not excited to any degree of applause. The performance occupied four hours— much too long, according to my notion, to listen to a language which one does not understand; but the house is superb, and the decorations of the proprietors' boxes (which occupy the whole of the second tier) are in a style of magnificence which even the extravagance of Europe has not yet equaled. I have one-third of box No. 8; Peter Schermerhorn one-third; James J. Jones one-sixth; William Moore one-sixth. Our box is fitted up with great taste with light blue hangings, gilded panels and cornice, armchairs, and a sofa. Some of the others have rich silk ornaments, some are painted in fresco, and each proprietor seems to have tried to outdo the rest in comfort and magnificence. The scenery is beautiful. The dome and the fronts of the boxes are painted in the most superb classical designs, and the sofa seats are exceedingly commodious. Will this splendid and refined amusement be supported in New York? I am doubtful.

The outcome justified Mr. Hone in his doubts. The season was advertised, to last forty nights. When they were at an end a supplementary season of twenty-eight nights was added, which extended the time to July 21, 1834. Besides "La Gazza ladra," the operas given were "Il Barbiere di Siviglia," "La Donna del Lago," "Il Turco in Italia," "Cenerentola," and "Matilda di Shabran"—all by Rossini; Pacini's "Gli Arabi nelli Gallie," Cimarosa's "Il Matrimonio segreto," and "La Casa do Pendere," by the conductor, one Salvioni. The season had been socially and artistically brilliant, but the financial showing at the end was one of disaster. The prices of admission were from $2 down to fifty cents, and when the house was completely sold out the receipts were not more than $1,400. The managers took their patrons into their confidence, Rivafinoli publishing the fact that the receipts for the entire season—including fifteen nights in Philadelphia, for that city's dependence on New York for Italian opera began thus early—were but $51,780.89, which were exceeded by the expenses $29,275.09. For the next season the house was leased by the owners to Signor Sacchi, who had been the treasurer of Rivafinoli and Da Ponte, and Signor Porto, one of the singers. These managers had an experience similar to that which Maretzek declaimed against twenty years later when troubles gathered about the new Academy of Music. Notwithstanding that there had been a startling deficit, though the audiences had been as large as could be accommodated, these underlings of Rivafinoli and Da Ponte, who were at least men of experience in operatic management, took the house, giving the stockholders the free use of their boxes and 116 free admissions every night besides. The second season started brilliantly, but just as financial disaster was preparing to engulf it the performances were abruptly brought to an end by the prima donna, Signora, or Signorina, Fanti, who took French leave—an incident which remains unique in New York's operatic annals, at least in its consequences, I think.

It is evident to a close student of the times that the reasons given were not the only ones to contribute to the downfall of the enterprise. Italian opera had found a vigorous rival in English, or rather in opera in the vernacular, for the old ballad operas were disappearing and German, French, and Italian opera sung in the vernacular, not by actresses who had tolerable voices, but by trained vocalists, was taking its place. The people of New York were not quite so sophisticated as they are to-day, and possibly were dowered with a larger degree of sincerity. Many of them were willing to admit the incongruity of behavior at which Addison made merry when he predicted that the time would come when the descendants of the English people of his day would be curious to know "why their forefathers used to sit together like an audience of foreigners in their own country and to hear whole plays acted before them in a tongue which they did not understand." We know that Addison was a poor prophet, for the people of Great Britain and America are still sitting in the same attitude as their ancestors so far as opera is concerned; but it is plain that arguments like his did reach the consciences of even the stockholders of the Italian Opera House, or at least the one of them who has taken posterity into his confidence. The season under Sacchi and Porto had scarcely begun when Mr. Hone wrote in his diary:

I went to the opera, where I saw the second act of "La Straniera," by Bellini. The house is as pretty as ever, and the same faces were seen in the boxes as formerly; but it is not a popular entertainment, and will not be in our day, I fear. The opera did not please me. There was too much reiteration, and I shall never discipline my taste to like common colloquial expressions of life: "How do you do, madame?" or "Pretty well, I thank you, sir," the better for being given with orchestral accompaniment.

I shrewdly suspect that Mr. Hone had been reading his Spectator. There were three years of opera in London, in Addison's day, when the English and Italian languages were mixed in the operas as German and Italian were in Hamburg when Handel started out on his career. "The king or hero of the play generally spoke in Italian and his slaves answered him in English; the lover frequently made his court and gained the heart of his princess in a language which she did not understand." At length, says Addison, the audience got tired of understanding half the opera, "and to ease themselves entirely of the fatigue of thinking, so ordered it that the whole opera was performed in an unknown tongue." Now listen to our diarist:

The Italian language is among us very little understood, and the genius of it certainly never entered into with spirit. To entertain an audience without reducing it to the necessity of thinking is doubtless a first-rate merit, and it is easier to produce music without sense than with it; but the real charm of the opera is this—it is an exclusive and extravagant recreation, and, above all, it is the fashion.

   Italian music's sweet because 'tis dear,
 Their vanity is tickled, not their ear;
 Their taste would lessen if the prices fell,
 And Shakespeare's wretched stuff do quite as well.

The recitative is an affront to common sense, and if there be any spectacle more than another opposed to the genius of the English character and unsuited to its taste it is the ballet of the opera house. Its eternal dumbshow, with its fantastic appeals to sense and to sense only, may be Italian perfection, but here it is in English a tame absurdity. What but fashion could tempt reasonable creatures to sit and applaud—what was really perpetrated—Deshayes dancing "The Death of Nelson"?

After the season of Sacchi and Porto Italian opera went into exile for ten years. Da Ponte pleaded for "the most splendid ornament" of the city in vain. English opera conquered, aided, no doubt, by the fact that the section of the city in which the Italian Opera House was situated was fatally unfashionable, and after standing vacant for a year the house was leased to James W. Wallack, father of John Lester Wallack, who turned it into a home for the spoken drama. In another year it went up in flames.

CHAPTER III
THE FIRST ITALIAN COMPANY

The beginnings of Italian opera in America are intimately associated with two men who form an interesting link connecting the music of the Old World with that of the New. These men were Manuel del Popolo Vicente Garcia and Lorenzo Da Ponte. The opera performed in the Park Theater on November 29, 1825, when the precious exotic first unfolded its petals in the United States, was Rossini's "Il Barbiere di Siviglia." In this opera Garcia, then in his prime, had created, as the French say, the rôle of Almaviva in Rome a little less than ten years before. The performance was one of the most monumental fiascos in Rossini's career, and the story goes that Garcia, hoping to redeem it, introduced a Spanish song to which he himself supplied a guitar accompaniment. The fiasco of the first performance was largely, if not wholly, due to the jealous ill will of the friends of Paisiello, who had written music for an opera on the same story, which was much admired all over Europe, and which in an adapted form had reached America, as had Rossini's, before Garcia came with the original version. But Rossini's music was too fascinating to be kept under a bushel, and in it Garcia won some of his finest triumphs in London and Paris. In the first New York season it was performed twenty-three times. Garcia was also a composer, and had made his mark in this field before he became famous as a singer, having produced at least seventeen Spanish operas, nineteen Italian, and Seven French, most, if not all of them, before he came to America.

Exactly what it was that persuaded Garcia to embark on the career of impresario in a new land does not appear in the story of his enterprise. There are intimations that he had long had the New York project in mind; also it used to be thought that Da Ponte had inspired him with the idea; the more general story is that Dominick Lynch, a New York importer of French wines, was at the bottom of the enterprise, but whether on his own account or as a sort of agent for the manager of the Park Theater, I have not been able to learn. Garcia's singing days were coming to an end, though his popularity was not yet on the wane if there is evidence in the circumstances that from 1823 to 1825 his salary in London had increased from 260 pounds to 1,250 pounds. But it was as a teacher and composer that he now commanded the greater respect. He had founded a school of singing of which it may truthfully be said that it was continued without loss of glory until the end of the nineteenth century by his son Manuel, who died in 1906, a few months after he had celebrated the hundredth anniversary of his birth. But, though we may not know all the reasons which prevailed with him to seek fortune as a manager after he had himself passed the half-century mark, it is easy to fancy that the fact that he had half the artists necessary for the undertaking in his own family had much to do with it. His daughter, Maria Felicita, had studied singing with him from childhood and at sixteen years of age had sung with him in Italy. His wife was an opera singer and his son Manuel had made a beginning in the career which he speedily abandoned in favor of that which gave him far greater fame than the stage promised. The future Malibran was singing in the chorus in London only a year before she disclosed her peerless talents in New York. In June, 1825, Pasta, who was Mr. Ebers's prima donna at the King's Theater, took ill. Garcia was a member of the company and came forward with an offer of his daughter as substitute. The offer was accepted, the girl effected her début as Rosina in "The Barber," and made so complete a hit that she was engaged for the remaining six weeks of the season at a salary of 500 pounds. This is the story as told by Fétis, which does not differ essentially from that told by Ebers in his account of his seven years of tenancy of the King's Theater, or by Lord Mount-Edgecumbe in his "Musical Reminiscences," except that these make no direct reference to Pasta's illness as the cause which gave Maria her opportunity. Lord Mount-Edgecumbe's account says that Ebers found it necessary, about the time of the arrival of Pasta, "to engage a young singer, the daughter of the tenor Garcia, who had sung here for several seasons. She was as yet a mere girl, and had never appeared on any public stage; but from the first moment of her appearance she showed evident talents for it, both as singer and actress. Her extreme youth, her prettiness, her pleasing voice and sprightly, easy action as Rosina in 'Il Barbiere di Siviglia,' in which part she made her début, gained her general favor; but she was too highly extolled and injudiciously put forward as a prima donna when she was only a promising débutante, who in time, by study and practice, would, in all probability, under the tuition of her father, a good musician, but (to my ears at least) a most disagreeable singer, rise to eminence in her profession."

I am not more than half persuaded that this view of the future Malibran's talents and prospects did not tally with that of her father, though her tremendous success in New York ought to have persuaded him that a future of the most dazzling description lay before his daughter. There is something of a puzzle in the fact that in the midst of her first triumph the girl should have married M. Malibran, who was only apparently wealthy, and was surely forty-three years her senior, and of a nature which was bound to develop lack of sympathy and congeniality between the pair. The popular version of the story of her marriage is that she was forced into it by her father, and it is more than intimated that he was induced to act as he did by the promise of 100,000 francs made by Malibran as a compensation for the loss of his daughter's services. Did Garcia oppose his daughter's marriage, and did she wilfully have her own way in a matter in which she was scarcely a proper judge? Or was the marriage repugnant to her, and was she sacrificed to her father's selfishness? I cannot tell, but it has been hinted that there was danger of her marrying a member of the orchestra in London before she came to New York, and it is as like as not that the affair Malibran was of her wishing. Who can know the ways of a maid fourscore years after? The marriage was as unfortunate as could be. In a few months Malibran was a bankrupt, his youthful wife's father was gone to distant Mexico, there to make money, only to be robbed of it at Vera Cruz on his home journey to England, and Maria Felicita, instead of living in affluence as the wife of a wealthy New York merchant, was supporting an unworthy husband, as well as herself, by singing in English at the theater in the Bowery and in Grace Church on Sundays. The legal claims bound the ill-assorted pair for ten years, but did not gall the artist after she returned to Europe in 1827, little more than a year later. In Paris the marriage was annulled in 1836, and the singer, now the greatest prima donna on the stage, married Charles de Bériot, the violinist, with whom she had been living happily for six years, and by whom she had a son, born in February, 1833. The world's Book of Opera must supply the other chapters which tell of the great Malibran, her marvelous triumphs and her early death; but it is a matter of pride for every American to reflect that this adorable artist began her career with the admiring applause of our people.

Manuel Garcia, the son, the senior of his sister by three years, survived her the whole span of life allotted to man by the Psalmist. Malibran died in 1836; Garcia in 1906. He achieved nothing on the stage, which he abandoned in 1829. Thereafter his history belongs to that of pedagogy. Till 1848 his field of operations was Paris; afterward, till his death, London. Jenny Lind was one of his pupils; Mme. Marchesi another.

The story that Da Ponte had anything to do with inspiring Garcia's New York enterprise is practically disposed of by the fact that Da Ponte, though intimately associated with the opera in London during his sojourn in that city, had already been a resident of New York three years when Garcia made his début as a singer and never returned thither. Personally Garcia was a stranger to him and he to Garcia when the latter came to New York in the fall of 1825. This gives color of verity to a familiar story of their meeting. As might easily be imagined, the man who had written the librettos of "Le Nozze di Figaro," "Don Giovanni," and "Cosi Fan Tutte" for Mozart, was not long in visiting Garcia after his arrival here. He introduced himself as the author of "Don Giovanni," and Garcia, clipping the old man in his arm, danced around the room like a child in glee, singing "Fin ch'han dal vino" the while. After that the inclusion of Mozart's masterpiece in Garcia's repertory was a matter of course, with only this embarrassment that there was no singer in the company capable of singing the music of Don Ottavio. This was overcome by Da Ponte going to his pupils for money enough to pay an extra singer for the part. Many a tenor, before and since, who has been cast for that divinely musical milksop has looked longingly at the rôle of Don Giovanni which Mozart gave to a barytone, and some have appropriated it. Garcia was one of these (he had been a tenor de forza in his day), and it fell to him to introduce the character in New York. Outside of himself, his daughter, and the basso Angrisani, the company was a poor affair, the orchestra not much better than that employed at the ordinary theater then (and now, for that matter), and the chorus composed of mechanics drilled to sing words they did not understand. It is scarcely to be wondered at, therefore, that at one of the performances of Mozart's opera, of which there were ten, singers and players got at sixes and sevens in the superb finale of the first act, whereupon Garcia, losing his temper, rushed to the footlights sword in hand, stopped the orchestra, and commanded a new beginning.

It has already been told how that Da Ponte was active in the promotion of the first Italian opera enterprise, that he inspired Montressor's experiment at the Richmond Hill Theater and was the moving spirit in the ambitious, beautiful but unhappy Italian Opera House undertaking. To do all these things it was necessary that he should be a man of influence among the cultured and wealthy classes of the community. As a matter of fact he was this, and that in spite of the fact that his career had been checkered in Europe and was not wholly free from financial scandal, at least in New York. The fact is that the poet's artistic temperament was paired with an insatiable commercial instinct. This instinct, at least, may be set down as a racial inheritance. Until seven or eight years ago nobody seems to have taken the trouble to look into the family antecedents of him whom the world will always know as Lorenzo Da Ponte. That was not his name originally. Of this fact something only a little better than a suspicion had been in the minds of those who knew him and wrote about him during his lifetime and shortly after his death. Michael Kelly, the Irish tenor, who knew him in Vienna, speaks of him as "my friend, the abbé," and tells of his dandyish style of dressing, his character as a "consummate coxcomb," his strong lisp and broad Venetian dialect; if he knew that he was a converted Jew, he never mentioned the fact. Later writers hinted at the fact that he had been born a Jew, but had been educated by the Bishop of Ceneda and had adopted his name. When I investigated his American history, a matter of twenty years ago, my statement in The Tribune newspaper that he was the son of a Hebrew leather dealer provoked an almost intemperate denial by a German musical historian, who quoted from his memoirs a story of his religious observances to confound me. My statement, however, was based, not only on an old rumor, but also on the evidence of a pamphlet published in Lisbon in the course of what seems to have been a peculiarly acrimonious controversy between Da Ponte and a theatrical person unnamed, but probably one Francesco. In this pamphlet, which is not only indecorous but indecent, he is referred to as "the celebrated Lorenzo Daponte, who after having been Jew, Christian, priest, and poet in Italy and Germany found himself to be a layman, husband, and ass in London." It remained for Professor Marchesan, his successor in the chair of rhetoric in the University of Treviso, to give the world the facts concerning his origin and early family history. From Marchesan's book ("Della Vita e delle Opere di Lorenzo da Ponte") published in Treviso in 1900 we learn that the poet's father was in truth a Hebrew leather dealer, and also that the father's name was Jeremiah Conegliano, his mother's Rachel Pincherle, and his own Emanuele Conegliano. He was fourteen years old when not he alone, but the whole family, embraced Christianity. They were baptized in the cathedral of Ceneda on August 20, 1763, and the bishop gave the lad, whose talents he seems to have observed, his own name. The rest of his story up to his departure for America may be outlined in the words of the sketch in Grove's "Dictionary of Music and Musicians" (second edition, Vol. III, p. 789).

After five years of study in the seminary at Ceneda (probably with the priesthood as an object) he went to Venice, where he indulged in amorous escapades which compelled his departure from that city. He went to Treviso and taught rhetoric in the university, incidentally took part in political movements, lampooned an opponent in a sonnet, and was ordered out of the republic. In Dresden, whither he turned his steps, he found no occupation for his talents, and journeyed on to Vienna. There, helped by Salieri, he received from Joseph II the appointment of poet to the imperial theater and Latin secretary. Good fortune brought him in contact with Mozart, who asked him to make an opera book of Beaumarchais's "Mariage de Figaro." The great success of Mozart's opera on this theme led to further co-operation, and it was on Da Ponte's suggestion that "Don Giovanni" was undertaken, the promptings coming largely from the favor enjoyed at the time by Gazzaniga's opera on the same subject, from which Da Ponte made generous drafts—as a comparison of the libretti will show. Having incurred the ill will of Leopold, Da Ponte was compelled to leave Vienna on the death of Joseph II. He went to Trieste, where Leopold was sojourning, in the hope of effecting a reconciliation, but failed; but there he met and married an Englishwoman who was thenceforth fated to share his checkered fortunes. He obtained a letter recommending him to the interest of Marie Antoinette, but while journeying toward Paris learned of the imprisonment of the Queen, and went to London instead. A year was spent in the British metropolis in idleness, and some time in Holland in a futile effort to establish an Italian theater there. Again he turned his face toward London, and this time secured employment as poet to the Italian opera and assistant to the manager, Taylor. He took a part of Domenico Corri's shop to sell Italian books, but soon ended in difficulties, and to escape his creditors fled to America, arriving in New York on June 4, 1805.

Da Ponte lives in the respect and admiration of Dante scholars as the first of American teachers and commentators on "The Divine Comedy." He gave himself the title, and in this case adhered to the truth, which cannot be said of all of his statements about himself. For instance, in a letter to the public to be set forth presently, he calls himself "poet of the Emperor Joseph II." He was in the habit of thus designating himself and it was small wonder that his biographers almost unanimously interpreted these words to mean that he was poet laureate, or Caesarian poet. After the mischief, small enough, except perhaps in an ethical sense, had been done, he tried to correct it in a foot note on one of the pages of his "Memorie," in which he says that he was not "Poeta Cesario," but "poet to the Imperial theaters." In his capacity as a teacher his record seems to have been above reproach; and it was in this capacity that he first presented himself favorably to New Yorkers. Within two years after his arrival he gave a pamphlet to the public entitled "Compendium of the Life of Lorenzo Da Ponte, written by Himself, to which is added the first Literary Conversatione held at his home in New York on the 10th day of March, 1807, consisting of several Italian compositions in verse and prose translated into English by his scholars." That this little brochure was designed as an advertisement is obvious enough; it was issued on his fifty-eighth birthday and its contents, besides the sketch of his life, which, so it began, he had promised to give his pupils, were specimens of their literary handicraft. In the biographical recital are echoes of the contentions in which he had been engaged in London a few years before. Although only two years had elapsed since his arrival in America, what may be called the first of his commercial periods was already over. He had sent his wife to New York ahead of him with some of the money which his English creditors were looking for. With this he promptly embarked in business, trafficking in tobacco, liquors, drugs, etc.—goods which promised large profits. In three months fear of yellow fever drove him to Elizabethtown, N. J., where he remained a year, by which time he was ruined. He came back to New York and began to teach the Italian language and literature, and the little "Compendium" recorded his first successes. He taught till 1811, by which time he had laid aside $4,000, with which he again went into business, this time as a distiller in Sunbury, Pa. After several years of commercial life he returned again to New York and resumed the profession which brought him into contact with people of refinement and social standing, who seem to have remained his friends, despite his complaints and importunities, till his death in 1838. Among those who were sincerely attached to him were Clement Clark Moore, Hebrew lexicographer, trustee of Columbia College, and (best of all) author of "'Twas the Night before Christmas." Through Moore he secured the privilege of calling himself Professor of Italian Literature at Columbia, though without salary, managed to sell the college a large number of Italian books, and was engaged to make a catalogue of the college library. Another friend was Henry James Anderson, who became Professor of Mathematics and Astronomy in the college in 1825, the year in which Garcia came to New York with his operatic enterprise. Professor Anderson married his daughter and became the father of Edward Henry and Elbert Ellery Anderson. Other friends were Giulian C. Verplanck, Dr. Macneven, Maroncelli, the Italian patriot, (whose wife was one of the members of the opera company which Da Ponte organized with Rivafinoli), Samuel Ward, Dr. John W. Francis, the Cottenet family, and H. T. Tuckerman, who wrote a sketch of him after his death in Putnam's Magazine. At the time of his operatic venture, 1833-34, he lived at No. 342 Broadway, and kept a bookstore at No. 336, which may then have been an adjoining house. The site is near the present Catherine Lane. Before then he had lived in dozens of different houses, moving, apparently, nearly every year. He died at No. 91 Spring Street, on August 17, 1838, and was buried in the Roman Catholic Cemetery in Eleventh Street, between First Avenue and Avenue A. When the centenary of the first performance of "Don Giovanni" was celebrated in many European cities, in 1887, I conceived the idea of sending a choir of trombones to the grave of the poet who had written the text to pay a musical tribute to his memory, and thus made the discovery that the place of his burial was as completely lost as the last resting place of the mortal remains of Mozart. Weeks of research were necessary to determine the fact that it was the old cemetery that had received his body, and that the location of the grave was no longer to be determined by the records. It was never marked.

Da Ponte's ambition to see Italian opera permanently established in New York seems to have received a crushing blow with the failure of the pretentious Italian Opera House enterprise. His dream I have referred to; he was again to be a "poet to the opera," to write works for season after season which his countryman Trajetta was to set to music. His niece was to be a prima donna. He did write one libretto; it was for an opera entitled, "L'Ape Musicale," for the musical setting of which he despoiled Rossini. His niece, Giulia Da Ponte, did sing, but her talents were not of the kind to win distinction. He persuaded Montressor to give his season, and, rushing into print, as was his custom—the period of the pamphleteer was to his liking—he discussed the failure of that undertaking in two booklets. After the successive failures of himself with Rivafinoli and his underlings, who attempted to succeed where he had come to grief, he appended a letter to his old supporters (who had plainly fallen away from him) to a pamphlet devoted to setting forth the miseries of his existence after the great things which, in his opinion, he had done for the people of New York. The letter has never seen the light of day from the time when it was printed in 1835 till now; but it deserves preservation. I found it twenty years ago in the library of the Historical Society of New York in a bound volume of miscellaneous pamphlets. It is as follows:

TO THOSE AMERICANS who love the fine arts I address myself. Hitherto I have vainly spoken and written. Never was more really verified the Latin proverb: Abyssus abyssum invocat.

Let the verses that I now present you rouse you from your lethargy; yet should they not, I will not cease to cry aloud. I cannot now remain in silence while my fellow countrymen are sacrificed, the citizens of two noble cities deceived, and an enterprise for which I have so long and ardently labored, so calculated to shed luster on the nation, and so honorable in its commencement, ruined by those who have no means, nor knowledge, nor experience. Answer at least these questions: Did you not request from me an Italian company? It will be readily understood with whom I speak. Why did you ask this of me? I was offered a handsome premium if I would introduce a troupe of select Italian artists in America. Did not I, and I alone procure them? Were they not excellent? Have I been compensated for my labor, reimbursed my actual expenses, or even honored by those most benefited by my losses and labors?

Had not I a right to expect thus much, or at least justice? And if you thought me competent to do what I have done, why should you not be guided by my counsels? Did I not tell you and reiterate in my writing and verbally that Rivafinoli was not to be trusted? That he was a daring, but imprudently daring, adventurer, whose failures in London, and in Mecico and Carolina were the sure forerunners of his failure in New York? And when deceived by him, whom did you take in place of him? PORTO! SACCHI! With what means? What talents? What judgment? What experience? What chances of a happy issue? Would you know why they wished it? I will tell you, with Juvenal—'Greculus esuriens si in coelum jusseris ibit.' But ignorant pretenders mostly have more influence than modest truth. You, gentlemen of the committee, gave the theater to them because, not having anything to lose, they could yield to everything, even to the promising of what they knew themselves unable to perform.

One of them it is said still has some hopes from you. Before another disgrace occurs I beg you to look at the effects. Nemo dat quod non habet. I brought a company from Italy by the mere force of my word. And why was this? Because they knew me for an honorable man, who would not promise what he could not perform, who had been eleven years the poet of the Emperor Joseph 2d, who for another equal space of time had been the poet to the theater in London, who had written thirty-six operas for Salieri, for Martini, for Storace and Mozzart (sic).

That these dramas still survive, you yourself have seen and thought its author not worthy of your esteem. For God's sake let the past become a beacon light to save you from the perils of the future. Do not destroy the most splendid ornament of your city. Rocco is obliged to visit Italy. Lease to him the theater, he will have for his advisers the talented and estimable Bagioli and myself. For me I wish for nothing, but it pains me to see spoiled by ignorance and imposture, and vanity that which cost me so much, or to speak more correctly, which cost me everything, and you so much, and it will cost you more in fame as well as in money.

What will they say, the Trollops and the Halls and Hamiltons who nodum in scripto quoerunt with the microscope of national aversion? Rocco and he only can redeem the fortunes of your disorganized, betrayed, dishonored establishment by giving you a new and meritorious company. Listen then to him and assist him—you will lose nothing by it; I pledge you the word of an old man whose lips have never uttered an untruth. Your servant and fellow citizen, Lorenzo Da Ponte

The theater was not leased to Rocco. It never echoed to opera after the second season.

CHAPTER IV
HOUSES BUILT FOR OPERA

"His wit was not so sharp as his chin, and so his career was not so long as his nose," says Richard Grant White of the impresario who, ten years after the failure of the Italian Opera House, made the third effort to establish Italian opera in New York of which there is a record. The man with a sharp chin and long nose was Ferdinand Palmo. He was the owner of a popular restaurant which went by the rather tropical name "Café des Milles Colonnes," and was situated in Broadway, just above Duane Street. Palmo knew how to cook and how to cater, and his restaurant made him fairly rich. What he did not know about managing an opera house he was made conscious of soon after the ambition to be an impresario took hold of him. His was an individual enterprise, like Mr. Hammerstein's, with no clogs or entangling alliances in the shape of stockholders, or managing directors, or amusement committees. He seems to have been strongly impressed with the idea that after the public had been total abstainers for ten years they would love opera for its own sake, and that it would not be necessary to give hostages to fortune in the shape of a beautiful house, with a large portion set apart for the exclusive use of wealth and fashion. Except in name, says Mr. White, there were no boxes. Palmo did not even build a new theater. He found one that could be modeled to his purposes in Stoppani's Arcade Baths, in Chambers Street, between Broadway and Center Street. The site is now occupied by the building of the American News Company. The acoustics of the new opera house are said to have been good, but the inconvenience of the location and unenviable character of the neighborhood are indicated quite as much as Signor Palmo's enterprising and considerate nature by his announcement that after the performances a large car would be run uptown as far as Forty-Second Street for the accommodation of his patrons; and also that the patrons aforesaid should have police protection. The house seated about eight hundred persons, the seats being hard benches, with slats across the back shoulder high. Opera lovers given to luxury were permitted to upholster their benches. The orchestra numbered "thirty-two professors," but their devotion to the art which they professed was not so great as to make them willing to starve for its sake or to refuse to resort to the methods of the more modern workingmen's unions to compel payment for their services, as we shall see presently. The first performance under Signor Palmo took place on February 3, 1844, the opera being the same one with which Mr. Hammerstein began his latest venture sixty-two years later—"I Puritani."

The prima donna soprano was Borghese, who was attractive in appearance, though not beautiful; who dressed well, sang with passionate intensity, and won a popularity that found vent in praise which may have been extravagant. One critic, "balancing her beauties against her defects," pronounced her the best operatic singer that the writer had yet heard on this side of the Atlantic. This remark leads Mr. White to surmise that the critic had not been five years in America, for, says he, Signora Borghese was not worthy to tie the shoes of Malibran, Pedrotti, Fanti, Garadori, or Mrs. Wood, the last two of whom had sung in English opera. Her chief defect seems to have been the tremolo—that vice toward which the American critics of to-day are more intolerant than those of any other people, as they are toward the sister vice of a faulty intonation. Mr. White talks sensibly on the subject in his estimate of Borghese.

She had a fine voice, although not a great one; her vocalization, regarded from a merely musical point of view, was of the corresponding grade, but as stage vocalization it had great power and deserved higher commendation. Her musical declamation was always effective and musico-rhetorically in good taste. She had a fine person, an expressive face, and much grace of manner. One might be content never to hear a better prima donna if one were secured against never hearing a worse. In her was first remarked here, among vocalists of distinction, that trembling of the voice when it is pressed in a crescendo, which has since become so common as greatly to mar our enjoyment of vocal music. This great fault, unknown before the appearance of Verdi, is attributed by some musical critics to the influence of his vociferous and strident style. It may be so; but that which follows is not always a consequence of that after which it comes. Certain it is, however, that from this time forward very few of the principal singers who have been heard in New York—only the very greatest and those whose style was formed before Verdi domineered the Italian lyric stage—were without this tremble. Grisi, Mario, Sontag, Jenny Lind, Alboni, and Salvi were entirely without it; their voices came from the chest pure, free and firm.

I can scarcely believe that the distressful vocal wabble either came in with Verdi's music or was greatly promoted by it. In the lofty quality of style Mme. Sembrich is the most perfect exemplar whom it is the privilege of New Yorkers to hear to-day; and she is the best singer we have of Verdi's music. Did anyone ever hear a tone come out of her throat that was not pure, free, and firm? Frequently the tremolo is an affectation like the excessive vibrato of a sentimental fiddler; sometimes it is the product of weakness due to abuse of the vocal organ. In all cases it is the sign of bad taste or vicious training, or both, and is an abomination. On the opera stage to-day Italian prima donnas are most afflicted with it. In turn Verdi,

Meyerbeer, and Wagner have been accused of having caused it, but anyone who has listened intelligently to the opera singers of the last forty years will testify with me that the truly great singers of their music have been as free from the vicious habit as have been those whose artistic horizons have been confined by the music of Bellini, Rossini, and Donizetti.

The tenor of the Palmo company was Antognini, who effected his entrance on the American stage five weeks after the opening of the season. In the opinion of Mr. White, he was the greatest tenor ever heard here, not excepting Mario and Salvi, and Mr. White's opinion is so judiciously expressed that one is fain to give it credence. Whether or not it can be extended over the period which he has covered, which is that reaching from the last days of the Academy of Music, when Campanini was still in his vocal prime but had not developed the dramatic powers which he put into play with the decay of his voice, I shall not undertake to say; taste in tenor voices has changed within the last generation in favor of the robust quality so magnificently exemplified in Signor Caruso. To judge from Mr. White's description Antognini, as a singer merely, was a Bonci of a manlier mould. His fame seems to have died with those who heard him, and perhaps this is a good reason for reprinting what Mr. White said about him in full:

He (Antognini) was an artist of the first class, both by natural gifts and by culture. His voice, although not of notable compass, was an absolute tenor of a delicious quality and great power. His vocalization was unexceptionably pure, and his style was manly and noble. As a dramatic singer I never heard his equal except Ronconi; as an actor, I never saw his equal, except Ronconi, Rachel, and Salvini. He had in perfection that power which Hamlet speaks of in his soliloquy, after he dismisses the players, when the speech about Pyrrhus is ended:

> Is it not monstrous that this player here,
> But in a fiction, in a dream of passion
> Could force his soul so to his own conceit
> That from her working all his visage wann'd;
> Tears in his eyes, distraction in's aspect,
> A broken voice, and his whole function suiting
> With forms to his conceit!

I have seen the blood fade not only from Antognini's cheeks, but from his very lips, as he strode slowly forward to interrupt the nuptials in "Lucia di Lammermoor," and then flame back again as he broke into defiance of his foes. The inflections of his voice in passages of tenderness were ravishing, and his utterance of anger and despair was terrible. Nor was any tenor that has been heard here, not even Mario in his prime, his superior in that great test of fine vocalization, a sustained cantabile passage. He was one of those blond Italians who are found on the northern border of the peninsula. Being all this he nevertheless soon disappeared, and was forgotten except by a few of the most exacting and cultivated among his hearers; the reason of which was that his voice could not be depended upon for two nights together—not, indeed, for one alone. On Monday he would thrill the house; on Wednesday he would go about the stage depressed, almost silent, huskily making mouths at his fellow actors and the audience. His voice would even desert him in the middle of an evening, thus producing an impression that he was trifling with his audience. No judgment could have been more unjust, for he was a conscientious artist, but the effect of this defect, as Polonius might say, was therefore no less disastrous, and he soon gave place to artists less admirable but more to be relied upon.

In this season there appeared a prima donna of the French school in the person of Laura Cinthe Montalant, known in the annals of opera as Cinti-Damoreau, who had come to America to sing in concerts with Artôt, the violinist. In the eyes of Fétis she was one of the greatest singers the world had known. Damoreau was the name of her husband, an unsuccessful French actor. When she came to America she had made her career in Paris and London, a great triumph coming to her in the French capital, where Rossini composed the principal female rôles in "Le Siège de Corinth" and "Moïse," and Auber those in "Domino Noir," "L'Ambassadrice," and "Zanetta."

[Repertory of the first season at Palmo's Opera House: "I Puritani" (Bellini), "Belisario" (Donizetti), "Beatrice di Tenda" (Bellini), "Il Barbiere di Siviglia" (Rossini), "La Sonnambula" (Bellini), "L'Elisir d'Amore" (Donizetti), "L'Italiana in Algeri" (Rossini). Repertory of the second season, 1844-1845: "Lucia di Lammermoor" (Donizetti), "Il Pirata" (Bellini), "Chiara de Rosemberg" (Luigi Ricci), "Lucrezia Borgia" (Donizetti), "Belisario" (Donizetti), "La Cenerentola" (Rossini), "Semiramide" (Rossini).]

It is not surprising that ill fortune became the companion of Palmo at the outset of his enterprise and dragged him down to the lowest depths before the end of his second season (according to the calendar).

The first season ran its course and a second one began in November, 1844. Amidst the usual vicissitudes it continued until January 25, 1845. On this momentous date Borghese was before the footlights and about to open her mouth in song when suddenly the orchestra ceased playing. Not a soft complaining note from the flute, not a whimper from the fiddles. Borghese raved and Palmo came upon the stage to learn the cause of the direful silence. A colloquy with the musicians, if not exactly in these words, was to this effect:

"What's the meaning of this? Is it a strike? Why?"

"No pay."

"I'll pay you to-morrow."

"To-night's the time"—the musicians packing up their instruments.

Palmo rushed to the box office to get the night's receipts. Alas! they were already in the hands of the deputy sheriff. Another opera manager had gone down into the vortex which had swallowed up Ebers, and Taylor, and Delafield, and others of their tribe in London, and Montressor and Rivafinoli in New York. Palmo, it is said, had literally to return to his pots and kettles; after serving as cook and barkeeper in the hotels of others the once enterprising manager of the Café of a Thousand Columns became a dependent upon the charity of his friends. There was another season of opera at Palmo's, among the managers of which were Sanquirico, a buffo singer, Salvatore Patti, and an Italian named Pogliagno. In the company were Catarina Barili and her two children, Clotilde and Antonio. Patti was a tenor singer. He was the husband of the prima donna, Catarina Barili, who was looked upon as a fine representative of the old school of singing, and from the pair sprang Carlotta and Adelina, who gave a luster to the name of Patti which the father would never have given it by his exertions as singer and manager. Both were born before their parents came to New York; Carlotta in Florence, in 1840, and Adelina in Madrid, in 1843. The childhood and youth of both were spent in New York, and here both received their musical training. Their artistic history belongs to the world, and since I am, with difficulty, trying just now to talk more about opera houses and those who built them to their own ruin, than about those who sang in them, I will not pursue it. The summer of 1847 saw Palmo's little opera house deserted. In 1848 it became Burton's Theater, where, as Mr. White observes, that most humorous of comedians made for himself in a few years a handsome fortune.

Who shall deny that Signor Palmo, though his fortunes went down in disaster, made a valuable contribution to that movement—which must still be looked upon as in an experimental stage—which has for its aim the permanent establishment of opera in the United States? Experimental in its nature the movement must remain until the vernacular becomes the language of the performances and native talent provides both works and interpreters. The day is still far distant, but it will come. The opera of Germany was still Italian more than a century and a half after the invention of the art form, though in the meanwhile the country had produced a Bach and a Handel. The Palmo venture (at the bottom of which there seems to have been a desire to popularize or democratize a form of entertainment which has ever been the possession of wealth and fashion) revived the social sentiment upon which Da Ponte had built his hopes. In the opinion of the upper classes's it was not Italian opera that had succumbed, but only the building which housed it. This certainly presented an aspect of incongruity. Fine talent came from England for the English companies, whose career continued without interruption, and the moment which saw the downfall of Palmo's enterprise saw also the influx of a company of Italian artists under the management of Don Francesco Marty y Torrens, of Havana, who deserves to be kept in the minds of opera lovers which go back to the days of the Academy of Music, if for no other reason than that he brought Signor Arditi to New York—the hawk-billed conductor whose shining pate used to glisten like a stage lamp from the conductor's seat in the fine old house at Fourteenth Street and Irving Place.

And so, in order that Italian opera might not perish from the earth, but live on, surrounded by the architectural splendor appropriate to it, one hundred and fifty men of social prominence got together and guaranteed to support it for five years, and Messrs. Foster, Morgan, and Colles built the Astor Place Opera House. Instead of the eight hundred seatings of Palmo's institution, this held 1,800. The theater had "a fine open front and an excellent ventilation." That it was an elegant playhouse and admirably adapted to the purpose for which it had been designed there are many people still alive in New York to testify. Mr. White says enthusiastically that it was "one of the most attractive theaters ever erected." Even Max Maretzek, who began his American career there, first as conductor, afterward as impresario, while throwing ridicule upon its management (his own administration excepted, of course) and its artistic forces, praises the architectural arrangement of the house. "Most agreeably surprised was I," he writes in his "Crotchets and Quavers," published in 1855, "on entering this small but comfortably arranged bonbonnière. It contained somewhere about 1,100 excellent seats in parquet (the Parisian parterre), dress circle and first tier, with some seven hundred in the gallery. Its principal feature was that everybody could see, and, what is of infinitely greater consequence, could be seen. Never, perhaps, was any theater built that afforded a better opportunity for a display of dress. Believe me" (he is indulging in the literary fiction of a letter to a journalistic friend in Paris), "that were the Funambules built as ably for this grand desideratum, despite the locality and the grade of performance at this theater, my conviction is that it would be the principal and most fashionable one in Paris." Maretzek is, of course, here aiming chiefly to cast discredit upon one of the vanities and affectations of society—the love of display; but if Mr. White is to be believed, the patrons of the Astor Place Opera House, on its opening (which means the fashionable element of New York society) were temperate and tasteful in the matter of dress. Speaking of the first performance at the new house, he says: "Rarely has there been an assembly, at any time or in any country, so elegant, with such a generally suffused air of good breeding; and yet it could not be called splendid in any one of its circles. At the Astor Place Opera House that form of opera toilet for ladies which is now peculiar to New York and a few other American cities came into vogue—a demi-toilet of marked elegance and richness, and yet without that display either of apparel and trimmings or of the wearer's personal charms which is implied by full evening dress in fashionable parlance. This toilet is very pleasing in itself, and it is happily adapted to the social conditions of a country in which any public exhibition of superior wealth in places set apart for common enjoyment of refined pleasure is not in good taste." Mr. White wrote in 1881; would he have been able to be so complimentary to the opera audiences of 1908? What relation does the present extravagance of dress, the vulgar ostentation which Mr. White would have us believe was foreign to the taste of New York's cultured society in 1847, bear toward the support which opera has received since the Metropolitan Opera House was opened? The factors which are to determine the question seem to be marshaling themselves since Mr. Hammerstein opened the Manhattan Opera House, but they are not yet fairly opposed to each other. There are features in which the new opera house recalls memories of the old Academy which met its downfall when the amalgamation between the old Knickerbockers and the newer New Yorkers was effected; but there are also other features which make a repetition of that occurrence under present circumstances very improbable, and the chiefest of these is that inculcated by the failure of the Palmo enterprise; opera must have an elegant environment if it is to succeed. But it had this in the Astor Place Opera House; why, then, did it live its little span only?

The question is easily answered—the Astor Place Opera House was killed by competition; not the competition of English opera with Italian, which had been in existence for twenty-five years, but of Italian opera with Italian opera. The first lessees of the new institution were Messrs. Sanquirico and Patti, who had first tried their luck in Palmo's Opera House. They endured a season. [At the Astor Place Opera House in its first season Sanquirico and Patti produced Verdi's "Ernani," Bellini's "Beatrice di Tenda," Donizetti's "Lucrezia Borgia," Mencadante's "Il Giuramento," and Verdi's "Nabucco." Mr. Fry's season in 1848 when Mr. Maretzek was the conductor, brought forward Donizetti's "Linda di Chamouni," "Lucrezia Borgia," "L'Elisir d'Amore," "Roberto Devereux," and "Lucia di Lammermoor" and Verdi's "Ernani."] Then the first American manager appeared on the field—I mean the first American manager whose thoughts were directed to opera exclusively as distinguished from the managers of theaters who took hold of opera at intervals, as they did any other sort of entertainment which offered employment for their houses. The manager in question was Mr. E. R. Fry, who came from the counting house to a position of which he can have known nothing more than what he could acquire from attendance upon opera, of which he was fond, and association with his brother, W. H. Fry, who was a journalist by profession (long the musical critic of The Tribune) and an amateur composer of more than respectable attainments. Mr. Maretzek, in his "Crotchets and Quavers"—a book generally marked by characteristic good humor, but not free from malevolence—tries to make it appear that Mr. Edward Fry went into operatic management for the express purpose of performing his brother's operas; but while the animus of the statement is enough to cause it to be looked upon with suspicion, the fact that none of William Henry Fry's operas was performed at the Astor Place Opera House during the incumbency of Edward Fry is a complete refutation. "Leonora," the only grand opera by a professional critic ever performed in New York, so far as I know, was brought forward at the Academy of Music a good nine years later. Apropos of this admirable and respected predecessor of mine, a good story was disclosed by Charles A. Dana some fifteen or twenty years ago in his reminiscences of Horace Greeley. Mr. Dana published a large number of letters sent to him at various times while he was managing editor of The Tribune and Mr. Greeley editor-in-chief. It was in the days just before the War of the Rebellion. A political question of large importance had arisen in Congress, and Mr. Greeley was so concerned in it that he went to Washington to look after it in person and act as a special correspondent of his own newspaper. Thence one day he sent two letters to The Tribune on the subject, but in the issue of the day in which he expected them to appear in The Tribune he sought in vain for his communication. Thereupon he indited an epistle to Mr. Dana in these wingèd words:

Friend Dana: What would it cost to burn the Opera House? If the price is reasonable have it done and send me the bill. . . . I wrote my two letters under the presumption (there being no paper on Wednesday) that the solid work of exposing their (Pierce and Gushing) perversion of history had of course been done by Hildreth. I should have dwelt with it even more gravely but for that. And now I see (the Saturday paper only got through last night) that you crowded out what little I did say to make room for Fry's eleven columns of arguments as to the feasibility of sustaining the opera in N. Y. if they would only play his compositions. I don't believe three hundred people who take the Tribune care one chew of Tobacco for the matter.

The "eleven columns" was an amiable exaggeration quite in consonance with the remainder of the letter; but I can testify from a consultation of the files of the newspaper which I have served as one of Mr. Fry's successors for more than a quarter of a century that on the date in question The Tribune's critic did occupy three and a half columns with a discussion of the Lagrange season just ended at the Academy of Music and a most strenuous plea for the permanent substitution of English for Italian opera! Also, that most of what Mr. Fry said would sound just as apposite to-day as it did then, and be backed by just as much reason. But a taste for the elegant exotic and reason do not seem to go hand in hand, and managers are still strangely averse to placing themselves for guidance into the hands of The Tribune's critics. How different might not musical history in New York have shaped itself had William Henry Fry, George William Curtis, John R. G. Hassard, and H. E. K. had their way during the last sixty years! The thought is quite overpowering.

The opposition which the Astor Place Opera House met was indeed formidable. It came from the company organized by Don Francesco Marty y Torrens for performances in Havana. This enterprising gentleman did not come to New York to make money, but mischief—as Messrs. Sanquirico, Patti, Fry, and Maretzek must have thought—and incidentally to keep his singers employed during the hot and unhealthy season in Havana. His aiders and abettors were James H. Hackett and William Niblo. The former, in his day an actor, was particularly famous for his impersonation of Falstaff. His interest in opera may have been excited more or less by the fact that his wife had been Catherine Leesugg, an English opera singer, who had sung the part of Rosina in an English version of Rossini's "Barber of Seville" as early as 1819. At Niblo's history I have already taken a glance. In the present chapter he is chiefly interesting, according to a story which has long had currency, as the manager who succeeded in putting an end to the Astor Place Opera House by a trick which took the bloom of caste off that aristocratic institution. I shall let Maretzek tell the story presently, pausing now to interject an anecdote which fell under my notice some years ago while I was turning over the records of the Grand Ducal Theater at Weimar. This always comes to my mind when the downfall of the Astor Place Opera House is mentioned, and also when, as has frequently been the case within the last sixteen years, I met a grandson of one of the principal actors in the incident in the streets of New York.

In April, 1817, there came to Weimar from Vienna a gifted dog, who assisted his master in the presentation of a play of the melodramatic order, entitled "The Dog of Aubri de Mont-Didier." The director of the Grand Ducal Theater at the time was one Wolfgang von Goethe. To him the dog's manager applied for the privilege of producing his edifying piece. Goethe refused permission, and there was danger that the patrons of the playhouse which had echoed to the first sounds of the plays of Schiller and Goethe were to be deprived of the inestimable privilege of seeing a dog dash out of the door of a tavern in which a murder had been committed, pull a bell rope to alarm the village, carry a lantern into the forest, discover the murderer just at the psychological moment, pursue him from rock to rock, capture him at the last, and thus bring about the triumph of justice. But the dog's manager was not thus to be put down. He went with a petition to Fräulein Jagemann (whose portrait in the character of Sappho my readers may still find hanging on a wall of the library at Weimar), and solicited her intervention with the Grand Duke, whose reign Schiller and Goethe made glorious. Fräulein Jagemann was a prima donna and the Grand Duke's mistress. ("The companion of my leisure moments," he called her with quite a pretty euphemism.) In the former capacity she had given Goethe, the director, a great deal of trouble, and in the latter her influence had caused him many an annoyance. It was the dog that broke the camel's back of his patience. Fräulein Jagemann saw an opportunity to get in a blow against her artistic tyrant, and she wheedled Charles Augustus into commanding the production of "The Dog of Aubri de Mont-Didier." The play was given twice, on April 12 and 14, 1817, with uproarious success, of course, and on April 17th Goethe resigned the artistic direction of the Weimar Court Theater. As for Fräulein Jagemann, she eventually got a title and estates as Frau von Heygendorf.

And now for the story of "The Dogs of Donetti: or, the Downfall of the Astor Place Opera House," by Max Maretzek; it must be prefaced by the statement that after Edward Fry had made a lamentable failure of his opera season at which he had the services of Maretzek as conductor, Maretzek became lessee of the house and thus remained for the years 1849 and 1850.

Bled to the last drop in my veins (I, of course, allude to my purse and my pocket), the doors of the Astor Place Opera House were closed upon the public. It was my determination to woo the fickle goddess Fortune elsewhere. Possibly her blinded eyes might not recognize her old adorer, and she might even yet bestow upon me a few of her faithless smiles.

Again, however, after my departure, was the opera house leased. But to whom do you imagine it was now abandoned by the exemplary wisdom of its proprietors?

To the identical William Niblo who had fostered and encouraged the opposition—the same William Niblo who had a theater (or let me give it his name, and call it—a garden) within the length of some three stone-throws from their own house. It must be granted they did not foresee that which was about to happen. But this will scarcely palliate the folly of taking the head of a rival establishment for their tenant.

This gentleman engaged the troupe of dogs and monkeys, then in this country, under the charge of a certain Signor Donetti.

Their dramatic performances were offered to the refined and intelligent proprietors and patrons of this classic and exclusive place of amusement. Naturally they protested. It was in vain. Then they sued out an injunction against this exhibition on the ground that in Niblo's lease of the premises only respectable performances were permitted to be given in the opera house. On the "hearing to show cause" for this injunction Mr. Niblo called up Donetti or some of his friends, who testified that his aforesaid dogs and monkeys had, in their younger days, appeared before princes and princesses and kings and queens. Moreover, witnesses were called who declared under oath that the previously mentioned dogs and monkeys behaved behind the scenes more quietly and respectably than many Italian singers. This fact I feel that I am not called on to dispute. . . . As might be supposed the injunction was dissolved.

As a matter of course, the house lost all its prestige in the eyes of the community. Shortly afterward its contents were sold, and the shell of the opera was turned into a library. Its deathblow had been given it as a place for theatrical amusement by the astute Mr. William Niblo.

Furthermore, Mr. Maretzek would have us believe that some year or two later, the Academy of Music having been projected meanwhile, he met Niblo and asked him what he thought of the prospects of the new enterprise.

"Why," answered the manager, in his nasal voice, "I suppose I shall have again to engage Donetti's dogs and monkeys."

CHAPTER V
MARETZEK, HIS RIVALS AND SINGERS

Of the operatic managers of fifty years ago Max Maretzek was the only one with whom I was personally acquainted, and it was not until near the close of his career that he swam into the circle of my activities or I into his. He died on September 17, 1897. His last years were spent in a home on Staten Island, and the public heard nothing about him after the memorable concert given for his benefit at the Metropolitan Opera House on February 12, 1889, the occasion being set down as the fiftieth anniversary of the beginning of his career as a conductor in America. All the notable conductors then living in New York took part in the concert—Theodore Thomas, Anton Seidl, Frank van der Stucken, Walter Damrosch, and Adolf Neuendorff. Maretzek was seventy-six years of age at the time of his death, and he had grown old, if not gracefully, at least good-naturedly. He did not quarrel with his fate, but even when he spoke of its buffetings it was in a tone of pleasant banter and with a twinkle in his eyes. His manner of accepting what the world brought him was illustrated at a meeting which I had with him in the season of 1883-84—the first of the Metropolitan Opera House. It was on a Saturday afternoon that I found him standing in front of the new establishment after the first act of the opera was over. Not having seen him in the house, I asked him if he was attending the performance. He said he was, but that, the house being sold out, he had no seat. Thereupon I offered him mine, saying that it might be a pleasure to occupy it since several of his professional acquaintances were seated in the neighborhood who would be glad to greet him. "Annie Louise Cary is right back of me," I said, "and Clara Louise Kellogg near by." But he did not care to accept my offer, and I fancied I saw a rather more serious and contemplative look come over his grizzled face. Naturally, I asked him what he thought of the new house and the new enterprise, adding that I regretted that he was not the manager. He began with apparent solemnity:

"Well, when I heard the house was to be built, I did think—I did think that some of the stockholders would remember what I had done for opera. Some of the old-timers, who used to go to the Academy of Music and Astor Place Opera House when I was manager there, I thought, would recollect what companies I gave them—Parodi, and Steffanone, and Marini, and Lorini, and Bettini, and Bertucca"—(how often I had heard him chant the list, counting off the singers on his chubby fingers!)—"and Truffi, and Benedetti, and Salvi. I thought somebody might remember this and the old man, and come to me and say, 'Max, you did a good deal for us once, let us do something for you now.' I didn't expect them to come and offer me the house, but I thought they might say this and add, 'Come, we'll make you head usher,' or, 'You may have the bar.' But nobody came, and I'm out of it completely."

Maretzek's managerial career continued at least until 1874; after that he conducted operas for others and did something toward the last in the way of teaching. It was seldom that one could get into a conversation with him but he could grow reminiscent, and, reverting to the olden time, begin tolling off the members of the companies which he had led to artistic victories and who had helped plunge him into financial defeat—"Parodi, and Steffanone, and Marini, and Bettini, and Lorini, and Bertucca," and so on. Poor Bertucca! Few of those who in later years saw Mme. Maretzek, portly and sedate, enter the orchestra at the Academy of Music and Metropolitan Opera House, and tune her harp while the audience was gathering in the gilded horseshoes above, recalled that she had been the sprightly and bewitching Bertucca of thirty years before.

I cannot recall that Maretzek ever grew bitter in discoursing on what once was and what might have been. He could be satirical and cutting, but his words were generally accompanied with a smile. His dominant mood and something of his style of expression are illustrated in his book, "Crotchets and Quavers, or Revelations of an Opera Manager in America," which he published in 1855, most obviously with the help of some literary hack who, I imagine, got the thoughts from Maretzek, but supplied the literary dress for them. A good many old scores are paid off in the book, and a good many grudges fed fat; but there are not many instances of bad humor. There is a sugar coating even to his malice. Shortly before I left Cincinnati, the College of Music of that city, having suffered a serious loss of prestige because of the resignation of Theodore Thomas, made a pretentious announcement of an operatic department, a practical school for opera, which was to be conducted by Maretzek. I think it was in the fall of 1880. At any rate, it was on the very eve of my departure from Cincinnati for New York. Maretzek came to the city somewhat late in the evening, and though I called upon him at the Burnet House as soon as I heard of his coming, he was already in bed when my card reached him. Nevertheless, I was asked up to his room. A tea tray still stood upon the table by the side of the bed when I entered. He held out his hand cordially and apologized for receiving me in bed. I told him that my newspaper, The Gazette, wanted to know, for the information of its readers, what he purposed doing at the college. The squabble between Mr. Thomas and the college authorities had kept the town in a ferment for months, all of which Maretzek seemed to know. It was no concern of his, but he could not help having artistic sympathies or predispositions, and these were obviously on the side of the musician Thomas, who had split with the business management of the college because of charlatanry in its methods. There was a merry twinkle in Maretzek's eyes as in reply to my question he answered: "I don't know what I am going to do, or what I'm here for. They made me an offer, and I came. I'm told that I am to run an opera school." Again he held out his hand at parting, and his last words were:

"Don't give me away!"

Not many months had passed before he, too, had followed Theodore Thomas back to New York, I met him in the lobby of the Academy of Music between the acts of the opera. It was in the consulship of Mapleson. "Hello!" I greeted him. "Back to New York so soon? What's the matter in Cincinnati?"

The quizzical smile with which he had greeted me grew wider as he replied sententiously:

"I'm not a hog. I know when I've got enough!"

Maretzek was a Hebrew, born in Brünn, Moravia, and educated in Vienna, where first he studied medicine, but, according to his own story, becoming disgusted with the sights of the dissecting room, he changed his purposes and devoted himself to music. He wrote an opera entitled "Hamlet" when he was twenty-two years old, and a year later, in 1844, found himself in London, employed under Balfe at Her Majesty's Theater. Thence he was brought to New York to conduct the opera for Mr. E. P. Fry, as has already been mentioned, in 1848. After one season as conductor he started in on his career as manager, which lasted twenty-five years, the first five of which are amusingly described in his book "Crotchets and Quavers." More than twenty years later he attempted to continue the story in a musical journal, and gathering the disconnected chapters together, issued them in an unattractive form under the title "Flats and Sharps." The first book is, to some extent, a contribution to musical history, though its strong personal equation and its effort to be entertaining mar its value and influence. The impression to which I have given utterance, that he was helped in its preparations by some penny-a-liner, is based upon the difference between its pages and the personal letters which I received from Maretzek in his later years, especially a brief autobiographical sketch which he prepared for me. To judge by the evidence of book and sketch, the latter in his own handwriting and delivered in person, one was forced to the conclusion either that he knew more about the English language six years after his first coming to New York than he did twenty years later or that he had hired somebody fluent but malignant of pen to put his thoughts into shape. It had long been the fashion for theatrical managers and opera impresarios to give the history of their administrations to the world, and

Maretzek was but following it, though why he should have done so before he had finally and definitely retired from the field it is not easy to see.

It was an unwise, even a dangerous, thing to do, for it involved the necessity of criticizing the acts of professional people and music patrons with whom a manager was more or less likely to come into contact if he expected to continue his enterprises. The style adopted in the book was the epistolary, the chapters being in the form of letters to European friends: Hector Berlioz (with whom Maretzek had been brought into connection in London), Fiorentino (an Italian, who had been musical critic of the Corsaire, of Paris), Luigi Lablache (the famous basso), Professor Joseph Fischof (of Vienna), Michael W. Balfe (of London, composer of "The Bohemian Girl" and other English operas), Frederick Gye (manager of the Royal Italian Opera, Covent Garden, London), and Carl Eckert (conductor of the Court Opera, Vienna). A final chapter is addressed to the public and is devoted to a recital of the troubles through which the Academy of Music passed in the earliest stages of its career. Eckert had been in America as conductor of the company headed by Henrietta Sontag, and the chapter over which his name is written tells of the career of that artist in the United States and her death in Mexico. Incidentally, also, Maretzek pays off a score owing to Bernard Ullmann, a manager with whom Maretzek was much in conflict and against whom he tried to turn the public by calling the attention of Americans to the sneers in which the delectable gentleman had indulged at their expense while he was trying to win the good graces of the Havanese. Nevertheless, within four years he was Ullmann's partner, for together they opened the season of 1859 at the Academy of Music. The quarrels of opera managers are very like those of lawyers inside the courtroom.

But when Maretzek was holding up the heinousness of Ullmann in the chapter entitled "Los Americanos y su gusto por la Musica," Ullmann was only an agent for Maurice Strakosch, who had entered the managerial field. It was different with Don Francesco Marty y Torrens, the impresario who invaded Maretzek's territory from Havana; and he remained Maretzek's pet aversion to the end of the chapter. In his memoirs Arditi, who came to New York as conductor of one of Marty's companies, says that Don Francesco was among impresarios the most generous of men, Maretzek the cleverest (though he sets down Maurice Grau as the "cleverest of entrepreneurs"), and Colonel Mapleson the most astute. It is not unlikely that Arditi's amiable opinion of the Cuban was influenced not a little by the circumstance that Marty, not caring to make money in New York, treated his artists with unusual liberality. That, naturally, would not tend to increase the admiration of a rival manager for him. He may have been the most generous of men in the eyes of Arditi, but in those of Maretzek he was worse than Barbaja, the Neapolitan manager, who owned the gambling monopoly in the kingdom of Naples, and who, after animating his acquaintances with music and singing, and diverting their eyes with the silk fleshings and short muslin jupons of his dancers, fleeced them at his gambling houses and became richer than the King of Naples himself. Maretzek intimates that in his youth Don Francesco had been the mate of a pirate vessel which preyed on the commerce of the Gulf of Mexico and adjacent waters; that he betrayed his captain to death, and was rewarded with a monopoly of the fish trade in Cuba; that he became possessed mysteriously of enough money to fit out a feet of fishing boats to supply the market which he controlled; that from that source alone his annual income rose to about $160,000; that then he embarked in the slave trade, bringing negroes from Africa and Indians from Yucatan, which he bribed the Spanish officials to permit him to land; was knighted by the Spanish Crown out of gratitude for pecuniary help extended in a crisis; and built an opera house in Havana in order to acquire a social position among the proud people who, despite his badge of nobility, refused to "swallow the fish and digest the negro," as Maretzek puts it. This was the manager who, in the summer of 1850, brought to New York what Maretzek characterizes as "the greatest troupe which had been ever heard in America," and which, "in point of the integral talent, number, and excellence of the artists composing it," had "seldom been excelled in any part of the Old World."

"This party consisted of three prime donne. These were the Signore Steffanone, Bosio, and Tedesco. Its only contralto was the Signora Vietti. There were three tenors—Salvi, Bettini, and Lorini. Badiali and Corradi Setti were the two barytones, while the two bassi were Marini and Coletti. At the head of this extraordinary company was the great contrabassist Bottesini, assisted by Arditi. It would be useless, my old friend, to attempt to indicate to you the excellence of this company. You have long since known their names, or been aware of their standing as artists in the world of music. The greater portion of them enjoy a wide and well-deserved European reputation, and their reunion anywhere would form an almost incomparable operatic troupe."

Some of these names are those of singers whom, in his later days, I have said Maretzek was in the habit of chanting while telling them off on his fingers. His was not the credit of having brought them to the country, but he did, a year after they had made their first appearance in the Havana company, succeed in enticing them away from their generous manager and enlisting them under his banner at the Astor Place Opera House. All but Tedesco.

Of these singers Maretzek has more or less to say in his book, but the point of view is that of the manager perpetually harassed by the jealousies, importunities, and recalcitrancy of his singers. Steffanone was a conscientious artist, but had an infirmity of body and mind which was exceedingly troublesome to her manager; Bosio was talented and industrious, but had a husband whose devotion to her interests was an affliction to her manager; Tedesco was husbandless, but had a father who was so concerned about her honorarium that he came to the opera house on payday with a small pair of scales in his pocket, with which he verified every coin that came out of the exchequer of the unfortunate manager, "subjecting each separate piece of gold to a peculiarly Jewish examination touching their Christian perfection;" Salvi was a mountain of conceit, who believed himself to be the Louis Quatorze of the lyric drama, and compelled his manager to imagine him exclaiming "L'opéra c'est moi!" Toward his manager Salvi was a despot, who rewarded favors bestowed upon himself by compelling the manager to engage persons who had served the tenor. Maretzek cites a ukase touching a singer named Sidonia:

Caro Max: Fa di tutto per iscriturare la Sidonia, altrimenti io non canto ne "Don Giovanni," ne "Norma," ne altri.

A 250 $ il mese, e che la scrittura porti 350 $. Amen, cosi sia. Il tuo, Salvi.

19. 4. 53.

(In English: "Dear Max: Do everything to engage the Sidonia, otherwise I shall not sing in 'Don Giovanni,' 'Norma' or other operas. At $250 per month, but let the writing bear $350. Amen, and so be it.")

"At $250 per month, but let the scrittura bear $350." I wonder how many of my readers think of this cheap device of singers and managers when they read about the honoraria received by opera singers to-day!

Bettini drank to excess and spent whole nights in the gambling room, rendering him unfit for duty ever and anon; Badiali was singularly conscientious as an artist, and became a favorite with the public, but not with his colleagues, because of his extraordinary meanness and avarice and a jealous disposition; Marini was the greatest living Italian basso, save Lablache, but his voice was occasionally unreliable, and he frequently ill-humored, capricious, splenetic, and peevish.

In private life Angiolina Bosio was Mme. Panayotis di Xindavelonis, the wife of a Greek gentleman, whom she had married in 1851. She was in her prime when she came to New York, though she had not reached the meridian of her reputation. Her features were irregular, and she was not comely. Richard Grant White claims credit for having given her the punning sobriquet "Beaux Yeux," by which she was widely known on account of her luminous and expressive eyes. "Her voice," says White:

was a pure, silvery soprano, remarkable alike for its penetrating quality and for its charm so fine and delicate that it seemed almost intellectual. But she was not a remarkably dramatic singer, even in light comedy parts, which best suited her; and her style was not at all declamatory. She *sang*; and in her vocalization she showed the results of intelligent study in the old Italian school. Her phrasing was incomparably fine, and the delicacy of her articulation has been surpassed by no modern prima donna, not even by Alboni. Thus much of her as a vocal artist; but her charm was greatly personal. Although her acting was always appropriate and in good taste, and at times—as, for example, in the saucy widow of "Don Pasquale"—very captivating, she never seemed to throw herself wholly into her part. She was always Angiolina Bosio, and appeared on the stage like a lady performing admirably in private theatricals. Her bearing was a delight to her audience, and seemed to be a performance, whereas it was only herself. She sang the music of all the great operatic composers to the admiration of the public and the critics of the most exacting disposition; but she was greatest in Rossini's operas, and in Bellini's and Donizetti's. Yet her exquisitely charming and finished performance of Zerlina should not be passed over unmentioned.

Tedesco, who came to New York with the first Havana company in April, 1847, presented herself to the always susceptible mind of Mr. White as a great, handsome, ox-eyed creature, the picture of lazy loveliness until she was excited by music; then she poured out floods, or rather gusts, of rich, clear sound. "She was not a great artist, but her voice was so copious and so musical that she could not be heard without pleasure, although it was not of the highest kind." Bettini left nothing here that remained in the memory of New Yorkers except the half of a name which he gave to his wife, the contralto Trebelli-Bettini, who was a member of Mr. Abbey's company on the opening of the Metropolitan Opera House in 1883. Salvi came over with the Havana company in the spring of 1848, and was one of the fish which Maretzek took from Marty's weirs. If we are to believe the testimony of contemporaneous critics he was the greatest tenor of his time, with the exception of Mario. That was the opinion of White, who wrote of him as follows in The Century Magazine for May, 1882:

Although Salvi was past his youth when he first sang in New York, his voice was yet in perfect preservation. It lacked nothing that is to be expected in a tenor voice of the first class; and it had that mingling of manliness and tenderness, of human sympathy and seraphic loftiness which, for lack of any other or better word, we call divine. As a vocalist he was not in the first rank, but he stood foremost in the second. His presence was manly and dignified, and he was a good actor. But it was as a vocalist, pure and simple, that he captivated and moved his audiences. He was heard in

America at brief intervals during a few years, and his influence upon the taste of the general music-loving public was very considerable and wholly good. Singing at Niblo's or Castle Garden and other like places at which the price of admission was never more than $1, and was generally 50 cents, he gave to multitudes who would otherwise have had no such opportunity that education in art which is to be had only from the performances of a great artist. In purity of style he was unexceptionable. He lacked only a little higher finish, a little more brilliancy of voice and impressiveness of manner to take a position among tenors of the very first rank. Of these, however, there are never two in the world at the same time, scarcely two in the same generation; and so Salvi prepared the public for the coming Mario. His forte was the cantabile and his finest effects were those in mezza voce, expressive of intense suppressed feeling. More than once when he sang "Spirto gentil," as he rose to the crescendo of the second phrase, and then let his cry pass suddenly away in a dying fall, I have heard a whole house draw suspended breath, as if in pain, so nearly alike in their outward manifestation and fine, keen pleasure.

Such were some of the singers whose names are associated in the musical annals of New York with that of Max Maretzek.

CHAPTER VI
THE NEW YORK ACADEMY OF MUSIC

Fifty-one years ago the center of operatic activity had shifted to the Academy of Music, at Fourteenth Street and Irving Place, and there it remained until the Metropolitan Opera House was built. From the opening of the Academy in 1854 to the opening of the Metropolitan in 1883 the former had no rival as an establishment, though the rivalry between managers and singers was the liveliest that New York has ever seen during the first decade of the time. For twenty years Burton's Theater revived its early traditions, and housed an opera troupe at intervals, and Niblo's Theater and Castle Garden were open to every manager who wished to experiment with the costly enterprise. English companies came and went, and a new competitive element, which soon became more dangerous than that which several times crushed the Italian exotic, entered in the shape of German opera, which, though it first sought a modest home in the lesser theaters of the Bowery and lower Broadway, soon achieved recognition at the fashionable Academy. The eagerness of the rivalry in the Italian field alone is indicated by the fact that the Academy had five different managers in the first three seasons of its history, and that thereafter, until the coming of James H. Mapleson in 1878, it was almost a rule that there should be a change of management every season. Maretzek was alternately manager and competitor over and over again, and the bitterest rivals of one season would be found associated with each other the next. Already in the first season the stockholders had to step in and assume some of the risks of management to save the enterprise from shipwreck, and, despite the attractiveness of the house, the excellence of the performances, the presence of such phenomenal artists as Mme. Grisi and Signor Mario, and generous public patronage, the first season cost the different managers between $50,000 and $60,000—three times as much as Maretzek had lost in the previous six years, if that gentleman's word is to be taken. The figures look modest now, but twenty years later their duplication at the Metropolitan Opera House sufficed to effect a revolution in methods, and eventually tastes, which had a profound influence upon musical life in New York.

The Academy of Music had its birth in the expiring throes of the Astor Place Opera House. The spirit of which it was the material expression seems to have been admirable. To this the name of the establishment bears witness. It was not alone the official title of the French institution, popularly spoken of as the Grand Opéra, which was in the minds of the promoters of the New York enterprise—the new opera house was to be a veritable academy of music, an educational institution. Not only was fashionable society to have a place in which to display and disport itself, but popular taste and popular knowledge were to be cultivated. To this end the auditorium was to be three times as commodious as that of the Astor Place Opera House, and the low prices which had been prevalent only at Niblo's, Burton's, and Castle Garden were to be the rule at the new establishment. In the charter granted by the State, dated April 10, 1852, the purposes of the Academy were set down as the cultivation of taste by entertainments accessible at moderate charges, by furnishing facilities for instruction and by rewards. These purposes were overlooked at the beginning, but before the first season had come to its end Ole Bull, for a few weeks a manager, proclaimed his intention to pursue them by promising to open a conservatory in the fall of 1855, and at once (January, 1855) offering a prize of $1,000 for the "best original grand opera by an American composer, and upon a strictly American subject." The competition ended with Ole Bull's announcement, for his active season endured only two weeks.

It is doubtful if the competition would have produced anything more than a curiosity had it been carried to a conclusion. On the spur of the moment I can think of only two American musicians whose capacity was adequate to such a task—Mr. W. H. Fry, who was then musical critic and an editorial writer for The Tribune, and Mr. George F. Bristow, both of whom had composed operas found worthy of performance. Mr. Fry's "Leonora" was performed at the Academy on March 29, 1858, with Mme. Lagrange in the principal rôle, but the score was already a dozen years old, and it is not likely that the composer's state of health would have permitted him to undertake the writing of a new opera even if he had been so disposed. Mr. Bristow's "Rip Van Winkle," which had a production in New York in the year of Ole Bull's announcement, may, for all that I know to the contrary, have been written for the prize. The scheme of uniting a training school for singers with an opera house was not heard of again, so far as I can recall, until Mr. Conried became director of the Metropolitan Opera House. It has much to commend it, and might be made a power for artistic good with an operatic establishment on a really public-spirited, artistic, and unselfish basis; as it is, its influence is apt to be pernicious morally, as well as artistically. How seriously Mr. Fry took the proposed educational feature of the institution is indicated by an article on the new opera house, which he published in The Tribune, in the course of which he said:

The expense of maintaining an opera house so nurtured at home will be at most not more than one-fourth what it would be if the artists were brought from Europe. American vocalists would be content with some few thousand dollars a year, and, if they were sought for and educated, boarded and lodged gratuitously the meanwhile, their services could be procured for several years in payment of the expenses of apprenticeship. In that way alone can the exorbitant demands of foreign artists be diminished; and the folly and extravagance of paying them from one to ten thousand dollars a night, as has been done in this city, will be forever avoided. In connection with this it may be mentioned that there are some Americans now studying for the operatic stage in Italy, and one lady of Boston has appeared in Naples with success. It may yet come to pass that art, in all its ramifications, may be as much esteemed as politics, commerce or the military profession. The dignity of American artists lies in their hands.

Mr. Fry's hopes, so far as the Academy of Music is concerned, were never realized, and after half a century his words are echoing wherever writers indulge in discussion of ways and means for promoting American music. Yet, without schools connected with opera houses American singers have made their mark, not only at home, but in the lyric theaters of Italy, France, Germany, and England. Names like Clara Louise Kellogg, Annie Louise Cary, Minnie Hauk, Alwina Valleria, Emma Nevada, Lillian Nordica, Adelaide Phillips, Emma Albani, and Josephine Yorke are connected more or less intimately with the history of the Academy of Music, but they do not exhaust the list. To them must be added those of Charles Adams, Suzanne Adams, David Bispham, Robert Blass, William Candidus, Emma Eames, Signor Foli, Geraldine Farrar, Julia Gaylord, Helen Hastreiter, Eliza Hensler (the daughter of a Boston tailor who became the morganatic wife of Dom Fernando of Portugal), Louise Homer, Emma Juch, Pauline l'Allemande, Marie Litta, Isabella McCullough, Frederick C. Packard, Jules Perkins, Signor Perugini, Mathilde Phillips, Susan Strong, Minnie Tracey, Jennie Van Zandt, Emma Abbott, Bessie Abott, Julia Wheatley, Virginia Whiting (Signora Lorini), Edyth Walker, Marion Weed, Zélie de Lussan, Clarence Whitehill, Allen Hinckley, Joseph F. Sheehan, and half a dozen or more singers now attracting attention in London and Germany.

Max Maretzek was the first lessee of the Academy of Music, but the company that opened it on October 2, 1854, was that engaged by J. H. Hackett to support Grisi and Mario, which had appeared at Castle Garden two months before. Maretzek sublet to Hackett, who thought that the brilliancy of his stars, and the new house, justified him in advancing the price of seats to $2. He had a rude awakening, for the audience on the first night was neither large nor brilliant. It numbered not more than 1,500, and on the second night the prices came down to the popular scale, with $1.50 as the standard. By the middle of December, though the stockholders had been obliged to come to the rescue of Hackett, the collapse of the opening enterprise was announced, and Hackett took Grisi and Mario to Boston for a brief season, and then came back for three or four performances at the Metropolitan Theater.

The last performance took place on February 20, 1855. Though many excellent singers had been heard in New York between the coming of Malibran and that of Grisi and Mario, the three months of their sojourn in America have ever since remained memorable. For a generation afterward all tenors were measured by Mario's standard. Grisi created a less enduring impression, because the audiences that heard her were within the space of a few years permitted also to hear such singers as Jenny Lind, Henrietta Sontag, and Marietta Alboni, three names that are still resplendent in operatic annals. There does not seem to be any reason for questioning the belief that Mario was the greatest tenor singer that ever gladdened the ears of American music lovers. Richard Grant White, who was then writing the musical reviews for The Courier and Enquirer newspaper, had chosen Benedetti as his ideal of a dramatic singer, and he found Mario lacking in passion, while confessing that he had the sweetest tenor voice in all the world. He retired from the stage in 1867, but came to America in 1872, under Strakosch, and sang in concert with Carlotta Patti, Annie Louise Gary, Teresa Carreño, and Sauret. He had always been a somewhat unreliable singer, frequently disappointing his audiences by not singing at all, or singing listlessly until he reached the air in which he could produce a sensational effect, and when he returned to America he had only a superb presence and bearing, and a magnificent reputation with which to arouse interest. He was sixty-two years old, and had accepted an engagement for the reason that frequently brings worn-out artists to the scenes of their earlier triumphs; he needed money. Eight years later his financial condition so distressed his old friends and admirers in London that they got up a benefit concert for him. He was living in Rome when he died in 1883.

Such satisfaction as can come to one from seeing a renowned artist was mine in 1872; but I can scarcely say that I *heard* Mario. With Annie Louise Gary he sang first in a graceful little duet, "Per valli, per boschi," by Blangini ("Dear old Mario had to warm up in a duet before he would trust himself in solo," said the admired contralto, many years afterward), and later attempted Beethoven's "Adelaide." Romances were Mario's specialty, and Beethoven's divine song ought to have been an ideal selection for him, but it was quite beyond his powers and I do not now know whether to be glad or sorry that I heard him attempt it. It is always unfortunate when great singers who have gone into decay are tempted again to sing. To the generation who knew them in their prime they bring a double measure of disappointment—grief for the passing away of the art which once gave pleasure, and regret that the younger generation should carry down to posterity a false impression of the singer's voice and style. Who shall measure the heartburnings left by Madame Patti's last visit to America when she sold herself to a trumpery balladist, and, affecting the appearance and manner which had been hers a quarter of a century before, tried to make a new generation believe that it was listening to the vocalist whom veterans maintained was the last one entitled to be called "la Diva." How much lovelier and more fragrant the memory of Annie Louise Cary, whose American career began during the Strakosch régime at the Academy of Music, and ended with her marriage to Charles Mon son Raymond, when she was still in the very plenitude of her powers. Many a time within the first few years after her retirement have I seen her surrounded by young women and old, as she was leaving the Academy of Music or the Metropolitan Opera House, and heard their pleading voices: "Oh, Miss Cary! aren't you ever going to sing for us again?" and "Please, Miss Cary, won't you let me kiss you?"

Ole Bull's management of the Academy of Music was but a fleeting incident, memorable only for the protestations with which it was begun and for its brevity. For the famous Norwegian violinist it was a Utopian dream with a speedy and rude awakening. After he had retired the Lagrange troupe came from downtown and completed the season with the help of the stockholders, and Maretzek, the erstwhile impresario and lessee, became the conductor. For four years, 1855, 1856, 1857, and 1858, the Academy saw Maretzek, Strakosch, and Ullmann alternately installed as impresarios, and then for a year there was no opera at the house, the three men at the head of as many different companies seeking their fortunes outside of the metropolis. With Ullmann Thalberg was associated for a space, the great pianist having come to America to make money under the management of Ullmann, and probably having been persuaded to risk some of his gains by his manager. It was but a brief interlude, however. Ullmann, whose activities in America extended over a quarter of century, lived to manage some of the artists who are still before the public. The beginning of his career, like that of Maretzek, fell in the period when Barnumism was at its zenith, and Ullmann was utterly unconscionable in the methods to which he resorted for the purpose of exploiting his artists. It was under his operatic consulship that the winsome Piccolomini came to New York—an artist of insignificant caliber, lovely to look upon and fascinating as an actress in soubrette parts. "A Columbine," said Chorley about her when she effected her début in London, "born to 'make eyes' over an apron with pockets, to trick the Pantaloon of the piece, to outrun the Harlequin, and to enjoy her own saucy confidence on the occasion of her success—with those before the footlights and the orchestra." But this was not all. "Never did any young lady, whose private claims to modest respect were so great as hers are known to be," said the same critic, "with such self-denial fling off their protection in her resolution to lay hold of the public at all risks. Her performances at times approached offense against maidenly reticence and delicacy. When she played Zerlina, in 'Don Giovanni,' such virtue as there was between the two seemed absolutely on the side of the libertine hero—so much invitation was thrown into the peasant girl's rusticity." Here was a capital subject for the methods dear to the heart of Ullmann. In London the Piccolomini had been proclaimed to be of a noble Roman family, the niece of a cardinal, who had quarreled with her relations because of her theatrical propensities. There may have been some truth in the statements, but Ullmann adorned her history still more, and proclaimed from every New York housetop that the lady was a lineal descendant of Charlemagne, and the great-grand-daughter of Schiller's tragic hero Max Piccolomini.

It was under the co-consulship of Maretzek and Ullmann that Adelina Patti made her operatic début at the Academy of Music. The date was November 24, 1859, the opera "Lucia di Lammermoor." Twenty-five years later Patti was again the prima donna of the Academy, though Mapleson was now the manager. It was the second year of the rivalry between the Academy and the Metropolitan Opera House, and Colonel Mapleson conceived the idea of profiting by the anniversary. At first it was planned that "Lucia" should be given, with Brignoli as Edgardo, the part he had sung in the opera at Patti's début, but two months before the time the tenor died. Instead, "Martha" was performed, in a manner wholly commonplace in all respects except as to the titular rôle, in which Mme. Patti appeared, as a matter of course. There was only a little perfunctory applause, but Colonel Mapleson had resolved that the scene should be enacted, of which we have often read, in which the devotees of the prima donna unhitch the horses from her carriage, and themselves drag it, with wild rejoicings, through the streets. To make sure of such a spontaneous ovation in staid New York was a question which Mapleson solved by hiring fifty or more Italians (choristers, probably) from the familiar haunts in Third Avenue, and providing them with torches, to follow the carriage, which was prosaically dragged along to its destination at the Windsor Hotel. As a demonstration it was the most pitiful affair that I have ever witnessed. In fact, it seemed to me such a humiliation of the great artist that on the next opera night I suggested to my colleague of The Times newspaper that something adequate and appropriate to so interesting an anniversary be arranged. He agreed and within a fortnight or so a banquet was given in Mme. Patti's honor at the Hotel Brunswick, under the auspices of a committee consisting of a number of well-known gentlemen, including Judge Daly, William Steinway, and Nahum Stetson. The committee of arrangements, having visited Mme. Patti and gained her consent, went to work right merrily, but before the invitations were issued an obstacle was met which threatened shipwreck to the amiable enterprise; the wives of several gentlemen who had been invited privately refused pointblank to break bread with the prima donna on account of the scandal caused by her separation from the Marquis de Caux and marriage to Nicolini, the tenor. Somewhat perplexed, the two critics visited her a second time, and put the matter to her as delicately as possible. Would she, under the circumstances, be the guest of a number of gentlemen, representative of the legal, artistic, and literary professions? Again she accepted, and without a moment's hesitation. So, instead of the gathering that had been planned, there was a stag party of about seventy gentlemen in the ballroom of the Brunswick, handsomely decorated and discreetly lighted with wax candles.

The preliminary reception was held in one of the rooms adjoining the banquet hall, and there a scene was enacted which brought into relief a trait of character which was extremely useful to the Colonel in the difficult task of managing his wilful and capricious prima donna. Mme. Patti received her hosts seated upon a divan. She looked radiant, and was wholly at ease after having taken a peep into the hall to see that the light would not be prejudicial to her complexion. One after another of the seventy gentlemen advanced to her, took the hand which she extended with a gracious smile, muttered the pretty compliment which he had rehearsed, and fell back to make room for the next comer. The room was pretty nearly full, when the Colonel appeared in the glory of that flawless, speckless dress suit, with the inevitable rose in the lapel of his coat. Not a glance did he give to right or left, but with the grace of a practised courtier, he sailed across the room, sank on his knees before the diva, and raised her hand to his lips. Such a smile as rewarded him! A score of breasts bulged out with envy and a score of brains framed the thought: "Confound it! Why didn't I think of doing that?"

The dinner passed off without a hitch, Mme. Patti managing by a hundred pretty coquetries to convince nearly every one of her three-score and ten hosts that he had received at least one smile that was more gracious than that bestowed upon his fellows. Speeches were made by Judge Daly, William Steinway, Dr. Leopold Damrosch, William Winter and others, but, as Colonel Mapleson had carried off the palm by his courtliness at the reception, Max Maretzek made himself the most envied of men at the dinner. Quite informally he was asked to say something after the set programme had been disposed of. Where the other speakers had brought forward their elegantly turned oratorical tributes the grizzled old manager told stories about the child life and early career of the guest. Amongst other things he illustrated how early the divine Adelina had fallen into the ways of a prima donna by refusing to sing at a concert in Tripler Hall unless he, who was managing the concert, would first go out and buy her a pound of candy. He agreed to get the sweetmeats provided she would give him a kiss in return. In possession of her box she kept both of the provisions of her contract. When the toastmaster declared the meeting adjourned Patti bore straight down on her old manager and said:

"Max, if I gave you a kiss for a box of candy then, I'll give you one for nothing now!"

And she did.

CHAPTER VII
MAPLESON AND OTHER IMPRESARIOS

Memories are crowding upon me, and I find there is much still to be said about the Academy of Music, and the operatic folk whom it housed between 1854 and 1886. Just now the incidents which have been narrated about the banquet given in honor of the twenty-fifth anniversary of Adelina Patti's début recall other characteristic anecdotes of Colonel Mapleson, who managed the Academy of Music from 1878 to the end of the disastrous season of 1885-'86. When Mapleson and Abbey were drawing up their forces for the battle royal between the Academy of Music and the Metropolitan Opera House in 1883, one of the New York newspapers reported Mme. Patti as saying: "Colonel Mapleson comes here when he wants me to sing, and he calls me 'My dear child,' and he goes down on both knees and kisses my hands, and he has, you know, quite a supplicating face, and it is not easy to be firm with a man of such suavity of manners." I have often thought of this in connection with the outcome of the disastrous rivalry between the two houses and their managers. When Colonel Mapleson let himself down so gracefully upon his knee and pressed the prima donna's hand to his lips, the act was not all unselfish adoration. It used to be said that there was no manager alive who had succeeded in becoming debtor to Adelina Patti. It was golden grain alone that persuaded this bird to sing. The story is old of how her personal agent once hovered between her dressing room and the manager's office, carrying the message one way: "Madame Patti will not put on her slippers until she is paid," returning the other way with a thousand dollars; coming again to the manager with: "Madame has one slipper on, but will not put on the other till she has her fee"—and so on. Doubtless apocryphal and yet only a bit fanciful and exaggerated. Yet it was known in the inner operatic circles in 1885 that Colonel Mapleson had succeeded in getting himself pretty deeply into her debt. How he did it the anecdotes of the reception and Mme. Patti's interview serve to indicate. In sooth, the persuasive powers of the doughty colonel were distinctly remarkable, and it was not only the prima donna who lived in an atmosphere of adulation who fell a victim to them. I have a story to illustrate which came to me straight from the lips of the confiding creditor. He was a theatrical costumer, moreover, and one of the tribe of whom it is said that only to a Connecticut Yankee will they lower the flag in a horse trade.

My friend was a theatrical costumer with a shop conveniently situated in Union Square. When the clouds began to lower upon the Academy around the corner he became curious to know whether or not he was likely to get a balance of some $1,500 owing him for costumes furnished to the establishment. He sent his bill many times, and, being on amicable terms with Colonel Mapleson, called on him at intervals to talk over the situation. When he left the impresario's office he always carried away profuse promises of speedy payment, but nothing more. Finally, he put the bill into the hands of his lawyer, who at once took steps to attach the property of the foreign debtor, and, to bring about pressure in a manner that seemed likely to be effective, he instructed the deputy sheriff, who was to serve the legal papers, to present himself at the office of Colonel Mapleson an hour or so before the beginning of the opera. The arrangements perfected, he informed his client of what had been done. But there remained a kindly spot in the costumer's soul, and of his own volition he called on the manager in the afternoon of the day set apart for the coup in order to give him one more opportunity to save himself from the impending catastrophe.

"I found the Colonel in his office," said he, in relating the incident, "cutting the corners off of tickets and sending them out to fill his house for the next performance. While he clipped he talked away at me in his cheerfullest and blandest style, told me how sorry he was that he could not pay me out of hand, and deplored the action which I had taken, but with such absence of all resentment that I began to feel ashamed of myself for having threatened to shut him up. After half an hour I agreed to send a messenger post-haste to my lawyer and call off the sheriff. This done he borrowed $75 cash from me, and I went away happy. I tell you I know lots of managers, but there's only one Colonel Mapleson in this world."

Whether or not my friend ever collected his bill I do not know; but this I do know, that when the colonel ended the campaign of 1884-'85 Mme. Patti's name was on his list of creditors for a considerable sum—$5,000 or $6,000, I believe. The next time I met him he was sauntering about in what passes for a foyer in Covent Garden Theater, London. The rose in his buttonhole was not more radiant than he.

"What are you up to now, Colonel?" I asked him.

"In what respect?"

"In a business way, of course."

"Well," with a twinkling smile, "just now I am persuading Adelina to sing at my benefit."

"Will she do it?"

"I think she will" And she did.

Mapleson was one of the last of the race of managers who had practical training in the art in which he dealt commercially. He was a graduate of the Royal Academy of Music in the violin class, and had played in the orchestra at the opera. He had also studied singing, and in his youth tried his luck as an operatic tenor. In this he was like Maurice Strakosch, who played the pianoforte prodigiously as a child, studied singing three years with no less an artist than the great Pasta, and after singing for a space at Agram turned his attention again to the pianoforte. He came to New York in 1848, and his first engagement was with Maretzek, at the Astor Place Opera House. Afterward he was a member of a traveling concert company, in which he was associated with Amalia Patti, whom he married, and it was thus that he became the teacher, and, eventually, the manager of his sister-in-law, Adelina Patti. When Ronconi first appeared in America at Burton's Theater (which had been Palmo's Opera House), in the spring of 1858, Strakosch was the conductor. The last of the old opera managers whom I recall at this moment who were practical musicians as well, was Dr. Leopold Damrosch, who directed the destinies of the Metropolitan Opera House after one year of warfare with the Academy of Music had put Henry E. Abbey hors du combat for a while. Abbey came out of the ranks of theatrical managers, like Heinrich Conried, his only practical experience in music being as a cornet player in a brass band in Akron, Ohio, whence he came.

Strakosch's associates, however, were not musical practitioners. Ullmann may have had some knowledge of music, but he was all showman. Thalberg, the pianist, was Ullmann's partner when Strakosch and Ullmann joined their forces in January, 1857, to manage the Academy of Music, but the new coalition was the sign of Thalberg's withdrawal from the managerial field.

Like Maretzek, in his Cincinnati experience, the virtuoso knew when he had enough. Strakosch's later associates were his brothers, Ferdinand and Max. The former was the European agent for the firm, and the latter what might be termed the acting house man in the United States, especially during the later years of the Strakosch régime.

In Europe Maurice Strakosch was also associated with Pollini, who afterward became a large factor in the field of German opera, as manager of the opera in Hamburg. Pollini had been Strakosch's office boy. His real name was Pohl, and he hailed from Cologne; but he, too, was a musician. Strakosch died in Paris in October, 1887. One night in July, 1886, I met him in the theater at Altona, whither I had gone to hear a performance of "Der Trompeter von Säkkingen," then the rage throughout Germany. He asked me to drive back to his hotel in Hamburg with him, for his physician had told him that day that he might drink a glass of beer, the first in six months, and he wanted a friend to share the pleasure with him. I brought him the latest news from the opera houses of New York, and, also, the intelligence that Pollini had just engaged Mme. Sembrich for a season at some 5,000 francs a night.

"We quit partnership," said he, "back in the 70's because Pollini thought that money was no longer to be made in Italian opera, and wanted to take up German opera exclusively. I didn't agree with him, and went on with Nilsson and the rest. He got rich and I got poor, and now he's going back into the Italian field. He'll rue it."

Call the roll of some of the best of the singers whose American careers are chiefly bound up with the history of the Academy of Music: Grisi, Mario, Vestvali (a much admired contralto), Badiali, Amodio (barytone), Steffanone, Brignoli, Lagrange, Mirate, D'Angri, Piccolomini, Adelina Patti, Kellogg, Nilsson, Campanini, Lucca, Cary, Parepa, Albani, Hauk, Gerster, Nevada. There are others whom fond recollection will call back, some belonging indubitably to the first rank, like Maurel, some who will live on because they gladdened the hearts of the young people of a generation ago, who were more impressionable than critical. Some men of middle age (as they think) now will not want to forget Mlle. Ambre or Mlle. Marimon, and will continue to forgive the homely features of Mme. Scalchi for the sake of her perfect physical poise and movement as the page in "Les Huguenots," as others forgave the many registers of her voice because of her joyous volubility of utterance. Doubtless, too, there are matrons of to-day who will remember the singing of Ravelli with as much pleasure as I recall it, and the shapely legs of the young tenor that walked off with the heart (we also had a story of a diamond ring) of a young singer from California, who afterward made a name for herself in Paris, with more enthusiasm than I could possibly feel.

Some of these singers became intimately associated with New York life in a social way. Annie Louise Cary, after her marriage to Charles Monson Raymond, lived for years in a cheery apartment at No. 20 Fifth Avenue, sang occasionally with the choir in the West Presbyterian Church, in Forty-second Street, and shed sunshine over a circle of friends who loved her as enthusiastically as a woman as they had admired her as an artist. Now her home is in Norwalk, Conn. Her first operatic engagement was at Copenhagen, and she spent two seasons in the opera houses of the Scandinavian peninsula, and one at Brussels before the Strakosch brothers brought her to the United States, in 1870. The first season she sang in concert with Nilsson, the second (1871-72) in opera, the third with Carlotta Patti and Mario in concert; and thereafter till her retirement in 1882 in both concert and opera, winning and holding an almost unparalleled popularity. In the Strakosch company of 1873-74 she was one of a galaxy of artists that the opera-goers of that period, who are still living, will never cease to think of without a swelling of the heart—Nilsson, Cary, Campanini, Capoul, Maurel, Del Puente, and others.

Campanini remained the tenor of tenors for New Yorkers for a decade longer. Abbey took him away from Mapleson for the first season of the Metropolitan Opera House, and, after the introduction of German opera there, his local career was practically at an end. He died in 1896 in Italy, whither he had returned on retirement. His dramatic style improved as his voice decayed. When he first came he was chiefly a lyrical singer; his Elvino was delicious beyond description. In his last years he had taken on robust stature, and his passionate utterances in "Carmen" and "Aïda" will live till the end in the memory of those who heard them. He was proud of his skill as a singer pure and simple, though he was more or less of a "naturalist," as the Germans call a singer who owes more to nature than to artistic training. How greatly he admired the perfection of his "attack" is illustrated in an incident which twice grieved the soul of Theodore Thomas and some other sticklers for the verities in classical music.

At the Cincinnati Music Festival, in May, 1880, Mr. Thomas brought forward Beethoven's Mass in D, the great "Missa Solemnis." In the first movement, "Kyrie," of this work Beethoven has created an effect of surpassing beauty in the successive introduction of the solo voices. At the outset there is a crashing chord from all the forces, including the full organ. The thundering sound ceases abruptly, leaving the solo tenor voice sustaining a tone seemingly in midair. Another loud crash projects the solo contralto voice, and so on. The effect is transporting; but the obvious intention of the composer and the loveliness of his device weighed nothing in Campanini's mind against the fact that it interfered with popular appreciation of the "attack," of which he was proud. So he calmly waited until the colossal D major chord was silenced, then intoned his D softly, and made a beautiful crescendo upon it. After a rehearsal I ventured to call his attention to the beautiful effectiveness of Beethoven's device, but he answered: "It is music for the head, not for the heart. If I sing it so the audience will not hear my beautiful attack."

And at the concert he perverted the text to gratify his vanity. I reminded Mr. Thomas of the incident two years later, when he gave the mass at the festival held in the Seventh Regiment Armory in New York. Campanini was to sing in it again. Mr. Thomas said he would set him right, but at the performance we were again cheated of Beethoven's effect in order that the tenor might make his. When Campanini died Philip Hale set down his estimate of him in these words:

No tenor who has blazed here above the opera horizon has fully equaled in brilliancy Campanini at his zenith. De Reszke, in point of personal refinement, is a greater artist, but his voice is inferior, and his dramatic action lacks the elementary force shown by Campanini when aroused. De Lucia is a greater actor of melodramatic parts, but his voice is too shrill. Tamagno in "Otello" is beyond comparison, but that is his one opera. . . . Of all tenors who have visited us since 1873 the greatest, viewed from all points, was Campanini.

The popular idol before Campanini was Brignoli, who held his own from the first days of the Academy until within less than a decade of its collapse. For some years before the Mapleson era, however, he had dropped out of the Italian operatic ranks and sung in English companies, and in concerts. It was in such organizations that I first heard him some twelve or fifteen years after he had become the popular "silver-voiced tenor" of New York. He came to New York in 1855, and his career was American, though it was in Paris that Strakosch heard him and turned his face toward America. He lived in New York, singing and occasionally managing companies in which he sang, till October, 1884, when he died. He was twice married, the first time to Kate Duckworth, an English contralto, known on the platform as Mlle. Morensi, and, after her death, to Isabella McCullough, an American soprano. Richard Grant White's mind was still obsessed by memories of Salvi, Benedetti, and Mario when Brignoli was basking in the sunshine of popular favor, and his estimate of the tenor in The Century Magazine for June, 1882, is scarcely flattering either to the singer or the public that liked him. It was Mr. White's observation that Brignoli came into the swim at the time that the young woman of New York became the arbiter of art and elegance. Says Mr. White:

Her admiration of Brignoli was not greatly to the credit of her taste. He had one of those tenor voices that seem like the bleating of a sheep made musical. His method was perfectly good; but be sang in a very commonplace style, and was as awkward as the man that a child makes by sticking two skewers into a long potato; and he walked the stage, hitching forward first one side and then the other, much as the child would make his creature walk. But he was a very "nice" young man, was always ready to sing, and faute de mieux it became the fashion with the very young to like him. But there never was a tenor of any note in New York whose singing was so utterly without character or significance and who was so deficient in histrionic ability. His high and long continued favor is one of those puzzling popular freaks not uncommon in dramatic annals.

Let us hope, in a spirit of Christian charity and something more selfish, that Brignoli never read these severely critical words. His vanity was that of a child, and they would have grieved him inordinately. There was truly something of the bleat in his voice, and his walk on the stage, whether in concert or opera, was provocative of the risibles, but even his mannerisms were fascinating. Shall we, because a critic did not like him, be ashamed for having thrilled a little when we heard his "Coot boy, sweetheart, c-o-o-o-t boy!" thirty years ago? I trust not. And if he were here again, and his manager were to come with the old request, "Do me a favor, won't you, and if you chance to meet dear old Brig say something pretty to him and help me keep him in a good humor against the concert to-night—admire his teeth and compliment him on his youthful appearance"—we should do it for old sake's sake, and with a heart full of gratitude. No one could know Brignoli and remain in ignorance of his frailties and foibles. He probably ate as no tenor ate before or since—ravenously as a Prussian dragoon after a fast. No contracts did he sign on a Friday or on a thirteenth day, and he lived in perpetual dread of the evil eye. Part of his traveling outfit was a pair of horns, which he relied upon to shield him in case the possessor of the jettatura should get into his room and he not have his fingers properly posed. I had been four years in the turmoil of New York's musical life when Brignoli died; I cannot recall an unkind word that was ever spoken of him.

CHAPTER VIII
THE METROPOLITAN OPERA HOUSE

Not the chronicler of musical doings but the historian of society should discuss the genesis of the Metropolitan Opera House, which came twenty-five years ago to displace the Academy of Music as the home of grand opera in New York. In the second of these "Chapters of Opera" I cited the Metropolitan Opera House as the last illustration of the creative impulse which springs from the growth of wealth and social ambition, and stated that it marked the decay of the old Knickerbocker régime, and its amalgamation with the newer order of society. Before this latter occurrence, however, it had become plain that the Academy of Music could not accommodate all the representatives of the two elements in fashionable society, who, for one reason or another, wished to own or occupy the boxes which were the visible sign of wealth and social position. There was no manifest dissatisfaction, either, with the Academy of Music or with the performances under the direction of Colonel Mapleson, though these were conventional enough and the dress of the operas looked particularly shabby in contrast with the new scenery and costumes at the new theater when once the rivalry had begun. The house being satisfactory, popular taste contented with the representations, and there being no evidences of insufficient room in any part of the audience room except the private boxes, it seems obvious to the merest observer from without that social and not artistic impulses led to the enterprise which produced the new establishment.

The Metropolitan Opera House was built in the summer of 1883. The corporation which built it was called the Metropolitan Opera House Company (Limited), and its leading spirits were James A. Roosevelt, the first president of the board of directors; George Henry Warren, Luther Kountze, George Griswold Haven, who remained the active head of the amusement committee from the beginning till he died last spring; William K. Vanderbilt, William H. Tillinghast, Adrian Iselin, Robert Goelet, Joseph W. Drexel, Edward Cooper, Henry G. Marquand, George N. Curtis, and Levi P. Morton. The building is bounded by Broadway, Seventh Avenue, Thirty-ninth and Fortieth Streets. About one-quarter of the space is devoted to the audience room, another quarter to the stage and accessories, and the rest to administrative offices, apartments, etc. Its cost, including the real estate, was $1,732,978.71, and so actively was the work of construction pushed that the portion of the building devoted to the opera was completed when the first performance took place on October 22, 1883. J. Cleaveland

Cady, the architect, had had no previous experience in building theaters, to which fact must be ascribed a few impracticable features of the house, most of which have since been eradicated, but he had made a careful study of the plans of the most celebrated opera houses of Europe, and the patrons of the house still have cause to be grateful to him for the care with which he looked after their safety and comfort. Since then the appearance of the interior has been changed very considerably. The two tiers of boxes were where they are now, but their fronts were perpendicular, and there was no bulging curve at the proscenium. Besides the two tiers of boxes, as they exist at present, there were twelve baignoirs, six on a side at the stage ends of the parquet circle, so-called. These were found to be unprofitable, and were abolished when the house was remodeled about ten years after the opening. The decoration of the interior was intrusted to E. P. Tredwill, an architect of Boston, who followed Mr. Cady's wishes in avoiding all garish display and tawdry effect. The deepest color in the audience room was the dark, rich red of the carpet on the floor. The silk linings of the boxes and the curtains between them and the small salons in the rear were of fabrics specially made for the purpose. They had an old gold ground and large, raised figures of conventional design in a darker shade, with dark red threads. The tier fronts, ceiling, and proscenium were of a light color, the aim having been to obtain a prevailing tint of ivory. Amid the filigree designs of the pilasters, which carried the work above the curtain opening, were pictures of singing and playing cherubs, and back of the bold consoles, which projected from the side walls, were figures called "The Chorus" and "The Ballet," painted by Francis Maynard, while above the middle of the opening, in a segmentary arch, was an allegory, with Apollo as the central figure, by Francis Lathrop. Statues of the Muses filled niches on both sides of the consoles. Over the ceiling, amidst the entwinings of ornamental figures, on a buff ground, were spread a large number of medallions of oxidized metal, which, in the illumination from the lights, shone with a copper luster. The house was lighted by gas, though preparations had been made for the installation of electrical appliances when that form of illumination should be found justified by economy. As originally built, the orchestra was sunk sufficiently below the level of the floor to conceal the performers from all but the occupants of the upper tiers. In the hope of attaining improved acoustic effects the floor of the orchestra was laid upon an egg-shaped sound-chamber of masonry. The innovation did not meet with the approval of Signor Vianesi, the first musical director at the opera house, and, after an experimental rehearsal, the floor was raised so that the old conditions obtained when the performances began. So the orchestra remained, the players spoiling the picture on the stage, until "Lohengrin" came to a performance. Then Signor Vianesi was prevailed upon to try the arrangement from which Mr. Cady had expected fine artistic results. The effect was good, and the device was adhered to for a space, and in more or less modified form ever since, though there has been continual experimentation with the disposition of the instrumentalists.

Operatic performances began at the new house on October 22, 1883, and after sixty-one representations, at which nineteen operas were produced, the first season came to an end. I shall tell the story of the season in greater detail in the next chapter, contenting myself for the present with an account of the results of the merry war which ensued between the rival establishments. Colonel Mapleson was intrenched in the Academy of Music, which opened its doors for its regular season on the same evening. The advantage lay with Mr. Henry E. Abbey, who had a new house, the fruit of an old longing, and the realization of long cherished social aspirations. With the Academy of Music there rested the charm of ancient tradition, more potent then than it has ever been since, and the strength of conservatism. There were stars of rare refulgence in both constellations, which met the Biblical description in differing one from another in their glory. With Colonel Mapleson was Mme. Adelina Patti, who, in so far as she was an exponent of the art of beautiful vocalization, was without a peer the whole world over. She served then to keep alive the old traditions of Italian song as Mme. Sembrich does now. At her side stood Mme. Etelka Gerster, with a voice youthful, fresh, limpid, and wondrously flexible, and a style that was ripening in a manner that promised soon to compass all the requirements of the Italian stage from the sentimental characters in which she won her first successes to the deeper tragic parts which had begun to make appeal to her ambition. With Mr. Abbey was Mme. Christine Nilsson. Mme. Patti, though she had grown to womanhood and effected her entrance on the operatic as well as concert stage in New York, was not so familiar a figure as Mme. Nilsson. Patti had begun her operatic career at the Academy of Music in 1859, and had gone to Europe, where she remained without revisiting her old home until the fall or winter of 1881, when she came on a concert trip. The trip was more or less a failure, the public not yet being prepared to pay ten dollars for a reserved seat to hear anybody sing. After singing at a concert for the benefit of the sufferers from forest fires in Michigan, she announced a reduction of prices to two dollars for general admission, and five dollars for reserved seats. Under these conditions business improved somewhat, but in February, 1882, she found it necessary to organize an opera company in order to awaken interest fairly commensurate with her great merit and fame. It was a sorry company, and the performances, only a few, took place in the Germania Theater, on Broadway, at Thirteenth Street, formerly Wallack's; but they were received with much enthusiasm. So far as London was concerned, she was under engagement at the time to Mr. Gye, Colonel Mapleson's rival at Covent

Garden. Mr. Abbey claimed that he had an option on any American engagement for opera, but she appeared next season at the Academy, and the doughty English manager held her as his trump card in the battle royal which ensued on the opening of the Metropolitan.

In the twenty years of Mme. Patti's absence from New York, Mme. Nilsson, who had come to the metropolis in the heyday of her European fame in 1870, had won her way deep into the hearts of the people. In 1883 she was no longer in her prime, neither her voice nor her art having stood the wear of time as well as those of Mme. Patti, who was six months her senior in age, and five years in stage experience, but she was more than a formidable rival in the admiration of the public. She was no less happy in the companionship of Mme. Sembrich as a junior partner than Patti was with Mme. Gerster. Both of the younger singers were fresh from their first great European successes. Three years later Mme. Gerster went back to Mme. Marchesi, her teacher, with her voice irreparably damaged. "The penalty of motherhood," said her friends; "the result of worry over the failure to hold her place in the face of opposition," said more impartial observers. Mme. Sembrich went back to Europe to continue her triumphs after disaster had overtaken her first American manager, and in a decade returned, to remain an ornament of the Metropolitan ever since.

In Mr. Abbey's ranks were also Mme. Fursch-Madi, Mme. Scalchi, Mme. Trebelli, Mme. Lablache (who gave way to her daughter till a quarrel over her between the impresarios was determined), and Mme. Valleria, who had come to the Academy some time before from London, though she was a Baltimorean by birth—a sterling artist who is remembered by all connoisseurs with gratitude and admiration. Chief among Colonel Mapleson's masculine forces was Signor Galassi, a somewhat rude but otherwise excellent barytone. At the head of the tenors was Signor Nicolini, the husband of Mme. Patti, who sang only when she did, but not always. The circumstance that Mme. Patti insisted upon his engagement, also, whenever she signed a contract gave rise to a malicious story to the effect that she had two prices, one of, let us say merely for illustration, 6,000 francs for herself alone, one of 4,000 francs for herself and Nicolini. The rest of the male contingent was composed mostly of small fry—Vicini, Perugini, and Falletti, tenors, Cherubini and Lombardini, basses, and Caracciolo, buffo. Mr. Abbey had carried off three admired men singers from the Academy—Campanini, Del Puente, and Novara—and brought an excellent barytone, Kaschmann, from Europe, and a redoubtable tenor, Stagno.

There was little to interest a public supposedly weary of the barrel-organ list in the promises made in the rival announcements. Colonel Mapleson held forth the prospect of Patti in Gounod's "Roméo et Juliette," and

"Mireille" (in Italian, of course), as well as in Rossini's "La Gazza ladra," a forgotten opera then and again forgotten now; other old works which were to be revived for her and Mme. Gerster were "Crispino e la Comare," and "L'Elisir d'Amore." Mme. Pappenheim's presence as the dramatic soprano of the company (a less necessary personage in the companies of that day than now) led to the promise of "Norma" and "Oberon." Only the Italian work was given. Mr. Abbey's book of good intentions embraced twenty-four operas, all of them familiar except "La Gioconda," which had been the novelty of the preceding London season.

The outcome of the battle between the opera houses was defeat for both. The Academy of Music survived for two more campaigns, out of which the new house came triumphant, while the old went down forever. It was different with the men. Mr. Abbey retired after one season, forswearing opera, as he said, for all time; Colonel Mapleson, though defeated, was a smaller loser, and he was not only brave enough to prepare for a second encounter, but also adroit enough to persuade Mme. Patti to place herself under his guidance again. Mr. Abbey's losses have been a matter of speculation ever since. It was known at the time that he had lost all the profits of three or four other managerial enterprises, and some years ago I feared that I might be exaggerating when I set down the deficit of the Metropolitan Opera House in its first season at $300,000. As I write now, however, I have before me a letter from Mr. John B. Schoeffel, who was associated with Mr. Abbey as partner, in which he says that the losses of the season were "nearly $600,000."

[The operas performed at the Academy of Music in the season 1883-1884 were: "La Sonnambula," "Rigoletto," "Norma," "Faust," "Linda di Chamouni," "La Gazza ladra," "Marta," "La Traviata," "Aïda," "L'Elisir d'Amore," "Crispino e la Comare," and "Les Huguenots" (in Italian).]

CHAPTER IX
FIRST SEASON AT THE METROPOLITAN

Twenty-five years ago there was no opera in the current repertory comparable in popularity with "Faust." If I am told that neither is there to-day I shall neither gainsay my informant nor permit the fact to give me heartburnings in spite of my attitude toward the modern lyric drama. To that popularity Mme. Nilsson contributed a factor of tremendous puissance. No singer who is still a living memory was so intimately associated in the local mind with Gounod's masterpiece as she, whose good fortune it had been to recreate the character of Marguerite, when, on March 3, 1869, the opera in a remodeled form was transferred from the Théâtre Lyrique to the Grand Opéra in Paris. Coming to New York soon afterward, it was she who set the standard by which, for a long time, all subsequent representatives of the character were judged. With her, Mme. Scalchi (who never had more than one rival in the part of Siebel so far as New Yorkers are concerned, viz., Annie Louise Cary), and Signor Campanini (the most popular Faust who has ever sung in New York) in the company, it was no wonder that the opera was chosen for performance on the opening night at the Metropolitan Opera House on October 22, 1883. The opera was sung in Italian, no manager's fancy having yet attained such a conception, as that all operas ought to be sung in the language in which they were composed—and might be; for this reason the names in the cast, though given in their familiar French forms may be transliterated into Italian if so they will better please the reader. The cast then was as follows: Marguerite, Mme. Nilsson; Siebel, Mme. Scalchi; Martha, Mlle. Lablache (whose mother had been expected to appear in the part, but was prevented by judicial injunction); Faust, Signor Campanini; Valentine, Signor Del Puente; Mephistopheles, Signor Novara.

The performance did not differ materially from many which had taken place in the Academy of Music when the same artists took part. All the principal artists, indeed, had been heard in the opera many times when their powers were greater. Mme. Nilsson had been thirteen years before the American public, and though in this period her art had grown in dignity and nobility, her voice had lost the fresh bloom of its youth, and her figure had begun to take on matronly contours. Still, she was a great favorite, and hers was an extraordinary triumph, the outburst of popular approbation coming, as was to have been expected, in the garden scene of the opera. Referring to my review of the performance which appeared in The Tribune of the next day, I note that till that moment there had been little enthusiasm. After she had sung the scintillant waltz, however, "the last film of ice that had held the public in decorous check was melted," and an avalanche of plaudits overwhelmed the fair singer. Bouquets rained from the boxes, and baskets of flowers were piled over the footlights till it seemed as if there was to be no end. In the midst of the floral gifts there was also handed up a magnificent velvet casket inclosing a wreath of gold bay leaves and berries, ingeniously contrived to be extended into a girdle to be worn in the classic style, and two gold brooch medallions, bearing the profiles of Tragedy and Comedy, with which the girdle was to be fastened. The donor was not mentioned, but an inscription told that the gift was in "commemoration of the opening of the Metropolitan Opera House." Signor Campanini had spent the year before the opening in retirement, hoping to repair the ravages made in his voice by the previous seasons at the Academy of Music, and, I regret to say, possibly his careless mode of life. His faults had been conspicuous for several seasons, and the hoped-for amendment did not discover itself. "Occasionally the old-time sweetness, and again occasionally the old-time manly ring was apparent in his notes, but they were always weighted down by the evidences of labor, and the brilliancy of the upper tones with which he used to fire an audience into uncontrollable enthusiasm was gone."

The regular subscription nights at the Metropolitan in the first season, and for all the seasons that followed down to that of 1907-08, were Mondays, Wednesdays, and Fridays, with afternoon performances on Saturdays. On the second night of the season, October 24, 1883, Mr. Abbey brought forward two of his new singers. The opera was "Lucia di Lammermoor," the first performance of which in the new house was made memorable by the introduction of Mme. Marcella Sembrich. She had been engaged by Mr. Abbey on the strength of the success achieved by her in the London season of 1883. She was almost at the beginning of her career, being little known outside of Athens, where she made her début, Dresden, where she had sung in German, and London. She had dazzled the British metropolis by her vocalization, especially in "Lucia," and it was for this reason that it was selected for her introduction to New York. Before the season came to an end she sang in "I Puritani," "Don Giovanni," "La Traviata," and "Hamlet." All the good qualities which have since then been extolled hundreds of times by the critics of the New York newspapers were noticeable in her first representation. I turn back to the files of The Tribune to see what I wrote while under the spell of her witching art, and find the following:

Mme. Sembrich is a lovely singer,—lovely of person, of address, of voice; and her artistic acquirements, in the limited field in which Donizetti's opera called them into activity, at least, are of the highest rank. Her style is exquisite, and plainly the outgrowth of a thoroughly musical nature. It unites some of the highest elements of art. Such reposefulness of manner, such smoothness and facility in execution, such perfect balance of tone and refinement of expression can be found only in one richly endowed with deep musical feeling and ripe artistic intelligence. She carries her voice wondrously well throughout a wide register, and from her lowest note to her highest there is the same quality of tone. It is a voice of fine texture, too; it has a velvety softness, yet is brilliant; and though not magnetic in the same degree as the voices of other singers still before the public, it has a fine, sympathetic vein. It wakens echoes of Mme. Patti's organ, but has warmer life-blood in it.

Of the musicianly qualities of this charming singer, recognized on this first acquaintance, we were to have a demonstration before her departure which was in the highest degree surprising. Sympathy for Mr. Abbey in his great losses, and admiration for the self-sacrificing manner in which he adhered to all his obligations to them as well as to the public, led the directors of the Metropolitan Opera Company to offer him a benefit concert. At this entertainment, which was successful beyond anything that local records had to show up to that time, the profits amounting to $16,000, Mme. Sembrich sang an aria; then came upon the stage and played a violin obbligato to Mme. Nilsson's performance of the familiar Bach-Gounod "Ave Maria"; again she appeared and this time played a Chopin Mazourka on the pianoforte. In every instance she was the complete artist, and the public, who had been charmed by her witcheries as Mozart's Zerlina and melted by the pathos of her singing in the last act of "La Traviata," were at a loss to say if she had shown herself a greater artist in song or in instrumental music, as a pianist or violinist. It was not until many years after she had returned to Europe to continue her operatic triumphs in St. Petersburg, Madrid, Vienna, Paris, and Berlin that I learned the story of her life, and with it the secret of her musical versatility; how she had started life as a player of the pianoforte and violin with her father at dances in the houses of the wealthy folk in her native town in Poland, gone to the conservatory in Lemberg to study the pianoforte, been taken to the Conservatory at Vienna by Professor Stengel (then her teacher, now her husband), because there was nothing left in his system of instruction from which she could profit, and there been advised to study singing instead of the pianoforte with Liszt, as her proud teacher had fondly hoped. It was Professor Epstein who gave the world one of the greatest singers of our generation, but in doing so he robbed it of a pianist of doubtless equal caliber. So far as I know, the story of Mme. Sembrich is without a parallel.

Signor Kaschmann was the barytone of the "Lucia" performance. He had a handsome face and figure, a good bearing, and disclosed familiarity with the stage, and considerable talent as an actor, but he was afflicted with that distressful vocal defect which singers of his school often call vibrato in order to affect to find a virtue in it. There is, indeed, artistic merit in a true vibrato which lends vitality to a voice, but when it degenerates into a tremolo, or wabble, it is a vice of the most unpardonable kind.

Another of the newcomers made his bow to the Metropolitan public on the third night of the season, October 26th, when "Il Trovatore" was brought forward. This was the tenor Signor Stagno, a stockily built, heavy, self-conscious man, of good stage features and bad stage manners. When his voice was first heard from behind the scenes, it sounded throaty, a squeezed-out, constrained tone, but later, when Manrico's display pieces came it rang out full and vibrant as a trumpet. It developed at once that he was a singer of the sideshow kind, with whom the be-all and end-all of his part and art lay in the high tones. So little of a musician was he that, being enthusiastically recalled after the "Di quella pira," he was unable to keep the key of C major in his head in spite of his stentorian proclamation of its tonic a few seconds before, and could not begin the repetition till the concert-master had plucked the first note of the air on his violin. A short time before I heard Mme. Patti perform the feat of beginning the trill which accompanies the melody by the orchestra in the middle of the dance song in "Dinorah" without a suggestive tone or chord after a hubbub and gladsome tumult that seemed, to have lasted several minutes. A new bass, Signor Mirabella, appeared in "I Puritani" on October 29th—a musical singer with a voice of large volume and ample range, and a self-possessed, easy, and effective stage presence.

On her second appearance Mme. Nilsson was seen in a part with which she was more intimately associated in the popular mind than any other singer in New York or London. The opera was "Mignon," the date October 31st. Ambroise Thomas's opera had its first American performance at the Academy of Music under the management of Maurice Strakosch, on November 22, 1871. With Mme. Nilsson, on that occasion as on this, was associated M. Capoul, the most ardent and fascinating lover known to opera in America, who not long before had risen from the ranks of French opéra bouffe. Mme. Trebelli, who had created the part of Frederick in London, where, as in New York, Mme. Nilsson was the original Mignon, and for whom the composer had written the rondo-gavotte, "In veder l'amata stanza" (taking its melody from the entr'acte music preceding the second act), was also a member of Mr. Abbey's company, but Mme. Scalchi, who could wear man's attire and walk in tights more gracefully than any woman who ever appeared on the American operatic stage within my memory, was too popular in the part to be set aside for the sake of a newcomer, and Mme. Trebelli had to wait until October 27th before getting a hearing in opera. Meanwhile she sang industriously in concerts. The changes which had taken place in Mme. Nilsson's person and voice during the dozen years between her first appearance as Mignon and the one under consideration might naturally have been expected to affect her performance of the part. Many were ready to perceive the loss of some of the charms of youthful freshness and grace, which are indissolubly connected with any conception of this most poetical of Goethe's creatures. The result fulfilled their anticipations in a measure, for Mme. Nilsson's impersonation was more remarkable for its deep feeling in the dramatic portions than for lightness and gracefulness in the lyric. This loss brought with it a compensation, however. Many protests have been felt, when not expressed, against the tendency of singers to make Mignon a mere wilful, pettish, silly young woman. The poet's ideal was sufficiently despoiled by the unconscionable French librettist without this further desecration which effectually dispelled the last glimmer of the poetical light that ought always to shine about this strange child of the South. Too much of tropical passion, too much of undefined longing, too much of tenderness the part could hardly be invested with, but it is easily made silly by over-acting in the very place where the tendency to do so is strongest. The whole opera is one that must either be represented with extreme care in avoiding extravagant expression, or all effort to approach even distantly the ideals of the poet must be abandoned and the piece be given as if Goethe had never lived, and "Wilhelm Meister" had never been written.

Perhaps the latter plan would be the better one, for it is hard to think of Goethe during the performance of the opera without taking violent offense, and it would only be a relief to have all thought of him studiously kept out of mind. Yet, we would not willingly lose the pleasure which Ambroise Thomas provided in this, his best opera. It is to his credit that he felt the embarrassments which his subject caused. At one time he thought seriously of permitting the heroine to go the way of Goethe's "Mignon," and of offering the opera to the Théâtre Lyrique instead of the Opéra Comique, for which he had undertaken to write it. He did not carry out the plan, however, but instead thought to silence the carping of the Germans by composing a second conclusion, a dénouement allemand, in which Mignon falls dead, while listening to Philine's polacca in the last scene. A tragic end to a piece treated in the comedy manner throughout was too ridiculous, however, and the Germans would have none of the dénouement allemand. They raised a hue and cry against the opera, then heard it for the sake of its music, and ended by admiring its admirable parts without changing their minds about the desecration of their great poet.

It is no wonder that the opera-book was made. Such scruples as distressed the Germans never trouble French librettists, and the characters which Carré and Barbier found in Goethe's romance are as if born for the stage. What lyric possibilities do not lie in the Harper? Was ever a more perfect musical coquette dreamed of than Philine? Have not Mignon's songs drawn forth music from nearly every composer of eminence since Beethoven? The filling-in parts were on the surface of the story, and the character of their music could not be misconceived. Wilhelm Meister himself, in his character of a strolling player, had only to sacrifice his habit of reflection to be a dashing tenor. The temptation was certainly strong; the sacrilege was committed, and the verbal skeleton constructed out of things which were dearest in German literature, was tricked out with piquant music and ear-tickling roulades by the man who was not awed even by Shakespeare. Think of "Le Songe d'une Nuit d'Été"! With such characters the play is easily acted, and the music never fails to fascinate.

"La Traviata" was the next opera, produced on November 5th, with Mme. Sembrich as Violetta, and Capoul as Alfredo, and then came "Lohengrin" on November 7th. In Wagner's opera the parts of the heroine and hero were enacted by Nilsson and Campanini, who had sung in its first Italian performance at the Academy a decade before. Excellently sung in the best manner as understood by singers of the Italian school—a manner fully justified, let it be said in passing, by Signor Marchesi's Italian text—and magnificently dressed, the opera attracted the most numerous and brilliant audience since the opening night, and remained one of the most pronounced successes of the season. It served also to introduce Mme. Fursch-Madi, a dramatic singer, who, although not attractive in appearance, was one of the finest singers in her style and most conscientious artists known to her period. She was a French woman, who was graduated from the Paris Conservatoire, married M. Madier, a chef d'orchestre in the French capital, came to America to join the French company in New Orleans in 1874, and sang for three seasons (1879-'81) at Covent Garden. She spent the last years of her life in and about New York, singing in opera and concert, always a noble example to youthful aspirants, and died in poverty after great suffering in September, 1894. "La Sonnambula" followed on November 14th, and "Rigoletto" on November 16th, without noteworthy incident, except the first American appearance of Gaudignini as the Jester, and "Robert le Diable" (in Italian), with Fursch-Madi as Alice, Valleria as Isabella, Stagno and Mirabella. This performance was enlivened by an amusing incident. It will be recalled by people familiar with the history of the opera that Scribe and Meyerbeer first designed "Robert" for the Opéra Comique, but remodeled it for the Grand. For a few moments in the incantation scene at this performance the audience seemed inclined to ignore the author's sober second thought, and accept the work as a comic instead of romantic opera. The wicked nuns, called back to life by the sorcery of Bertram, amid the ruins of the cloister, appeared to have been stinted by the undertaker in the matter of shrouds, and the procession of gray-wrapped figures in cutty sarks caused the liveliest merriment until the transformation took place, and serious interest was revived by the lovely face, form, and dancing of Mme. Cavalazzi.

"Il Barbiere," with Sembrich as a delightfully piquant Rosina, nevertheless moved with leaden feet in many of its scenes, because of the ponderous and lugubrious Stagno, who essayed a part far from his province, when he tried to sing the Count. On November 28th "Don Giovanni" was reached with the finest distribution of women's rôles, I dare say, that New York has ever seen, and one that ranked well with the famous London one of Tietjens, Nilsson, and Patti. Mme. Fursch-Madi was Donna Anna, Mme. Nilsson Donna Elvira, and Mme. Sembrich Zerlina. For delvers in musical history the performance had curious interest because it partook somewhat of an anniversary character. It fell within a day of exactly fifty-eight years after Italian opera had first been heard in America (November 29, 1825). Save Mme. Patti we have heard no Zerlina comparable with Mme. Sembrich, and Mme. Nilsson's singing of the airs, "Ah, che mi dice mai," and "Mi tradi quell' alma ingrata" lingers in my memory as an impeccable exemplification of the true classic style. The performance suffered shipwreck, however, in the famous first finale, because of the untunefulness of the orchestra, and the incapacity of the enlisted stage bands. In "Mefistofele," on December 5th, Nilsson appeared as Marguerite and Helen of Troy, and Trebelli as Marta and Pantalis. Nilsson had fixed the ideal of Helen in Europe and New York, and it is she, I believe, who started the questionable practice of having one performer impersonate both Marguerite and the classic Queen. Boito has given us so little of Goethe's Gretchen in his delightful, but sketchy, opera that it does not make much difference how the part is acted; but Helen is a character that seemed cut to the very form of Nilsson—regal in beauty and carriage, soul-moving in voice, serene in pose and gesture. She fitted perfectly into the fairest picture that a lover of ancient Greek life could conjure up, and moved through the classic act like a veritable Hellenic queen. The beauty, majesty, the puissant charm of a perfect woman of the antique type—all were hers. Campanini, who, like Nilsson, had been seen in the opera before the Metropolitan Opera House entered the lists, sang on this evening with peculiar enthusiasm; and with reason. Not only had he been instrumental in giving the opera to the people of London and New York, but, on this occasion, he was singing under the baton of his younger brother, Cleofonte, then a modest maestro di cembalo trying his 'prentice hand at conducting; now the redoubtable leader of Mr. Hammerstein's forces at the Manhattan. Four years later Cleofonte Campanini came again to New York as conductor of his brother's company organized for the production of Verdi's "Otello."

On December 20th the one real novelty of Mr. Abbey's list had production. It was Ponchielli's "La Gioconda," with the following distribution of parts: La Gioconda, Mme. Nilsson; Laura Adorno, Mme. Fursch-Madi; La Cieca, Mme. Scalchi; Enzo Grimaldo, Signor Stagno; Barnaba, Signor Del Puente; Alvise Badiero, Signor Novara. Ponchielli's opera had been the principal novelty of the London season in the summer of 1883, where it was brought out by Mr. Gye. On this occasion it was performed with a gorgeousness of stage appointments, and a strength of ensemble which spoke volumes for the earnestness of the effort which Mr. Abbey was making to give grand opera in a style worthy of the American metropolis, and the reception which the public gave to the work afforded convincing proof of the eagerness for a change from the stale list which had so long constituted its operatic pabulum. The house was crowded from floor to ceiling, and the audience, having assembled for the enjoyment of an unusual pleasure, was soon wrought into an extremely impressionable state, which the striking pictures, excited action, and ingenious music intensified with every act.

The score of "La Gioconda" is full of ingeniously applied harmonical and orchestral devices, but they are all such as were learned from Ponchielli's great predecessor and successor, Verdi. As a matter of fact, Ponchielli, though he has been discovered as the father of the young veritist school of Italy, which seems already to have exhausted itself, was less original than Boito, who has distinguished himself above all the rout of Verdi's traducers and followers (for a space the category included the same names) by continence and self-criticism. As I write more than two decades have elapsed since he became known in New York, and in the interim we have seen the rise, and, also, the considerable fall of such imitators as Mascagni, Leoncavallo, and their superior, Puccini. We are now more able to see than we were twenty-five years ago how much Ponchielli, and all his tribe, owe to Verdi; and also how much ruder and less attentive to real beauty they were. Then we could hear besides his voice, that of Verdi in his music; now we can hear also tones which awaken echoes in Mascagni, Leoncavallo, and Puccini. Of a sometimes mooted Wagnerian influence, there is only so much in this score as is to be found in all scores, German and French, and Italian, since the shackles of instrumental form were cast off. Ponchielli makes a little use of a recurring melodic phrase from La Cieca's "Voce di donna," but he pursues the device even less consistently than Verdi, and in a manner that is older than Meyerbeer. In melody he is wholly Italian, and of Wagner's use of typical phrases "La Gioconda" is as guiltless as Pergolesi's "Serva padrona."

What is admirable to the popular appreciation of to-day is the hot vigor of the drama, and the quick co-operation of music in its climacteric moments. This co-operation is most obvious in the employment of the device of contrast, which dominates the work and seems to have been the feature which has been most effectively seized upon by Ponchielli's pupils. It marks every climax in the opera, and becomes almost tiresome in its reiteration. In the first act the blind woman's prayer is set against a background composed of a gambling chorus and the wild whirl of the furlano, which ends abruptly with organ peals and a pious canticle—an effect repeated since in "Cavalleria Rusticana" and "Tosca." In the second act in the twinkling of an eye, Gioconda is transformed from a murderous devil into a protecting saint; in the third Laura's accents of mortal woe commingle with the sounds of a serenade in the distance, and the disclosure of a supposed murder is made at the climax of a ball; in the fourth the calls of passing gondoliers break in upon Gioconda's soliloquies, which have for their subject suicide, murder, and self-sacrifice. The device is of a coarse tissue, but it is of the opera operatic, and it is now more familiar than it was when first disclosed to the patrons of the Metropolitan Opera House, twenty-five years ago.

If it were necessary one might look for the source of this device of contrast in the literature to which Verdi directed attention when he turned his thoughts to Victor Hugo, and composed "Ernani" and "Rigoletto." Hugo was the prince of those novelists and dramatists who utilized glaring contrasts and unnatural contradictions to give piquancy to their creations and compel sympathy for monsters by uniting monumental wickedness with the most amiable of moral qualities. The story of "La Gioconda" is drawn from "Angelo, Tyrane de Padoue." In transforming this tragedy into an opera the librettist removed the scene from Padua to Venice, changed a wealthy actress into a poor street singer, and made the blind mother, who is barely mentioned in the play, into a prominent and moving character. There can be no question but that Boito ("Tobia Gorria" is but an anagramatic nom de plume of Arrigo Boito) was highly successful in remodeling the tragedy for operatic purposes, but he did not palliate its moral grossness or succeed in inviting our compassionate feelings for anyone entitled to them. The only personages who in this opera escape disaster are a pair of lovers, whose sufferings, as depicted or inferred, cannot be said to have refined the guilt out of their passion. We might infer that once the attachment of Enzo and Laura was pure and lovely, but all that we see of it is flauntingly criminal and doubly wicked. The happiness of Enzo, who to elope with another man's wife cruelly breaks faith with a woman whose love for him is so strong that she gives her life to save his, is hardly a consummation that ought to be set down as justifying so many blotches and blains, pimples and pustules, on the face of human nature. Laura's treachery is to Gioconda as well as to her husband, and has no redeeming trait. In fact, the blind woman is the only character in the opera who has moral health, and she seems to have been brought in only that her sufferings might intensify the bloody character of Barnaba, the spy. Even Gioconda, a character that has latent within it many effective elements, is sacrificed by the librettist to the one end—sensational effect through contrast and contradiction. Nowhere does she illustrate the spirit of blitheness which is put forth by her name, and only once does she allude to it. From the moment of her entrance till her death she is filled with torturing passion and conflicting emotions. Not la Gioconda she, but la Dolorosa—except for the bookmaker's desire for dramatic paradox. Against the desire to sympathize with her is thrust the revelation that her rival is never saved from death at her hands because of any repugnance of hers to murder. She would kill in an instant were it not that her vengefulness is overcome by gratitude to the benefactress of her mother. So it comes that the strongest feeling excited by the heroine, who dies a sacrifice to filial affection and passionate love, is one of simple pity— a feeling that is never absent from tender hearts, no matter how depraved the victim of misfortune.

But opera in the estate illustrated by "La Gioconda" scarcely justifies even an elementary moral disquisition. Moreover, what Ponchielli provoked is so much worse than what he himself did that his condemnation can go no further than purgatorial fires. It is in the operas of his pupils and would-be imitators, like Giordano, Tasca, and others, that filth and blood are supposed to fructify the music which rasps the nerves, even as the dramas revolt the moral stomach. In view of the products of the period in which began operatic veritism, so-called, "La Gioconda" seems almost washed in innocency, and if its music is at times highly spiced, it is at least frankly and simply melodious. Naturally he has followed his librettist in aiming at contrast, at higgledy-piggledy finales, at garish orchestration, at strenuous declamation in the dialogue not cast in melodic forms and at abrupt changes. But he has plenty, if not profound melodiousness. La Cieca's air, Enzo's romance, Laura's "Stella del Marinar," Barnaba's barcarole, and the ballet music have lived on in our concert rooms from that day to this.

"La Gioconda" was the last opera brought forward in the winter season, which ended on December 22d, leaving two out of thirty promised subscription performances to be supplied on the return of Mr. Abbey's forces from Boston, whither they went for the holidays. When he came back in a fortnight he gave "Carmen," on January 9th, with Trebelli, Campanini, and Del Puente (who had been in the cast of the original London production); repeated it on January 11th, and "La Gioconda" on January 12th.

On March 10th a spring season began, which lasted till April 12th. It added four operas to the list. Ambroise Thomas's "Hamlet" (March 10), Flotow's "Martha" (March 14th), Meyerbeer's "Huguenots" (March 19th), and "Le Prophète" (March 21st). The last, which had first been heard in New York at the Astor Place Opera House four years after its original production in Paris, on April 16, 1849, had been absent from the current operatic list so long that it was to all intents and purposes a novelty to Mr. Abbey's patrons. The last week of the season brought two disappointments: Mmes. Nilsson and Sembrich both fell ill, the indisposition of the latter (or something else) causing the abandonment of Gounod's "Roméo et Juliette," an opera that was new to New Yorkers, and was promptly brought out by Colonel Mapleson with Mme. Patti in his spring season at the Academy of Music.

As has already been set forth, Mr. Abbey made a monumental financial fiasco; but his was a heroic effort to galvanize Italian opera, which seemed moribund, into vitality. He showed an honest desire to keep all his promises to the public made when he asked support for his enterprise, and all in all, his administration was signalized by virtues too frequently absent in the doings of operatic managers. His stage sets were uniformly handsome, and some of them showed greater sumptuousness than the people had seen for many years; his orchestra, though faulty in composition as well as execution, did some admirable work under Signor Vianesi; his chorus was prompt, vigorous, and tuneful; his ensembles were carefully and intelligently composed, and his selection of operas was judicious from a managerial point of view. He gave to New York the strongest combination of women singers that the city had ever known; nor has it been equaled in any one season since. The financial failure of the enterprise caused no surprise among intelligent and impartial observers. One needed not to be prophetically gifted to foretell twenty-five years ago that New York could not support two such costly establishments as the Academy of Music and the Metropolitan Opera House. The world of fashion, which in the nature of things is the supporter of Italian opera, and has been ever since the art form was invented, was divided in its allegiance, and divided, moreover, in a manner which made an interchange of courtesies all but impossible. This threw the burden of maintaining the rival houses upon two limited groups of persons, and the loss was mutual.

In Mr. Abbey's prospectus he promised to produce twenty-four operas, which he named; he kept his promise as to all but five, these being "Lucrezia Borgia," "Linda di Chamouni," "Fra Diavolo," "Otello," and "Le Nozze di Figaro." "Roméo et Juliette," which he attempted to give, but failed at the last, was not in the original list. Besides these performances, he gave fifty-eight outside of New York in visits to Brooklyn, Boston, Philadelphia, Chicago, Cincinnati, St. Louis, Washington, and Baltimore. The local record may be tabulated as follows:

Opera First performance Times given

"Faust" ………………….. October 22 …………. 6
"Lucia di Lammermoor" …… October 24 …………. 3
"Il Trovatore" …………. October 26 …………. 3
"I Puritani" ……………. October 29 …………. 1
"Mignon" ………………… October 31 …………. 4
"La Traviata" ………….. November 5 …………. 4
"Lohengrin" ……………. November 7 …………. 6
"La Sonnambula" ………… November 14 ……….. 2
"Rigoletto" ……………. November 16 ……….. 2
"Robert le Diable" ……… November 19 ……….. 3
"Il Barbiere di Siviglia" .. November 23 ……….. 3
"Don Giovanni" …………. November 28 ……….. 5
"Mefistofele" ………….. December 5 …………. 2
"La Gioconda" ………….. December 20 ……….. 4
"Carmen" ……………….. January 9 …………. 5
"Hamlet" ……………….. March 10 ………….. 1
"Martha" ……………….. March 14 ………….. 3
"Les Huguenots" ………… March 19 ………….. 2
"Le Prophète" ………….. March 21 ………….. 1

There was one performance with a mixed program.

CHAPTER X
OPERATIC REVOLUTIONS

Colonel Mapleson and the stockholders of the Academy of Music and their friends were little disposed to yield to the new order of things without a struggle. The Academy was refurnished and a season of Italian opera begun on the same night on which Mr. Abbey opened his doors. Colonel Mapleson's company comprised Mmes. Patti, Gerster, Pappenheim, Pattini, and Josephine Yorke, and Signori Falletti, Nicolini, Perugini, Cherubini, Vicini, Lombardini, and Caracciolo. The performances were like those that had been the rule for years, except for the brilliancy which Mme. Patti lent to those in which she took part. But not even she could hold the fickle public. On the nights when she sang the house was two-thirds full; Mme. Gerster had established herself as a prime favorite, but when she sang on the "off nights" the house was two-thirds empty. The season was financially disastrous, though Colonel Mapleson's losses were not comparable to Mr. Abbey's, and he was not only brave enough to prepare for the next season's campaign, but adroit enough to persuade Mme. Patti to place herself under his guidance again. But, while he held out against Mr. Abbey and the new house, he was compelled to yield to the Metropolitan and German opera as established by Dr. Damrosch. Of the singers who helped Colonel Mapleson make his fight, one is still in enjoyment of popular favor. This is Mme. Nordica, who, though not a regular member of the company, effected her American operatic début at the Academy on November 26, 1883, in Gounod's "Faust." She was announced as Mme. Norton-Gower, and of her performance I wrote at the time in The Tribune:

Of Mrs. Norton-Gower the first statement must be that she gives abundant evidence of having been admirably trained in the spirit of Gounod's music and the tragedy. Nearly every number in the score which falls to the part of Margherita she sang with commendable intelligence and taste. The most obvious criticism was that the spirit so excellently conceived by her put a severe strain upon the matter in her control. It cost her a manifest effort to do what she well knew how to do, for she is not a phenomenal vocalist. She has a voice of fine texture, and her tones are generally sympathetic. She sings with feeling, but acts with more. Her performance was meritorious beyond the performances of any of Mr. Mapleson's women singers, Mmes. Patti and Gerster excepted.

That Mr. Abbey had made losses which were so great as to make him unwilling to remain at the head of the operatic forces at the Metropolitan

Opera House was known long before the close of the first season. Before the spring representations began he made answer to the proposal of the directors of the Metropolitan Opera Company by saying that he would act as their manager without compensation for the next year, provided they would pay the losses which the first season would entail upon him. The directors had agreed in their original contract to save him whole to the extent of $60,000—a pitiful tenth part of what, according to Mr. Schoeffel, the losses finally aggregated; I am inclined to think, however, that Mr. Schoeffel has included the losses made in the other cities visited by the company. There were only sixty-one representations at the Metropolitan Opera House, and it is inconceivable that they averaged a deficit of over $9,000 each. They could not have cost that sum in fact, and many of the performances drew houses which at the prevailing prices (orchestra $6) must have yielded handsome returns. Whatever the sum which loomed up as a prospective loss, however, it was great enough to dissuade the directors from adopting Mr. Abbey's suggestion. Instead, they made up their minds cheerfully to pay their own loss, and at the beginning of the spring season, all negotiations having come to an end, sent Mr. Abbey a letter which read as follows:

> Metropolitan Opera House, New York,
> Secretary's Office, March 14, 1884.

My Dear Sir: It gives me much pleasure to say that I am instructed by the president to tender you the use of the Opera House on April 21, 1884, for a benefit performance to yourself. I beg also to express my hope that the results of the benefit may in some measure be commensurate with the manner you have presented Italian opera and to say that it will give me great pleasure to do anything I can to aid in making the benefit a great success. Most sincerely yours,

> Edmund C. Stanton, Secretary.

To Henry E. Abbey.

In the meantime negotiations had already begun looking to the transfer of the house for the next season to Mr. Ernest Gye, who was manager at the time of Covent Garden, London. These negotiations were continued till deep in the summer and came to naught at the end. Of the reasons for the failure several became known to the public. One was the unwillingness of the directors to give Mr. Gye a free hand in the engagement of artists. The directors, who were active in determining the policy of the opera, were all devoted admirers of Mme. Nilsson; they were, in fact, the donors of the laurel wreath of gold which she received on the first night of the season. They were desirous that she should be re-engaged, though the weight of her contract had done much to break Mr. Abbey's financial back, and they were also a little fearful that Mr. Gye, the husband of Mme. Albani, would, not unnaturally, seek to put that singer in Mme. Nilsson's place. Meanwhile, the opera season at Covent Garden came to a close, and though Mr. Gye had not had Colonel Mapleson at Her Majesty's Theater to cope with, as in former seasons, but only English opera at Drury Lane, under the direction of Carl Rosa, the financial outcome was such as to suggest that Mr. Gye's attitude toward opera at the Metropolitan was something like that which the Germans describe as a cat walking about a dish of hot porridge.

At intervals bits of gossip reached New York by cable, but none of them was of a comforting character. One week it was said to be the exorbitance of Mme. Nilsson's demands which gave Mr. Gye pause, and the next the difficulty of finding a tenor worthy of succeeding Signor Campanini and capable of satisfying the captious, critical, and fastidious people of New York. There were suspicions, too, that some of the embarrassments which confronted Mr. Gye and the Metropolitan directors were due to the machinations of that sly and persuasive old dog, Colonel Mapleson. Nilsson had but one rival, and she was Mme. Patti. Her Colonel Mapleson had secured; not only her, but, report said, Scalchi, Tremelli, and Tamagno also. Mme. Scalchi had been a strong prop of the first Metropolitan season, and Tremelli and Tamagno, though they had not been heard in America, had names to conjure with. Tremelli never came, and it was not until 1890, when Mr. Abbey was again in the traces of an Italian opera manager, and was exploiting both Mme. Patti and Mme. Albani, that Tamagno was heard in New York.

Failures of such magnitude as those of Mr. Gye in London, Colonel Mapleson at the Academy of Music, and Mr. Abbey at the Metropolitan Opera House, naturally set the beards of the wiseacres a-wagging. Clearly the world of opera was out of joint and a prophet with a new evangel seemed to be needed to set it right. In New York the efforts had been made along old lines, but Mr. Gye had ventured on an experiment which suggested the polyglot scheme which became the fixed policy of the Metropolitan Opera House some ten years later. Along with the old Italian list Mr. Gye gave some of Wagner's lyric dramas in German, and even ventured an English opera done into German—C. Villiers Stanford's "Savonarola." Was Italian opera dead? So it almost seemed; but the incidents attending its demise were familiar to operatic history and as old as Italian opera in London and New York. When the art form was making its first struggles for habilitation in the British metropolis Addison thought the spectacle so amusing that he wrote an essay in which he pictured the amazement of the next generation on learning that in the days of its predecessors English men and women had sat out entire evenings listening to an entertainment in a foreign tongue. And he said in that essay many other excellent things, the truth and force of which are just as deserving of appreciation (and just as needful) now as they were in the time of the writer.

The consciousness of the absurdity of Italian opera transported in the "original package" (to speak commercially) to England and America seems to have been constant with the Anglo-Saxon peoples. Of this the legion of managerial wrecks which strew the operatic shores or float as derelicts bear witness. Bankers, manufacturers, and noblemen have come to the rescue of ambitious managers, or become ambitious managers themselves, only to go down in the common disaster. Mr. Delafield wrote his name high among his fellows across the water by losing half a million of dollars in a single season—a feat which no man equaled till Mr. Abbey came. Taylor got himself into the King's Bench Prison by his venturesomeness, and, once there, found consolation in a philosophy which taught him that of all places in the world the properest one for an opera manager was a prison. But I have mentioned this before.

Time was when the popular taste found complete satisfaction in the melodies of the Italian composers. Time was when the desire for novelty in the operatic field could be satisfied only by importations from Italy. Time was when Germans, Frenchmen, and Englishmen went to Italy to study operatic composition and wrote in the Italian manner to Italian texts. All this had changed at the period of which I am writing—Germans, Frenchmen, and Englishmen had operas in their own languages and schools of composition of their own. But still New York and London clung to Italian sweets.

And Italy had become sterile. Verdi seemed to have ceased writing. There were whisperings of an "Iago" written in collaboration with Boito, but it was awaiting ultimate criticism and final polish while the wonderful old master was engaged in revamping some of his early works. Boito was writing essays and librettos for others, with the unfinished "Nerone" lying in his desk, where it is still hidden. Ponchielli had not succeeded in getting a hearing for anything since "La Gioconda." Expectations had been raised touching an opera entitled "Dejanice," by Catalani, but I cannot recall that it ever crossed the Italian border. The hot-blooded young veritists who were soon to flood Italy with their creations had not yet been heard of. The champions of a change from Italian to German ideals seemed to have the argument all in their favor. The spectacle presented by the lyric stage in Germany and France seemed to show indubitably what course opera as an art form must needs take if it was to live. Gluck, Weber, and Wagner, all Germans, had pointed the way. In 1883 five new operas by English composers reached the dignity of performance, and it was significant that two of them—Mr. Mackenzie's "Colomba" and Mr. Stanford's

"Savonarola"—were performed in German, the former in Hamburg, the latter in London. There were many lovers of opera in New York besides the musical reviewer for The Tribune who believed that if America was ever to have a musical art of its own the way could best be paved by supplanting Italian performances by German at the principal home of opera in the United States. We should, it is true, still have foreign artists singing foreign works in a foreign tongue, but the change in repertory would promote an appreciation and an understanding of truthful, dramatic expression in a form which claimed close relationship with the drama.

This was the state of affairs when, negotiations having failed with both Mr. Abbey and Mr. Gye, the summer days of 1884 being nearly gone and the prospect of a closed theater confronting the directors of the Metropolitan Opera House, Dr. Leopold Damrosch submitted to them a proposition to give opera in German under his management, but on their account. Either the forcefulness and plausibility of his arguments or the direfulness of their need led the directors to make the venture. Dr. Damrosch went to Germany toward the end of August; toward the end of September he was back in New York, ready to announce a season of opera in German, with a completely organized company and a promising list of operas. Few persons knew what was coming, and the information brought with it a shock of surprise. Dr. Damrosch had been a vigorous factor in the musical life of New York for twelve years, but he had never been identified with opera in the public mind, and, in fact, his practical familiarity with it was little. He had come to New York from Breslau, where he was conductor of the Orchesterverein (a symphonic organization) in 1871. He had had some practical experience with the theater at Weimar, where he played with the orchestra of the Court Theater under the direction of Liszt, had been musical director at the Municipal Theater in Posen and Breslau, but for short periods only. He had not gone through the career of the typical German conductor for the reason that he was not a musician "vom Hause aus"—as the Germans express it. He was a physician turned musician—a member of one of the scientific professions who had abandoned science for art.

Dr. Damrosch was a remarkable man. He was born in Posen, Prussia, on October 22, 1832. He studied music in the home circle, like the generality of German lads, but his parents had chosen the profession of medicine for him, and he had acquiesced in the choice, matriculating in the medical department of the University of Berlin after he had completed the usual gymnasial course of studies. He had not abandoned his love for music, though he so devoted himself to medicine that in due course he was graduated with honors and received his degree. Incidentally, like Schumann at Heidelberg, he continued to study music, Hubert Ries being his teacher in violin playing, and the venerable Professor Dehn in counterpoint and composition. After graduation he returned to his native Posen to practise medicine, and remained there thus occupied till 1854.

In 1855 the physician's earlier and stronger love for music achieved the mastery over his adopted profession, and he started out into the world as a concert violinist. He played at Magdeburg and at Berlin, where his talents were so much admired that on the recommendation of friends in the Prussian capital he went to Weimar, where he won the friendship of Liszt and joined the body of enthusiastic young musicians—Peter Cornelius and others—who had rallied around the great musician and were fighting the battles of the new German school. His musical creed was formed here, as he himself confessed in a series of articles written for the Neue Zeitschrift für Musik. His first official appointment was as director of the music at the Stadttheater in Posen, and in 1866 he was called to fill the same post at Breslau. After he had resigned this position he remained in Breslau as director of the Orchesterverein, which he called into existence until he accepted the call of the Männergesangverein Arion in New York in 1871. Though Dr. Damrosch had achieved a European reputation before he came to New York, his best and most enduring work was accomplished here, where he organized the Oratorio Society, which has had a continuous existence since 1873, and the Symphony Society, which, amid many vicissitudes and with several reincarnations, has lived since 1877. The establishment of German opera, though it did not endure, was yet his crowning achievement, and at the culmination of the glory which it brought him he died. But of that presently and in its proper place.

The artistic basis of the scheme which Dr. Damrosch put into effect was essentially German. It dispensed with the star system (except so far as the engagement of Mme. Materna was a deference to it) and substituted instead a good ensemble, unusual attention to the mounting of operas, and the bringing out of dramatic effects through other stage accessories. The change of base brought with it of necessity a change of repertory, and the Italian operas which had formed the staple of New York lists for years were put aside for the masterpieces of German and French composers. One or two efforts to include works of a lighter lyrical character sufficed to demonstrate the wisdom of a strict adherence to the list of tragic works of large dimensions and spectacular nature, and the sagacity of Dr. Damrosch was shown in nothing more clearly than in his choice of operas for representation.

There were few familiar names in the list of singers printed in the prospectus. The most familiar, and the greatest, was that which has already been announced as the one concession made to the star system—Mme. Amalia Materna. Twenty-five years ago the story of Bayreuth was a household word throughout the civilized world, and Mme. Materna had been associated with the Wagner festivals since the first held, in 1876. In May, 1882, she was brought to New York by Theodore Thomas for the Music Festival, held in the Seventh Regiment Armory, and with her Bayreuth colleagues—Winkelmann, tenor, and Scaria, bass—she took part in concerts and festivals which Mr. Thomas gave in 1884 in Boston, New York, Philadelphia, Cincinnati, and Chicago. After returning to Europe after the American engagement of 1882, she had gone straight to Bayreuth, where she "created" the part of Kundry in the original production of "Parsifal," alternating afterward in the character with Fräulein Brandt, who was associated with her in Dr. Damrosch's Metropolitan company. When she came to the Metropolitan (she made her first appearance after the season was well under headway, in January, 1885) Mme. Materna was thirty-eight years old and her splendid powers were at their zenith. She had sung in public since her thirteenth year, at first in church, then in comic opera in Graz and Vienna. While singing at a small theater in the Austrian capital she became a member of the Court Opera, attracted wide attention by her dramatic abilities in the grand operas of its repertories, and at once leaped into fame by her impersonation of Brünnhilde at the first Bayreuth festival, in 1876.

Next in significance in the first Metropolitan German Company was Marianne Brandt, whose influence in creating new ideals and developing new tastes among the opera-goers of New York was even greater than that of Mme. Materna, because her powers were no less and her labors of longer duration. She came here after having won praise from the critics of London, where she had sung at the first performance in England of "Tristan und Isolde" at Drury Lane in 1882. That was ten years after she had effected her London début. The principal Coloratursängerin of the company was Frau Marie Schroeder-Hanfstängl, then a member of the Frankfort Opera, who was a native of Breslau and a friend of the Damrosch family while they were there. As Mlle. Schroeder she had already established a reputation at that time in Paris, where she had sung at the Théâtre Lyrique through the mediation of her teacher, Mme. Viardot-Garcia. The jugendlich Dramatische was Frau Auguste Seidl-Krauss, who was announced throughout the season by her maiden name, but had been married for about a year to Anton Seidl, then conductor at the Stadttheater in Bremen, who was soon to become a most puissant factor in the sum of New York's musical activities. The principal tenor was Anton Schott, who had made a considerable reputation as a Wagnerian singer in the opera houses of Munich, Berlin, Schwerin, Hanover, and London, and had made the Italian tour with Angelo Neumann's Wagner company which Seidl conducted in 1882. Earlier in life he had been an artillery officer in the German army, which fact coupled with his explosive manner of singing prompted one of Dr. von Bülow's witticisms. The doctor had been conductor of the opera in Hanover when Schott was there and had conceived a violent dislike for him. Some years after the latter's New York season, conversing socially with von Bülow, I chanced to mention Schott's name.

"Ah! do you know Schott?" asked the irascible little doctor; "ein eigenthümlicher Sänger, nicht war? Eigentlich ist er ein Militärtenor—ein Artillerist. Sie wissen er singt manchmal zu hoch—da distonirt er; gewöhnlich singt er zu tief—da destonirt er; und wenn er gelegentlich rein singt—da detonirt er!" The ingenious play on words is quite untranslatable, but my readers who understand German but are unfamiliar with musical terms will be helped to an appreciation of the fun by being told that "dis," "des," and "de" are the German names applied respectively to D sharp, D flat, and D natural. No doubt Dr. von Bülow had perpetrated his little joke before he shot it off for my benefit. It was a habit of his to have such brilliant impromptus ready and ingeniously to invite an occasion for their introduction. But they always had the effect of brilliant spontaneity. It was on another occasion, when he was praising the performance of another German tenor, and I had interposed the suggestion that to me he seemed to lack virility, that he burst out with:

"But, my dear fellow, a tenor isn't a man; it's a disease!"

I supplied the quotation marks in my mind, for though the remark was his, it had served him on at least one other occasion, as I chanced to know.

Other members of the company were Anna Slach, Anna Stern, Hermine Bely, Adolf Robinson, barytone (another of Dr. Damrosch's professional friends from Breslau); Josef Staudigl (bass, son of the great Staudigl); Josef Koegel, bass; Emil Tiffero, Herr Udvardi, Otto Kemlitz, Ludwig Wolf, Josef Miller, and Herr Schneller. John Lund, who came from Kroll's, in Berlin, and Walter Damrosch, were chorus masters and assistant conductors. The first season began on November 17, 1884, with a performance of "Tannhäuser."

CHAPTER XI
GERMAN OPERA AT THE METROPOLITAN

After German opera began at the Metropolitan Opera House it endured seven years. It was only at the outset that it had the opposition of what had been the established régime of Italian opera at the Academy of Music, but it was pursued throughout its career by desultory enterprises and hampered greatly by the fact that the stockholders were never unitedly and enthusiastically in favor of it or the principles of art which it represented. Throughout the period there was a hankering for the fleshpots of Egypt in the region of the Metropolitan boxes. It seems desirable, therefore, that, though it is my purpose more specifically in the next few chapters to tell the story of the seven years of German opera, I should turn the light occasionally on the doings at rival institutions. The first of the seven years at the Metropolitan Opera House was the seventh year of Colonel Mapleson's tenancy of the Academy of Music. He opened his season on November 10, 1884, but before then James Barton Key and Horace McVicker experimented with Italian opera for three weeks at the Star Theater. The organization was composed of operatic flotsam and jetsam, such as is always to be found plentifully in New York after operatic storms in South America or Mexico, and was neither better nor worse than scores of other companies heard here before and since. Like most of these, too, it had a mouth-filling name—the Milan Grand Opera Company—but, like few of them, it had a capital tenor, Signor Giannini, who at a somewhat later period we shall find in Colonel Mapleson's forces. Other members of the company whose names are worthy of preservation were Maria Peri (soprano leggiero), Signora Damerini (dramatic soprano), Signora Mestress (contralto), and Signor Serbolini (bass). The experiment resulted in financial failure, but it introduced to New York the South American opera, "Il Guarany," by Señor Gomez. In Colonel Mapleson's company were Mme. Patti, Signora Ricetti, Mme. Emma Nevada, Signor Nicolini, Signor Vicini, and Signor Cardinali (tenors), Mme. Scalchi, Mme. Fursch-Madi, Signori de Pasqualis, Cherubini, Caracciolo (bassos), Signor de Anna (barytone), and Signor Bassetti (tenor), otherwise Mr. Charles Bassett, like Mme. Nevada, an American singer. The subscription ended on December 27th, and in the following week he gave four extra performances, at two of which he reduced the prices, though they were of a higher artistic order than the others. The relations between Mapleson and the stockholders of the Academy were becoming strained, and in a speech which he made at his annual benefit he remarked upon their absence sarcastically. It was plain that their patience had given out and that they were weary of extending to him the financial support which had helped him through the season. In my review of the season I find this remark, which is indicative of their indifference to the fate of their lessee: "The condition of the house gives evidence of an unwillingness to sink money in an unlucrative enterprise. It is somewhat discouraging to the patrons of the house to sit in ramshackle chairs which threaten to deposit them incontinently on the floor at any moment, and the collapse of a stall has frequently accentuated a musical or dramatic climax in the season just ended."

The season ended with many promises unfulfilled, for which the impresario placed the blame upon the directors, who, he said, had not given him sufficient use of the Academy stage. His explanations were not always wholly ingenuous, however. Thus he had announced that "Lakmé" would be given, with the composer, M. Delibes, in the conductor's chair. Now, in the season before, Mme. Gerster had been so desirous to create the part of the heroine in America (it being one which afforded fine scope for her lovely powers, and which she had studied with the composer) that she had bought the performing rights. But nothing came of her ambition, and it was an open secret that Heugel, the publisher, had quarreled with Mapleson because of unwarranted practices with his scores in London. In the midst of his troubles Colonel Mapleson announced that he had engaged Mme. Nilsson for the season of 1885-86. There was as little foundation for this announcement as for the promise of "Lakmé."

With ruin staring him in the face, Mapleson concluded the season. He bettered his fortunes a trifle in Boston and Philadelphia, but failed again in New Orleans and St. Louis. Then he went to San Francisco, where the fact that Mme. Nevada was a native of the Pacific Slope was a helpful factor. After the close of the season at the Metropolitan Opera House he gave a "spring season" of six performances in one week, beginning on April 20th. He repeated the performance in Boston and then sailed for Europe, stopping in New York only long enough to institute two suits at law—one against Signor Nicolini to recover $10,000 for failing to sing, and one against Mme. Nevada for $3,000, alleged to have been overpaid her. The suits, in all likelihood, were merely moves in the managerial game which he was playing in London and New York. In the seventh of these "Chapters of Opera" I described as the crowning achievement of Colonel Mapleson in the season full of noteworthy incidents the circumstance that he had succeeded in owing Mme. Patti some $5,000 or $6,000. Nicolini was Patti's husband.

More than ever it looked in the spring of 1885 as if Italian opera had received its quietus. The demoralization of the Academy of Music was complete. In London there prevailed a state of affairs so anomalous and startling that the newspaper critics were cudgeling their brains in a vain effort to find an explanation. For the first time in one hundred and fifty-eight years the British metropolis was without opera; for the first time in thirty-nine years (except in 1856, when fire made it impossible) the Royal Italian Opera at Covent Garden had failed to open its doors on Easter Tuesday. Mr. Gye and his backers refused to venture their fortunes again, and the lease of Her Majesty's was also going begging. In New York Colonel Mapleson had held one good card which he did not seem to know how to play: the season compassed the twenty-fifth anniversary of the operatic début of Mme. Patti. There ought, for excellent and obvious reasons, to have been a fitting celebration of the event; but there was not. On November 26th, two days after the date, Colonel Mapleson gave a performance of "Martha," with Mmes. Patti and Scalchi in the principal women's parts. After the opera a rout of supernumeraries, choristers, and other boys and men engaged for the purpose, carrying torches, followed the diva's carriage to the Windsor Hotel, where she was serenaded. That was all. It was so undignified and inadequate that it provoked some of Mme. Patti's friends to arrange the banquet in her honor which I have described in Chapter VI. Had Signor Brignoli, who was the Edgardo to Adelina Patti's Lucia at the Academy on November 24, 1859, been spared in life and health a few weeks longer (Signor Brignoli died in October, 1884), his friends would probably have urged an association of the two artists in a gala performance of Donizetti's opera. This would have provided an appropriate and delightful celebration, and it would not have been difficult to marshal a number of interesting relics of the period which saw the operatic advent of Mme. Patti, though all of them would have appeared much worse for the wear of a quarter-century than she. Of the valiant champions who were leading the contending operatic armies of the time, Arditi, Maretzek, and Strakosch were still with us. The first was filling, as of yore, the leader's chair at the Academy and doing yeoman's service in the unobtrusive and modest manner which always characterized him; the second, withdrawn from all connection with operatic management, was watching the boiling and bubbling of the caldron with amused interest and spicing his comments with capitally told reminiscences of opera a generation before; the third was still chasing the fickle goddess with fugitive essays as impresario. There were even remains of the critics of those days still active in the world of letters—Richard Grant White, for instance, and George William Curtis, one of my predecessors on The Tribune—and they would undoubtedly have grown young again and been warmed into enthusiastic utterance by eager memories of the dainty débutante and the singers who had preceded her—Grisi, Bosio, Piccolomini, and the rest.

A vast amount of reminiscences would have been justified by such a celebration, for it would have thrown a bright sidelight on the marvelous career of Mme. Patti, a career without parallel in the history of the last half-century. Within three years after she made her first essay "our little Patti," as she was then fondly spoken of, had achieved the queenship of the lyric stage; and, now, twenty-two years later, her title had not suffered the slightest impairment. Within the time singers who had won the world's admiration had been born, educated, and lifted to the niches prepared for them by popular appreciation, but all far below the place where Patti sat enthroned. Stars of great brilliancy had flashed across the firmament and gone out in darkness, but the refulgence of Patti's art remained undimmed, having only grown mellower and deeper and richer with time. Truth is, Mme. Patti was then, and is still, twenty-five years later, a musical miracle; and the fact that she was in New York to sing in the very spot in which she began her career twenty-five years before should have been celebrated as one of the proudest incidents in the city's musical annals. For the generation of opera-goers who grew up in the period which ought to be referred to for all time in the annals of music as The Reign of Patti, she set a standard by which all aspirants for public favor were judged except those whose activities were in a widely divergent field. Not only did she show them what the old art of singing was, but she demonstrated the possibility of its revival. And she did this while admiring enthusiastically the best results of the dramatic spirit which pervades musical composition to-day. Her talent was so many-sided and so astonishing, no matter from which side it was viewed, that rhapsody seems to be the only language left one who attempts analysis or description of it. Her voice, of unequaled beauty, was no more a gift of nature than the ability to assimilate without effort the things which cost ordinary mortals years of labor and vexation of soul. It was perpetually amazing how her singing made the best efforts of the best of her contemporaries pale, especially those who depended on vocal agility for their triumphs. Each performance of hers made it plainer than it had been before that her genius penetrated the mere outward glitter of the music and looked upon the ornament as so much means to the attainment of an end; that end, a beautiful interpretation of the composer's thought. No artist of her time was so perfect an exponent as she of the quality of repose. So far as appearances went it was as easy for her to burden the air with trills and roulades as it was to talk. She sang as the lark sings; the outpouring of an ecstasy of tones of almost infinite number and beauty seemed in her to be a natural means of expression. Her ideas of art were the highest, and it was a singular testimony of her earnestness that, while educated in the old Italian school of vocalization and holding her most exalted supremacy as a singer of Rossini's music, her warmest love, by her own confession, was given, not to its glittering confections, but to the serious efforts of the most dramatic writers. This must be remembered in the list of her astonishing merits now when her voice can no longer call up more than "the tender grace of a day that is dead"; mine was the proud privilege and great happiness of having heard her often in her prime. But I must get down to the real business of this chapter.

The first German performance at the Metropolitan took place on November 17, 1884. The opera was "Tannhäuser" and the distribution of parts as follows: Elizabeth, Mme. Krauss; Venus, Fräulein Slach; a Young Shepherd, Fräulein Stern; the Landgrave, Josef Koegel; Tannhäuser, Anton Schott; Wolfram, Adolf Robinson; Walther von der Vogelweide, Emil Tiffero; Biterolf, Josef Miller; Heinrich der Schreiber, Otto Kemlitz; Reinmar, Ludwig Wolf. The performance made no claim upon special analysis or description. Its highest significance consisted in the publication which it made with reference to the new ideals in operatic representation which came in with the new movement. No doubt to a large portion of the audience, still judging by the old standards, much of it must have been inexplicable, much of it (especially the singing of Herr Schott) little short of monstrous. To a smaller portion, familiar with the opera, the language of its book and the spirit of the play, as well as the music, it came as a vivid realization of the purposes of the poet-composer. To all but the German element in the audience the opera itself was practically a novelty. "Tannhäuser" had not been incorporated in the Italian repertory as "Lohengrin" had, and only those knew it who had attended the sporadic German performances of earlier decades conducted by such men as Bergmann, Anschütz, and Neuendorff. The first New York performance took place on August 27, 1859, at which the Männergesangverein Arion supplied the choruses.

Wagner once described his Tannhäuser as "a German from head to foot," and it was doubtless because Dr. Damrosch saw in it a representative quality that he chose it for his opening. There was patriotism as well as lovely artistic devotion, too, in the choice of "Fidelio" for the second performance, on November 19th. Beethoven's opera had almost as little association with Italian opera as "Tannhäuser," and it was noteworthy that the only portion of the audience room which was not filled was that occupied by the stockholders' boxes. It was an English company that, in September, 1839, had introduced "Fidelio" to New York, and with it made such successful competition with the Italian company of the day that it was performed fourteen times in succession. Mr. Mapleson made a pitiful essay with it in March, 1882, at the Academy, but to recall as vivid and vital a performance as that under discussion one had to go back to the days of Mme. Johannsen and her associates, who gave German opera in 1856. In Dr. Damrosch's performance Marianne Brandt effected her entrance on the

American stage, and the memory of her impersonation of the heroine is still one of the liveliest and most fragrant memories of those memorable days. The dramatic framework of "Fidelio" is weak, its construction faulty. Only one ethical idea is presented in it with real vividness, but it is an idea which is peculiarly dear to the German heart—the saving power of woman's love. "Fidelio" is a tale of wifely devotion, and Beethoven bent all his energies to a glorification of his heroine's love and fidelity. To represent the character faithfully has been the highest ambition of German singers for a century. In that time not many more than a dozen have achieved high distinction in it; and Marianne Brandt is among the number. On its musical side her performance was thrillingly effective, but on its histrionic it rose to grandeur. Every word of her few speeches, every note of her songs, every look of her eyes and expression of her face was an exposition of that world of tenderness which filled the heart of Leonore. Nine-tenths of the action which falls to the part of Leonore is by-play, and by-play of the kind which is made particularly difficult by the time consumed by the music, which is not wisely adjusted with reference to the promotion of the action. Yet all these waits while Leonore is in view were filled by Fräulein Brandt with little actions which tended to develop the character so sadly left in the background by the playwright, but so lovingly treated by the composer. It was down to its smallest detail a picture of a woman impelled by one idea, in which her whole soul had been resolved, and which had grown out of a lofty conception of love and duty. There was nothing of the petty theatrical in Fräulein Brandt, and it was only an evidence of the sincerity of her devotion to the art work which made her bend over and stroke the wrist which she had freed from manacles while the powerful personages of the play were bowing before her as a pattern of conjugal love and the mimic populace were shouting their jubilations over salvation accomplished.

At the third representation, on November 21st, Meyerbeer's "Huguenots" was brought forward to introduce Mme. Schroeder-Hanfstängl; and at the fourth tribute to the characteristic German spirit was paid by the production of Weber's "Der Freischütz." From the day of its birth this has been the opera in which the romantic spirit of the German race has found its most vivid reflection. The sombre lights and mysterious murmurings of the German forests pervade it; the spectres of that paganism from which the sturdy Northerners could be weaned only by compromise and artifice flit through it. The Wild Huntsman overshadows it and, though he says not a word, he powerfully asserts his claim upon the trembling admiration of those who keep open hearts for some of his old companions of pre-Christian days—especially for the burly fellow who under a new name is welcomed joyfully every Christmastide. In another sense, too, "Der Freischütz" is a national opera; the spirit of its music is drawn from the art-form which the people created. Instead of resting on the highly artificial product of the Italian renaissance, it rests upon popular song—folk-song, the song of the folk. Its melodies echo the cadences of the Volkslieder in which the German heart voices its dearest loves. Instead of shining with the light of the Florentine courts it glows with the rays of the setting sun filtered through the foliage of the Black Forest. Yet "Der Freischütz" failed on this its revival—failed so dismally that Dr. Damrosch did not venture upon a single repetition. The lesson which it taught had already been suggested by "Fidelio," but now it was made plain and Dr. Damrosch paid heed to it at once. The dimensions of the Metropolitan Opera House forbade the intimacy which operas founded on the German Singspiel demand for appreciation, and spoken dialogue, especially in a foreign tongue, was painfully destructive of artistic illusion. The operas which followed were more to the purpose: "William Tell," on November 28th, with Robinson as the hero, Schroeder-Hanfstängl as Mathilde, Slach as Gemmy, Staudigl as Gessler, Koegel as Walter, Udvardi as Arnold, and Brandt exemplifying a new spirit in opera by her assumption of the unimportant part of Tell's wife; "Lohengrin," on December 3d, with Krauss, Brandt, Schott, and Staudigl in the principal parts; "Don Giovanni," on December 10th, with Schroeder-Hanfstängl as Donna Anna, Hermine Bely as Zerlina, Brandt as Elvira, Robinson as the Don, Koegel as the Commander, and Udvardi as Ottavio; "Le Prophète," on December 17th, with Brandt as Fidès (one of her greatest rôles), Schroeder-Hanfstängl as Bertha, and Schott as John of Leyden; "La Muette de Portici" (otherwise "Masaniello") on December 29th, with Schott as the hero and Isolina Torri as Fenella. There was an interruption of this spectacular list on January 2, 1885, when "Rigoletto" was given to gratify the ambition of Herr Robinson to be seen and heard as the Jester, and of Mme. Schroeder-Hanfstängl to sing the music of Gilda. In this opera Fräulein Brandt played the part of Maddelena and interpolated a Spanish song sung in German. Then, on January 5th, came Mme. Materna's first operatic appearance in America, in a repetition of "Tannhäuser."

Before continuing the record a few notes on some of these operas and their performance may not be amiss. There was little that was noteworthy about the representation of "Don Giovanni" except Dr. Damrosch's effort to do justice to the famous finale, the full effectiveness of which failed nevertheless because of the arrangement of the stage, which was that of the preceding season. "Les Huguenots" was a distinct disappointment. "La Muette de Portici," which was as good as new to the majority of the audience, acquired historical interest from close association with "William Tell." It was something of an anomaly that, though Rossini's opera had made its appearance during the many years of Italian domination whenever a tenor came who could be counted on to make a sensation with his high notes in the familiar trio of men, Auber's opera, its inspiration as a type, had

had so few representations that it had passed out of memory except for its overture. But the history of "La Muette" is full of anomalies. Its story is Neapolitan and there is Neapolitan color in its music; but it is nothing if not French. It inspired Rossini to write "William Tell" and Meyerbeer to write "Les Huguenots" for the French stage, and is the masterpiece of its author; but Auber is the only Frenchman among the great composers for the Académie in the first half of the nineteenth century. Wagner defended it against the taste of the Parisians, who preferred Rossini and Donizetti, and was snubbed for his pains by the editor of the Gazette Musicale, who was an officer of the French government. Von Weber condemned as coarse the instrumentation which Wagner praised for its fire and truthfulness. Its heroine is dumb; yet to her is assigned the loveliest music in the score.

"Lohengrin" better than "Tannhäuser" gave the public an opportunity to study the change in matter and spirit which had been introduced into local opera by the coming of the Germans to the Metropolitan.

Mme. Materna's first appearance on January 5th was followed by a second on January 7th as Valentine in "Les Huguenots," and a third on January 16th in Halévy's "La Juive." By this time Dr. Damrosch was ready with the first of the large Wagnerian productions which were a part of the dream which it was fated should be realized, not by him, but by his successor, whose name was thereby made illustrious in the operatic annals of New York. On January 30th "Die Walküre" was performed, with the following cast: Brünnhilde, Amalia Materna; Fricka, Marianne Brandt; Sieglinde, Auguste Krauss; Siegmund, Anton Schott; Wotan, Josef Staudigl; Hunding, Josef Koegel; Gerhilde, Marianne Brandt; Ortlinde, Fräulein Stern; Waltraute, Fräulein Gutjar; Schwertleite, Fräulein Morse; Helmwige, Frau Robinson; Siegrune, Fräulein Slach; Grimgerde, Frau Kemlitz; Rossweise, Fräulein Brandl.

"Die Walküre" had been presented before in New York at a so-called Wagner festival at the Academy of Music on April 2, 1877, under the direction of Adolf Neuendorff; but the memories of that production were painful when they were not amusing, and, though much of the music of the Nibelung trilogy had been heard in the concert room, this was practically the first opportunity the people of New York had to learn from personal experience what it was that Wagner meant by a union of arts in the lyric drama. Dr. Damrosch had made an earnest effort to meet the standard set by the Bayreuth festivals. The original scenery and costumes were faithfully copied, except that for the sake of increased picturesqueness Herr Hock, the stage manager, had draperies replace the door in Hunding's hut, which, shaking loose from their fastenings, fell just before Siegmund began his love song, and disclosed an expanse of moonlit background. In the third act, too, there was a greater variety of colors in the costumes of the

Valkyrior. Fräulein Brandt again disclosed her artistic devotion by enacting the part of Fricka and also leading the chorus of Valkyrior; but Mme. Materna was the inspiration of the performance. It was a surprise to those who had already learned to admire her to see how in the character of Brünnhilde she towered above herself in other rôles. Both of the strong sides of the character had perfect exemplification in her singing and acting—the wild, impetuous, exultant freedom of voice which proclaimed the Valkyria's joy in living and doing until the catastrophe was reached, and the deep, unselfish, tender nature disclosed in her sympathy with the ill-starred lovers and her immeasurable love for Wotan. Her complete absorption in the part fitted her out with a new gamut of expression. "If anything can establish a sympathy between us and the mythological creatures of Wagner's dramas," I wrote at the time, "that thing is the acting and singing of Materna." The drama made a tremendous impression, and in the three weeks which remained of the season (including some supplementary performances) "Die Walküre" had seven representations.

The remaining incidents of the season may now be hurried over to make room for a record of the catastrophe which marked its close. By the middle of January it was reported that the receipts were double those of the corresponding period in the previous year, notwithstanding that the price of admission had been reduced nearly one-half. By this time, too, the board of directors had decided to continue the policy adopted at the suggestion of Dr. Damrosch and engage him as director for the next year. This decision had not been reached, however, without consideration of other projects. Charles Mapleson, a son of the director of the Academy of Music, and doubtless only his go-between, submitted a proposition for the directorship, and so did Adolf Neuendorff, a man of indefatigable energy and enterprise, who had given New York its first hearing of "Lohengrin" at the Stadt Theater, in the Bowery, in April, 1871. In January there was also a strike of the chorus, which was quickly settled, and all but the ringleaders in the disturbance taken back into favor on signing an apology.

Rejoicings over the success of the enterprise gave way to general grief and consternation with the unexpected death of Dr. Damrosch on February 15th. On Tuesday, February 10th, he contracted a cold from having thrown himself upon a bed in a cold room for a nap before dinner on returning from a rehearsal at the opera house. He had neglected to open the furnace register or cover himself, and he awoke thoroughly chilled. After dinner he went to a rehearsal of the Oratorio Society, which was preparing Verdi's Manzoni Requiem for performance the following week. Before the conclusion of the rehearsal he was so ill that he was forced to hurry home in a carriage. The next morning it was found that pneumonia had set in, complicated by pleurisy, and a consultation of physicians was held. Only one of the subscription performances at the Metropolitan Opera House remained to be given, but there were still before the director in the way of operatic work five supplementary performances and seasons at Boston, Chicago, and Cincinnati. This naturally caused the sick man a great deal of concern. He deferred to the wishes of his physicians and sent his son Walter, in whose talent and skill he felt great confidence and pride, to conduct the remaining subscription performance in the evening, hoping in the meantime to secure such good care as to enable him to be in his chair on Thursday evening when "Die Walküre" was to be repeated. In this hope, too, he was disappointed and had to send his son a second time to conduct a performance of the drama which had put the capstone to the astonishingly successful season which his zeal, learning, skill, enterprise, and perseverance had brought about. As on the previous day he went through the score with his son and called his attention to some of the details of the responsible and difficult task before him. The young man's knowledge of the score and aptitude in grasping the suggestions made to him comforted and quieted the father, and the representations at the opera house went off in a manner which caused complimentary comments on Thursday evening and Saturday afternoon. On Sunday, February 15th, at 3 o'clock A.M., a change in the sick man's condition set in, and the physicians, realizing that the case was hopeless, so informed the family early in the day. Dr. Damrosch was not disturbed by the prospect of death. He retained consciousness until one o'clock in the afternoon, and within an hour before that time called Walter to his bedside and asked that an opera score be brought that he might give a few more suggestions for the concluding representations in New York. He was assured that all would go well. His last thoughts and words were with his family and work. In disjointed phrases he repeatedly asked that nothing be permitted to suffer because of his sickness; that the preparations for the operas and concerts of the societies of which he was conductor should go on. With his mind thus occupied he sank into unconsciousness and died at a quarter after two o'clock in the afternoon of Sunday, February 15, 1885. His funeral took place at the opera house on February 18th, amidst impressive ceremonies, addresses being made by the Rev. Horatio Potter (Assistant Bishop of New York), the Rev. Henry Ward Beecher, and Professor Felix Adler. The remaining performances of the supplementary season were conducted by Mr. Lund, after which the company went on tour, Mr. Lund and Walter Damrosch sharing the work of conducting. The season had begun on November 17th, one week after Colonel Mapleson opened his seventh season at the Academy of Music. It lasted until February 21st, but the last subscription performance was that on the evening of the day after Dr. Damrosch had fallen ill. The subscription was for thirty-eight nights and twelve Saturday matinées. There was no Christmas interregnum. The list of operas produced, the date of first representation, and the number of times each opera was given can be read in the following table:

Opera First performance Times given

"Tannhäuser" .... November 17 9
"Fidelio" .... November 19 3
"Les Huguenots" .... November 21 5
"Der Freischütz" .... November 24 1
"William Tell" .... November 28 3
"Lohengrin" .... December 3 9
"Don Giovanni" .... December 10 2
"Le Prophète" .... December 17 9
"La Muette de Portici" .... December 29 3
"Rigoletto" .... January 2 1
"La Juive" .... January 16 5
"Die Walküre" .... January 30 7

Total number of representations 57

Twelve out of twenty-two works promised in the prospectus were given, the unperformed operas being "Rienzi," "Der Fliegende Holländer," "Le Nozze di Figaro," "Die Zauberflöte," "Il Barbiere di Siviglia," Gounod's "Faust," "Die Lustigen Weiber von Windsor," "La Dame Blanche," "Hans Heiling," and Kreutzer's "Nachtlager von Granada." The failure to produce all the operas promised was largely due to the teachings of the first month of the season. In the list were a number of peculiarly German works, in which the musical numbers alternated with spoken dialogue. The experience made with "Fidelio" and "Der Freischütz" showed that works of this character were unedifying to the persons of native birth in the audience, and this was one reason why it was decided to omit several of them. Another reason was that it was found that the large dimensions of the opera house detracted from even good performances of light works; and still another was that the style of the singers was adapted to vigorous and declamatory music, rather than to that which depends for effect upon purity and beauty of voice and excellence of vocalization. A comparison of the last performances with those which were given when the company was continually engaged in studying new works suggests another reason: "Der Freischütz" was poorly performed; the first representations of "William Tell" and "Les Huguenots" threatened the loss of all the prestige won by the performances of "Tannhäuser"; and "Fidelio" and "Don Giovanni" called for a vigorous exercise of good nature. Whatever disappointment came, therefore, from the failure to produce such interesting works as "Hans Heiling," one of the finest products, if not the finest, of the epigonoi of Weber, and "Die Lustigen Weiber von Windsor," unquestionably the best Shakespearian opera extant (Verdi's "Otello" and "Falstaff" excepted), was compensated for by the excellence which marked the performances of "Tannhäuser," "Lohengrin," "Le Prophète," and "Die Walküre." The production of this great work was a fitting end to Dr. Damrosch's artistic career. It marked the beginning of a new era in New York's operatic affairs, and led to the execution in the years which followed of his large plan to produce the entire Nibelung tragedy, "Tristan und Isolde" and "Die Meistersinger"—a plan carried out by his successor. For "Tannhäuser," "Fidelio," "William Tell," "La Muette de Portici," "La Juive," and "Die Walküre" new stage decorations had to be provided, and this was done on a scale of great liberality, in comparison with what New York had been accustomed to. The largest expenditure on a single representation was $4,000, and the average cost was $3,400. These sums were much smaller than those expended in the previous season on the hurdy-gurdy Italian list, and the stage pictures were all much finer. The saving was in the salaries of the artists, no two of which cost together as much as Mme. Nilsson alone.

CHAPTER XII
END OF ITALIAN OPERA AT THE ACADEMY

The season 1885-86 witnessed the collapse of the Italian opposition at the Academy of Music, but also the rise of an institution in its place, which, had it commanded a higher order of talent and been more intelligently administered, might have served the lofty purposes set for the German opera. This was the American Opera Company, which, after an extremely ambitious beginning, made a miserable end a season later, leaving an odor of scandal, commercial and artistic, which infected the atmosphere for years afterward. German opera was also given throughout a large part of the season at the Thalia Theater, the manager being Mr. Gustav Amberg, and the conductor John Lund, who had come into notice at the Metropolitan Opera House by reason of the death of Dr. Damrosch. These performances were unpretentious, and divided between operetta and the type of opera which grew out of the Singspiel. Their significance, so far as this history is concerned, lay in the evidence which they bore of a considerable degree of interest on the part of the public outside of the patrons of the Metropolitan Opera House in German opera. There were also commendable features in the repertory. Thus, the performances began on October 13, 1885, with "Der Freischütz," in which appeared Ferdinand Wachtel, a son of the famous "coachman tenor," Theodore Wachtel, whose sensational career in Europe and America had come to an end a decade before, though he did not die till 1893. The father's battle horse, "Le Postillon de Lonjumeau," was brought out for the son, but the public were not long in discovering that the latter had all the faults and none of the merits of the former, and he failed to become even a nine days' wonder. Among the operas brought forward by Mr. Amberg was Nicolai's "Lustigen Weiber von Windsor," and Emil Kaiser's "Trompeter von Säkkingen," a production obviously prompted by the sensational success in Europe of Nessler's opera of the same name. Nicolai's opera, which has never lost its popularity with the Germans, was probably given on its merits alone, but the fact that Dr. Damrosch had abandoned it after putting it in his prospectus, may have had something to do with its performance by Mr. Amberg's modest troupe, as well as by the proud American Opera Company, which brought it out in a specially prepared English version. Mr. Amberg's company also brought forward a German version of Maillart's "Les Dragons de Villars," under the title, "Das Glöckchen des Eremiten."

Colonel Mapleson, having spent the summer bickering and negotiating with the directors of the Academy, after having failed to get into the Metropolitan Opera House under the cloak of his son Charles, began his eighth season in the Academy of Music, which had been furbished up for the occasion, on November 2, 1885. Mme. Patti had deserted him, and if he ever had made overtures to Mme. Nilsson, whose engagement he had announced, they came to naught. He now made a virtue out of necessity and proclaimed the merits of "good all 'round" opera, and the iniquity of the star system. His company, however, was the old one, with Alma Fohström and Minnie Hauk in place of Mme. Patti, Gerster, and Nevada. Among the familiar names in the prospectus were those of Mme. Lablache, Ravelli, de Anna, Del Puente, Cherubini, and Carraciolo; among the newcomers were Signor Giannini, an extremely serviceable tenor, who had sung in the previous season in the "Milan Grand Opera Company," compiled by James Barton Key and Horace McVicker, as related in the preceding chapter; also a Mlle. Felia Litvinoff, whom we shall meet again as Mme. Litvinne, sister-in-law of M. Édouard de Reszke, and member of a company singing at the Metropolitan Opera House. Mapleson opened with "Carmen," the heroine represented by Mme. Hauk. She had created the character in London and New York, and set a standard which prevailed in England and America until the coming of Mme. Calvé; but time had dealt harshly with Mme. Hauk during the nineteen years which had elapsed since she, a lissome creature, had first sung at the Academy of Music (she had effected her operatic début in Brooklyn a few weeks before), and much of the old charm was gone from her singing, and nearly all from her acting. The opening was distinctly disappointing, and the season came to an end on November 28th, after twelve evening and four afternoon performances. There could scarcely have been a more convincing demonstration of how completely the fashionable world had abandoned the Academy of Music than the giving of a subscription season of only four weeks' duration. Within this period, moreover, there was no sign of effort to get out of the old rut into which Colonel Mapleson's repertory had sunk. "Carmen" was given three times, "Il Trovatore" twice, "Lucia di Lammermoor" twice, "L'Africaine" twice, "La Sonnambula" once, "La Favorita" once, "Fra Diavolo" twice, "Don Giovanni" twice, and "Faust" once. Mlle. Fohström effected her American début in a performance of "Lucia" on November 9th. She had been announced for the second night of the season in "Il Trovatore," but was taken ill. She had been little heard of previous to her coming, though diligent observers of musical doings knew that she had sung for several seasons in Europe, and, I believe, South America, and had figured in Colonel Mapleson's spring season in London in 1885. She was a small creature, with features of a markedly Scandinavian type—she was a native of Finland—and had evidently studied the traditions of the Italian operatic stage to as much purpose as was necessary to present, acceptably, the stereotyped round of characters. But her gifts and attainments were not great enough to take her impersonations out of the rut of conventionality, nor to save her singing from the charge of nervelessness and monotony of color. Three seasons later (1888-89) she was a member of the German company at the Metropolitan Opera House, and sang such rôles as Marguerite de Valois ("Les Huguenots"), Mathilde ("William Tell"), Marguerite ("Faust"), Bertha ("Le Prophète"), and Eudora ("La Juive"), giving place at the beginning of February to Mme. Schroeder-Hanfstängl, who had returned, to the delight of her admirers. In the interim she increased her artistic stature very considerably, her voice proving more effective in the new house than in the Academy of Music, which was incomparably better acoustically. Mapleson's singers came back to the Academy on December 20th to sing Wallace's "Maritana" in Italian (with Tito Mattei's recitatives in place of the spoken dialogue), and at the manager's benefit on December 23d Massenet's opera "Manon" was performed for the first time in America. Under the circumstances the cast deserves to be set forth: The Chevalier des Grieux, Signor Giannini; Lescaut, Signor del Puente; Monfontaine, Signor Rinaldini; the Count des Grieux, Signor Cherubini; du Bretigny, Signor Foscani, (Mr. Fox, an American); an innkeeper, Signor de Vaschetti; attendant of the Seminary of St. Sulpice, Signor Bieletto; Poussette, Mlle. Bauermeister; Javotte, Mme. Lablache; Rovette, Mlle. de Vigne; Manon, Mme. Hauk.

From January 4th to April 17th the Academy of Music was occupied by the American Opera Company, the artistic director of which was Theodore Thomas, who had long stood at the head of orchestral music in America. As I have already intimated, rightly managed this institution might have become of the same significance to the future of opera in the United States as the German company, which had just established a domicile at the Metropolitan Opera House. Indeed, it might have become of greater significance, for the best friends of the German enterprise looked upon it as merely a necessary intermediary between the Italian exotic and a national form of art, with use of the vernacular, which every patriotic lover of music hoped to see installed some day in the foremost operatic establishment in the land. Unfortunately, its claims to excellence were put forward with impudent exaggeration, and there was no substantial or moral health in its business administration. It could not expect to cope with foreign organizations or local aggregations of foreign artists in respect of its principal artists, but it could, and did, in respect of scenic investiture, and in its choral and instrumental ensemble. Unhappily, even in these elements it was unwisely directed, though with a daring and a degree of confidence in popular support which may be said to have given it a characteristically American trait. In three respects the season was unique in the American history of English opera (or opera in English, as it would better he called, since there was not an English opera in its repertory), viz.: in the brilliancy of the orchestra, the excellence of the chorus (numerous and fresh of voice), and the sumptuousness of the stage attire.

There were sixty-six performances in the season of light operas, and one ballet, the latter Delibes's "Sylvia." The operas were Goetz's "Taming of the Shrew" (five times), Gluck's "Orpheus" (thirteen times), Wagner's "Lohengrin" (ten times), Mozart's "Magic Flute" (six times), Nicolai's "Merry Wives of Windsor" (nine times), Delibes's "Lakmé" (eleven times), Wagner's "Flying Dutchman" (seven times), and Massé's "Marriage of Jeannette" (in conjunction with the ballet, five times). "The Taming of the Shrew" received its first performance in America on January 4, 1886; "Lakmé" on March 1st; "The Marriage of Jeannette," on March 24th, and "Lohengrin" (in English), on January 20th.

Immediately on the death of Dr. Damrosch, trouble broke out in the Metropolitan company. There had been some jealousy among the women singers because of the large honorarium paid to Mme. Materna. It was her third visit to America, and she had learned to say dollars when at home she was accustomed to think of florins. Moreover, in the spring of the year she had made an extensive concert tour with Mme. Nilsson, under the direction of Mr. Thomas, and knew something about the liberality of Americans in the matter of artists' fees. Herr Schott (Dr. von Bülow's dis-, des-, and detonating tenor), developing a large and noisy managerial ambition, scarcely waited for the burial of Dr. Damrosch before beginning an agitation looking toward his installation in the dead director's place. All this might have been done in a seemly manner, and if it had been so done might have been carried through successfully and with popular approbation, for Herr Schott's project, in the main, was the one acted on by the directors. But Herr Schott, in an effort to promote his scheme, made an ungallant attack upon the artistic character of Mme. Materna, and this the public found to be "most tolerable and not to be endured." The occasion soon presented itself for Schott to show that he had an overweening sense of his own importance and popularity. At the end of the fourth of the five supplementary performances there was a demonstration of applause. Herr Schott interpreted it as a curtain call for himself, and promptly showed himself, and bowed his thanks. The applause was renewed, and he repeated this performance. Then came a third call, and again the tenor stepped out before the footlights. Now the applause of his friends was mingled with cries of "Materna!" but on a fourth call, and a fourth appearance of Schott, the popular feeling exploded in hisses and calls for the soprano. He retired unabashed, but Mme. Materna, answering the next call, was tumultuously greeted. So far as the overwhelming majority of the patrons of the house was concerned, Herr Schott's cake was now dough. Foolishly he, or his friends for him, proceeded to anger the directors from whom they were expecting favors. It was given out that he had submitted a proposition concerning the management of the opera house at the request of the directors. This met with prompt denial at the hands of Mr. Stanton, the secretary of the board, and by some of the directors themselves.

Herr Schott had submitted a proposition, however, and had coupled it with a hint, which sounded like a threat, that in case it was not promptly accepted it would go to the directors of the Academy of Music. This vexed some of the stockholders of the older institution, who made public denial that they were considering German opera, even as a remote possibility. Herr Schott's proposition was dismissed with little ceremony by the Metropolitan directors, who, however, sent Mr. Stanton and Mr. Walter Damrosch to Europe to organize a company to carry out the lines already established during the coming season. In doing so they adopted several valuable suggestions contained in Herr Schott's plan. In this plan Schott was to be the musical director of the company, of course, but not the conductor. For this post he contemplated engaging Anton Seidl, then conductor of the Municipal Theater of Bremen and husband of the jugendlich Dramatische, who had successfully gone through the ordeal of one season—Auguste Krauss. Walter Damrosch was to be assistant conductor, Mme. Schroeder-Hanfstängl, Frau Krauss, Fräulein Brandt, and Herren Staudigl and Blum, of the old company, were to be kept, and the new singers were to be a Fräulein Gilbert, Fräulein Koppmeyer, Ferdinand Wachtel (son of Theodore, already referred to), and Carl Hill, bass.

The organization, as finally effected, placed Mr. Stanton at its head as director, acting for the stockholders; Walter Damrosch, as assistant director, and also conductor; Lilli Lehmann, of Berlin, was the principal soprano; Marianne Brandt, principal contralto; Albert Stritt, principal tenor; Emil Fischer, of Dresden, principal bass, and Adolf Robinson, principal barytone. Other singers were Auguste Krauss (who now became Seidl-Krauss), Max Alvary, tenor; Fräulein Slach, mezzo-soprano; Eloi Sylva, tenor; Kemlitz, tenor; Lehmler, bass; Frau Krämer-Wiedl, dramatic soprano; Herr Alexi, barytone, and Fräulein Klein, soprano. With this company the second season of German opera was opened on November 23, 1885, the opera being "Lohengrin." I shall not take up the features of the season seriatim, nor make detailed record of the consecutive productions of the operas on its list. Only special incidents shall be recorded; but before this is done something may be said touching the newcomers:

Anton Seidl was a young man when he came to New York, but he had filled the position of secretary to Richard Wagner, and been a member of his household for six years. Before then he had studied at the Leipsic Conservatory (which he entered in October, 1870), and been a chorus master or accompanist at the Vienna Opera. There he came under the eyes of Hans Richter, who sent him to Wagner when the latter asked for a young man who could give him such help on "The Ring of the Nibelung" as Richter had given him on "Die Meistersinger"—that is, to write out the clean score from the composer's hurried autograph. The period which he spent with Wagner was from 1872 to 1879. During all the preparations for the first Bayreuth Festival in 1876 he was one of the poet-composer's executive officers. He was one of the assistant conductors on the stage during the festival, and afterward conducted the preliminary rehearsals for the concerts which Wagner gave in London and elsewhere to recoup himself for the losses made at the festival. Then, on Wagner's recommendation, he was appointed conductor at the Municipal Theater at Leipsic (his associates being Victor Nessler and Arthur Nikisch), later on of Angelo Neumann's "Richard Wagner Theater," which gave representations of "Der Ring des Nibelungen" in many cities of Germany, Holland, England, and Italy, and still later of the Municipal Theater in Bremen—the post which he held when the death of Dr. Damrosch created the vacancy which brought him to New York. All this he had accomplished before his thirty-fifth year (he was born in Pesth on May 7, 1850), and he was not yet thirty when Wagner, in a speech delivered in Berlin, alluded to him as "the young artist whom I have brought up, and who is now accomplishing astounding things." Naturally, when he came to New York, he was looked upon as a prophet, priest, and paladin of Wagner's art. For twelve years he filled a large place in the music of New York, in concert room as well as opera house, and when he died it was like his predecessor, in the fulness of his powers, and in the midst of his activities. But this belongs to a later chapter of this story.

Lilli Lehmann brought to New York chiefly the fame which she had won in Bayreuth at the first Wagner festival, of 1876, at which she was one of the Rhine daughters (Woglinde), and one of the Valkyrior (Helmwige), and where she also sang the music of the Forest Bird in "Siegfried." At that period in her career she was still classed among the light sopranos, and so she continued to be classed until she broke violently away from the clogs which tradition puts upon artists in the theaters of Germany. She felt the charm of freedom from the old theatrical conventions when she sang Isolde at Covent Garden on July 2, 1884, and her growth to a lofty tragic stature was rapid. She was filled with fervor for the large rôles of Wagner when she came to New York, and her success in them was so gratifying to her ambition that it led her at the expiration of her leave of absence from the Court Opera at Berlin (where she had been fifteen years as erste Coloratursängerin) to extend her stay in America beyond the period of her furlough, and involved her in difficulties with the Berlin Intendant, and the federation of German theatrical managers, called the Cartellverband. Having carried to her an offer from the president of the Cincinnati Festival Association to sing at the festival of May, 1886, which was the ultimate reason for her action, I am in a position to give the details of the story of what became a cause célèbre, and led to a wide discussion of the relations between the German managers and their singers. A short time before Miss Lehmann had declined an offer from the committee of the North American Sängerbund to take part in the Sängerfest, which was to be held in Milwaukee in June, 1886. She had also been asked by the artistic manager of the house of Steinway & Sons to go on a concert tour with Franz Rummel and Ovide Musin. When I came to her with the dispatch from Cincinnati she spoke of her unwillingness to break her contract with Berlin, and of the loss of the lifelong pension to which her period of service at the Court Opera would eventually entitle her. I declined to advise her in the premises, but made a calculation of her prospective net earnings from the three engagements which were offering, and suggested that she compare the income from their investment with the pension which she would forfeit. I also agreed, if she wished it, to reopen the negotiations with the Sängerfest officials at Milwaukee. She took the matter under advisement, and in a few days, having concluded the engagement with a representative of the Cincinnati association, she told me she had determined to stay in America during June. In July, against the advice of some of her American friends, she paid a fine imposed upon her by the Intendant of the Court Opera. The amount of the fine was 13,000 marks ($3,250), and this amount she had received from the Milwaukee engagement. I had written to Mr. Catenhusen, the director of the Sängerfest, as promised, and he had reopened negotiations with more than willingness. Asked for her terms, she replied: "Three thousand three hundred dollars," and turning to a friend said: "I'll let the festival pay my Berlin fine." After she had paid the money into the royal exchequer, the manager of Kroll's Theater engaged her for a series of representations, but met an unexpected obstacle in the form of a refusal of the Intendant of the Court Theater to restore her to the privileges which she had forfeited by breaking her contract. It was long before she succeeded in making peace with the Governmental administration of the Court Opera, and in the public discussion which accompanied her efforts she took part in an eminently characteristic way. The newspapers were open to her, and in the Berlin Tageblatt (I think it was) she defended her course on the ground that America had enabled her to exercise her talent in a field which the hidebound traditions of the German theaters would have kept closed to her. Once a florid singer, always a florid singer, was her complaint, and she added: "One grows weary after singing nothing but princesses for fifteen years." Though she began in "Carmen," and followed with "Faust," Miss Lehmann soon got into the Wagnerian waters, in which she was longing to adventure, and in them set some channel buoys which the New York public still asks Brünnhildes and Isoldes to observe. It was then, however, and still is, characteristic of her broad ideals in art, that, while winning the highest favor in tragic parts, she preserved not only her old skill, but her old love for good singing in the old sense. When, at the height of her Wagnerian career, she sang at a performance for her own benefit, she chose "Norma."

From 1885 till the time when her operatic experiences had become the exception to her rule of concert work, the greater part of her career was spent in New York; and during the whole of the period she was in all things artistic an inspiration, and an exemplar to her fellow artists. For industry, zeal, and unselfish devotion in preparing an opera I have never met an artist who could be even remotely compared with her. When "Siegfried" was in rehearsal for its first American production, she took a hand in setting the stage. Though she had nothing to do in the second act, she went into the scenic lumber room and selected bits of woodland scenery, and with her own hands rearranged the set so as to make Siegfried's posture and surroundings more effective. When the final dress rehearsal of "Götterdämmerung" was reached a number of the principal singers were still uncertain of their music. Miss Lehmann was letter perfect, as usual, but without a demur repeated the ensembles over and over again, singing always, as was her wont, with full voice and intense dramatic expression. This had been going on literally for hours when the end of the second act was reached. When she came into the audience room for the intermission I ventured to expostulate with her:

"My dear Miss Lehmann, pray have a care. You are not effecting your début in New York, nor is this a public performance. Think of to-morrow. You will weary your voice. Why do you work so? Markiren Sie doch!"

"Markiren thu Ich nie!" ("Markiren," it may be explained, is the technical term for singing in half-voice, or just enough to mark the cues.) "As for the rest, rehearsals are necessary, if not for one's self, then at least for the others. Don't be alarmed about my voice. It is easier to sing all three Brünnhildes than one Norma. You are so carried away by the dramatic emotion, the action, and the scene that you do not have to think how to sing the words. That comes of itself. But in Bellini you must always have a care for beauty of tone and correct emission. But I love 'Norma,' and Mozart's 'Entführung.'"

Very different this from the conduct of Max Alvary after he had begun to grow into public favor. He was a son of the Düsseldorf painter, Andreas Achenbach, and came to New York without reputation, and engaged to sing second rôles. Early in the season Stritt, the first tenor, after creating the part of Assad in Goldmark's "Königin von Saba" yielded it up to Alvary, finding the range of the music a little too trying for his voice. Alvary's handsome face and figure, especially the latter, his gallant bearing, and his impeccable taste in dress, made a deep impression, and it was not long before he developed into a veritable matinée girl's idol. He developed also an enormous conceit, which near the end of his New York career led him to think that he was the opera, and that he might dictate policies to the manager and the directors back of him. So in the eyes of the judicious there were ragged holes in his shining veneer long before his career in New York came to a close. The preparation of "Siegfried" for performance led to an encounter between him and Mr. Seidl, in which the unamiable side of his disposition, and the shallowness of his artistic nature were disclosed. At the dress rehearsal, when alone on the stage, he started in to go through his part in dumbshow. Seidl requested him to sing.

"It is not necessary; I know my part," was the ungracious reply.

"But this is a rehearsal. It is not enough that you know your part or that you know that you know your part. I must know that you know it. Others must sing with you, and they must hear you."

He started the orchestra again. Not a sound from the puffed up little tenor in his picturesque bearskin and pretty legs. Seidl rapped for silence, and put down his baton.

"Call Mr. Stanton!" he commanded.

Mr. Stanton was brought from his office, and Mr. Seidl briefly explained the situation. He would not go on with the rehearsal unless Mr. Alvary sang, and without a rehearsal there would be no first performance of "Siegfried" to-morrow. Mr. Alvary explained that to sing would weary him.

"I shall not sing to-day and to-morrow. Choose; I'll sing either to-day or to-morrow."

"Sing to-day!" said Stanton curtly, and turned away from the stage. Like a schoolboy Alvary now began to sing with all his might, as if bound to incapacitate himself for the next day. But he would have sacrificed a finger rather than his opportunity on the morrow, and the little misses and susceptible matrons got the hero whom they adored for years afterward.

Next to Miss Lehmann, the most popular singer in the company in this second year of German opera at the Metropolitan was Emil Fischer, the bass. Except for a short period spent abroad in an effort to be an opera manager in Holland, Fischer has remained a New Yorker ever since he came in 1885. This has not been wholly of his own volition, however. He came from Dresden, where he was an admired member of the Court Opera. His coming, or his staying, involved him in difficulty with the Royal Intendant, and though the singer began legal proceedings against his liege lord, the King of Saxony, for rehabilitation, he never regained the privileges which he had forfeited in order to win the fame and money which came to him here. The fame was abiding; the money was not. Twenty-one year after his coming his old admirers were still so numerous, and their admiration so steadfast, that a benefit performance at the Metropolitan Opera House, in which he took part in an act of "Die Meistersinger," yielded nearly $10,000.

The season of 1885-86 at the Metropolitan Opera House began on November 23d, and lasted till March 6th, with an interregnum of two weeks from December 19th to January 4th, during which the company gave performances in Philadelphia, with woeful financial results, the loss to the stockholders being $15,000. The excellence of the management and the wisdom and honesty of the artists were attested by the circumstance that not once was an opera changed after it was announced. Nine operas were performed, and of these three were wholly new to the Metropolitan stage, two were absolutely new to America, and two were provided with considerable new scenery. The table of performances was as follows:

Opera	First performance	Times given
"Lohengrin"	November 23	4
"Carmen"	November 25	2
"Der Prophet"	November 27	3
"Die Walküre"	November 30	4
"Die Königin von Saba"	December 2	15
"Tannhäuser"	December 11	4
"Die Meistersinger"	January 4	8
"Faust"	January 20	5
"Rienzi"	February 5	7
Total representations		52

The attractive charm of a new work was shown in the success achieved by Goldmark's "Queen of Sheba," which was given with great pomp in its externals, but also finely from a musical point of view. It brought into the box office an average of $4,000 for fifteen performances, and was set down as the popular triumph of the season, though, considering that "Die Meistersinger von Nürnberg" had a month less to run, its record was also remarkable. The average difference in attendance on the two works which led the list was about one hundred and fifty. The directors had fixed the assessment on the stockholders in October at $2,000 a box, and their receipts from this source were $136,700; from the general public,

$171,463.13; total, $308,163.13. The cost of producing the operas, omitting the charges for new scenery and properties, but including the expenses of the Philadelphia season, was $244,981.96. The fixed charges on the building (taxes, interest, and rental account) were about $85,000 in the preceding year, and the financial outcome was so satisfactory to the stockholders that the directors promptly re-engaged Mr. Seidl, and adopted a resolution empowering the managing director, Edmund C. Stanton, to make contracts with artists for three years. It was interesting to note the effect upon the opera houses and artists of Germany. I cannot recall that there were any more difficulties like those which attended the disruption of their contracts by Fräulein Lehmann and Herr Fischer. Instead, the managers of the municipal theaters of Germany especially (and, I doubt not, court theaters also) found that they, too, could come in for a share of the American dollars by granting leaves of absence for the New York season, and taking a percentage of the liberal fees received by their stars.

CHAPTER XIII
WAGNER HOLDS THE METROPOLITAN

The incidents of the early history of the Metropolitan Opera House come to me in such multitude that I find it difficult to apportion seasons and chapters in this record. Later, it may be, when the new order of things shall have been established, and again given place to the old, the relation may make more rapid progress. I have already devoted much space to the second German season, but there are a few details which deserve special consideration. The first of these (if the reader will accept the instantaneous popularity of Mr. Seidl as a conclusion from the remarks made in his introduction in these annals) was the first appearance of Lilli Lehmann. Circumstances would have it that she should show herself first, not as the singer of old-fashioned florid rôles, with which (except for her Bayreuth experience) she was associated, nor yet as the Wagnerian tragedienne which she became later, but in a transitional character—that of Carmen in Bizet's opera of that name. Lehmann as the gipsy cigarette maker, with her Habanera and Seguidilla, with her errant fancy wandering from a sentimental brigadier to a dashing bull fighter, is a conception which will not come easy to the admirers of the later Brünnhilde and Isolde; and, indeed, she was a puzzling phenomenon to the experienced observers of that time. Carmen was already a familiar apparition to New Yorkers, who had imagined that Minnie Hauk had spoken the last word in the interpretation of that character. When Fräulein Lehmann came her tall stature and erect, almost military, bearing were calculated to produce an effect of surprise of such a nature that it had to be overcome before it was possible to enter into the feeling with which she informed the part. To the eye, moreover, she was a somewhat more matronly Carmen than the fancy, stimulated by earlier performances of the opera or the reading of Mérimée's novel, was prepared to accept; but it was in harmony with the new picture that she stripped the character of the flippancy and playfulness popularly associated with it, and intensified its sinister side. In this, Fräulein Lehmann deviated from Mme. Hauk's impersonation and approached that of Mme. Trebelli, which had been brought to public notice at the first Italian season at the Metropolitan Opera House. In her musical performance she surpassed both of those admired and experienced artists. Her voice proved to be true, flexible, and ringing, and, also, of a most particularly telling quality. She disclosed ability to fill the part with the passionate expression and warmth of color which it called for, and utilized that ability judiciously and tastefully. M. Eloi Sylva, the new tenor, effected his American introduction in Meyerbeer's "Prophet" on November 27th. He was an exceedingly robust singer, with an imposing stage presence, a powerful voice, which, in its upper register, especially, was vibrant, virile, and musical. Two seasons later he essayed English opera, with about the same results, so far as his pronunciation was concerned, as he achieved in German. Fräulein Lehmann was first seen and heard as Brünnhilde in "Die Walküre" on November 30th. She was statuesquely beautiful, and her voice glorified the music. In the first scene she brought into beautiful relief the joyful nature of the Wishmaiden; her cries were fairly brimming with eager, happy vitality. While proclaiming his fate to Siegmund, she was first inspired by a noble dignity, then transformed instantaneously into a sympathetic woman by the hero's devotion to the helpless and hapless woman who lay exhausted on his knees.

The first of the two novelties of the season was Goldmark's opera "Die Königin von Saba," which had its first performance in America on December 2d. The cast was as follows: Sulamith, Fräulein Lebmaun; Königin, Frau Krämer-Wiedl; Astaroth, Fräulein Brandt; Solomon, Herr Robinson; Assad, Herr Stritt; Hohepriester, Herr Fischer; Baal Hanan, Herr Alexi. Mr. Seidl conducted. The opera (which had had its first production in Vienna ten years before, and had achieved almost as much success in Germany as Nessler's "Trompeter von Säkkingen") was produced with great sumptuousness, and being also admirably sung and acted, it made a record that provided opera-goers in New York with a sensation of a kind that they had not known before, and to which they did not grow accustomed until the later dramas of Wagner began their triumphal career at the Metropolitan. Twenty years afterward (season 1905-06) Mr. Conried revived the opera at the Metropolitan, but it was found that in the interim its fires had paled. In 1885 there were reasons why the public should not only have been charmed, but even impressed by the opera. In spite of its weaknesses it was then, and still is, an effective opera. Thoughtfully considered, the libretto is not one of any poetical worth, but in its handling of the things which give pleasure to the superficial observer it is admirable. It presents a story which is fairly rational, which enlists the interest, if not the sympathy, of the observers, which is new as a spectacle, and which is full of pomp and circumstance. Looked at from its ethical side and considered with reference to the sources of its poetical elements, it falls under condemnation. The title of the opera would seem to indicate that the Bible story of the visit of the Queen of Sheba to Solomon had been drawn on for the plot. That is true. The Queen of Sheba comes to Jerusalem to see Solomon in his glory, and that is the end of the draft on the Biblical story; the rest is the modern poet's invention. But that is the way of operas with Biblical subjects—a few names, an incident, and the rest of invention. In Gounod's "Reine de Saba" the magnificently storied queen tries to elope with the architect of Solomon's temple like any wilful millionaire's daughter. Salome is a favorite subject just now that the danse du ventre is working its way into polite society, but save for the dance and the names of the tetrarch and his wife, the Bible contributes nothing to the Salome dramas and pantomimes. Sulamith, who figures like an abandoned Dido, in the opera of Mosenthal and Goldmark, owes her name, but not her nature or any of her experiences, to the pastoral play which Solomon is credited with having written. The Song of Songs contributes, also, a few lines of poetry to the book, and a ritualistic service celebrated in the Temple finds its prototype in some verses from Psalms lxvii and cxvii, but with this I have enumerated all that "Die Königin von Saba" owes to the sacred Scriptures. Solomon's magnificent reign and marvelous wisdom, which contribute factors to the production, belong to profane as well as to sacred history, and persons with deeply rooted prejudices touching the people of Biblical story will be happiest if they can think of some other than the Scriptural Solomon as the prototype of Mosenthal and Goldmark, for in truth they make of him a sorry sentimentalist at best. The local color of the old story has been borrowed from the old story; the dramatic motive comes plainly from "Tannhäuser"; Sulamith is Elizabeth, the Queen Venus, Assad Tannhäuser, and Solomon Wolfram. Goldmark's music is highly spiced. At times it rushes along like a lava stream, every measure throbbing with eager, excited, and exciting life. He revels in instrumental color; the language of his orchestra is as glowing as the poetry attributed to the veritable King whom the operatic story celebrates. Many composers before him made use of Oriental cadences and rhythms, but to none did they seem so like a native language. It has not been every Jew who could thus handle a Jewish subject. Compare Halévy, Meyerbeer, and Rubinstein with Goldmark.

The first performance of Wagner's "Meistersinger" fell on the same night as the production for the first time in America of Goetz's "Widerspänstigen Zähmung" in English by the National Opera Company. We thus had in juxtaposition an admirable operatic adaptation of a Shakespearian comedy and a modern comedy, of which I thought at the time I could not speak in higher praise than to say that it was truly Shakespearian in its delineation of character. In my book, "Studies in the Wagnerian Drama," I have analyzed Wagner's comedy from many points of view, and printed besides the results of investigations of the old Nuremberg mastersingers made on the spot. The significance of this record is that it tells of the introduction in America of a comedy which, though foreign in matter and manner to the thoughts, habits, and feelings of the American people, has, nevertheless, held a high place in their admiration. Later we shall see that this admiration was based on the sound understanding of the play which the original, performers inculcated. Let their names therefore be preserved. They were: Hans Sachs, Emil Fischer; Veit Pogner, Josef

Staudigl; Kunz Vogelsang, Herr Dworsky; Konrad Nachtigal, Emil Sänger; Sixtus Beckmesser, Otto Kemlitz; Fritz Kothner, Herr Lehmler; Balthasar Zorn, Herr Hoppe; Ulrich Eisslinger, Herr Klaus; Augustin Moser, Herr Langer; Hermaun Ortel, Herr Doerfer; Hans Schwartz, Herr Eiserbeck; Hans Foltz, Herr Anlauf; Walther von Stolzing, Albert Stritt; David, Herr Kramer; Eva, Auguste Seidl-Krauss; Magdalena, Marianne Brandt; Nachtwächter, Carl Kaufmann. Mr. Seidl conductor.

I modulate to the Metropolitan season 1886-87 through the performances of the opposition, which began at the Academy of Music, but ended in the house which was now definitely acknowledged to be the home, and only home, of fashionable opera. Mme. Patti provided the last bit of evidence. In the two preceding seasons she had led Colonel Mapleson's forces at the Academy; yet the public would have none of his opera. Now, after a year's absence, she returned to America under the management of Mr. Abbey, who had opposed Nilsson to her when the rivalry of the houses began. She gave operatic concerts, one, two, three, and four, at the Academy of Music, with old favorites of the New York public—Scalchi, Novara, and a French tenor named Guille—in her company, besides Signor Arditi; and she gave fragments of opera ("Semiramide" and "Martha"), besides a miscellaneous concert. The experiences of Mme. Patti on her return to her old home in 1881 were measurably repeated. The great singer was admired, of course, and half an operatic loaf was accepted as better than no bread. This was in November, 1886, and in April, 1887, Mr. Abbey decided to offer the operatic loaf, such as it was, but to cut it, not at the house with which Patti's name had been intimately associated, but at the Metropolitan Opera House. He was conjuring with the legend (then new, but afterward worn threadbare), "Patti's Farewell." I am writing in July, 1908, and have just been reading the same legend again in the London newspapers—twenty-one years after it served Mr. Abbey a turn. In April, then, Mr. Abbey came to the Metropolitan Opera House with Mme. Patti to give six "farewell" operatic performances. The company consisted of Scalchi, Vicini, Galassi, Valerga, Del Puente, Novara, Abramoff, Corsi, and Migliara, some of them recruited from an earlier company that had come and departed like a shadow in the fall season. Also Miss Gertrude Griswold, whom I mention because she was an American singer who had given promise of good things in Europe, and who helped Mme. Patti with the one and doubly singular performance of "Carmen," in which she was seen and (occasionally) heard in the United States. Mr. Abbey gave six performances, in all of which Mme. Patti appeared, the operas being "La Traviata," "Semiramide," "Faust," "Carmen," "Lucia," and "Marta." The financial results were phenomenal. The public paid nearly $70,000 for the six operas! Had Colonel Mapleson been able to do fifty per cent. of such business the Academy of Music might have been saved. But Mr. Abbey, to use the slang of the stage, was playing Patti as a sensation. Prices of admission were abnormal, and so was the audience. Fashion heard Patti at the Metropolitan, and so did suburban folk, who came to $10 opera in business coats, bonnets, and shawls. Such audiences were never seen in the theater before or since.

This was a little Italian opera season, but a successful one, and one housed at the Metropolitan. In the fall there had been another at the Academy of Music, which was not a success, and which ended in a quarrel between prima donna and manager that contributed a significant item to the popular knowledge of the status of Italian opera. On October 18th an Italian named Angelo began a season of Italian opera at the Academy. The name of the company was the Angelo Grand Italian Opera Company, and its manager's experience had been made, as an underling of Mapleson in the luggage department. The season, as projected, was to last five weeks, and a virtue proclaimed in the list was to be a departure from the hurdy-gurdy list which had been doing service so long. There were smiles among the knowing that a trunk despatcher should appear as the successor of his former employer, and that employer so polished a man of the world as James H. Mapleson; but opera makes strange bedfellows, and there have been stranger things than this in its history. A Hebrew boy named Pohl was little more than a bootblack when he entered the service of Maurice Strakosch, but as Herr Pollini a couple of decades later he was a partner of that elegant gentleman and experienced impresario, and one of the operatic dictators of Germany. Eventually, in the case of the Angelo Grand Italian Opera Company, it turned out that the Deus ex machina was the prima donna, Giulia Valda (Miss Julia Wheelock), an American singer, who had chosen this means of getting a hearing in her native land. The list of operas sounded like an echo of half a century before. Five operas were given, and four of them were by Verdi: "Luisa Miller," "I Lombardi," "Un Ballo in Maschera," and "I due Foscari;" the remaining opera was Petrella's "Ione." Here was an escape from the threadbare with a vengeance. It made the critics rub their eyes and wonder if Mme. Valda had not been in the company of the Seven Sleepers of Ephesus. Five weeks were projected, but trouble came at the end of a fortnight—that is to say, it came to public notice at the end of a fortnight; it began probably with the season. On November 3d the persons who came to hear a promised performance of "La Juive" found the doors of the Academy closed. A few spasmodic efforts to galvanize the corpse into the semblance of life were made, but in vain; the Angelo Grand Italian Opera Company was dead. Some of its members had been heard before in other organizations; some were heard later. They were Giulia Valda, Mlle. Prandi, Mme. Valerga, Mlle. Corre, Mathilde Ricci, Mme. Mestress, Mme. Bianchi-Montaldo, Signor Vicini, Lalloni, Bologna, Greco, Giannini, Pinto, Corsi, Migliara, and Conti. The conductors were Logheder and Bimboni, the latter of whom was discovered as a young conductor of surprising merit twenty years later by Boston.

One season of the American Opera Company sufficed to involve it in such financial difficulties that its managers deemed a reorganization necessary. It appeared, therefore, in the season of 1886-87 under the title, National Opera Company. Mr. Theodore Thomas was still its musical director, and Mr. Gustav Hinrichs and Arthur Mees assistant conductors; Charles E. Locke was the business manager. The company spent the greater part of the season in other cities, but gave two series of representations in Brooklyn, at the Academy of Music, and one series at the Metropolitan Opera House. The first Brooklyn season was of one week, from December 27th to January 1st, when the German company was idle; the second embraced the Thursday evenings from February 28th to March 26th, during which period the company gave a regular series of representations in New York. Among the singers were Pauline L'Allemand, Emma Juch, Laura Moore, Mathilde Phillips (sister of Adelaide Phillips, one of the singers of first rank sent out into the world by America), Jessie Bartlett Davis, Mme. Bertha Pierson, William Candidus, Charles Bassett (The Signor Bassetti of Colonel Mapleson's company in the previous season), William Fessenden, William Ludwig, Myron W. Whitney, Alonzo E. Stoddard, and William Hamilton. The notable feature of the repertory was the first production in America of Rubinstein's opera "Nero," on March 14, 1887. The book had been translated for the production by Mr. John P. Jackson. Mr. Thomas conducted, and the cast was as follows: Nero Claudius, William Candidus; Julius Vindex, William Ludwig; Tigellinus, A. E. Stoddard; Balbillus, Myron W. Whitney; Saccus, William Fessenden; Sevirus and a Centurion, William Hamilton; Terpander, William H. Lee; Poppaea, Bertha Pierson; Epicharis, Cornelia van Santen; Chrysa, Emma Juch; Agrippina, Emily Sterling; Lupus, Pauline L'Allemand. So far as I can recall, "Nero" is the only opera of Rubinstein's that has been given in the United States. Its performance by the National Opera Company did greater justice to its spectacular than its musical features, but in this there was not a large measure of artistic obliquity. The opera seems to have been constructed with the idea that mimic reproductions of scenes from Rome in its most extravagant, debauched, and luxuriant period would prove more fascinating to the public than an effort to present the moral and intellectual life of the same place and period through the medium of an eloquent, truthful, compact, well-built, and logically developed drama with its essentials further vitalized by music. From whatever side he is viewed, Nero is an excellent operatic character, and the wonder is that the opera of Barbier and Rubinstein did not have sixty instead of only six predecessors. Not only is it a simple matter to group around him historical pictures of unique interest, brilliancy, variety, and suggestiveness, but, as the historians present him to us, he is as made for the stage. His cruelty, profligacy, effeminacy, cowardice, and artistic vanity are traits which invite dramatic illustration, and for each one of them the pages of Suetonius afford incidents which accept a dramatic dress none the less willingly because they are facts of historical record. Besides all this, there is something like poetical justice in the conceit of making a stage character out of the emperor who hired himself to a theatrical manager for 1,000,000 sesterces (say $40,000—a pretty fair honorarium for the time, I should say), and who employed a claque of 5,000 young men. To throw a sequence of the characteristic incidents in the life of Nero into the form of a dramatic poem, logical in its development, and theatrically effective, ought not to be a difficult thing to do. And yet, in the case of this opera, Barbier did not do it, and by a singularly persistent and consistent fatality Rubinstein apparently found every weak spot in the poet's fabric, and loosened and tangled his threads right there. The operas and ballets performed by the National Opera Company in this season besides "Nero" were "The Flying Dutchman," "The Huguenots," "Faust," "Aïda," "Lakmé," "The Marriage of Jeannette," Massé's "Galatea," "Martha," "Coppélia," and Rubinstein's "Bal Costumé," an adaptation.

"Galatea" had its first New York performance at the Academy of Music in Brooklyn, on December 30, 1886, under the direction of Arthur Mees; Delibes's ballet "Coppélia" at the Metropolitan on March 11, 1887, under the direction of Gustav Hinrichs. It is likely that both works were previously given by the National Opera Company on tour.

The fourth regular subscription season of opera at the Metropolitan Opera House (third season of opera in German) began on November 8, 1886, under the management of the board of directors, the direction of Edmund C. Stanton, with Anton Seidl and Walter Damrosch, conductors. It extended over fifteen weeks, the closing date being February 26, 1887, and comprised forty-five subscription nights, and fifteen matinées, no opera having been given from December 5th to January 3d. In the prospectus the directors had promised to produce fourteen operas, and the promise was kept as to number, though two operas, "Tristan und Isolde" and "Fidelio," were substituted for "Siegfried" (which had been completely staged) and "Les Huguenots." The operas thus substituted were the most successful of the list, "Fidelio" being received with so much favor on the two occasions for which it had been announced that an extra performance had to be given to satisfy the popular demand. Of this incident more presently. This extra performance raised the number of representations to sixty-one, which were distributed through the list of operas as follows:

Opera First performance Times given

"Die Königin von Saba" .... November 8 4
"Die Walküre" .... November 10 3
"Aïda" .... November 12 4
"Der Prophet" .... November 17 5
"Das Goldene Kreutz" and ballet .. November 19 4
"Tannhäuser" .... November 28 6
"Tristan und Isolde" .... December 1 8
"Faust" .... December 8 3
"Lohengrin" .... December 15 4
"Merlin" .... January 3 5
"Fidelio" .... January 14 3
"Die Meistersinger" .... January 21 5
"Rienzi" .... January 31 5
"La Muette de Portici" .... February 16 2
—
Total performances 61

The cost of representation was $288,400, and of maintaining the opera house about $154,000; in this total of about $442,000 was included the cost of the scenery, wardrobe, and properties. The company's receipts comprised $202,751 from subscriptions and box office sales, about $33,000 from rentals, and about $175,000 from an assessment of $2,500 from each of the stockholders; in all about $410,751 I am able to be thus explicit about the financial affairs of the German régime because of courtesies received at the time from Mr. Stanton, with the sanction of the stockholders, who were inclined then to look upon their undertaking as one of public, not merely of private, concern. The figures will enable the student of this history to view intelligently some of the happenings at a later period, when the giving of opera became a business speculation pure and simple. In attendance, the measure of public patronage was represented by 137,399. The prices of admission ranged from fifty cents to four dollars, and the average receipts were $1.47 1/2 per individual.

The incidents of a particularly interesting character in the season were the first American performances of "Tristan und Isolde," and Goldmark's opera "Merlin," and the coming and going of Albert Niemann; secondary in importance were the production of Wagner's "Rienzi," with which was connected the return of Anton Schott to the ranks of the company, the surprising triumph of "Fidelio," and the production of Brüll's opera, "Das goldene Kreutz," and the ballet, "Vienna Waltzes." "Tristan und Isolde" was brought forward on December 1, 1886, under the direction of Anton Seidl. The distribution of characters was as follows: Tristan, Albert Niemann; Isolde, Lilli Lehmann; König Marke, Emil Fischer; Kurwenal, Adolf Robinson; Melot, Rudolph von Milde; Brangäne, Marianne Brandt;

Ein Hirt, Otto Kemlitz; Steuermann, Emil Sanger; Seemann, Max Alvary. The interesting character of the occurrence was fully appreciated by the public, and the drama was seen and heard by a remarkable assembly. The last seat had been sold four days before, and the vast audience room was crowded in every portion. The tenseness of the attention was almost painful, and the effect of Herr Niemann's acting in the climax of the third act was so vivid that an experienced actress who sat in a baignoir at my elbow grew faint and almost swooned. At the request of Mr. Stanton, or Mr. Seidl, he never ventured again to expose the wound in his breast, though the act is justified, if not demanded, by the text. The enthusiam after the first act was tremendous. The performers came forward three times after the fall of the curtain, and then Mr. Seidl, who had won the greenest laurels that had yet crowned him, was called upon to join them, and twice more the curtain rose to enable the performers to receive the popular tribute. Five recalls after an act would have meant either nothing or a failure in an Italian theater; it was of vast meaning here. The reception accorded Wagner's love drama was not such an one as comes from an audience easily pleased or attracted by curiosity alone. It told of keen and lofty enjoyment and undisguised confession of the power of the drama. The applause came after the last note of the orchestral postludes. The drama was performed eight times in seven weeks, and took its place as the most popular work in the repertory, though in average attendance it fell a trifle short of the three representations of "Fidelio," which also served to signalize the season.

I shall have something to say presently about Herr Niemann, and a criticism of his interpretation of the character of the hero of the tragedy can be spared. From a histrionic point of view it has been equaled only by his performances of Siegmund and Tannhäuser; nothing else has shown such stature that has been witnessed on the operatic stage of New York. Nor has his declamation of the text been equaled, though the compelling charm of Wagner's melody was potently presented years later by Jean de Reszke. Herr Niemann was long past the prime of life when he came to New York, and when he went back to Berlin after his last visit there was very little left of his public career; but the youngest artist in the company might have envied him the whole-souled enthusiasm with which he set about his tasks. How completely he dedicated himself to the artistic duty was illustrated when, in the season of 1887-88, he realized what had been the ambition of years, and gave a first performance of Siegfried in "Götterdämmerung." He had studied the part a dozen years before in the hope of appearing in it at the first Bayreuth festival; but Wagner did not want the illusion spoiled by presenting the actor of Siegmund on one evening as the actor of Siegfried on another, and Niemann's Siegmund was a masterpiece that must not be despoiled. In New York, on Niemann's second visit, he asked for the privilege of enacting the Volsung's part in the last division of the tetralogy, and studied the part ab initio with Seidl. I chanced one evening to be a witness of his study hour—the strangest one I ever saw. It was at the conductor's lodgings in the opera house. There was a pianoforte in the room, but it was closed. The two men sat at a table with the open score before them. Seidl beat time to the inaudible orchestral music, and Niemann sang sans support of any kind. Then would come discussion of readings, markings of cues, etc., all with indescribable gravity, while Frau Seidl-Krauss, a charming ingénue budding into a tragedienne, sat sewing in a corner. After the performance of the drama, I sat again with Niemann and Seidl over cigars and beer. I thanked Niemann for having discarded a universal trick in the scene of Siegfried's murder, and for carrying out Wagner's stage directions to the letter in raising his shield and advancing a step to crush Hagen, and then falling exhausted upon it.

"I am glad you noted that," said Niemann in his broad Berlinese. "Years ago I was angered by the device which all Siegfrieds follow of lifting the shield high and throwing it behind themselves before they fall. Das hat doch gar kein Sinn. There's no sense in that; if he has strength enough to throw the shield over his head, he certainly has strength enough to hurl it at the man he wants to kill. He lifts the heavy shield for that purpose, but his strength gives way suddenly, and he falls upon it with a crash. It's dangerous, of course. A fellow might easily break a finger or a rib. But if you do a thing, do it right. I have waited more than ten years to sing Siegfried, and now I've done it; but, youngster (to Seidl), if we meet again years from now, and I've fifty marks in my pocket, I'll get an orchestra, and you will conduct just enough to let me sing 'Ach! dieses Auge, ewig nun offen,' and then I'll die in peace! That's the climax of Siegfried's part, and it must sound red, blood red—Siegfried is red; so is Tristan. Vogl sings Tristan well, but he's all yellow—not red, as he ought to be."

I recall another bit of Niemann's characteristic criticism: Adolf Robinson, the barytone of the first few German seasons, was an excellent singer and also actor; but he belonged to the old operatic school, and was prone to extravagant action and exaggerated pathos. He was, moreover, fond of the footlights. At one of the last rehearsals for "Tristan und Isolde," Robinson, the Kurwenal of the occasion, was perpetually running from the dying hero's couch to the front of the stage to sing his pathetic phrases with tremendous feeling into the faces of the audience. Niemann, reclining on the couch, immovable as a recumbent statue, as was his wont, without a gesture, all evidence of the seething impatience which is consuming him mirrored in the expression of his face, and particularly his eyes, watched the conventional stage antics of his colleague till he could endure them no longer. He gave a sign to Seidl, who stopped the orchestra to hear the dying knight addressing his squire in wingèd, but un-Wagnerian, words to this effect:

"My dear Robinson, this scene is not all yours—Tristan has also something to say here; but how am I to make my share of the dramatic effect if you are always going to run down to the audience and sing at it? After a while there will be nothing left for me to do but to get up and hurl my boots into the audience room. And I'm a very sick man. Now, there's a good fellow, come over here to the couch; stay by me and nurse me, and you'll see there's something in my part, too."

Niemann's first American appearance was on November 10th in "Die Walküre." From the criticism of his performance, which I wrote for The Tribune on that occasion, I reprint the following extract as the best summing up which I am able to make of the great dramatic singer's art:

The creation of a Wagnerian musical drama created also the need of Wagnerian singers. Those who go to see and hear Herr Niemann must go to see and hear him as the representative of the character that he enacts. It is only thus that they can do justice to themselves, to him, and to the artwork in which he appears. A drama can only be vitalized through representation, and the first claim to admiration which Herr Niemann puts forth is based on the intensely vivid and harmonious picture of the Volsung which he brings on the stage. There is scarcely one of the theatrical conventions which the public have been accustomed to accept that he employs. He takes possession of the stage like an elemental force. Wagner's dramas have excited the fancy of painters more than any dramatic works of the century, because Wagner was in a lofty sense a scenic artist. Niemann's genius, for less it can scarcely be called, utilizes this picturesque element to the full. His attitudes and gestures all seem parts of Wagner's creation. They are not only instinct with life, but instinct with the sublimated life of the hero of the drama. When he staggers into Hunding's hut and falls upon the bearskin beside the hearth a thrill passes through the observer. Part of his story is already told, and it is repeated with electrifying eloquence in the few words that he utters when his limbs refuse their office. The voice is as weary as the exhausted body. In the picturesque side of his impersonation he is aided by the physical gifts with which nature has generously endowed him. The figure is colossal; the head, like "the front of Jove himself"; the eyes large and full of luminous light, that seems to dart through the tangled and matted hair that conceals the greater portion of his face. The fate for which he has been marked out has set its seal in the heroic melancholy which is never absent even in his finest frenzies, but in the glare of those eyes there is something that speaks unfalteringly of the godlike element within him. This element asserts itself with magnificent force in the scene where Siegmund draws the sword from its gigantic sheath, and again when he calmly listens to the proclamation of his coming death, and declines the services of the messenger of Wotan who is sent to conduct him to Walhalla.

There are aspects in which, even from a literary point of view, Wagner's "Ring of the Nibelung" seems to be the most Teutonic of the several German versions of the old legend which is its basis. It is a primitive Teutonism, however, without historical alloy; such a Teutonism as we can construct by letting the imagination work back from the most forceful qualities of the historical German to those which representatives of the same race may have had in a prehistoric age. The period of Wagner's tetralogy, it must be remembered, is purely mythical. The ruggedness of the type which we obtain by such a process is the strong characteristic of Herr Niemann's treatment of Wagner's musical and literary text. It is, like the drama itself, an exposition of the German esthetic ideal: strength before beauty. It puts truthful declamation before beautiful tone production in his singing and lifts dramatic color above what is generally considered essential musical color. That from this a new beauty results all those can testify who hear Herr Niemann sing the love song in the first act of "Die Walküre," which had previously in America been presented only as a lyrical effusion and given with more or less sweetness and sentimentality. Herr Niemann was the first representative of the character who made this passage an eager, vital, and personal expression of a mood so ecstatic that it resorts to symbolism, as if there was no other language for it. The charm with which he invests the poetry of this song (for this is poetry) can only be appreciated by one who is on intimate terms with the German language, but the dramatic effect attained by his use of tone color and his marvelous distinctness of enunciation all can feel.

The defects in Herr Niemann's singing, the result of the long and hard wear to which his voice has been subjected in a career of thirty-five years' duration, are so obvious that I need not discuss them. To do so would be as idle as to attempt to deny their presence. He must be heard as a singing actor, as a dramatic interpreter, not as a mere singer.

Niemann said farewell to the New York public at a notable performance of "Tristan und Isolde," the last of the season, on February 7, 1887. I doubt if the history of opera in New York discloses anything like a parallel to the occasion. Out of doors the night was distressingly dismal. A cold rain fell intermittently; the streets were deep with slush, and the soft ice made walking on the pavements uncomfortable, and even dangerous. But these things were not permitted to interfere with the determination of the lovers of the German lyric drama to bear testimony to their admiration for the artist who had done so much for their pleasure. The house was crowded in every part. Every seat had been sold days before. Many of the tickets had been bought by speculators, who, in spite of the untoward weather, reaped a rich harvest. During the day the prices obtained varied from ten dollars to fifteen dollars for the orchestra stalls (regular price, four dollars), and at night seats in the topmost gallery fetched as much as three dollars, which was six times the regular tariff. There were delegations in the audience from Boston, Philadelphia, and Cincinnati. The enthusiasm after each act was of the kind that recalled familiar stories of popular outbursts in impressionable Italy. Herr Niemann husbanded his vocal resources in the first act, but after that both he and Fräulein Lehmann threw themselves into the work with utter abandon, such abandon, indeed, as made some of the prima donna's friends tremble for her voice. After two recalls had followed the second fall of the curtain a third round was swelled by a fanfare from the orchestra. To acknowledge this round Herr Niemann came forward alone, and was greeted with cheers, while a laurel wreath, bearing on one of its ribbons the significant line from "Tannhäuser," "O, kehr zurück, du kühner Sänger," was handed up to him. The third act wrought the enthusiasm to a climax. After the curtain had been raised over and over again, Herr Niemann came forward and said, in German: "I regret exceedingly that I am not able to tell you in your own language how sincerely I appreciate your kindness toward me. I thank you heartily, and would like to say 'Auf wiedersehn.'" His place for the rest of the season was filled by Herr Anton Schott.

I have referred to the "Fidelio" incident of the season, which may now be told, since Herr Niemann also figured in it. To Beethoven "Fidelio" was a child of sorrow; that fact is known to every student of musical history. On its first production it failed dismally. With his heart strings torn, the composer yielded to the arguments and prayers of his friends and revised the opera. In the new form it was revived, and made a better impression; but now Beethoven quarreled with his manager, and withdrew his opera from the Vienna theater. He offered it in Berlin, and it was rejected. For seven years it slept. Then it was taken in hand again by the composer, and adapted to a revised text. Some of the music elided at the first revision was restored. By this time four overtures had been written for it. Again it was brought forward; and this time the Viennese awoke to an appreciation of its splendor. Since 1814 its name has been almost the ineffable word for the serious musician. But sorrow and disaster have followed upon innumerable efforts to habilitate it in the opera houses of the world. We have seen that Dr. Damrosch made haste to produce it at the Metropolitan Opera House, but the financial results were so direful that two years later it was only upon the urgent entreaty of a few friends who stood close to him that Mr. Stanton consented to include it in the repertory for 1886-87.

"But," said the director to his petitioners, "if I give it once I must give it twice, for I have two Leonores in my company, and there must be no quarrel."

So he gave the opera on Friday, January 14th, with Fraulein Brandt as the heroine, and on Wednesday, January 19th, with Fräulein Lehmann—Niemann being the Florestan on both occasions. The enthusiasm was boundless, though the silly laugh of a woman in one of the boxes at the first performance so disconcerted Fräulein Brandt at the beginning of the duet in the dungeon scene that she broke down in tears, and Mr. Seidl had to stop the orchestra till she could sufficiently recover her composure to begin over again. Now, the popular interest was so great that Mr. Stanton gave an extra performance, with Fräulein Lehmann, and when the record of the season was made up, lo! Beethoven's opera led all the rest in average receipts and attendance. In Berlin, Dr. Ehrlich preached a sermon to the people of Germany with the incident as a text.

As a novelty "Tristan und Isolde" had been preceded on November 19th by Brüll's pretty little opera, "Das goldene Kreuz," and the ballet, "Vienna Waltzes." It was succeeded on January 3d by Goldmark's "Merlin," conducted by Walter Damrosch, with the parts distributed as follows: Artus, Robinson; Modrid, Kemlitz; Gawein, Heinrich; Lancelot, Basch; Merlin, Alvary; Viviane, Lehmann; Bedwyr, Von Milde; Glendower, Sieglitz; Morgana, Brandt; Dämon, Fischer. Much interest centered in the opera because of its newness (it had received its first production in Vienna less than two months before), and the great success achieved by its predecessor, "The Queen of Sheba;" but it failed of popular approval, eight operas preceding it in popularity, as evidenced by the attendance, and but one of them—"Tristan"—a novelty.

CHAPTER XIV
WAGNERIAN HIGH TIDE

In this chapter I purpose to tell the story of a period of three years, from 1887 to 1890, and in order to cover the ground I shall leave out what appertains to the repetition of works incorporated in the repertory of the Metropolitan Opera House during the preceding three seasons.

The period was an eventful one and marked the high-water of achievement and also of popularity of the German régime, but also the beginning of the dissatisfaction of the boxholders, which resulted two years later in a return to the Italian form. It witnessed the introduction of the "Ring of the Nibelung" in its integrity and illustrated in a surprising manner the superior attractiveness of Wagner's dramas to the rest of the operatic list. Outside of the Nibelung dramas it brought two absolute novelties to the knowledge of the public and revived several old operas of large historical and artistic significance, which had either never been heard at all in New York, or heard so long ago that all memory of them had faded from the public mind. It saw the light of competition flicker out completely at the Academy of Music, and after a year of darkness it beheld the dawn of Italian rivalry in what had become the home of German art.

Twenty operas were brought forward in the first three years of the German régime. They were "Tannhäuser," "Fidelio," "Les Huguenots," "Der Freischütz," "William Tell," "Lohengrin," "Don Giovanni," "The Prophet," "Masaniello," "Rigoletto," "La Juive," "Die Walküre," "Carmen," "The Queen of Sheba," "Die Meistersinger," "Rienzi," "Aïda," "Das Goldene Kreutz," "Tristan und Isolde," and "Merlin." (In this list I have set down the titles in the language in which they live in the popular mouth in order to avoid what might seem like an affectation were I to use the German form always in the story simply because the Italian and French works were sung in German.) Additions to the list in the season of 1887-88 were "Siegfried," "Der Trompeter von Säkkingen," "Euryanthe," "Ferdinand Cortez," and "Götterdämmerung"; in the season of 1888-89, "L'Africaine," "Das Rheingold," and "Il Trovatore"; in 1889-90, "Der Fliegende Holländer," "Un Ballo in Maschera," "Norma," and "Der Barbier von Bagdad."

The record of the last two years indicated a falling off in energy, but though it caused disaffection at the time, it seems notable enough compared with the activities of the establishment twenty years later under much more favorable circumstances. For the last of the three seasons under discussion seven additions to what was called by courtesy the established list had been promised; but counting in "Norma," (a special performance for the benefit of Lilli Lehmann) and "The Flying Dutchman," which had been promised only by implication in the plan of a serial representation of Wagner's works, only four additions were made. Two causes operated toward the disappointing outcome. One was an epidemic of influenza which prevailed during the greater part of the winter and caused much embarrassment to the singers; the other was the inefficiency of the chorus—a defect which has not yet been remedied, but was greater in the season 1907-08 than a decade earlier. "Otello" was in readiness so far as the principals were concerned, but the chorus consumed so much time restudying old works that it had to be abandoned; also Lalo's "Le Roy d'Ys." Though the stockholders were giving opera themselves for themselves, they took no steps toward making it a permanent institution. Their decision to give German opera was made from year to year, and the end of every season brought with it practically a complete disruption of the company. There had to be a reorganization each fall. The directors were unwilling to give their own manager the degree of permanence which they bestowed without hesitation upon a lessee, and the policy of the house was thus kept continually in controversy. The fact is that the activities of the Germans were not to the taste of the stockholders, who were getting serious art where they were looking for fashionable diversion. This became painfully obvious when the conduct of the occupants of the boxes scandalized the institution to such a degree that the directors were compelled to administer a public rebuke to themselves and their associates, and a stigma was placed upon the institution from which it has suffered, very unjustly, ever since. But a discussion of these incidents can be more intelligently and profitably introduced later in this narrative.

The fourth German season began on November 2, 1887, and ended on February 18, 1888, and consisted of forty-seven subscription nights, sixteen subscription matinées, and one extra matinée. In all fourteen operas were produced. The two Wagnerian novelties, "Götterdämmerung" and "Siegfried," were the most popular features of the season, the former being given seven times, though it was the last of the season's productions. It brought into the treasury a total of $30,324, or an average of $4,332, and was heard by audiences averaging 2,871. "Siegfried" was a good second. It had nine weeks' advantage of "Götterdämmerung" and was performed eleven times, with total receipts amounting to $37,124.50, or an average of $3,374.95. Pursued by its old fatality, "Fidelio" dropped to the foot of the list with four performances, which yielded only $8,997. The receipts for the season were $411,860.24, of which $190,087.24 came from the box office sales and subscriptions, $170,180 from the stockholders' assessment of $2,500 on each box, and $51,593 from rentals. This assessment was only

$24,000 more than the cost of maintaining the opera-house, which was about $146,000. The staging of new operas cost $19,727.27, more than half of which was expended on Spontini's "Ferdinand Cortez." The scenery for "Siegfried" had been purchased the year before and also the costumes for that drama and "Götterdämmerung." The principal members of the company were Lilli Lehmann, Marianne Brandt, Auguste Seidl-Krauss, Biro di Marion, Louise Meisslinger, Albert Niemann, Max Alvary, Emil Fischer, Adolf Robinson, Rudolph von Milde, Johannes Elmblad, Herr Ferenczy, and Herr Alexi.

The first American representation of Wagner's "Siegfried" took place on November 9, 1887. Anton Seidl conducted and the parts were distributed as follows: Siegfried, Max Alvary; Mime, Herr Ferenczy; der Wanderer, Emil Fischer; Alberich, Rudolph von Milde; Fafner, Johannes Elmblad; Erda, Marianne Brandt; Brünnhilde, Lilli Lehmann; Stimme des Waldvogels, Auguste Seidl-Krauss. The production of this drama was an invitation to the people of New York to take the longest and most decisive step away from the ordinary conventions of the lyric theater that had yet been asked of them. At the time it seemed foolishly presumptive to attempt a prediction of what the response would be. A season before "Tristan und Isolde" had been received with great favor and under conditions which did not admit a question of the honesty and intelligence of the appreciation. This was encouraging to the lovers of Wagner's dramas, but the difference between opera of the ordinary type and "Tristan und Isolde" is not so great as between "Tristan und Isolde" and "Siegfried," notwithstanding that in the love tragedy Wagner took as uncompromising a stand as ever did a Greek poet, and hewed to the lines of his theoretical scheme with unswerving fidelity. In the subject-matter of the drama lies the distinction. Despite the absence of the ethical element which places "Tannhäuser" immeasurably higher than "Tristan" as a dramatic poem, the latter drama contains an expression of the universal passion which is so vehement, so truthful, and so sublime that it seems strange that anybody susceptible to music and gifted with emotions could ever have been deaf to its beauties or callous to its appeals. Besides this, the sympathies are stirred in behalf of the personages of the play who stand as representatives of human nature, and, though the co-operation of a chorus, which has always been considered an essential element of the lyric drama, is restricted to a single act, the dramatic necessity of the restriction is so obvious that an audience, once engrossed in the tragedy, must needs resent such a violation of propriety as the introduction of a chorus in any scene except that of the first act would be. In "Siegfried," however, the case is not so plain. Here there is not only no chorus, but scarcely more than five minutes during which even two solo voices are blended in a duet. Except Siegfried and Brünnhilde, the personages of the play have no claim upon human sympathy, and their actions can scarcely arouse a loftier feeling than curiosity. Through two acts and a portion of the third, save in a dozen measures or so, the music of woman's voice and the charm of woman's presence are absent from the stage, and, instead, we are asked to accept a bear, a dragon, and a bird, a sublimely solemn peripatetic god who asks riddles and laughs once, and two dwarfs, repulsive of mind and hideous of body.

These are the drawbacks concerning which there can be no controversy. To them are to be added the difficulties which result from a desire to employ in a serious drama mechanical devices of a kind that custom associates only with children's pantomimes and idle spectacles. A bear is brought in to frighten a dwarf; a dragon sings, vomits forth steam from its cavernous jaws, fights and dies with a kindly and prophetic warning to its slayer; a bird becomes endowed with the gift of human speech through a miraculous process which takes place in one of the people of the play. Surely these are grounds on which "Siegfried" might be stoutly criticized from the conventional as well as a universal point of view; but I have not enumerated them for the purpose of disparaging Wagner's drama, but rather to show the intellectual and esthetic attitude of the patrons of the Metropolitan Opera House twenty years ago, who, through all these defects, saw in "Siegfried" a strangely beautiful and impressive creation, which, under trying circumstances, challenged their plaudits at the outset and soon won their enthusiastic admiration.

More direct and emphatic was the appreciation of "Götterdämmerung," the last of the season's novelties, as "Siegfried" was the first. It was produced on January 25, 1888, only three weeks before the close of the season, yet it was given six times in the subscription performances and once outside the subscription, with the financial results already mentioned. The cast was as follows: Siegfried, Albert Niemann; Gunther, Adolf Robinson; Hagen, Emil Fischer; Alberich, Rudolph von Milde; Brünnhilde, Lilli Lehmann; Gutrune, Auguste Seidl-Krauss; Woglinde, Sophie Traubmann; Wellgunde, Marianne Brandt; Flosshilde, Louise Meisslinger. Mr. Seidl conducted. It was but natural that the concluding drama of the tetralogy should have excited warmer sympathy than its immediate predecessor. In it the human element becomes really active for the first time. This circumstance Mr. Seidl accentuated by two bold excisions. One of the things for which Wagner has been faulted is that in his treatment of the Siegfried legend he has sacrificed historical elements in order to bring it into closer relationship with Norse mythology; has, in fact, made the fate of the gods and goddesses of our ancestors the chief concern of the prologue and succeeding dramas. Except for those who prefer to see only ethical symbols in the characters there is some force in the objection. Like Homer in his

"Iliad," Wagner has a celestial as well as a terrestrial plot in his "Ring of the Nibelung," and the men and women, or semi-divine creatures, in it are but the unconscious agents of the good and evil powers typified in the gods and dwarfs.

    The criticism, however, is weaker here than in Germany, where ten or a dozen dramas (chief of which is Geibel's "Brünnhild"), as well as the medieval epics, have accustomed the people to think of their national hero with something like historical surroundings. In these writings the death of Siegfried is brought about by his alliance with the Burgundians, whose seat was at Worms; and the Gunther of the legend is easily identified with King Gundikar, who was overcome by Attila and died A.D. 450. Wagner's original draft of "Götterdämmerung" (an independent drama which he called "Siegfried's Death") followed the accepted lines, and it was not until the tetralogy was planned that the mythological elements from the Eddas were drawn into the scheme, the theater of the play changed, its time pushed back into a prehistoric age, and the death of the hero made to bring about the destruction of the old gods—the Ragnarök of the Icelandic tales. The connection between the death of Siegfried and the fate of the gods is set forth in the two scenes which were eliminated at this production of "Götterdämmerung." The first is the prologue in which the Nornir (the Fates of Northern mythology), while twisting the golden-stranded rope of the world's destiny, tell of the signs which presage the Twilight of the Gods. The second is the interview between Brünnhilde and Waltraute, one of the Valkyrior, who comes to urge her sister to avert the doom which threatens the gods by restoring the baneful ring to the Rhine daughters. Both scenes are highly significant in the plan of the tragedy as a whole, but a public largely unfamiliar with German and unconcerned about Wagner's philosophical purposes can much more easily spare than endure them. In later years they were restored at the Metropolitan performances, but I make no doubt that Mr. Seidl's wise abbreviation had much to do with the unparalleled success of the drama in its first season. Persons familiar with the German tongue and the tetralogy, either from study of the book and music or from attendance on performances in Germany, were justified in being disappointed at the loss of two scenes highly important from a dramatic point of view and profoundly beautiful from a musical; but it was better to achieve success for the representations by adapting the drama to the capacity of the public than to sacrifice it bodily on the altar of integrity.

    Nessler's opera, "Der Trompeter von Säkkingen," which had for nearly five years fairly devastated the German opera houses, receiving more performances than any three operas in the current lists, won only a succès d'estime. It was performed for the first time on November 23d, dressed most sumptuously and effectively cast (Robinson as Werner, Elmblad as

Conradin, Kemlitz as the Major-domo, Sänger as the Baron, Frau Seidl-Krauss as Marie, Von Milde as Graf von Wildenstein, and Meisslinger as Gräfin), but it reached only seven performances, was fourth from the bottom in the list arranged according to popularity, and in the following year it was not included in the repertory. In 1889-90 it was revived and received four performances, but its rank was seventeenth in a list of nineteen. Weber's "Euryanthe" fared but little better, though a work immeasurably greater. It, too, received four performances, and it was but one remove in advance of "Der Trompeter." To all intents and purposes it was new to the American stage when it was produced on December 23, 1887, with Lehmann, Brandt, Alvary, Fischer, and Elmblad in the parts of Euryanthe, Eglantine, Adolar, Lysiart, and the King, respectively. Mr. Seidl conducted. Twenty-four years before there had been some representations of the opera under the direction of Carl Anschütz in Wallack's Theater, at Broadway and Broome Street, but of this fact the patrons of the Metropolitan Opera House had no memory. It was a beautiful act of devotion on the part of Herr Anschütz and his German singers to produce "Euryanthe" at that time, and, had it been possible to break down the barriers of fashion and reach the heart of the public, the history of the lyric theater in America during the quarter of a century which followed would, no doubt, read differently than it does. "Tannhäuser" and "Lohengrin" were produced under similar circumstances, and even "Die Walküre"; but "Lohengrin" was popularized by the subsequent performances in Italian, and "Tannhäuser" and "Die Walküre" had to wait for appreciation until fortuitous circumstances caused fashion, fame, and fortune to smile for a space upon the German establishment at the Metropolitan. It may have been a benignant fate which preserved "Euryanthe" from representation in the interval. The work is one which it is impossible for a serious music lover to approach without affection, but appreciation of all its beauties is conditioned upon the acceptance of theories touching the purpose, construction, and representation of the lyric drama which did not obtain validity in America until the German artists at the Metropolitan had completed their missionary labors. Indeed, there are aspects of the case in which Weber's opera, with all its affluence of melody and all its potency of romantic and chivalric expression, is yet further removed from popular appreciation than the dramas of Wagner. In these there is so much orchestral pomp, so much external splendor, so much scenic embellishment, so much that is attractive to both eye and ear, that delight in them may exist independently of a recognition of their deeper values. "Euryanthe" still comes before us with modest consciousness of grievous dramatic defects and pleading for consideration and pardon even while demanding with proper dignity recognition of the soundness and beauty of the principles that underlie its score and the marvelous tenderness, sincerity, and intensity of its expression of passion. When it was first brought forward in Vienna in October, 1823, Castelli observed that it was come fifty years before its time. He spoke with a voice of prophecy. It was not until the fifty years had expired that "Euryanthe" really came into its rights, and it was the light reflected upon it by the works of Weber's great successor at Dresden that disclosed in what those rights consisted. After that the critical voices of the world agreed in pronouncing "Euryanthe" to be the starting point of Wagner, and, as the latter's works grew in appreciation, "Euryanthe" shone with ever-growing refulgence. No opera was ever prepared at the Metropolitan with more patience, self-sacrifice, zeal, and affection than this, and the spontaneous, hearty, sincere approbation to which the audience gave expression must have been as sweet incense to Mr. Seidl and the forces that he directed. But "Euryanthe" is a twin sister in misfortune to "Fidelio"; the public will not take it to its heart. It disappeared from the Metropolitan list with the end of the season which witnessed its revival.

A dozen or more circumstances combined to give the first performance of Spontini's "Ferdinand Cortez," which took place on January 6, 1888, a unique sort of interest. In one respect it was a good deal like trying to resuscitate a mummy, for whatever of interest historical criticism found in the opera, a simple hearing of the music was sufficient to convince the public that Spontini was the most antiquated composer that had been presented to their attention in several years. Compared with him Gluck and Mozart had real, dewy freshness, and Weber spoke in the language of to-day. Nevertheless, Spontini still stands as the representative of a principle, and if it had been possible for Mr. Stanton to supplement "Ferdinand Cortez" with "Armida" or "Iphigenia in Aulis," the Metropolitan repertory would admirably have exemplified the development of the dramatic idea and its struggle with simple lyricism in opera composition. The public would have been asked to take the steps in the reverse order, it is true—Wagner, Weber, Spontini, Gluck—but this circumstance would only have added to the clearness of the historical exposition. The light which significant art works throw out falls brightest upon the creations which lie behind them in the pathway of progress. "Euryanthe" was understood through the mediation of "Tristan und Isolde." "Ferdinand Cortez" has an American subject; the conqueror of Mexico is the only naturalized American with whom we had an acquaintance till Pinkerton came on the stage in Puccini's "Madama Butterfly," and Mr. Stanton surpassed all his previous efforts in the line of spectacle to celebrate the glories of this archaic American opera. The people employed in the representation rivaled in numbers those who constituted the veritable Cortez's army, while the horses came within three of the number that the Spaniard took into Mexico. This was carrying realism pretty close to historical verity. A finer sense of dramatic propriety, however, was exhibited in the care with which the pictures and paraphernalia of the opera were prepared. The ancient architecture of Mexico, the sculptures, the symbols of various kinds carried in the processions, the banners of Montezuma and some of the costumes of his warriors were copied with painstaking fidelity from the remains of the civilization which existed in Mexico at the time of the conquest. The cast of the opera was this: Cortez, Niemann; Alvarez, Alvary; High Priest, Fischer; Telasko, Robinson; Montezuma, Elmblad; Morales, Von Milde; Amazily, Fräulein Meisslinger.

The prospectus for the season of 1888-89 announced sixteen weeks of opera between November 28th and March 16th, the subscription to be for forty-seven nights and sixteen matinées. The last two weeks were set apart for two consecutive representations of the dramas constituting "The Ring of the Nibelung." The difficulties involved in an effort to compass the tetralogy in a week combined with other circumstances to compel an extension of the season for a week, much to the advantage of the enterprise. The final record showed that fifty evening and eighteen afternoon performances had taken place between the opening night and March 23, 1889. Sixteen works were performed, the relative popularity of which is indicated in the following list: "Götterdämmerung," "Tannhäuser," "Das Rheingold," "La Juive," "Il Trovatore," "Lohengrin," "Aïda," "Siegfried," "L'Africaine," "Die Meistersinger," "Les Huguenots," "Die Walküre," "Faust," "Le Prophète," "Fidelio," and "William Tell." The most significant new production—indeed the only significant one—was "Das Rheingold," which completed the acquaintance of the New York public with the current works of Wagner, "Parsifal" being still under the Bayreuth embargo, although it had several times been given in concert form. The total cost of the representations, not including scenery, costumes, properties, and music, was $333,731.31, or an average of $4,907.78 a representation. The total receipts from the opera were $213,630.99, divided as follows: Box office sales, $149,973.50; subscriptions, $59,607.50; privileges, $4,049.99. The average receipts a representation were $3,141.63. The loss to the stockholders on the operatic account was $1,766.15 a representation, which was covered by the receipt of $201,180.00 from the stockholders for the maintenance of the establishment, the fixed charges on the building, and the cost of scenery, music, etc., amounting to $144,455.81.

"Das Rheingold" was produced for the first time on January 4, 1889, under the direction of Mr. Seidl, and was performed nine times in the ten weeks of the season which remained. The artists concerned in the production were Emil Fischer as Wotan, Max Alvary as Loge, Alois Grienauer as Donner, Albert Mittelhauser as Froh, Joseph Beck as Alberich, Wilhelm Sedlmayer as Mime, Eugen Weiss as Fafner, Ludwig

Mödlinger as Fasolt, Fanny Moran-Olden as Fricka, Katti Bettaque as Freia, Sophie Traubmann as Woglinde, Felice Kaschowska as Wellgunde, Hedwig Reil as Flosshilde, and again, Hedwig Reil as Erda.

The sixth season of opera in German began on November 27, 1889, and ended on March 22, 1890. Within this period fifty evening and seventeen afternoon subscription performances were given and there was an extra performance on February 27th for the benefit of Lilli Lehmann, who had stipulated for it in her contract in lieu of an increase in her honorarium, demanded and refused. The sixty-seven subscription performances were devoted to nineteen operas and dramas which are here named in the order of popularity as indicated by attendance and receipts: "Siegfried," "Don Giovanni," "Die Meistersinger," "Tristan und Isolde," "Lohengrin," "Das Rheingold," "Der Barbier von Bagdad," "Tannhäuser," "Der Fliegende Holländer," "Götterdämmerung," "Die Königin von Saba," "William Tell," "Aïda," "Die Walküre," "Rienzi," "Il Trovatore," "Der Trompeter von Säkkingen," "Un Ballo in Maschera," and "La Juive." The ballet "Die Puppenfee" was performed in connection with the opera "Der Barbier von Bagdad." The last three weeks of the season were devoted to representations in chronological order (barring an exchange between "Tristan" and "Meistersinger") of all the operas and lyric dramas of Wagner from "Rienzi" to "Götterdämmerung," inclusive. The total receipts from subscriptions, box office sales, and privileges were $209,866.35; average, $3,132.34. The total cost of producing the operas (not including scenery, costumes, properties, and music) was $352,990.32, or an average of $5,268.52 per representation. On this showing the loss to the stockholders on operatic account was $2,136.18 a representation, which was met by an assessment of $3,000 a box; of this sum $1,200 went to the fixed charges on the opera house.

The one novelty of the season was Peter Cornelius's "Barbier von Bagdad," which had its first performance on January 4, 1890. The production was embarrassed by mishaps and misfortunes. It had been announced for December 25th, but Mr. Paul Kalisch, the tenor, fell ill with the prevailing epidemic and a postponement became necessary. It was set down for January 4th, but when that day came Mr. Seidl was ill. He had prepared the opera with great care and loving devotion, but at the eleventh hour had to hand his baton to his youthful assistant, Walter Damrosch. The beautiful work had only four representations. The original cast was as follows: Caliph, Josef Beck; Mustapha, Wilhelm Sedlmayer; Margiana, Sophie Traubmann; Bostana, Charlotte Huhn; the Barber, Emil Fischer. "Die Puppenfee," ballet by J. Hassreiter and F. Gaul, music by Joseph Bayer, followed the opera and was conducted by Frank Damrosch. The most important addition to the forces in this season was Theodor

Reichmann, who effected his entrance on the American stage on the first evening in Wagner's "Flying Dutchman." Herr Reichmann was known to American pilgrims to the Wagnerian Mecca as the admired representative of Amfortas in "Parsifal," but his impersonation of the Dutchman was equally famous in Vienna and the German capitals. On this occasion Mr. Seidl restored the architect's original design with reference to the band. Mr. Cady's device had never had a fair trial. Signor Vianesi condemned it in the first season. When Dr. Damrosch took the helm he tried it, but abandoned it and resorted to the compromise suggested by Vianesi, which raised the musicians nearly to the level of the first row of stalls in the audience room. The growth of the band sent the drummers outside the railing, but no one was brave enough to restore the original arrangement till the opening of the sixth German season.

I come to the operatic activities of the period beyond the walls of the Metropolitan. They scarcely amounted to opposition at any time, though at the end of the third year there came a brief season of Italian opera in the home of the German institution which whetted the appetites of the boxholders and, no doubt, had much to do with the revolution which took place two years later. In 1887, beginning on October 17th and ending in December, there was a series of performances at the Thalia Theater which served again to indicate that German opera had a following among the people who could not afford to patronize the aristocratic establishment. This season was arranged to exploit Heinrich Bötel, a coachman-tenor of the Wachtel stripe, who came from the Stadttheater, in Hamburg. The prima donna was Frau Herbert-Förster, the wife of Victor Herbert, who had been a member of the Metropolitan company while her husband, afterward the most successful of writers for the American operetta stage, sat in Mr. Seidl's orchestra. The operas given were "Trovatore," "Martha," "The Postilion of Lonjumeau," Flotow's "Stradella," "La Dame Blanche," and "Les Huguenots." At other theaters, too, there were performances of operas and operettas by the Boston Ideal Opera Company and other troupes, but with them these annals have no concern. The National Opera Company, stripped of the prestige with which it had started out, abandoned by Mr. Thomas and reorganized on a co-operative basis, made its last struggle for existence at the Academy of Music between April 2 and April 6, 1888. The decay of the institution seemed to fill it with the enterprise and energy of despair. It produced (but in anything but a commendable fashion) English versions of Goldmark's "Queen of Sheba," Rubinstein's "Nero," "Tannhäuser" (first performance of the opera in English in New York on April 4th), and "Lohengrin." In the company, besides some of the singers who had belonged to it in the previous two years, were Eloi Sylva, Bertha Pierson, Amanda Fabbris, Charles Bassett, and Barton McGuckin, the last a tenor who had made a notable career in Great Britain with Mr. Carl Rosa's companies.

This season also saw the introduction of Verdi's "Otello" by a company especially organized for the purpose by Italo Campanini, who, his singing days being practically over, turned impresario. He had been in Milan when Verdi's opera was produced, on February 5, 1887, and made haste to procure the American rights of performance. It was a laudable ambition, but the enterprise was overwhelmed with disaster. Campanini brought from Italy a tenor named Marconi for the titular rôle; his sister-in-law, Eva Tetrazzini, to sing the part of Desdemona, and his brother, Cleofonte (who was maestro di cembalo at the Metropolitan Opera House during its first season), as conductor. With these he associated Signora Scalchi and Signor Galassi (Emilia and Iago). The first performance took place on April 16, 1888, in the Academy of Music, and four representations were given on the established opera nights and Saturday afternoons. The public's attitude was apathetic. The tenor did not please, the fashionable season was over, the music was not of the kind that had been expected from Verdi, and the prices of admission were too high for a popular audience. Signor Campanini essayed a second week and now threw his own popularity into the scale. Signor Marconi was dismissed and returned at once to Europe, never to be heard again in New York; Campanini, who had been the most popular tenor with New Yorkers since the palmy days of Brignoli, took his part; the prices of admission were reduced. All to no avail; ruin had overtaken the manager, and the eighth performance was the last. It was truly pitiable. Signor Campanini deserved better for his bold embarkation in a noble enterprise; but reasons for the failure were easily found. It was unwise to give opera on an ambitious scale after the amusement season had worn itself out; it was nothing less than foolish to do so with an ill-equipped company, in a house that had lost its fashionable prestige and at prices so large that a fatal blunder had to be confessed by their reduction at the end of a week. Two seasons later, the opera was announced by the Metropolitan director, Mr. Stanton, but was not given, for reasons already mentioned. How it entered the fashionable home of opera we shall see presently.

After the lapse of twenty years it is still impossible to say that "Otello" has really been habilitated in New York. Its fate has not been quite so pitiful as that of "Falstaff," because it has been more frequently performed, and performed, moreover, in better style; but it has not won the popular heart. It is admired by the knowing, but not loved by the masses, as the earlier operas, especially "Aïda," is loved. The reason? I am still inclined to look for it where I thought I found it a score of years ago. At that time it seemed to me that the public, if it concerned itself with the matter at all (which I doubt), was at a loss for a point of view from which to consider it. Was it an Italian opera? Certainly not, if that type was represented by any of the works of Rossini, Bellini, Donizetti, or of Verdi himself when he was the popular idol. Was it a French opera? A German opera? A lyric drama in the Wagnerian manner? To the connoisseur, if not to the idle prattler about music, each of these designations suggests a distinct idea—a form, a style, a manner. Which of them might with most propriety be applied to this work? The circumstance that the book was in the Italian language had little to do with the question, no matter how loudly an excitable individual (as on this occasion) might shout "Viva l'Italiano!" to testify his admiration for Verdi's music. "The style—it is the man." "Otello" was composed and first brought forward under anomalous conditions, and though it first saw the stage lamps at Milan, its style is not distinctively Italian. Neither is it distinctively French or German. It is of its own kind, Verdian; characteristic of the composer of "Rigoletto," "Trovatore," and "Traviata" in its essence, though widely different from them in expression. The composer himself indicated that he desired it to be looked upon as outside of the old operatic conventions. According to its title page it is "Dramma lirico in quattro Atti." "Aïda" was still an "Opera in quattro Atti." The distinction was not undesigned. There are many other indications that he desired his work to be looked upon as something as far from old-fashioned opera as were Wagner's later dramas; that he aimed in the first instance at a presentation of its dramatic contents, and considered the music as a means, and not entirely as an end. In this he followed a Wagnerian precept. His score is filled with instrumental interludes designed to accompany actions or to depict emotions. He leaves no question in our minds on this point, but as fully as Wagner in his "Lohengrin" period he indicates the bodily movements that are to go hand in hand with the music. In the picture of a storm which opens the opera the manipulator of the artificial lightning is not left to his discretion as to the proper moment for discharging his brutum fulmen; in the love duet, at the close of the first act, the appearance of the moon and stars is sought to be intensified by descriptive effects in the music; and when, in the last scene, Otello kisses the sleeping Desdemona, and the one typical phrase of the opera (drawn from the love scene) is repeated, the composer indicates on what beat of each measure he wants each kiss to fall. These are only a few instances of Verdi's appreciation of the necessity of suiting the action to the music, the music to the action; and they sink into insignificance when compared with his treatment of the murder in the last act. Then Otello's entrance and actions up to the waking of Desdemona are accompanied by a solo on double basses, interrupted at intervals by energetic passages from the other strings. It is not difficult to recall other melodramas written since "Fidelio" in which similar dramatic effects are sought, but the audacity of Verdi's procedure is unexampled in Italian opera. I make no doubt that had this scene been written twenty years earlier it would have been received by his countrymen with hisses and catcalls. Yet we were told that at the opera's first performance in Milan the audience redemanded it uproariously and the Italian critics could not sufficiently express their admiration for it. The fact is that "Otello" disclosed an honest, consistent, and in many respects successful effort to realize the higher purposes which we associate in the conception of a lyric drama as distinguished from the opera. With this conception nationalism had nothing to do; Verdi's superb artistic nature, everything.

In the season of 1888-89 there was but a single performance of Italian opera in New York, a circumstance singular enough to deserve special mention. On April 24th Signor Campanini appeared with Clementine De Vere in "Lucia di Lammermoor," the performance being for the once-popular favorite's benefit. Memories of a period in which Italian singers were tremendously active were called up in the minds of opera-goers of the older generation by an entertainment given in the Metropolitan Opera House on February 12th, in honor of the fiftieth anniversary of Max Maretzek's entrance in the American field as a conductor of operas. The affair was generously patronized and participated in on its professional side by Theodore Thomas, Anton Seidl, Frank van der Stucken, Adolf Neuendorff, and Walter Damrosch as conductors; Mme. Fursch-Madi, Miss Emily Winant, Miss Maud Powell, Rafael Joseffy, Max Alvary, Signor Del Puente, Julius Perotti, Wilhelm Sedlmayer, and Mrs. Herbert-Foerster. Scenes from "Siegfried," "Il Trovatore," and "Carmen" were performed.

There were some performances of operas in English in the early part of the next season (1889-90) by the Emma Juch English Opera Company (Nessler's "Trumpeter of Säkkingen" being brought forward as a novelty), at the Harlem Opera House, owned and managed by Oscar Hammerstein. This house also, for a week after the close of the regular season at the Metropolitan, was the scene of an unsuccessful effort to prolong the German performances, or rather to provide German opera at popular prices to the residents of Harlem. The company, headed by Miss Lehmann and conducted by Walter Damrosch, was made up of singers from the Metropolitan company. The operas given were "Norma," "Les Huguenots," and "Il Trovatore."

The Italian company which took possession of the Metropolitan Opera House immediately on its vacation by the German singers was under the management of Henry E. Abbey and Maurice Grau. During the fall and winter months it had been giving representations in some of the larger cities of the United States and Mexico City. Arditi and Sapio were the conductors, and most of the singers were familiar to the public—Patti,

Albani, Nordica, Fabbri, Ravelli, Vicini, Perugini, Del Puente, Castelmary, Novara, Migliara; newcomers were Hortense Synnerberg, mezzo-soprano; Signora Pettigiani, soprano leggiero; Zardo, barytone, and Francesco Tamagno, tenor. The presence of this singer in the troupe served to indicate that its purpose, outside the exploitation of Madame Patti, was the production of Verdi's "Otello," with which the season was opened on March 24th, Madame Albani being the Desdemona. Tamagno had created the title rôle in Milan two years before.

The subscription was for sixteen evenings and four matinées, which were to be encompassed in a period of four weeks; but the illness of Madame Patti compelled a postponement of one of the performances until the fifth week after the opening, and then to the twenty subscription representations was added, a twenty-first as a "farewell" to Madame Patti. The operas in which this artist appeared were "La Sonnambula," "Semiramide," "Lakmé," "Martha," "Lucia di Lammermoor," "Roméo et Juliette," "Il Barbiere," "Linda di Chamouni," and "La Traviata." The other operas were "Otello," "Il Trovatore," "Tell," "Aïda," "Faust," "L'Africaine," "Rigoletto," and "Les Huguenots."

There was no novelty in the list, unless the fact that "Lakmé" was transformed into a novelty by the Italian version; it had been heard before in English, and the performance was so desperately slipshod, notwithstanding that Mme. Patti impersonated the heroine, that it awakened only pity for Delibes's work. It would be extremely interesting and doubtless instructive also were I able to give such a detailed financial statement of the outcome of this season as Mr. Stanton's courtesy enabled me at the time to give of the German seasons. But here I am thrown on conjecture. On the evenings and afternoons when Patti sang the audiences unquestionably represented vast receipts to the management. An estimate made at the time from a study of the character and size of the audiences placed the receipts in round numbers at $100,000. It was significant as bearing on the artistic problem suggested by the succession of German and Italian opera—a problem that was destined to become of paramount interest soon—that on scarcely a single Patti performance were all the orchestra stalls sold, and that there were always unsold boxes in the tier not occupied by the stockholders. The bulk of the money came from the occupants of the balconies and gallery. The musical and fashionable elements in the city's population had comparatively small representation. The audiences, in fact, were largely composed of curiosity seekers, impelled by the desire to be able in the future to say that they, too, had heard the greatest songstress of the last generation of the nineteenth century. The "Patti's Farewell" trick was still effective; a few years later it was found that it would work no longer, and the great singer disappeared in a black cloud of failure, followed by the grief of all who had been her admirers.

CHAPTER XV
END OF THE GERMAN PERIOD

The season of 1890-91 was full of incidents, some exciting, some amusing, but they were all dwarfed by the announcement which came in the middle of January that the directors of the Metropolitan Opera House had concluded a contract of lease with Henry E. Abbey (or Abbey and Grau) under which opera was to be given in the next season in Italian and French. The alleged reason was that Mr. Abbey was willing to assume all risk of failure for the same subvention which the stockholders as individuals were paying themselves in their capacity as entrepreneurs; the real reason was that the stockholders, or a majority of them, were weary of German opera, and especially of the dramas of Wagner. This reason spoke out of the action which had been taken looking to the eighth season of opera (seventh in German) before an agreement had been reached with Mr. Abbey. Wagner had supplied the financial backbone to all the seasons since German opera had been introduced, as will appear presently; but the directors were unwilling to admit that fact until, as a result of their change of policy, disaster stared them in the face. Then they made haste to reverse their action as far as possible and did other works of repentance which enabled them to save a modicum of prestige and some money; but the hands of the clock had been set back, and the goal of a national opera, toward which the German movement was leading, was forgotten. It has never been seen since.

When Mr. Stanton went to Germany in the spring of 1890 to engage singers and select a repertory he carried with him a definite policy, formulated by the directors, which was the fruit of a sentimental passion for the amiable Italian muse and a spirit of thrift. Italian opera under their own management seeming still impracticable because of its expensiveness, the directors conceived what they thought would prove to be a happy compromise; they would continue to give German opera, but would make a radical change in the character of the repertory. Wagner was to be shelved as to all but his earlier operas, such as "Tannhäuser" and "Lohengrin," and the season enriched with new works by Italian and French composers. With this purpose in view, Mr. Stanton completed his arrangements, and the season of 1890-91 was opened on November 26th in a manner that looked like a bold and successful stroke in favor of the new policy. "Asrael," an opera by an Italian composer, which had stirred up some favorable comment in Germany and Italy, was given with a great deal of sumptuousness in stage attire and with a company which critics and amateurs agreed in recognizing as, on the whole, stronger than any of recent years. Mme. Lehmann-Kalisch was not at its head, it is true, but instead there was a singer of excellent ability and considerable personal and artistic charm in the person of Antonia Mielke. Emil Fischer was retained, and also Theodor Reichmann and some of the lesser members of the old company, and to them were added Heinrich Gudehus, Jennie Broch (soprano leggiero), Marie Ritter-Goetze (mezzo-soprano), Andreas Dippel, Marie Jahn (soprano), and others. Mme. Minnie Hauk joined the forces later in the season.

"Asrael" was in every respect a surprise—as strange to the audience as if it had been composed for the occasion. The name of the composer, Alberto Franchetti, had never appeared in any local list save once, in April, 1887, when a symphony in E minor, bearing it, had been performed at a concert of the Philharmonic Society under the direction of Theodore Thomas. The Tribune newspaper contributed all that the public learned about him then and since. This was to the effect that he was a young Italian (or, rather, Italianized Hebrew), a member of one of the branches of the Rothschilds, who had studied in Munich and lived much of his time in Dresden, where Kapellmeister Schuch sometimes gave him opportunities to hear his orchestral music. Also that he was very wealthy, having a purse as large as his artistic ambition, and was not disinclined, when a work of his composition was accepted for performance, to care for its sumptuous production by paying for the stage decorations out of his own pocket. He resembled Meyerbeer in being a Jew, and also in that it was possible for his mother to say of him: "My son is a musical composer, but not of necessity." The book of the opera proved to be a most bewildering conglomeration of scenes and personages from familiar operas, and though the pictures were magnificent and much of the music was pleasing, "Asrael" had only five performances, and when the record of the season was made up it was found to stand thirteenth in a list of seventeen operas.

At the bottom of this list stood the two other novelties of the season, and if the public were bewildered by "Asrael" they were thrown into consternation by "Der Vasall von Szigeth," and into contemptuous merriment by "Diana von Solange." Both of these operas were sung in German, of course, but "Der Vasall," not only had an Italian (Anton Smareglia) for its composer, like "Asrael," but had originally been composed in Italian and borne an Italian name—"Il Vassallo di Szigeth." Here plainly was a concession to the Italian predilections of the stockholders. But the composer of "Der Vasall," or "Il Vassallo"—as you like it—was a Dalmatian, like Von Suppé, the operetta composer. His native tongue was Italian, but the influence of Austrian domination and Austrian art had deeply affected his nationalism, and enabled him to infuse an Hungarian subject (the story of "Der Vasall" was Hungarian) with Hungarian musical color. It therefore chanced that in this instance, when the stockholders seemed to have bargained for Italian sweets, they got a strong dose of Magyar paprika. As for the libretto, it offered such a sup of horrors as had never been seen on an operatic stage before, and has never been seen since. "Der Vasall von Szigeth," which was brought forward on December 12th, had four performances in the season and took in $7,805.50, which was probably not much more than the cost of staging the opera.

The amused gossip touching the potency of new influences which had begun with "Asrael" was given fresh fuel by the production of "Diana von Solange." Why an opera which had lain "so lange" (to make an obvious German pun) in the limbo of forgotten things, which, indeed, had never enjoyed a popularity of any kind, though it was thirty or forty years old, should have been resurrected for production in New York was a question well calculated to irritate curiosity and provoke many an ill-natured sally of wit. "Diana von Solange" was the work of Ernest II, Duke of Saxe-Coburg-Gotha. The family to which the duke belonged had long dallied with music; that the public knew. His ducal highness's brother, the British Prince Consort, affected the art in his time, and left evidences of good, sound taste in the story of English music, and it was known that the Duke of Edinburgh (son of the Prince Consort and Queen Victoria) was an amateur fiddler, quite capable of leading the band at a London smoking concert. A complacent German lexicographer had even admitted Ernest II into the fellowship of Beethoven, but that fact was not widely known, and after "Diana von Solange" had been produced the most cogent argument in explanation of its production among the theatrical wits was based on familiar German stories of the lavishness of the Duke of Saxe-Coburg-Gotha in the distribution of orders, especially among musicians. No anecdote was more popular for the rest of the season in the corridors than that which told of how a concert party driving away from the ducal palace discovered that the chamberlain had handed over one more decoration than the artists who had entertained the duke. "Never mind," quoth the chamberlain; "give it to the coachman!" The production of an opera composed by the duke without the obbligato distribution of orders was inconceivable, even in democratic America, but the tongues of waggish gossips wagged so furiously that it was said only the stage manager was willing to accept his bauble. Brahms's bon mot touching the danger of criticizing the music of royalty, "because no one could tell who composed it," not being current at the time, the music of "Diana von Solange" was mercilessly faulted, as was also the libretto. It was certainly right royal poetry set to right royal music—an infusion of immature Verdi and Meyerbeer plentifully watered. Archaic research discovered that the opera had been written some thirty-five years before, and that the composer, possessing, quite naturally, some influence with the management of the ducal theaters at Coburg and Gotha, had succeeded in having it performed in those cities in December, 1858, and May, 1859, and that Dresden had also honored it with a performance in January, 1859. Why New York blew the dust of generations off its score was never learned by the inquisitive newspaper scribes.

The story of the opera concerned itself with the succession to the throne of Portugal on the death of Enrique, with whom the old Burgundian line became extinct in 1580. A wicked man plotted to give the crown to Philip II of Spain (who really got it), and employed a Provençal adventuress to help keep it from the nephew of the dying king. But the adventuress, who lent her name to the opera, lost heart in the enterprise because she fell in love with the nephew and was stabbed to death for her pains. The wicked man was shot by the nephew, and there was thus a proper amount of bloodshed to justify the historical character of the work, the grewsomeness of which was modified by much edifying declamation on the part of the dying king, expressive of the lofty sentiments which, the world knows, always fill the breasts of monarchs. The opera was performed on January 9, 1891, and received two representations. A third was announced for a Saturday afternoon, but called forth so emphatic a popular request for "Fidelio" that the representative of the stockholders adjudged it to be the course of wisdom to set aside Ernest II in favor of Beethoven.

For six weeks Mr. Stanton followed the line of policy laid down by his directors, and within that time brought forward the three novelties which I have described, besides "Tannhäuser," "Lohengrin," "The Flying Dutchman," "Les Huguenots," "Le Prophète," and "Fidelio." Already in the third week of the season, however, it became manifest that the policy of the directors did not meet with the approbation of the public. One result of the German representations in the preceding six years had been to develop a class of opera patrons with intelligent tastes and warm affections. A large fraction of this public had become season subscribers, and among these dissatisfaction with the current repertory was growing daily. It may be that the panicky feeling in financial circles had something to do with a falling off in general attendance in the early part of the season, but this is scarcely borne out by the fact that the advance subscription amounted to $72,000, representing about one thousand persons, and that, though the novelties would not draw, the three Wagnerian works proved to be as attractive as ever they had been. The significance of the popular attitude, indeed, was obvious enough, although the directors chose to close their eyes and ears to it. It was, in fact, so obvious that The Tribune newspaper did not hesitate to predict a tremendous success for "Fidelio" when it was announced "for one performance only" on December 26th, and to assert in advance of the performance that it would have to be repeated to satisfy the demand for good dramatic music which had grown up because of the Wagner cult and been whetted by Mr. Stanton's neglect to put on the stage a few works imbued with the modern dramatic spirit. Two repetitions of "Fidelio" and the lifting of that opera to fourth place in the list attested the soundness of The Tribune's diagnosis of the situation.

By a coincidence, on the night of the first representation for the season of one of the latter-day works of Wagner, which, had the directors chosen to read the signs of the times aright and be guided by them, might have ushered in the era of prosperity which they were sighing for but repelling by their course, the decision was reached to turn over the opera house to Mr. Abbey for performances in Italian and French. This date was January 14th. So far as the subscribers to the opera and the majority of its patrons were concerned, this action of the directors seemed like nothing else than the culmination of a conspiracy to set back the clock of musical progress in New York a quarter of a century at least. The news came upon the public like a bolt from the blue. The plan had been laid early in the summer (was, in fact, the fruition of the postprandial Patti season of 1889-90), but all concerned had been pledged to secrecy. Mr. Abbey seized the right moment to strike, and when he had bagged his game he exhibited it forthwith, and it was received with a loud chorus of cheers from the enemies of the German institution. The directors gleefully continued their course for a little while longer, though the handwriting on the wall had begun to blaze forth when all the canons of art and the fruit of years of serious effort were insulted by the production of the amorphous creation of one whose sole claim on popular attention as a composer was that he was a royal duke and the brother-in-law of the Queen of England.

At the first performance, after the announcement of the projected change had been made, the public took it upon themselves to show their disapproval of the action of the directors. There seemed to be but one way to do this effectually without injury to the form of art which the public had learned to love, and that way was adopted: After January 14th not a single representation was conducted by Mr. Seidl at which the conductor was not compelled to appear upon the stage and accept a tribute of popular admiration. Mr. Seidl had come to be the representative in an especial manner of the new spirit as opposed to the directors, who, by their action, had shown that they stood for the old. And so the directors were rebuked in the honors showered upon the conductor. It needed as little prophetic gift to predict what course Mr. Stanton would pursue in view of the new developments as it had required to predict the success of "Fidelio" after the experiences of 1888-89 had seemed to indicate that the opera had lost all charm for the public. On January 20th, only six days after Mr. Abbey had captured the directors, The Tribune, commenting editorially on the "Operatic Revolution," remarked:

Financially Wagner must save this season or it will suffer shipwreck. Mr. Stanton knows that, and it is not a rash prediction to say that the whole unperformed list will be sacrificed from this time forth to the production of Wagner's works. The policy will be voted wise by the directors because it will go further than anything else to save the season; it will be welcomed by the public because of their disappointment with the novelties which a shortsighted policy attempted to foist upon them.

The prediction was fulfilled to the letter; after January 20th thirty-five representations took place, and all but ten of them were devoted to Wagner's works, notwithstanding that within this period Mme. Minnie Hauk was added to the company and that the two operas in which she appeared ("L'Africaine" and "Carmen") proved more popular than any works of the non-Wagnerian list, with the single exception of "Fidelio." An amusing evidence of the enforced change of heart in the directors was a promulgation of an order requesting the occupants of the boxes to discontinue the conversation during performances which had grown to be a public scandal. The resolution to publish the order was adopted, either at the meeting of the directors at which the agreement was reached with Mr. Abbey, or the day after; the order bore date January 15; the contract with Mr. Abbey was made on January 14th.

It is proper that I devote some attention to the story of the growth of the spirit which eventually overthrew German opera at the Metropolitan Opera House, or, rather, not German opera, but opera exclusively in the German tongue; for it was not long in developing that the new régime stood no show of success unless to Italian and French German opera was also added. The vicissitudes which brought with them this demonstration must be reserved for a subsequent chapter, but before I tell the story of the institution's retrogression I owe to the student of history an outline of the doings of the season 1890-91. The season began on November 26th and lasted till March 21st. There were sixty-seven subscription performances, an extra performance of "Fidelio" for the benefit of the chorus, which yielded $1,849, giving each chorister $18.20, and a Sunday night performance of excerpts from "Parsifal," which brought in $1,872. I have enumerated the operas which had been given up to the production of "Diana von Solange"; after this date came "Die Meistersinger," "L'Africaine," "Siegfried," "Der Barbier von Bagdad," "Die Walküre," "Götterdämmerung," "Carmen," and "Tristan und Isolde." Arranged in the order of their popularity as indicated by attendance and receipts, the entire list was as follows: "Siegfried," four times; "Tannhäuser," seven times; "Götterdämmerung," four times;

"Fidelio," three times; "Die Meistersinger," six times; "Die Walküre," four times; "Lohengrin," seven times; "Carmen," three times; "The Flying Dutchman," four times; "L'Africaine," three times; "Le Prophète," once; "Tristan und Isolde," three times; "Asrael," five times; "Barber of Bagdad," four times; "Les Huguenots," three times; "Der Vasall von Szigeth," four times; "Diana von Solange," twice. The total receipts for the season (box office sales and subscriptions) were $198,119.25; the average, $2,957.

The last performance of the season was given to "Die Meistersinger" on a Saturday afternoon. The house was crowded from floor to ceiling and there were signs from the beginning that there was to be a large expression of public opinion. After the first and second acts there were calls and recalls for the singers and for Mr. Seidl. But this was but a preparation. After the fall of the curtain on the last act the multitude remained in the audience room for over half an hour (remained, indeed, till laborers appeared on the stage to get it ready for a concert in the evening), and called for one after another of the persons who were in one way or another representative of the system that was passing away. The greatest bursts of enthusiasm were those which greeted Mr. Stanton (whose sympathies were with the German movement), Mr. Seidl and Mr. Fischer, though Mr. Walter Damrosch, Mr. Habelmann, Mr. Dippel, Fräulein Jahn, and other singers were not neglected. Mr. Stanton's unwillingness to receive the distinction which the audience plainly wished to shower upon him caused disappointment; but Mr. Stanton stood in an awkward position between the stockholders and the public. Finally, after an unusual outburst of plaudits for Mr. Fischer, that singer came forward carrying a gigantic wreath and half a dozen bouquets and said:

Ladies and Gentlemen: It is impossible for me to express what I feel for your kindness and love; and I hope it is not the last time (here a tremendous uproar interrupted the speaker for a space) that I shall sing for you here, on this stage, in German.

Had one been able to explode a ton of dynamite when Mr. Fischer ended it would have been accepted by the audience as not more than a fitting amount of approbative noise. Twenty minutes later, the audience still clamoring for a speech, Mr. Seidl came forward, for perhaps the twentieth time, and spoke as follows:

Believe me, ladies and gentlemen, I understand the meaning of this great demonstration. For myself, the orchestra, and the other members of the company, I thank you.

To understand the story of the overthrow of German opera managed by the owners of the opera house, and the reversion to the system which had proved disastrous at the beginning and was fated to prove disastrous again, it is well to bear the fact in mind that instability was, is, and always will be an element in the cultivation of opera so long as it remains an exotic; that is, until it becomes a national expression in art, using the vernacular and giving utterance to national ideals. The fickleness of the public taste, the popular craving for sensation, the egotism and rapacity of the artists, the lack of high purpose in the promoters, the domination of fashion instead of love for art, the lack of real artistic culture—all these things have stood from the beginning, as they still stand, in the way of a permanent foundation of opera in New York. The boxes of the Metropolitan Opera House have a high market value to-day, but they are a coveted asset only because they are visible symbols of social distinction. There were genuine notes of rejoicing in the stockholders' voices at the measure of financial success achieved in the first three seasons of German opera, but the lesson had not yet been learned that an institution like the Metropolitan Opera House can only be maintained by a subvention in perpetuity; that in democratic America the persons who crave and create the luxury must contribute from their pockets the equivalent of the money which in Europe comes from national exchequers and the privy purses of monarchs. This fact did eventually impress itself upon the consciousness of the stockholders of the Metropolitan Opera House, but when it found lodgment there it created a notion—a natural one, and easily understood—that their predilections, and theirs alone, ought to be humored in the character of the entertainment. I have displayed a disposition to quarrel with the artistic attitude of the directors, but I would not be an honest chronicler of the operatic occurrences of the last twenty-five years if I did not do so. The facts in the case were flagrant, the situation anomalous. The stockholders created an art spirit which was big with promise while rich in fulfilment, and then killed it because its manifestation bored them. An institution which seemed about to become permanent and a fit and adequate national expression in an admired form of art, was set afloat again upon the sea of impermanency and speculation. About the middle of the fourth German season the directors formally resolved to continue the German representations. Not long afterward it developed that the receipts for the season would be considerably less than had been counted on, and immediately a clamor arose against the management. The champions of Italian opera joyfully proclaimed that the knell of German opera had rung, and attributed the falling off in popular support to the predominance of Wagner's operas and dramas in the repertory. The disaffection threatened mischief to the enterprise and had to be met; the directors met it by formally asking for an expression of opinion from the stockholders as to the future conduct of the institution. On January 21, 1888, they sent out a circular letter to the stockholders, in which they submitted two propositions, on which they asked for a vote. One was "To go on with

German opera with an assessment of $3,200 a box"; the other, "To give no opera the next season, with an assessment of $1,000 a box, and to resume, if possible, the following season." The letter, which was signed by James A. Roosevelt, president, stated that the giving of Italian opera was not suggested because the directors "were convinced that to do so in a satisfactory manner will require a much larger assessment upon the stockholders than to give German opera." It was also set forth that the directors had estimated that the opera could be maintained for the assessment ($2,500 on each box), provided the receipts from the public amounted to $3,000 a performance. The subscription was 50 per cent. larger than the previous year (about $80,000, against $52,000), and larger receipts had been expected than in 1886-87, when the average was about $3,300. Instead, the receipts had fallen off and indicated an average of only $2,500. Rentals, however, had increased $14,000.

The answer of the stockholders was a vote of over four to one in favor of continuing German opera under the first proposition of the circular letter. Then, while the Italinissimi were still proclaiming that the Metropolitan opera had been killed by Wagnerism, there came the announcement of two weeks of consecutive representations of the three dramas of "The Ring of the Nibelung" (all but the prologue), which were in the repertory of the company. The two weeks, and a third in which "Götterdämmerung" was performed three times, brought more money into the exchequer of the opera than any preceding five weeks of the season. The average of $2,500 apprehended by the directors was raised to over $3,177.

During the next season the average receipts were practically the same, nor was there anything to change the situation from a financial point of view. The stockholders had voted themselves into a mood of temporary quiescence, and the opera pursued its serious course unhampered by more than the ordinary fault-finding on the part of the representations of careless amusement seekers in the public press, and the grumbling in the boxes because the musical director and stage manager persisted in darkening the audience room in order to heighten the effect of the stage pictures.

The aristocratic prejudice against gloom extended to the operas which contained dark scenes, and when Mr. Stanton once exercised his authority as director and had the stage lights going at almost full tilt in the dungeon scene of "Fidelio," the effect of Florestan's exclamation, "Gott! welch' Dunkel hier!" upon an audience fully three-fourths of which was composed of Germans or descendants of Germans the ludicrous effect may be imagined. Many stories were current among the artists of the blithe indifference of the occupants of the boxes to artistic proprieties when they interfered with the display of gowns and jewels. One of them was that the chairman of the amusement committee of the directors had requested that the last act of "Die Meistersinger" be sung first, as it was "the only act of the opera that had music in it," and the boxholders did not want to wait till the end. The conduct of the occupants of the boxes now grew to be so intolerable that there were frequent demonstrations of disapproval and rebuke from the listeners who sat in the parquet and balconies. The matter became a subject for newspaper discussion; in fact, it had been such a subject ever since the loud laugh of a woman at the climacteric moment of "Fidelio" had caused Fräulein Brandt to break down in tears in the opening measures of the frenetically joyous duet, "O namenlose Freude!" In the course of this extraordinary discussion one of the directors boldly asserted the right of the stockholders in the boxes to disturb the enjoyment of listeners in the stalls. Not only did he repeal the old rule of "noblesse oblige," but he also intimated that the payment of $3,000 acquitted the box owner and his guests of one of the simplest and most obvious obligations imposed by good breeding. At length the directors were forced to rebuke their own behavior. On the night of January 21, 1891, the following notice was found hung against the wall in each of the boxes:

January 15, 1891. Many complaints having been made to the directors of the Opera House of the annoyance produced by the talking in the boxes during the performances, the board requests that it be discontinued. By Order of the Board of Directors.

This was the first sop to Cerberus after the directors had concluded a contract with Mr. Abbey, leasing the house to him a second time and substituting opera in Italian and French for opera in German. The public had begun to speak its mind, not only by making a mighty demonstration in honor of Mr. Seidl and the singers when a German opera was given, but in remaining away when the weak-kneed novelties were given; in requesting by petition a performance of "Fidelio" on a Saturday afternoon for which the opera by the royal composer had been set down, and in crowding the house and giving an ovation to the singers when their petition was granted. The next sop was to set aside all the works which it had been projected should take the place of the later dramas of Wagner, which the stockholders (or the majority of them) did not like, and to devote the remainder of the season almost exclusively to Wagner. The operas thus sacrificed were Marschner's "Templer und Jüdin," Massenet's "Esclarmonde," Lalo's "Le Roi d'Ys," Goetz's "Taming of the Shrew," and Nicolai's "Merry Wives of Windsor." Not love of Wagner but fear of financial consequences dictated the step, which was successful in extricating the institution from the slough into which it had fallen. How much the Wagner operas and dramas did to keep the Metropolitan Opera House alive can be shown by the statistics of the last five German seasons, which I compiled at the close of the season of

1890-91, and printed in The Tribune of March 25th of the latter year. Here is the table:

Season Season Season Season Season 1886-1887 1887-1888 1888-1889 1889-1890 1890-1891 Total representations ………. 61 64 68 67 67 Wagnerian representations ………. 31 36 35 37 39 Non-Wagnerian representations ………. 30 28 33 30 28 Total receipts …….. $202,751.00 $185,258.50 $209,581.00 $204,644.70 $198,119.25 Average receipts ……….. 3,323.78 2,894.66 3,141.63 3,054.39 2,957.00 Wagnerian receipts ……… 111,049.50 116,449.75 115,784.50 121,568.70 125,169.25 Non-wagnerian receipts ………. 91,701.50 68,808.75 93,796.50 83,076.00 72,950.00 Wagnerian average ……….. 3,582.21 3,234.72 3,308.13 3,285.65 3,209.46 Non-Wagnerian average ……….. 3,056.71 2,457.45 2,842.32 2,769.20 2.605.37 Average difference in favor of Wagner … 525.50 777.27 465.81 516.45 604.09

CHAPTER XVI
ITALIAN OPERA AGAIN AT THE METROPOLITAN

The figures which I have printed showing a loss to the stockholders of the Metropolitan Opera House on opera account year after year during the German period, do not tell the whole story of the financial condition into which the Metropolitan Opera House Company (Limited) had fallen. This condition had much to do with creating a desire on the part of the stockholders for a change of policy. The first German season cost the stockholders only about $42,000 above the amount realized from the box assessment, which was, I believe, $2,000—two-thirds of the sum that has ruled ever since. There were seventy stockholders, and in view of the loss made by Mr. Abbey the year previous this deficit was a trifle scarcely worth considering. The growth in popular interest as indicated by the support of the subscriptions for the season of 1890-91 was promising; but the stockholders themselves were not all prompt in meeting their obligations to their own organization. By 1890 there was an account of unpaid assessments amounting to $46,328. Of this, $21,112 was canceled by the acquisition of two boxes by the company, but the balance sheet at the end of the last German season still showed $25,216 due from stockholders on assessment account. The floating debt at this time amounted to $84,044.48. The prices of admission had been greatly reduced in the German years, and the capacity of the house, represented in money, was not more than fifty per centum of what it is to-day. The demands of singers were growing greater year after year, and were not lessened, as may easily be imagined, by the thrifty complacency of those German managers who granted furloughs to their singers in consideration of a share of their American earnings. Under the circumstances it is not to be wondered at that Mr. Abbey's agreement to give Italian and French opera at his own risk was alluring, especially to those who had never sympathized with the serious tendency of German opera.

The contract of the directors for opera in the season of 1891-92 was made with Henry E. Abbey and Maurice Grau, who figured in all the announcements as the managers. With them was associated as silent partner Mr. John B. Schoeffel, of Boston, who had shared in all of Mr. Abbey's daring theatrical ventures since 1876, and, consequently, also in the unfortunate season of 1883-84, when Maurice Grau acted as manager at a salary of $15,000. Mr. Abbey's mind was not closed to the lessons of the

German seasons. A few days after he had signed the contract he told me that he had had a project in contemplation to bring Materna, Winkelmann, Scaria, and others to America for Wagnerian opera before Mr. Thomas had brought them for concert work; that he looked upon German opera as more advantageous to the manager, not only on account of its smaller costliness, but, also, because it enabled a manager to adjust his singers to a repertory instead of the repertory to the singers. But he had speculated successfully with Patti under the "farewell" device, the managerial virus was again in his veins, and he cherished a foolish belief that, as one of the results of the German régime, he would be able to exact different service from the artists of Italian and French opera than they had been wont to give. On this point he was soon painfully disillusionized. Had it not been for the presence in his company of Mme. Lehmann, M. Lassalle, and the brothers Jean and Édouard de Reszke, whose instincts and training kept them out of the old Italian rut, his performances would never have gotten away from the old hurdy-gurdy list. As it was, when he wanted to give "L'Africaine," in order to present M. Lassalle in one of his most effective rôles, though he had Emma Eames, Marie Van Zandt, Albani, the sisters Giulia and Sophia Ravogli, Pettigiani, and Lillian Nordica in his company (the last hired specially for the purpose), he was obliged to ask Mme. Lehmann to learn the part of Selika. She did so, but the strain, combined with other things, broke down her health, and she was useless to her manager for the second half of the season. She had been engaged as a lure for the German element among the city's opera patrons, and to it also were offered propitiatory sacrifices in the shape of performances in Italian of "Fidelio," "The Flying Dutchman," and "Die Meistersinger" under the direction of Mr. Seidl. After the lesson had been still more thoroughly learned a German contingent was added to the Italian and French, and German opera was added to the list, making it as completely polyglot as it has ever been since. But before then many financial afflictions were in store for the enterprise.

Mr. Abbey began his season December 14, 1891, after having given opera for five weeks in Chicago. In his company, besides the sopranos just named, were Mme. Scalchi and Jane de Vigne, contraltos; Jean de Reszke, Paul Kalisch, M. Montariol, and a younger brother of Giannini, tenors; Martapoura, Magini-Coletti, Lassalle, and Camera, baritones; Édouard de Reszke, Vinche, and Serbolini, basses, and Carbone, buffo. As conductor, Vianesi, known from the season of 1883-84, returned. The subscription season came to a close on March 12th, and presented thirty-nine subscription evening performances, thirteen matinées, three extra evenings, and one extra afternoon—in all, fifty-six representations. The list of operas contained not a single novelty, unless Gluck's "Orfeo," which had been heard in New York in 1866, and Mascagni's "Cavalleria Rusticana," which had been performed by two companies in English earlier in the season, were changed into novelties by use of the Italian text. But under such a classification Wagner's comic opera would also have to be set down as a novelty. The list included ten operas not in the repertories of the German companies, which had occupied the opera house between the two administrations of Mr. Abbey. Inasmuch as a new departure was signalized by this season, I present herewith a table of performances in the subscription season, with the extra representations mentioned:

Opera First performance

"Roméo et Juliette" .... December 14
"Il Trovatore" .... December 16
"Les Huguenots" .... December 18
"Norma" .... December 19
"La Sonnambula" .... December 21
"Rigoletto" .... December 23
"Faust" .... December 25
"Aïda" .... December 28
"Orfeo" and "Cavalleria Rusticana" .... December 30
"Le Prophéte" .... January 1
"Martha" .... January 2
"Lohengrin" .... January 4
"Mignon" .... January 8
"Otello" .... January 11
"L'Africaine" .... January 15
"Don Giovanni" .... January 18
"Dinorah" .... January 29
"Hamlet" .... February 10
"Lakmé" .... February 22
"I Maestri Cantoni" .... March 2
"Carmen" .... March 4

The first and most obvious lesson of the season, so far as it was an index of popular taste, may be seen by a critical glance at the list of performances. A beginning was made on the old lines. The familiar operas of the Italian list were brought forward with great rapidity, but not one of them drew a paying house. The turning point came with the arrival of M. Lassalle on January 15th. Messrs. Abbey and Grau then recognized that salvation for their undertaking lay in one course only, which was to give operas of large dimensions, and in each case employ the three popular men who had taken the place in the admiration of the public usually monopolized by the prima donna—the brothers de Reszke, and M. Lassalle. How consistently they acted on that conviction is shown by the circumstance that, though seventeen operas had been brought out between

December 14th and January 15th, only six were added to them in the remaining two months.

It was not a "star" season in the old sense. The most popular artists were the three men already mentioned, but it required that they should all be enlisted together with Miss Eames and Mme. Scaichi to make the one "sensation" of the season—Gounod's "Faust," which had six regular performances, and two extra. Of the women singers the greatest popularity was won by Miss Eames, whose youthfulness, freshness of voice, and statuesque beauty, compelled general admiration. The smallness of her repertory, however, prevented her from helping the season to the triumphant close which it might have had if the company had been enlisted to carry out the policy adopted when the season was half over. Miss Eames's début was made on the opening night in Gounod's "Roméo et Juliette." In many ways she was fortunate in her introduction to the operatic stage of her people—her people, though she was born in China. She was only twenty-four years old, and there was much to laud in her art, and nothing to condone except its immaturity. Her endowments of voice and person were opulent. She appeared in the opera in which she had effected her entrance on the stage at the Grand Opéra in Paris less than three years before, and for which her gifts and graces admirably fitted her. She appeared, moreover, in the company of Jean de Reszke, who was then, and who remained till his retirement, in all things except mere sensuous charm of voice, the ideal Romeo. She came fresh from her first successes at Covent Garden, which had been made in the spring of the year, and disclosed at once the lovely qualities which, when they became riper, gave promise of the highest order of things in the way of dramatic expression. At the end of the period whose history I am trying to set down she was still one of the bright ornaments of the Metropolitan stage, though she had not realized all the promises which she held out at the close of the first decade of her career.

Curiosity was piqued, and a kindly spirit of patriotism enlisted by the début of Miss Marie Van Zandt on December 21st. She, too, was an American, but she had been before the European public ten years, and had won as much favor as any American artist ever enjoyed in Paris. Mr. Abbey had pointed to her engagement (and that of Mme. Melba, whose star was just rising above the horizon) as a persuasive argument with the directors. Everything about the little lady, not excepting some unfortunate experiences which put an end to her Parisian career, invited to kindliness of utterance touching her début. Those of her hearers who had followed the history of opera in America for a score of years remembered her mother with admiration. Long before the days when every effort to produce opera in the vernacular was heralded as a great patriotic undertaking, Mme. Jenny

Van Zandt headed companies which exploited as varied and dignified repertories as those of the German companies at the Metropolitan Opera House, barring the Wagnerian list. Miss Van Zandt, diminutive, but winsome in voice as well as figure, and ingratiating in manner, recalled an old observation about precious things being done up in small parcels. Her coming seemed to betoken the return of the day of small things. She appeared in "La Sonnambula," and it was not until two months had passed that the patrons of the opera were privileged to hear her in "Lakmé," the opera with which her name was chiefly associated in Paris. Meanwhile she appeared in "Martha," "Mignon," "Don Giovanni," and "Dinorah," without rousing the public out of the apathy which it felt toward operas of their character. And when her battle-horse was led into the ring the task of sustaining interest in the season had fallen upon the shoulders of the masculine contingent in the company.

Curious questionings were raised by the production of "Fidelio" and "Die Meistersinger" in Italian. It was generally recognized that Mr. Abbey offered them as sops to Cerberus; but the German element in the population, which they were designed to appease, plainly were lacking in that peculiar bent of mind necessary to understand why Beethoven's opera done in Italian with a cast one-half good was supposed by the management to be worth two-thirds more than the same opera done in a language which it could understand with a cast all good (two of the principals, Mme. Lehmann and Mr. Kalisch, being the same), during the preceding seven years. Was the Italian language sixty-seven per cent. more valuable than the German in an opera conceived in German, written in German, and composed in the German spirit by a German? The public thought not, and "Fidelio" had only two performances. A more kindly view was taken of the Italian "Meistersinger," Which enabled the Germans to give expression to their feelings by making demonstrations over Mr. Seidl. There was much to admire, moreover, in the singing and acting of Jean de Reszke as Walther, and M. Lassalle as Hans Sachs. There was nothing of the conventional operatic marionette in these men. One night while they and Édouard de Reszke were on the stage at the same time I expressed my admiration at the sight of three such fine specimens of physical manhood to Mme. Lehmann, who sat near my elbow in a baignoir.

"Inspiring, isn't it?"

"Yes," was the reply, "and they might be as fine artists as they are men if they would but study."

We all know that their American experience was as little lost on the brothers de Reszke as it was on Mme. Lehmann herself, who stepped into the foremost rank of tragic singers so soon as America offered her the opportunity to shuffle off the obligation of "singing princesses," as she called it.

Mascagni's "Cavalleria Rusticana," the hot-blooded little opera which was destined to make so great a commotion in the world (had already begun to make it, indeed), had its first production at the Metropolitan Opera House on December 30th. The opera was no novelty, having already made an exciting career before the Metropolitan opera season opened; but there were two features of the performances calculated to live in the memory of serious observers as characteristic of the change in spirit which had come over the institution since the departure of the German artists: Miss Eames wore a perfectly exquisite accordion-pleated skirt as the distraught Sicilian peasant, and Signor Valero sang the siciliano on the open stage, the overture being stopped and the curtain raised so that he might sing his serenade to Lola with greater effect. He sang behind Lola's house, and winning a call in spite of his stridulous voice and singular phrasing, he stepped out from cover, bowed his acknowledgments, and, returning to his hiding place, serenaded his love over again. After he had come forward a second time Signor Vianesi found his place in the score and resumed the overture.

"Cavalleria Rusticana" precipitated an amusing but extremely lively managerial battle when it reached New York. Those who watched the operatic doings of Europe were aware of the fact that the opera spread like wildfire from town to town immediately after its first success at Rome. Fast as it traveled, however, the intermezzo traveled faster. Seidl had seized upon it in the summer of 1891, and made it a feature of his concerts at Brighton Beach. Then came simultaneous announcements of the production of the opera by Rudolph Aronson and Oscar Hammerstein in the fall. Mr. Aronson wanted to open the season at the Casino with it, and let it introduce a change in the character of the entertainments given at that playhouse. Mr. Hammerstein had also announced the work, but he had no theater at his ready disposal. He thought Aronson was poaching on his preserves, and there began a diverting struggle for priority of performance, from which nobody profited and the opera suffered. Amid threats of crimination Aronson precipitated what he called a dress rehearsal of the work at the Casino in the afternoon of October 1, 1891. Like the king in the parable, he sent out into the highways, and bade all he could find in to the feast. Especially did his servants labor on the Rialto, and the affair had all the appearance of a professional matinée. Nothing was quite in readiness, but Mr. Hammerstein had announced his first performance for the evening of that day, and must be anticipated at all hazards. Yet there were singers and scenes and musicians in the orchestra, and Mr. Gustav Kerker to steer the little operatic ship through the breakers. On the whole, the performance was fair. Laura Bellini was the Santuzza of the occasion, Grace Golden the Lola, Helen von Doenhoff the Lucia, Charles Bassett the Turiddu, and William Pruette the Alfio. Heinrich Conried staged the production. In the evening Oscar Hammerstein pitchforked the opera on to the stage of the Lenox Lyceum—an open concert room, and a poor one at that. There was a canvas proscenium, no scenery to speak of, costumes copied from no particular country and no particular period, and a general effect of improvisation. But the musical forces were superior to Mr. Aronson's, and had there been a better theater the Casino performance would have been greatly surpassed. There was a really fine orchestra under the direction of Mr. Adolph Neuendorff, but it sat out on the floor of the hall, which reverberated like a drum. Mme. Janouschoffsky, an exceedingly capable artist, was the Santuzza, Mrs. Pemberton Hincks the Lola, Mrs. Jennie Bohner the Lucia, Payne Clarke the Turiddu, and Herman Gerold the Alfio. While all this pother was making, "Cavalleria Rusticana" was already three weeks old in Philadelphia, where Mr. Gustav Hinrichs had brought it forward with his American company at the Grand Opera House; Minnie Hauk, with a company of her own, had given it in Chicago the night before the New York struggle, and Emma Juch and her company were rushing forward the preparations for a production in Boston.

"Cavalleria Rusticana" came upon the world like the bursting of a bomb, and its effect was so startling that it bewildered and confounded the radical leaders of musical thought. There were few, indeed, who retained calmness of vision enough to perceive that it was less a change of manner than of subject-matter, which had whirled the world off its critical feet. Outside of Italy there was no means of seeing the work of preparation which had preceded it. The annual output of hundreds of operas made no impression beyond the Alpine barrier, and it was easy to believe that the entire product was formed after the old and humdrum manner. No sooner had "Cavalleria Rusticana" broken down the old confines, however, than it was discovered that a whole brood of young musicians had been brought up on the same blood-heating food, and a dozen composers were ready to use the same formulas. Most of them, indeed, got the virus from the same apothecary who uttered the mortal drug to Mascagni—that is to say, from Amilcare Ponchielli. Had we but listened twenty-five years ago to "La Gioconda" as we are able to listen to "Cavalleria Rusticana," and its swift and multitudinous offspring now, we might have recognized the beginnings of what has been termed "Mascagnitis," not in an essentially new manner of musical composition, but in the appeal to the primitive passion for violence and blood which found expression in the operatic paraphrase of Victor Hugo's story, and the invitation which that passion extended to the modern musician suddenly emancipated from a lot of cumbersome formularies, and endowed with a mass of new harmonic and instrumental pigments with which to produce the startling contrasts and swift contradictions for which the new field of subjects clamors.

Seventeen years ago "Cavalleria Rusticana" had no perspective. Now, though but a small portion of its progeny has been brought to our notice, we, nevertheless, look at it through a vista which looks like a valley of moral and physical death through which there flows a sluggish stream thick with filth, and red with blood. Strangely enough, in spite of the consequences which have followed it, the fierce little drama retains its old potency. It still speaks with a voice which sounds like the voice of truth. Its music still makes the nerves tingle, and carries our feelings unresistingly on its turbulent current. But the stage picture is less sanguinary than it looked in the beginning. It seems to have receded a millennium in time. It has the terrible fierceness of an Attic tragedy, but it also has the decorum which the Attic tragedy never violated. There is no slaughter in the presence of the audience, despite the humbleness of its personages. It does not keep us perpetually in sight of the shambles. It is, indeed, an exposition of chivalry, rustic, but chivalry, nevertheless. It was thus Clytemnestra slew her husband, and Orestes his mother. Note the contrast which the duel between Alfio and Turiddu presents with the double murder to the piquant accompaniment of comedy in "Pagliacci," the opera which followed so hard upon its heels. Since then piquancy has been the cry; the piquant contemplation of adultery, seduction, and murder amid the reek and stench of the Italian barnyard. Think of Cilèa's "Tilda," Giordano's "Mala Vita," Spinelli's "A Basso Porto," and Tasca's "A Santa Lucia!"

The stories chosen for operatic treatment by the champions of verismo are all alike. It is their filth and blood which fructifies the music, which rasps the nerves even as the plays revolt the moral stomach. I repeat: looking back over the time during which this so-called veritism has held its orgy, "Cavalleria Rusticana" seems almost classic. Its music is highly spiced and tastes "hot i' th' mouth," but its eloquence is, after all, in its eager, pulsating, passionate melody—like the music which Verdi wrote more than half a century ago for the last act of "Il Trovatore." If neither Mascagni himself, nor his imitators, have succeeded in equaling it since, it is because they have thought too much of the external devices of abrupt and uncouth change of modes and tonalities, of exotic scales and garish orchestration, and too little of the fundamental element of melody, which once was the be-all and end-all of Italian music. Another fountain of gushing melody must be opened before "Cavalleria Rusticana" finds a successor in all things worthy of the succession. Ingenious artifice, reflection, and technical cleverness will not suffice even with the blood and mud of the Neapolitan slums as a fertilizer.

Messrs. Abbey and Grau had no rival opera organizations to contend with at any time after they opened their doors, so they created a bit of competition themselves. In January they brought Mme. Patti and her operatic concert company into the house for a pair of concerts in which scenes from operas were sung in costume, the famous singer's companions being Mlle. Fabbri, M. Guille (tenor), Signor Novara (bass), and Signor Del Puente. The occasion offered an opportunity to study the impulses which underlie popular patronage. The entertainments being concerts, not operas, the stockholders were not entitled to their boxes under the terms of their contract with Abbey & Grau, and were conspicuous by their absence. Nevertheless, at the second concert, which took place on an afternoon, I estimated the audience at four thousand—nine-tenths women. Mme. Patti also appeared in performances of "Lucia di Lammermoor" and "Il Barbiere" in a supplementary season, one feature of which, on March 31, 1892, was the production of Wagner's "Flying Dutchman" in Italian, with M. Lassalle in the titular part, which he sang for the first time in his life. "A marvelous artist indeed is this Frenchman," was my comment in The Tribune, "and if he and the brothers de Reszke are in next year's company, the lovers of the lyric drama as distinguished from the old sing-song opera will look into the future without trepidation." Unhappily there was no "next year's company."

In August, 1892, the Metropolitan Opera House had a visitation of fire, which brought operatic matters to a crisis, caused a postponement of the performance for a season, a reorganization of the corporation which owned the building, and a remodeling of the stage and portions of the interior of the theater. For a considerable space before the building of the Metropolitan the public mind was greatly exercised over the awful loss of life at recent theater fires, especially the destruction of the Ringtheater in Vienna. When Mr. Cady planned the New York house, he set about making it as absolutely fireproof as such a structure can be. It was to be non-combustible from the bottom up. There was not a stud partition in it. The floors were all of iron beams and brick arches, the masonry being exposed in the corridors, passages and vestibules, but for comfort having a covering of wood in the audience room. The roof was of iron and masonry, the outer covering of slate being secured to masonry blocks. The iron roof beams of over one hundred feet span, were mounted on rollers to allow for contraction and expansion. The ceiling of the audience room was of iron. The ornamental work of the proscenium, the tier balustrades, and the frames of the partitions between the boxes were all of metal. The stage was supported by a complex iron system of about four thousand light pieces so adjusted as to be removable in sections when it was desired to open the stage floor. Theater fires almost invariably originate on the stage, and, as an additional safeguard, Mr. Cady contrived an apparatus for flooding the stage in the case of a threatened conflagration. A large skylight was weighted to fall open in case of fire, and a great water tank placed over the rigging loft and connected with a network of pipes with apertures stopped with extremely fusible solder, so that the heat of even a small fire would open the holes and release a drenching shower.

One after another these precautions were rendered inutile. The iron support of the stage troubled the stage mechanics, who wanted something that could be more easily handled, so wooden pieces were substituted for the iron. The location of the tank was such that the water was in danger of freezing in winter, and steam pipes were arranged to keep the water warm. Mr. Abbey did not like the expense of warming the water, and therefore emptied the tank. There was a fireproof curtain, which was cumbrous to handle, and Mr. Abbey's men chained it up. The commodious stage made a superb paint shop in summer, and Mr. Abbey used it for painting scenery for his other theaters. It was being thus used on August 27, 1892, when a workman carelessly threw a lighted match among the "green" scenery. It caught fire, the stage was burned out, and the auditorium sadly disfigured. When, eventually, the building was repaired, the interior of the theater, all that had suffered harm, was thoroughly remodeled, the stockholders' boxes were reduced to a single row, the proscenium was given its present shape, the apron of the stage was removed, and the stage itself was made more practicable in many ways. This did not happen, however, until the question whether or not the opera house should be restored to its original uses had occupied the minds of the stockholders and public for nearly a year. In the middle of the season Messrs. Abbey and Grau, while protesting that they were satisfied with the financial outcome of their venture, announced that they did not intend to give opera the next year. They were shaken in this determination, if they ever seriously harbored it, by the success of "Faust" and one or two other operas, which enlisted what in the next season of opera came to be called the "ideal cast." But there was a division of opinion as to the proper course for the future among the stockholders, especially after Mr. Abbey, late in September, sent word from London that his firm would not undertake opera in the United States without a subvention from the Metropolitan Opera Company. Also that he had already canceled his contracts with singers for the American season of 1892-93. There was some vague talk before this on the part of Mr. Schoeffel of a season of opera in Mexico City, and a longer season than usual in Chicago, the intimation plainly being that grand opera might be emancipated from dependence on the metropolis. One effect of this indecision was to bring forth a discussion of the feasibility of endowed opera in New York, Boston, Chicago, Philadelphia, and one or two other of the large cities of the country. Another was to call into new life an agitation in favor of the establishment of another German company. The first project died of inanition; the second developed in another year into an actuality, which created more stir than the close of the opera house had done. The Metropolitan Opera Company reached a decision some time in January, 1893. The directors had neglected to insure the building against fire, and provision had to be made for funds to rebuild, as well as to pay off existing liabilities. The opera lovers among the stockholders reorganized the company under the style of the Metropolitan Opera and Real Estate Company, and purchased the building under foreclosure proceeding for $1,425,000, then raised $1,000,000 by a bond issue, and the summer of 1893 was devoted to a restoration of the theater, an agreement having also been reached for a new lease to Mr. Abbey and his associates.

CHAPTER XVII
THE ADVENT OF MELBA AND CALVÉ

For the reasons set forth at the close of the last chapter there was no opera at the Metropolitan Opera House in the season of 1892-93, but the fall of the latter year witnessed the beginning of a new period, full of vicissitudes. With many brilliant artistic features, it was still experimental to a large extent on its artistic side, the chief results of its empiricism being the restoration of German opera in the repertory on an equal footing with Italian and French. It also brought the largest wave of prosperity to the house that it had experienced since its opening, yet ended in the shipwreck of the lessees, and disaster that was more than financial. The lessees were again Messrs. Abbey, Schoeffel and Grau, with whom the reorganized Metropolitan Opera and Real Estate Company (Limited) effected an agreement, the essential elements of which remained unchanged for fifteen years; that is, down to the close of the season of 1907-08. The term was five years. The lessees took the house for an annual rental of $52,000, and pledged themselves to give opera four times a week for thirteen weeks in the winter and spring. The lessors paid back to the lessees the $52,000 for their box privileges, and to insure representations which would be satisfactory to them, reserved the right to nominate six of the singers, two of whom were to take part in every performance in the subscription list.

The first season under the new lease was enormously successful, Abbey, Schoeffel, and Grau realizing about $150,000, including the visits to other cities, and a supplementary spring season of two weeks. They made great losses on their other enterprises, however, especially on Abbey's Theater (now the Knickerbocker), and the American tours of Mounet-Sully and Mme. Réjane. Like results attended the seasons of 1894-95, and 1895-96, the drag in the latter instance being the Lillian Russell Opera Company, which, together with other ventures, brought the firm into such a financial slough that it made an assignment for the benefit of its creditors, who were forced to take over its business to protect themselves. Chief of these was William Steinway, who had accommodated Abbey, Schoeffel and Grau with loans to the extent of $50,000. Under his guidance as chairman of the committee of reorganization, the stock company, Abbey, Schoeffel & Grau (Limited), was formed, he becoming president, and Henry E. Abbey, John B. Schoeffel, and Maurice Grau managing directors at a salary of $20,000 a year. Ernest Goerlitz, who had been in the employ of the firm for some time, was made secretary and treasurer. He remained in an executive capacity at the Metropolitan until the expiration of the consulship of

Conried in 1908. Mr. Steinway got rid of the debts of the company (or, perhaps, it would be more correct to say, changed their character) by issuing certificates of stock and notes to the creditors. In this manner some of the principal artists of the company became financially interested in opera giving.

Before the reorganized company began the next series of performances Mr. Abbey died, and the season was only a fortnight old when Mr. Steinway followed him into the grave. A very puissant personage in the managerial field was Mr. Abbey during a full quarter-century of theatrical life in America. He was a purely speculative manager, who never permitted his own likes or dislikes to influence him in his chosen vocation of purveying amusements, so-called, to the public, though his tastes led him generally into the higher regions, and there is little doubt that an inherent love for music for its own sake made him take to opera. As a young man in his native city of Akron, Ohio, where he was born in 1846, he played cornet in the town band. When he revoked his resolution never to embark in an operatic enterprise again after the disastrous season of 1883-84, I met him in Broadway, and asked him about the artists he intended to bring to the Metropolitan Opera House. He gave me the names of those whom he had in view, and I expressed my regret that one, whom I admired very greatly indeed, was missing. His reply was prompt: "There is no woman in the world I would rather engage, and no woman whose singing gives me greater pleasure; but she doesn't draw. I never made any money with her." It was an illuminative observation. As a youth he was interested with his father in the jewelry business in Akron, and on the death of his father, in 1873, the business became his; but by that time he was already a theatrical manager, though on a small scale. In 1869 he had assumed charge of the Akron theater. In 1876 he associated himself with John B. Schoeffel, and with him gradually acquired theatrical properties in several of the principal cities of the East, and entered upon enterprises of a character which were his undoing in the end. The Abbey, Schoeffel & Grau Company carried through the season of 1896-97 with a profit of about $30,000 in New York, despite the fact that the financial affairs of the country were in a bad way. A four weeks' season in Chicago, however, was ruinous, and Mr. Gran was compelled to fall back on some of the artists of the company and friends to enable him to bring the Chicago season to a close. Jean and Édouard de Reszke and Lassalle were among the subscribers to a guarantee fund of $30,000, which he needed to carry him through. All the guarantors were repaid in full, when, at the end of the season, the affairs of Abbey, Schoeffel & Grau (Limited) were wound up, and Mr. Schoeffel bought the principal asset, the Tremont Theater, in Boston. Thereupon Mr. Grau and his associates formed a new company, which gave opera under the conditions which seemed to have become traditional until the end of the season of 1902-3. Mr. Grau was compelled by ill health to withdraw from active duty before the end of the last season, and the story of his company's doings falls naturally into another chapter of this history. We must now survey the artistic incidents of the period between the reconstruction of the opera house and the beginning of the new régime. This will be the business of this and the following chapter.

Simply for the sake of convenience in the record, I shall devote the chief statistical attention in the remaining chapters of this history to the subscription seasons, and discuss the supplementary spring seasons only as they offer features of special interest. The seasons, generally a fortnight long, and given after the return of the singers from visits to Boston and Chicago, are distinguished from the subscription seasons very much as the fall seasons in London are from the summer seasons, though there is not the sharp line of demarcation so far as fashion goes, which the adjournment of Parliament makes on the other side of the Atlantic.

The tenth regular season of opera then began at the Metropolitan Opera House on November 27, 1893, and ended on February 24, 1894. Officially the languages of the performances were Italian and French, but the operas given were, for the greater part, French and German, and the representations were dual in language in all cases, except the Italian works. I mention this fact, not because of its singularity, for it is a familiar phenomenon all over the operatic world, except perhaps Italy, but in order to point out hereafter a betterment, which came in with a more serious artistic striving later. The chorus always sang in the "soft bastard Latin," whether the principals sang in Italian or French; and the occasions were not a few when two languages were sung also by the principals—when lovers wooed in French, and received their replies in Italian, thus recalling things over which Addison made merry generations ago. The season was planned to embrace thirty-nine subscription nights and thirteen matinées. To these were added two matinées and sixteen evening representations, two of the latter being for the benefit of popular charities. In all, New York had sixty performances of opera within the period covered by the regular subscription, which was a smaller number than had been shown by any season since that of 1886-87. Eighteen operas were brought forward in full (that is to say, without more than the conventional cuts), and parts of three others. Thus of "La Traviata," though I have included it in the list to be presented soon, only the first and fourth acts were performed. There was not a single opera in the repertory which had not been heard in New York before, though several were new to the house. The nearest approach to a novelty was Mascagni's "L'Amico Fritz," which disappeared from the list after two representations, and had been heard at an improvised performance, which scarcely deserves to be considered in a record of this character. In the supplemental season, however, a novelty of real pith and moment was brought forward in the shape of Massenet's "Werther," which had been promised to the regular subscribers, and which, while it made no profound impression, was accepted as an earnest of the excellent and honorable intentions of the managers, and a proof of the difficulties which hampered them at times.

The principal members of the company were Mesdames Melba, Calvé, Eames, Nordica, Arnoldson, Scalchi, and Mantelli, and Messrs. Jean and Édouard de Reszke, de Lucia, Vignas, Ancona, Plançon, Castelmary, and Martapoura. The subscription for the season amounted to $82,000, which was $10,000 more than the largest subscription in the German period. A great ado was made over this fact by the managers and their friends. Not unnaturally the lovers of German opera took up the cudgels against the Italianissimi, and pointed out the indubitable fact that owing to the difference in prices of admission and seats the subscription, instead of showing a large advance in popular interest, indicated a falling off to the extent of an attendance of six thousand in the season. Not money, but attendance, they argued, was the real standard of popularity. The managers also very unwisely, as it proved (since two years later they found themselves obliged to include German performances in their scheme), put forward a public boast that the receipts for the last month of the opera "nearly equaled the average gross receipts for the entire term of any German opera ever given in New York." Of course, the reference went only to the German seasons at the Metropolitan Opera House, for there was no record that could be consulted touching the many sporadic German enterprises of the earlier periods at the Academy of Music and other theaters. It was not at all unkind, but simply in the interest of historical verity that in The Tribune I called attention to the fact that it was scarcely ingenuous in Abbey, Schoeffel & Grau to choose the last month in the season for the comparison, for in that month there were twenty-two representations, including two for popular charities (at one of which, managed by the opera house directors, the public contributed $22,000), and six representations of "Carmen," which, with Mme. Calvé in the principal character, was enjoying the most sensational triumph ever achieved by any opera or singer. Moreover, most of 'these performances were outside the subscription, and the prices, as I have repeatedly said, were nearly double those which prevailed during the German régime. Besides, it was an easy task to prove from the figures which I had printed from year to year in my "Review of the New York Musical Season," that, in order to surpass the German record with their last month, Abbey, Schoeffel & Grau would have had to show average nightly receipts of over $9,000, whereas only once had they, in a spirit of boastfulness, claimed that as much as $11,000 had been taken at a single performance, and that at a phenomenal "Carmen" matinée.

Without Calvé and "Carmen" the bankruptcy which came two years later might have been precipitated in this season. Thanks to Bizet's opera, and its heroine, and the popularity of Mme. Eames and the brothers de Reszke in "Faust," the season was prodigiously successful, the receipts from all sources (including the Sunday night concerts and opera in Philadelphia and Brooklyn) being in the neighborhood of $550,000, and the profits, as I have already said, $150,000. The twelve performances of "Carmen," I make no doubt, brought at least $100,000 into the exchequer of the managers in the subscription season, and in the supplemental post-Lenten season of a fortnight there were three performances more. The success of the opera remained without a parallel in the history of opera in New York till the coming of Wagner's "Parsifal."

Mme. Melba effected her entrance on the operatic stage in America on December 4, 1893, in Donizetti's "Lucia." Five years before she had made her London début in the same opera, and between that time and her coming to New York she had won fragrant laurels in Paris in company with the brothers de Reszke and M. Lassalle in "Roméo et Juliette" and "Faust," both of which operas she had prepared with the composer. Her repertory was small when she came, but in it she was unique, both for the quality of her voice and the quality of her art. She did not make all of her operas effective in her first season, partly because a large portion of the public had been weaned away from the purely lyric style of composition and song, in which she excelled, partly because the dramatic methods and fascinating personality of Mme. Calvé had created a fad which soon grew to proportions that scouted at reason; partly because Miss (not Mme.) Eames had become a great popular favorite, and the people of society, who doted on her, on Jean de Reszke, his brother Édouard, and on Lassalle, found all the artistic bliss of which they were capable in listening to their combined voices in "Faust." So popular had Gounod's opera become at this time with the patrons of the Metropolitan Opera House, that my witty colleague, Mr. W. J. Henderson, sarcastically dubbed it "das Faustspielhaus," in parody of the popular title of the theater on the hill in the Wagnerian Mecca.

When Mme. Melba came she was the finest exemplar of finished vocalization that had been heard at the opera house since its opening, with the single exception of Mme. Sembrich. Though she had been singing in opera only five years, she had reached the zenith of her powers. Her voice was charmingly fresh, and exquisitely beautiful. Her tone-production was more natural, and quite as apparently spontaneous, as that of the wonderful woman who so long upheld the standard of bel canto throughout the world. In the case of Mme. Patti, art had already begun to be largely artifice, a circumstance that needed to cause no wonder inasmuch as her career on the operatic Stage already compassed a full generation; but Mme. Melba neither needed to seek for means nor guard against possible mishap. All that she needed—more than that: all that she wanted to humor her amiable disposition to be prodigal in utterance—lay in her voice ready at hand. Its range was commensurate with all that could be asked of it, and she moved with greatest ease in the regions which most of her rivals carefully avoided. To throw out those scintillant bubbles of sound which used to be looked upon as the highest achievement in singing seemed to be an entirely natural mode of expression with her. With the reasonableness of such a mode of expression I am not concerned now; it is enough that Mme. Melba came nearer to providing it with justification than any one of her contemporaries of that day, except Mme. Sembrich, or any of her contemporaries of to-day. Added to these gifts and graces, she disclosed most admirable musical instincts, a quality which the people had been taught to admire more than ever while they were learning how to give reverence due to the dramatic elements in the modern lyric drama.

I have already intimated that Mme. Melba's operas found little favor with the public compared with "Carmen" and "Faust," and, perhaps, there was in this more than a mere indication of the educational influence left by the German period. I should have no hesitation whatever in saying so had not the "Carmen" craze reached proportions which precluded the thought that artistic predilections or convictions had anything to do with it. So much of a mere fad did Mme. Calvé in "Carmen" become that the public remained all but insensible to the merits of her immeasurably finer impersonation of Santuzza in "Cavalleria Rusticana." It was in Mascagni's opera that she effected her début on November 29, 1893, in company with Señor Vignas, a Spanish tenor, squat and ungraceful of figure, homely of features, restricted in intelligence, and strident of voice. New York knew very little of Mme. Calvé when she came, though she had already been twice as long on the stage as Mme. Melba, and even after her first appearance Mr. Abbey met my congratulations on her achievement with a dubious shake of the head, and the remark that, while he hoped my predictions touching her popularity would be fulfilled, he placed a much lower estimation on her powers than I. Not he, but Mr. Grau, was responsible for her engagement, and his hopes were all centered on Mme. Melba. Like most of our singers at the time, Calvé came to New York by way of London. The rôle of Santuzza, which she had created in Paris in January, 1892, and in London in the following May, had been hailed with gladness in both cities, but her Carmen was as inadequately appreciated in Paris as it was overestimated in New York and London, especially in later years, when the capriciousness which led her originally to break away from some of the traditions of the rôle created by Galli-Marié. and thus cost her the understanding of the Parisians, had become a fixed habit, which she pursued regardless of decent moderation, sound principles, and good taste.

The Parisians attested their artistic Bourbonism not only in declining to recognize the excellence of the good features of Calvé's Carmen, but, also, in failing to appreciate her touchingly beautiful Ophelia, to the great grief of Ambroise Thomas, who went to Italy to see her in the part, and believed that had she but been given the proper support in Paris "Hamlet" would have ranked with "Faust" in popularity. Of course, this was a fond composer's too good opinion of his opera, but the trait of the Paris public which is unwilling to find merit in any change from a performance which first won their admiration has frequently stood in the way of first-class talent. To illustrate this I can relate an anecdote which was repeated to me at an artistic dinner table in the French capital in 1886. It is not for me to vouch for the truth of the story, but give it as it was told to me in explanation of some amused comments which I had made on the stiff conventionality of a performance of "L'Africaine" which I had witnessed at the Grand Opéra. Faure, the original of Ambroise Thomas's Hamlet, had been succeeded in the rôle by Lassalle, whose fine art in newer works had met with full recognition from press and public. To Lassalle's great surprise, his Hamlet, a remarkably fine performance within the limit set by the pitiable operatic travesty of Shakespeare's play, was received coldly, and there was wide comment on the circumstance that he had ignored traditions of performance, especially in the scene between the Prince and his mother. In considerable distress he went to Faure, who had set the fashion:

"What pose, gesture, effect of yours is it that I have failed to copy?" he asked of his confrère.

And Faure explained:

At the first performance when he reached the scene in question, he had found his throat suddenly clogged. Only by an act neither pleasant to observe nor polite to describe, could he remove the obstruction, and at a supreme moment he had improvised a movement which carried his face out of sight of the audience, so that he might free his throat unnoticed. Knowing nothing of the cause, the public applauded the effect, and the singular nuance became a part of the "business" of the piece.

When Mme. Calvé flashed upon New York in "Cavalleria Rusticana," her impersonation startled me into the declaration that no finer lyrico-dramatic performance had been witnessed in America within a generation. Unhesitatingly I placed it by the side of Materna's Brünnhilde, Brandt's Fidès, Niemann's Tristan and Siegmund, and Fischer's Hans Sachs, without, of course, presuming to compare the relative value of the dramatists' conceits. Even now I cannot recall anything finer in the region of combined action and song. She held her listeners so completely captive and swayed them so powerfully that she compelled even the foolishly and affectedly frantic claquers, who had seats near the stage, to hold their peace. They could only make their boisterous clamor in response to the old-fashioned appeal made by a high tone screeched by the stridulous tenor. There was as little conventionality in her singing as in her acting, though she had not yet adopted that indifference to rhythm which has marked her singing in more recent years. She saturated the music with emotion. Much of it she seemed to sing to herself, declaiming it like dramatic speech whose emotional contents had been raised to a higher power by the melody. In moments of extreme excitement one scarcely realized that she was singing at all. Carried along by the torrent of her feelings, her listeners accepted her song as the only proper and efficient expression for her emotional state. The two expressions, song and action, were one; they were mutually complemental. It was not nature subordinated to art, but art vitalized by nature. It is not possible for me to compare her Carmen with Galli-Marié's, which stood in the way of her appreciation in the part in Paris. I have heard that that was so frank in one of its expressions that it invited the interference of the Prefect of the Seine. To me, at least, in Mme. Calvé's impersonation, it seemed that I was enjoying my first revelation of some of the elements of the character of the gypsy as it had existed in the imagination of Prosper Mérimée when he wrote his novel. To me she presented a woman thoroughly wanton and diabolically equipped with the wicked witcheries which explained, if they did not palliate, the conduct of Don José. Here we had a woman without conscience, but also without the capacity for even a wicked affection; a woman who might have been the thief whom the novelist describes, who surely carried a dagger in her corsage, and who in some respects left absolutely nothing to the imagination, to which even a drama like "Carmen" makes appeal. She came upon the stage as Mérimée's heroine stepped into his pages: "poising herself on her hips, like a filly from the Cordovan stud," and with a fine simulation of unconsciousness, she seemed every moment about to break into one of those dances which the satirist castigated in the days of the Roman Empire:

 Nec de Gadibus improbis puellae
Vibrabunt sine fine prurientes
Lascivos docili tremore lumbos.

 Alas! Mme. Calvé's admiration for herself was stronger than her devotion to an artistic ideal, and it was not long before her Carmen became completely merged in her own capricious personality.

 Massenet's "Werther" (performed in Chicago, March 29) had its first New York performance at the Metropolitan, April 19, 1894, with Mme. Eames, Sigrid Arnoldson, Jean de Reszke, M. Martapoura, and Signor Carbone. Signor Mancinelli conducted. The opera had one performance, and was repeated once in the season of 1896-97. Then it disappeared from the repertory of the Metropolitan, and has since then not been thought of, apparently, although strenuous efforts have been made ever and anon to give interest to the French list. I record the fact as one to be deplored. "Werther" is a beautiful opera; as instinct with throbbing life in every one of its scenes as the more widely admired "Manon" is in its best scene. It has its weak spots as have all of Massenet's operas, despite his mastery of technique, but its music will always appeal to refined artistic sensibilities for its lyric charm, its delicate workmanship, its splendid dramatic climax in the duo between Werther and Charlotte, beginning: "Ah! pourvu que de voie ces yeux toujours ouverts," and its fine scoring. It smacks more of the atmosphere of the Parisian salon than of the sweet breezes with which Goethe filled the story, but no Frenchman has yet been able to talk aught but polite French in music for the stage, Berlioz excepted, and the music of "Werther" is of finer texture than that of most of the operas produced by Massenet since.

The season of 1894-95, consisting again of thirteen weeks, began on November 19th, and closed on February 16th. It was marked by a number of incidents, some of which made a permanent impression on the policy of the Metropolitan Opera House. Chief of these was a remarkable eruption of sentiment in favor of German opera—so vigorous an eruption, indeed, that it led to the incorporation of German performances in the Metropolitan repertory ever after, though the change involved a much greater augmentation of the forces of the establishment than the consorting of French with Italian had involved. To this I shall give the attention which it deserves presently. Other features were the introduction of Saturday night performances of opera at reduced prices (a feature which became permanent), the appearance of several new singers, and the production of two novelties, one of them Verdi's "Falstaff," of first-class importance.

In their prospectus the managers promised a reformation of the chorus, and announced the re-engagement of "nearly all the great favorites of last year." The improvement of the chorus was not particularly noticeable except in appearance; a number of young and comely American women were enlisted, but their best service was to stand in front of the old stagers who knew the operas, and could sing but who seemed to have come down through the ages from the early days of the old Academy. The phrase "nearly all" was an ominous one, for it betokened the absence from the company of Mme. Calvé. The newcomers were Lucille Hill, Sybil Sanderson, Zélie de Lussan, Mira Heller, and Libia Drog, sopranos; G. Russitano and Francesco Tamagno, tenors, and Victor Maurel, who had been a popular favorite twenty years before at the Academy of Music. Luigi Mancinelli and E. Bevignani were the conductors, and Mr. Seidl was engaged to give éclat to the Sunday evening concerts. Mme. Melba's chief financial value to the management in the preceding season had been found to lie in these concerts, which this year were begun earlier than usual, and made a part of Melba's concert tour. The first opera was "Roméo et Juliette," with the cast beloved of society, and on the second night the introduction of the newcomers began. But woefully. The opera was "William Tell," and Signorina Drog sang the part of the heroine in place of Miss Hill, indisposed. Mathilde (or Matilda—the opera was sung in Italian), does not appear in the opera until the second act, and then she has the most familiar air in the opera to sing—"Selva opaca," an air which then belonged to the concert-room repertory of most florid sopranos. When Signorina Drog came upon the stage, it is safe to say that no one regretted her substitution for the English singer except herself. She was an exceedingly handsome person, who moved about with attractive freedom and grace, and disclosed a voice of good quality, especially in the upper register. She began her aria most tastefully, but scarcely had she begun when her memory played her false. For a few dreadful seconds she tried to pick up the thread of the melody but in vain. Then came the inevitable breakdown. She quit trying, and appealed pitifully to Signor Mancinelli for help. He seemed to have lost his head as completely as the lady had her memory. So had the prompter, who pulled his noddle into his shell like a snail and remained as mute. Signor Tamagno entered in character, and indulged in dumbshow to a few detached phrases from the orchestra. Then the awfulness of the situation overwhelmed him, and he fairly ran off the stage, leaving Matilda alone. That lady made a final appeal to the conductor, switched her dress nervously with her riding whip, went to the wings, got a glass of water, and then disappeared. The audience, which had good-humoredly applauded till now, began to laugh, and the demoralization was complete. It would have been a relief had the curtain fallen, but as this did not happen Signor Tamagno, Signor Ancona, and Édouard de Reszke came upon the stage and began the famous trio, in which Signor Tamagno sang with tremendous intensity and power. It was a remarkable performance of a sensational piece, and had it not been preceded by so frightful a catastrophe, and interrupted by Tamagno himself to bow his acknowledgments, pick up a bunch of violets thrown from a box, and repeat his first melody, its effect would have been dramatically electrifying. There was a long wait after the act to enable Signor Mancinelli to arrange the necessary cuts, and after the stage manager had made an apology on behalf of Signorina Drog, and explained that she had been seized with vertigo, but would finish the opera in an abbreviated form, the representation was resumed. It is due to the lady to add that she had never before attempted to sing the part, and that on the third evening she materially redeemed herself in "Aïda." Miss de Lussan, a native of New York, who had begun her operatic career a few years before in the Boston

Ideal Opera Company, and had won a commendable degree of favor at Covent Garden as Carmen, had been engaged in the hope of continuing the prosperous career of Bizet's opera, but the hope proved abortive. It was the singer, not the song, which had bewitched the people of New York—Calvé, not Bizet. "Carmen" was excellently given, the charm of Melba's voice being called on for the music of Micaela's part; but the sensation had departed, and was waiting to be revived with the return of Calvé in the succeeding season.

The first novelty in this season was "Elaine," an opera in four acts, words by Paul Ferrier, music by Herman Bemberg, brought forward on December 17, 1894. "Elaine" was produced because Mme. Melba and the brothers de Reszke wanted to appear in it out of friendship for the composer, who had dedicated the score to them, and come to New York to witness the production, as he had gone to London when it was given in Covent Garden. In America Bemberg was a small celebrity of the salon and concert room. His parents were citizens of the Argentine Republic, but he was born in Paris, in 1861. His father being a man of wealth, he had ample opportunity to cultivate his talents, and his first teachers in composition were Bizet and Henri Maréchal. Later he continued his studies at the Conservatoire, under Dubois and Massenet. In 1885 he carried off the Rossini prize, and in 1889 brought out a one-act opera at the Opéra Comique, "Le Baiser de Suzon," for which Pierre Barbier wrote the words. "Elaine" had its first performance at Convent Garden in July, 1892, with Mme. Melba, Jean and Édouard de Reszke, and M. Plançon in the cast. It was then withdrawn for revision, and restored to the stage the next year. If there is anything creditable in such a thing it may be said, to Mr. Bemberg's credit, that, so far as I know, he was the first musician who wrote music for Oscar Wilde's "Salome." The public, especially the people of the boxes, lent a gracious ear to the new opera, partly, no doubt, because of its subject, but more largely because of Mme. Melba, Mme. Mantelli, the brothers de Reszke, Plançon, and M. Castelmary, who were concerned in its production. All of Mr. Bemberg's music that had previously been heard in New York was of the lyrical order, and it seemed but natural that he was less successful in the developing of a dramatic situation than in hymning the emotions of one when he found it at hand. A ballad in the first act ("L'amour est pur comme la fiamme"), the scene at the close ("L'air est léger"), a prayer in the third act ("Dieu de pitié"), and the duets which followed them are all cases in point. They mark the high tide of M. Bemberg's graceful melodic fancy, and exemplify his good taste and genuineness of feeling. It is not great music, but it is sincere to the extent of its depth. For the note of chivalry which ought to sound all through an Arthurian opera M. Bemberg has chosen no less a model than "Lohengrin"; but his trumpets are feebler echoes of the original voice than his harmonies on several occasions, as, for instance, the entrance of Lancelot into the castle of Astolat. In general his instrumentation is discreet and effective. He has followed his French teachers in the treatment of the dialogue, which aims to be intensified speech. He has also trodden, though at a distance, in the footsteps of Bizet and Massenet in the device of using typical phrases; but so timidly has this been done that it is doubtful if it was discovered by the audience. The resources of the opera house in reproducing the scenes of chivalric life were commensurate with the music of the opera in its attempt to bring its spirit to the mind through the ear. It is more exciting to read of a tournament in Malory than to see a mimic one on the stage. It is true that there were men on horses who rode together three times, that a spear was broken, and that they afterward fought on foot; but they struck their spears together as if they had been singlesticks, instead of receiving each his opponent's weapon on his shield, and when the spear broke it was not all "toshivered." Then, when they had drawn their swords, they did not "lash together like wild boars, thrusting and foining and giving either other many sad strokes, so that it was marvel to see how they might endure," as the gentle Sir Thomas would doubtless have had them do. Still, the opera was enjoyed and applauded, as it deserved to be for the good things that were in it, and the Lily Maid had more lilies and roses and holly showered about her than she could easily pick up and carry away.

Miss Sybil Sanderson, who had gone to Paris from the Pacific Slope some years before, and had achieved considerable of a vogue, particularly in Massenet's operas, made her American début on January 16, 1895, in Massenet's "Manon," in which M. Jean de Reszke sang the part of the Chevalier des Grieux for the first time. The opera had been heard at the Academy of Music, in Italian, nine years before, and this was its first performance in the original French, a language which the fair débutante used with admirable distinctness and charmingly modulated cadences, a fact which contributed much to the pretty triumph which she celebrated after the first act. She did not maintain herself on the plane reached in this act. The second had scarcely begun before it became noticeable that she was wanting in passionate expression as well as in voice, and that her histrionic limitations went hand in hand with her vocal. But she was a radiant vision, and had she been able to bring out the ingratiating character of the music she might have held the sympathies of the audience, obviously predisposed in her favor, in the degree contemplated by the composer. This quality of graciousness is the most notable element in Massenet's music. As much as anything can do so it achieves pardon for the book, which is far less amiable than that of "Traviata," which deals with the same unlovely theme. Another quasi novelty was Saint-Saëns's "Samson et Dalila," which had one performance—and one only—on February 8th to afford Mme. Mantelli an opportunity to exhibit her musical powers, and Signor Tamagno his physical. The music was familiar from performances of the work as an oratorio; as an opera it came as near to making a fiasco as a work containing so much good and sound music could.

The most interesting event in the whole administration of Mr. Abbey and his associates happened on February 4th, when Verdi's "Falstaff" was presented. Signor Mancinelli conducted, and the cast was as follows:

```
Mistress Ford ..................... Mme. Emma Eames
Anne ............................... Mlle. de Lussan
Mistress Page ...................... Mlle. Jane de Vigne
Dame Quickly ....................... Mme. Scalchi
Fenton ............................. Sig. Russitano
Ford ............................... Sig. Campanari
Pistol ............................. Sig. Nicolini
Dr. Caius .......................... Sig. Vanni
Bardolph ........................... Sig. Rinaldini
Sir John Falstaff .................. M. Victor Maurel
        (His original creation.)
```

To construct operas out of Shakespeare's plays has been an ambition of composers for nearly two centuries. Verdi himself yielded to the temptation when he wrote "Macbeth" forty years ago. Probably no one recognized more clearly than he did when he wrote "Falstaff" how the whole system of lyrico-dramatic composition should undergo a transformation before anything like justice could be done to the myriad-minded poet's creations. Who would listen now to Rossini's "Otello"? Yet, in its day, it was immensely popular. A careless day it was—the day of pretty singing, and little else; the day when there was so little concern for the dramatic element in opera that the grewsome dénouement of Rossini's opera is said once to have caused a listener to cry out in astonishment: "Great God! the tenor is murdering the soprano!" Then it might have been possible for a composer, provided he were a Mozart, to find a musical investment for a Shakespearian comedy, but assuredly not for a tragedy. No literary masterpiece was safe from the vandalism of opera writers at that time, however, and Shakespeare simply shared the fate of Goethe and their great fellows. With the dawn of the new era there came greater possibilities, and now it may be said we have a few Shakespearian operas that will endure for several decades at least: let us say Nicolai's "Merry Wives of Windsor," Gounod's "Romeo and Juliet," Verdi's "Othello" and "Falstaff." Ambroise Thomas's "Hamlet" and Saint-Saëns's "Henry VIII" seem already to have outlived their brief day, at least in all countries save France, where the personal equation in favor of a native composer seems strong enough to keep second-class composers afloat while it permits genius to perish. As for Goetz's "Taming of the Shrew," it was too much like good Rhine wine, and too little like champagne to pass as a comic opera. When Verdi's last opera appeared the only Falstaff who had vitality was the fat knight of Nicolai's work. Yet he had had many predecessors. Balfe composed a "Falstaff" for the King's Theater in London, which was sung with the capacious-voiced Lablache in the titular part, and Grisi, Persiani, and Ivanoff in the cast. That was in 1838. Forty years earlier Salieri had composed an Italian "Falstaff" for Vienna. In 1856 Adolphe Adam produced a French "Falstaff" in Paris, and the antics of the greasy knight amused the Parisians eighty-six years earlier in Papavoine's "Le Vieux Coquet." Nicolai's predecessors in Germany were Peter Ritter, 1794, and Dittersdorf, 1796.

Verdi's return to Shakespearian subjects after reaching the fulness of his powers in his old age, and after he had turned from operas to lyric dramas, is in the highest degree significant of the thoroughness of the revolution accomplished by Wagner. The production of "Otello" and "Falstaff" created as great an excitement in Italy as the first performance of "Parsifal" did in Germany; and it must have seemed like the irony of fate to many that Wagner should have to be filtered through Verdi in order to bear fruit in the original home of the art form. But that is surely the lesson of "Otello," "Falstaff," and the fervid works of Leoncavallo, Mascagni, and Puccini.

Even more strikingly than "Otello" this comic opera of the youthful octogenarian disclosed the importance which Boito had assumed in the development of Verdi. That development is one of the miracles of music. In manner Verdi represents a full century of operatic writing. He began when, in Italy at least, the libretto was a mere stalking horse on which arias might be hung. All that he did besides furnishing vehicles for airs was to provide a motive for the scene painter and the costumer. Later we see the growth of dramatic characterization in his ensembles, and the development of strongly marked and ingeniously differentiated moods in his arias without departure from the old-fashioned forms. In this element lay much of the compelling force of his melodies, even those commonplace ones which were pricked for the barrel organ almost before the palms were cool which first applauded them—like "Di quella pira" and "La donna è mobile." Then set in the period of reflection. The darling of the public began to think more of his art and less of his popularity. Less impetuous, less fecund, perhaps, in melodic invention, he began to study how to wed dramatic situations and music. This led him to enrich his harmonies, and to refine his instrumentation, which in his earlier works is frequently coarse and vulgar in the extreme. At this stage he gave us "La Forza del Destino" and "Aïda." Now the hack writers of opera books would no longer suffice him. He had already shown high appreciation of the virtue which lies in a good book when he chose Ghislanzoni to versify the Egyptian story of "Aïda." But the final step necessary to complete his wonderfully progressive march was taken when he associated himself with Boito. Here was a man who united in himself in a creditable degree the qualifications which Wagner demanded for his "Artist of the Future"; he was poet, dramatist, and musician. No one who has studied "Otello" can fail to see that Verdi owes much in it to the composer of "Mefistofele"; but the indebtedness is even greater in "Falstaff," where the last vestige of the old subserviency of the text to the music has disappeared. From the first to the last the play is now the dominant factor. There are no "numbers" in "Falstaff"; there can be no repetition of a portion of the music without interruption and dislocation of the action. One might as well ask Hamlet to repeat his soliloquy on suicide as to ask one of the characters in "Falstaff" to sing again a single measure once sung. The play moves almost with the rapidity of the spoken comedy. Only once or twice does one feel that there is an unnecessary eddy in the current.

And how has this play been set to music? It has been plunged into a perfect sea of melodic champagne. All the dialogue, crisp and sparkling, full of humor in itself, is made crisper, more sparkling, more amusing by the music on which, and in which, it floats, we are almost tempted to say more buoyantly than comedy dialogue has floated since Mozart wrote "Le Nozze di Figaro." The orchestra is bearer of everything, just as completely as it is in the latter-day dramas of Richard Wagner; it supplies phrases for the singers, supports their voices, comments on their utterances, and gives dramatic color to even the most fleeting idea. It is a marvelous delineator of things external as well as internal. It swells the bulk of the fat knight until he sounds as if he weighed a ton, and gives such piquancy to the spirits of the merry women (Mrs. Quickly monopolizing the importance due to Mrs. Page), that one cannot see them come on the stage without a throb of delight. In spite of the tremendous strides which the art of instrumentation has made since Berlioz mixed the modern orchestral colors, Verdi has in "Falstaff" added to the variegated palette. Yet all is done so discreetly, with such utter lack of effect-seeking, that it seems as if the art had always been known. The flood upon which the vocal melody floats is not like that of Wagner; it is not a development of fixed phrases, though Verdi, too, knows the use of leading motives in a sense, but a current which is ever receiving new waters. The declamation is managed with extraordinary skill, and though it frequently grows out of the instrumental part, it has yet independent melodic value as the vocal parts of Wagner's "Die Meistersinger" have. Through this Verdi has acquired a comic potentiality for his voice parts which goes hand in hand with that of his instrumental parts.

But Verdi is not only dramatically true and melodious in his vocal parts, he is even, when occasion offers, most simple and ingenuous. There is an amazing amount of the Mozartian spirit in "Falstaff," and once we seem even to recognize the simple graciousness of pre-Gluckian days. Thus the dainty fancy and idyllic feeling which opens the scene in Windsor Forest, with its suggestion of fays and fairies and moonlight (a scene, by the way, for which Verdi has found entrancing tones, yet without reaching the lovely grace of Nicolai), owes much of its beauty to a minuet measure quite in the manner of the olden time, but which is, after all, only an accompaniment to the declamation which it sweetens. The finales of "Falstaff" have been built up with all of Verdi's oldtime skill, and sometimes sound like Mozart rubbed through the Wagnerian sieve. Finally, to cap the climax, he writes a fugue. A fugue to wind up a comic opera! A fugue—the highest exemplification of oldtime artificiality in music! A difficult fugue to sing, yet it runs out as smoothly as the conventional tag of Shakespeare's own day, whose place, indeed, it takes. It is a tag suggested by "All the world's a stage," and though it is a fugue, it bubbles over with humor.

CHAPTER XVIII
UPRISING IN FAVOR OF GERMAN OPERA

In marshaling, in the preceding chapter, the chief incidents of the period with which I am now concerned I set down the restoration of German performances at the Metropolitan Opera House as the most significant. There was a strong influence within the company working to that end in the person of M. Jean de Reszke, who, though the organization was not adapted to such a purpose, nevertheless strove energetically to bring about a representation of "Tristan und Isolde" in the supplementary spring season of 1895. Through him "Die Meistersinger" in an Italian garb had been incorporated into the repertory, and he was more than eager not only that it and the popular operas "Tannhäuser" and "Lohengrin" should recover their original estate as German works, but that he might gratify a noble ambition and demonstrate how the tragic style of "Tristan" could be consorted with artistic singing. He achieved that purpose in the season of 1895-96, and set an example that will long be memorable in the annals of the Wagnerian drama in America. But the force which compelled the reform was an external one. It came from the public. To the people, as they spoke through the box office, Abbey, Schoeffel & Grau were always readier to give an ear than the stockholders or the self-constituted champions of Italian opera in the public press.

There had been talk of a rival German institution when Mr. Abbey restored the Italian régime in 1891; but it was wisely discouraged by the more astute friends of the German art, who felt that the influence of seven years would bear fruit in time, and who placed the principles of that art above the language in which they were made manifest. The interregnum following the fire had led Mr. Oscar Hammerstein to enter the field as an impresario on a more ambitious scale than ordinary, and on January 24, 1893, he opened a Manhattan Opera House with a representation in English of Moszkowski's "Boabdil." The "season" lasted only two weeks, and the opera house has long since been forgotten. It stood in the same Street as the present Manhattan Opera House, and its site is part of that covered by Macy's gigantic mercantile establishment. Though he had no opposition, Mr. Hammerstein showed little of that pluck and persistence which have distinguished him during the two seasons in which he has conducted a rival establishment to the Metropolitan Opera House. After two weeks, within which he produced "Boabdil," "Fidelio," and some light-waisted spectacular things, he turned his theater over to Koster & Bial, who ran it as a vaudeville house until the end of its short career. There were English performances of the customary loose-jointed kind in the summer at the Grand Opera House, the first series of which, beginning in May, 1893, derived some dignity from the fact that it was under the management of Mr. Stanton, who had conducted the Metropolitan Opera House for the stockholders during the German seasons; and in November the Duff Opera Company anticipated Mr. Abbey's forces by bringing out Gounod's "Philémon et Baucis" in an English version.

These things, however, contained no portents for the future of opera in New York; they were the familiar phenomena which flit by in the metropolis's dead seasons. Pregnant incidents came in the midst of the regular season. It chanced that Mme. Materna, Anton Schott, Emil Fischer, and Conrad Behrens, who had been identified with the earlier German seasons, were in New York in February, 1894, and taking advantage of that fact Mr. Walter Damrosch arranged two performances of "Die Walküre," in the Carnegie Music Hall, for the benefit of local charities. They were slipshod affairs, with makeshift scenery and a stage not at all adapted for theatrical performances; but the public rose at them, as the phrase goes, and Mr. Damrosch felt emboldened to give a representation of "Götterdämmerung," with the same principals at the Metropolitan Opera House, on March 28th. Again there was an extraordinary exhibition of popular interest which the German Press Club turned to good account by improvising a performance of "Tannhäuser" for its annual benefit on April 9. Soon there was a great stir in the German camp, but united action was hindered by the rivalry between Mr. Damrosch and Mr. Seidl. The supplementary season at the Metropolitan ended on April 27th, and under date of April 28th there appeared a circular letter, signed individually by friends of Mr. Seidl, soliciting subscriptions for a season of German opera in 1904-05. The plan contemplated forty performances between November and May, on dates which were not to conflict with the regular performances of Italian and French opera. At the same time announcement was made of the organization of a Wagner Society, whose purpose it was to support a season of Wagner's operas at the Metropolitan Opera House, beginning on November 19, 1894, and continuing for four weeks—twelve evening performances and four matinées, the company to include "the greatest Wagnerian singers from Bayreuth and other German opera houses." Personal friends of the two conductors attempted to unite the rival enterprises, and a conference was held at the office of William Steinway. The attempt failed because Messrs. Seidl and Damrosch could not agree on a division of the artistic labors and credits. Mr. Seidl withdrew from the negotiations. In less than a week Mr. Damrosch announced that he had secured subscriptions for his season amounting to $12,000, and also a guarantee against loss of $10,000 more. On May 10th he sailed for Europe to engage his company. When he returned in the fall he announced a season of twelve evening and four afternoon performances, to be devoted wholly to Wagner's operas and dramas, to begin on February 25, 1895. The prices ranged from $4 for orchestra stalls to $1 for seats in the gallery. In his company were Rosa Sucher, Johanna Gadski, Elsa Kutscherra, Marie Brema, Max Alvary, Nicolaus Rothmühl, Paul Lange, Franz Schwarz, and Rudolph Oberhauser, besides Emil Fischer and Conrad Behrens, who had been identified with the earlier German regime. Adolf Baumann, of the Royal opera at Prague, was engaged as stage manager, but lost his life in the wreck of the North German Lloyd steamship Elbe on the voyage hitherward.

The season began, as advertised, on February 25th and ended on March 23d, the sixteen performances receiving an additional representation to enable Max Alvary to effect his one hundredth performance of Siegfried in the drama of that name in the city where he "created" it, as the French say. There were also an additional performance of "Lohengrin" and three extra performances at reduced prices after the subscription. The whole affair was Mr. Damrosch's own venture, he being at once manager, artistic director, and conductor, but, as I have intimated, he had the backing of an organization called the Wagner Society, which was chiefly composed of women. The season came hard on the heels of the Italian and French season. Mr. Damrosch's leading singers were familiar with Wagner's works, but practically he had to build up his institution from the foundation and to do it within an incredibly short time. With such rapid work we are familiar in America, but in Germany to have suggested such an undertaking as the organization of a company, the preparation of a theater, and the mounting, rehearsing, and performing of seven of the most difficult and cumbersome works in the repertory of the lyric drama within the space of five or six weeks would have been to have invited an inquest de lunatico. I do not wish to be understood as mentioning these things wholly in the way of praise—the results from an artistic point of view disclosed much too often that they were blameworthy—but what credit they reflect upon the tremendous energy, enterprise, and will power of Mr. Damrosch must be given ungrudgingly and enthusiastically. Plainly he was inspired with a strength of conviction quite out of the ordinary line of that spirit of theatrical speculation upon which we have so often depended for the large undertakings in music. It was a belief based on something like religious zeal, and under the circumstances what he did was an even more remarkable feat than that accomplished by his father in 1884. I sometimes thought at the time that he was driven into the enterprise more by impulse than by reason, and the fact that he occasionally had the same sort of a notion is evidenced by a letter which I received from him in response to one of mine to him near the close of the season. "Thanks for your congratulations on the financial success so far," wrote the young manager. "I shall breathe more freely after the next four weeks are over. The responsibility has been a heavy one, and it is curious that no one seemed to share my almost fatalistic belief in Wagner opera. Neither Abbey & Grau, nor Seidl, nor anyone was willing to touch it, and I was finally driven into it myself by an irresistible impulse which, so far, seems to have led me right. I am glad now, for many reasons, that events have so shaped themselves, and I think that the season will be productive of much good for the future. A curious and interesting fact in connection with the performances has been that the public came to hear the operas, and not the singers."

And such a success! Not only far in advance of what the fondest Wagnerites had dared to hope for as a tribute to their master's art, but one which compelled them to rub their eyes in amazement and grope and stare in a search for causes. Twenty-one times in succession was the vast audience room crowded, and when the time was come for striking the balance on the subscription season there was talk, only a little fantastic if at all, of receipts aggregating $150,000, or nearly $9,000 a performance. I should like to keep the thought of this unparalleled financial success separate from that of the artistic results attained. Between the financial and artistic achievements there was a wide disparity; but that fact only sufficed to emphasize the obvious lesson of the season, namely, the vast desire which the people of New York felt again to enjoy Wagner's dramas. Fortunately I can make a record of the capaciousness of that hunger without necessarily lauding its intelligence and discrimination. Great indeed must have been the hunger which could not be perverted by the vast deal of slipshod work in the scenic department of the representations, and the vaster deal of bungling and makeshift in the stage management. Many an affront was given to the taste and intelligence of the audiences, and dreadful was the choral cacophony which filled some of the evenings. Yet the people came; they came, as Mr. Damrosch observed in his letter, to hear the dramas instead of the singers, and though "Lohengrin" had been beautifully performed in the Italian season by artists like Nordica, Jean and Édouard de Reszke, and Maurel in the cast, the public crowded into the German representation as if expecting a special revelation from Fräulein Gadski, a novice, and Herr Rothmühl, a second-rate tenor, Of all the singers only Miss Marie Brema, a newcomer, and the veteran, Emil Fischer, were entirely satisfactory. For the beautiful dramatic art of Frau Sucher and for her loveliness of person and pose there was much hearty admiration, but this could not close the ears of her listeners to the fact that her voice had lost its freshness. The subscription repertory, including the Alvary anniversary, was as follows: "Tristan und Isolde," three times; "Siegfried," four times; "Lohengrin," twice; "Götterdämmerung," twice; "Tannhäuser," twice; "Die Walküre," twice, and "Die Meistersinger," twice. In a letter recently received from Mr. Damrosch he says: "My first spring season of thirteen weeks in New York, Chicago, Boston, and a few Western cities gave a profit of about $53,000, leaving me with a large stock of Vienna-made scenery, costumes, and properties."

Mr. Damrosch had won the first battle of his campaign and taught a lesson of lasting value to his old and experienced rivals. Warned by the success of his experiment and stimulated by a petition signed by about two thousand persons asking that German representations under Mr. Seidl be included in the Metropolitan scheme, Messrs. Abbey, Schoeffel & Grau made German opera a factor in the next season; but they did so in a half-hearted way, which defeated its purposes and brought punishment instead of reward. Nevertheless, German opera had returned to the Metropolitan to stay, and henceforth will call for attention along with the Italian and French performances in this history. Meanwhile, since I have begun it, let me finish the tale of the impresarioship of Mr. Damrosch.

Flushed with victory, the young manager prepared a five months' campaign for the year 1896, and sought for new worlds to conquer. Philadelphia, in which city he began operations on February 20th, treated him shabbily, but he did fairly well in New York and other cities in the East and West. Unfortunately for him, he made an invasion of the South, which was not ripe for serious opera, either financially or artistically. A performance in one city of that section which cost him over $3,000 brought him exactly $220. The difference between the sums was what Mr. Damrosch paid to learn that knowledge and love of Wagner's operas had not penetrated far into Tennessee.

Experience is always purchased at large cost in the operatic field. Abbey, Schoeffel & Grau refused Mr. Damrosch the use of the Metropolitan Opera House for his second New York season, and he was driven to the old, socially discredited Academy of Music. They did not look with favoring eyes upon an enterprise which had achieved so tremendous a triumph at its very start, and they provided a large percentage of the wormwood which filled the cup which Mr. Damrosch drank in 1896; but they embittered their own goblet by the procedure, and when the time came for laying out the campaign of 1896-97 they were quite as ready as Mr. Damrosch to sign a treaty of peace whose provisions promised to make for the good of both sides instead of the injury of either. The rivals agreed to keep out of each other's way as much as possible and even to help each other by an occasional exchange of singers. By this means it was purposed to widen the repertories of both companies, Mr. Damrosch providing the Metropolitan establishment with a Brünnhilde and an Isolde for Jean de Reszke's Siegmund, Siegfried, and Tristan, and the Metropolitan company lending him in return Melba, Eames, and Calvé, or others, to enable him to perform some of the Italian and French operas which he had included in his list. Mr. Damrosch yielded Chicago to his rivals and took Philadelphia in exchange. It was a wise compromise. Mr. Damrosch lost $40,000 in 1896; he made $14,000 in 1897. The next year, the Metropolitan Opera House being closed during the regular subscription period, as will appear later in this record, Mr. Damrosch entered into partnership with Charles A. Ellis, manager of the Boston Symphony Orchestra, who had undertaken the management also of Mme. Melba's American affairs, and Italian and French operas were added to the German repertory. The regular season showed a good profit, most of which, however, was frittered away in a spring tour made by Melba with a portion of the company. By this time Mr. Damrosch had concluded that he was too good a man and musician to surrender himself to the hateful business of managing a traveling opera company, and he withdrew from the partnership with Ellis, to whom he sold all his theatrical properties, and returned to concert work and composition, though for two weeks in the next season he was conductor of Mr. Ellis's company.

And now to some of the details of the artistic work of these Damroschian enterprises. The year 1896 was signalized by the appearance in America of two singers who rapidly achieved first-class importance. These were Katherina Klafsky and Milka Ternina. Mme. Klafsky was the wife of Herr Lohse, whom Mr. Damrosch also engaged as assistant conductor. She came here under a cloud, so far as the managerial ethics of Germany were concerned. How much respect those ethics were entitled to may be judged from the story. I have already said, in discussing the case of Mme. Lehmann and her violation of contract with the Opera at Berlin, that a speedy result of the success of German opera under Mr. Stanton was a change of attitude on the part of the Intendanten of German theaters toward the New York institution so soon as it was found that a handsome proportion of the American earnings might be diverted into the pockets of those Intendanten or the managers of municipal theaters. When Mr. Damrosch engaged his second company Mme. Klafsky was a member of the Municipal Theater in Hamburg, of which Pollini was director. When the offer of an American engagement came to her she consulted with Herr Pollini, who graciously gave his consent to her acceptance of it on condition that she pay him one-half of her earnings. She refused to agree to do this, and, fearing that Pollini would invoke the aid of the courts to restrain her from coming to New York, she took French leave of Germany more than two months before she was needed here. Her success in America was emphatic, and after she had effected a reconciliation with Pollini she was re-engaged by Mr. Damrosch to alternate with Mme. Lehmann in the season of 1896-97. Within a fortnight of the re-engagement she died in

Hamburg from a trephining operation undertaken to relieve her from the results of an injury to her skull, received while in America.

Mme. Klafsky and Mr. Alvary had sung in "Tristan und Isolde," with which Mr. Damrosch began his campaign in Philadelphia on February 20th. Her success was instantaneous, and her tremendous dramatic forcefulness, the natural expression of an exuberant temperament, placed her higher in public favor during the season than Mme. Ternina, whose refined and ingratiating art did not receive full appreciation till later. Other members of the Damrosch troupe of 1896 were Wilhelm Grüning, tenor, and Demeter Popovici, bass, beside Gadski, Fischer, Alvary, and other persons already known, but of smaller importance. The New York season began at the Academy of Music on March 2d and ended on March 28th. The operas were "Fidelio," "Lohengrin," "Siegfried," "Tannhäuser," "Die Meistersinger," "Die Walküre," "Der Freischütz," and (in the original English) Mr. Damrosch's "The Scarlet Letter." This opera had its first performance in New York on March 6. Its libretto was written by George Parsons Lathrop, a son-in-law of Hawthorne, who wrote the romance on which it was based. The cast included Johanna Gadski as Hester Prynne, Barron Berthald as Arthur Dimmesdale, Conrad Behrens as Governor Bellingham, Gerhard Stehmann as the Rev. John Wilson, and William Mertens as Roger Chillingworth. The greater part of the music had been performed at concerts of the Oratorio Society on January 4 and 5, 1895. The book of the opera proved to be undramatic in the extreme, a defect which was emphasized by the execrable pronunciation of nearly all the singers at the performance on the stage at the Academy. In the music Mr. Damrosch essayed the style of Wagner, and did it so well, indeed, as to deserve hearty admiration. He was helped, it is true, by factors frankly and copiously copied from the pages of his great model. The nixies of the Rhine peeped out of the sun-flecked coverts in the forest around Hester Prynne's hut, as if they had become dryads for her sake; ever and anon the sinister Hunding was heard muttering in the ear of Chillingworth, and Hester wore the badge of her shame on the robes of Elsa, washed in innocency. But such things are venial in a first work. In frankly confessing his model (for it cannot be thought for a moment that Mr. Damrosch expected his imitations to be overlooked) he illustrated a rule which applies to all composers at the outset of their careers. The fact must be noted, but it is much more to the purpose that the young composer blended the elements of his composition with a freedom and daring quite astonishing in their exhibition of mastery. There is no sign of doubt or timorousness anywhere in the work, though the moments are not infrequent when the utterance is more fluent than significant. The typical phrases which he chose to symbolize the persons and passions of the play are most of them deficient in plasticity, and nearly all of them lack that expressiveness which Wagner knew so well how to impress upon his melodic elements; the greater, therefore, was the surprise that Mr. Damrosch was able to weave them together in a fabric which moved steadily forward for more than an hour, and reflected more or less truthfully and vividly the feeling of the dramatic situations. Unfortunately there is little variety in this feeling, so that in spite of Mr. Damrosch's effort, or, perhaps, because of it, there is a deal of monotony in the music of the first act. There is a fine ingenuity of orchestration throughout, however, and an amount of daring in harmonization which sometimes oversteps the limits of discretion. In an agonizing scene between Chillingworth and Hester at the close of the first act the orchestra and the two chief personages are wholly engrossed with an exposition of the dramatic feeling of the moment, while the chorus (supposed to be worshiping in the neighboring meeting-house) sing the "Old Hundredth" in unison and without instrumental support. It is an admirable historical touch, and the device is the approved one of using a psalm tune as a cantus firmus to the remainder of the music; but Mr. Damrosch's harmonization of the ensemble is such that we seem to hear two distinct and unsympathetic keys. There was, after the second act, a scene upon the stage in honor of Mr. Damrosch, in which, after several large wreaths had been bestowed upon him, a representative of the Wagner Society came forward, and on behalf of that body presented him with a handsome copy of Hawthorne's story and the incorrect statement that the honor was paid to him as the first American who had composed a grand opera on an American theme which had been publicly produced. In this there were as many errors of statement as in the famous French Academician's description of a lobster. George F. Bristow's "Rip Van Winkle" was composed by a native American and was brought out at Niblo's Garden long before Mr. Damrosch was born in Breslau; while Signor Arditi, who hailed from Europe, like Mr. Damrosch, brought out under his own direction and with considerable success an opera entitled "La Spia," based on Cooper's novel. This merely in the interest of the verities of history.

The German season of 1907, a part of whose story I have already told, began at the Metropolitan Opera House on March 8th and lasted four weeks. It added no novelty to the local list, but had some interesting features, among them a serial performance of the dramas of Wagner's "Ring of the Nibelung," the first appearance of Mme. Nordica in the Brünnhilde of "Siegfried" on March 24th, and the joint appearance of Mmes. Lehmann and Nordica in "Lohengrin," the German singer, true to her dramatic instincts, choosing the part of Ortrud. On April 1st Xavier Scharwenka, who had taken a residence with his brother Philip in New York, borrowed the company from Mr. Damrosch and on his own responsibility gave a performance of his opera, entitled "Mataswintha." The opera was produced under difficulties. It had withstood its baptism of fire in Weimar seven months before, and Mr. Scharwenka had performed portions of it at a concert for the purpose of introducing himself to the people of New York. But the singers had to learn their parts from the beginning, there was a great deal of pageantry which had to be supplied from the stock furniture of the Metropolitan stage, the tenor Ernst Kraus took ill and caused a postponement, and even thus the chapter of accidents was not exhausted. When the performance finally took place Herr Stehmann, a barytone, had to sing Herr Kraus's part, which he had learned in two days. Under the circumstances it may be the course of wisdom to avoid an estimation of the opera's merits and defects and to record merely that it proved to be an extremely interesting work and well worth the trouble spent upon its production. Under different circumstances it might have lived the allotted time upon the stage, which, as the knowing know, is a very brief one in the majority of cases. The story of the opera was drawn from Felix Dahn's historical novel "Ein Kampf um Rom."

It is high time to get back again to the story of opera at the Metropolitan Opera House under the direction of the lessees; but before then chronological orderliness requires that attention be paid to an incident outside the category of prime importance. This was the first production in New York of Humperdinck's delightful fairy opera "Hänsel und Gretel" at Daly's Theater on October 8, 1895. The production was in English. The venture looked promising, and great interest was felt in it. Mr. Seidl was charged with the musical direction. A company of singers was brought together, partly from London, partly enlisted here. Sir Augustus Harris, director of the opera at Covent Garden, was the financial backer of the enterprise. As numerous an orchestra as the score calls for could not be accommodated in the theater, but Mr. Seidl did the best he could, and the band was commendable. Three of the singers, Miss Jeanne Douste, Miss Louise Meisslinger, and Mr. Jacques Bars, disclosed ample abilities; but the English manager had no knowledge either of the needs of the opera or the demands of the New York public; Sir Augustus's speech on the opening night, indeed, disclosed ignorance also of the name of the composer and the history of the work which he had clothed with considerable sumptuousness. It was long remembered with amusement that to him Herr Humperdinck was "Mr. Humperdinckel" and the opera some "beautiful music composed for this occasion." And so great expectations were disappointed, and, after worrying along from October 8th to November 15th, the opera was withdrawn with a record of failure, not deserved by the work and only partly deserved by the performance. We shall meet the opera again in the story of opera at the Metropolitan Opera House a decade later, when it came into its rights, and the public were able to testify their admiration in the presence of the composer.

The prospectus of Henry E. Abbey and Maurice Grau (which continued to be the official style of the managers) for the season 1895-96, contained this announcement: "The management has also decided to add a number of celebrated German artists and to present Wagner operas in the German language, all of which operas will be given with superior singers, equal to any who have ever been heard in the German language. The orchestra will be increased. . . . The chorus will be strengthened by a number of young, fresh voices, to which will be added an extra German chorus." Signor Mancinelli was not re-engaged as conductor, but Anton Seidl was. After what I have told thus far in this chapter the causes which led to this change of policy will be readily understood. The augmented company was a formidable host, though its strength remained in the French and Italian contingent. Had the German singers been equally capable, the story of Mr. Damrosch's enterprise might have read differently. Mme. Calvé returned and revived the furor over "Carmen"; Mesdames Melba, Nordica, Scaichi, Mantelli, and Messrs. Jean and Édouard de Reszke, Pol Plançon, Victor Maurel, and Castelmary remained; newcomers were Lola Beeth, Frances Saville, Marie Brema (who had been brought from Europe by Mr. Damrosch), Giuseppe Cremonini, Adolph Wallnöfer, Giuseppe Kaschmann (who had been a member of Mr. Abbey's first company twelve years before), and Mario Ancona. The regular subscription season consisted of thirteen weeks (fifty-two performances), beginning on November 18th, and there was a special subscription, at the same scale of prices, for a season of ten performances of German operas, beginning on December 5th. There were also performances at popular prices on Saturday evenings, and the entire season, excluding the spring season, which developed but little interest, compassed seventy-four representations. For these and thirteen Sunday night concerts the public paid about $575,000.

"Oh! how far are we from Covent Garden!" cried Jean de Reszke on the night of November 27th, and he clipped in his arms the friend who had come to offer his congratulations to the thunderous plaudits of the audience. M. de Reszke was in a fine glow of enthusiasm. He had sung and played Tristan and opened a new era in the style of Wagnerian performances in New York. A few days later, while the drinking horn was going from hand to hand at a medieval dinner given in honor of the principal interpreters of Wagner's love drama (Mme. Nordica, Miss Brema, the brothers de Reszke, and Mr. Seidl), he responded to a toast, and in four languages, English, German, French, and Italian, celebrated the advent of what he called "international opera." Why he neglected to throw in a few Polish phrases for the benefit of his countryman Paderewski, who sat opposite him at table, his hosts could not make out, unless it was because he wanted his expressions of delight at the achievement and prospect to be understood by all his hearers. High hopes filled the hearts of all local lovers of the lyric drama at the period. The promises of Abbey and Grau had stimulated the kindliest, heartiest, cheeriest feeling on all hands. All bickerings between the adherents of the various schools were silenced by the promulgation of a policy which seemed as generous and public-spirited as it was liberal. Whenever it was practicable New York was to have performances which should respect not only the tongue, but also the spirit of the works chosen for representation. That M. de Reszke had been an active agent in the inauguration of the new régime was an open secret to his acquaintances, and he bore public testimony when he supplemented his impersonation of Tristan with a German Lohengrin. The significance of such an act, coupled with Mme. Nordica's support of him in both performances, seemed extraordinary even in the minds of those who were not inclined to attach much importance to the language used in performance, so long as the performance was imbued with a becoming spirit of sincerity and a desire to make artistic purpose replace idle diversion. It looked as if through the example of these two artists, seconded by the liberality of the management, the people of New York were to take a long step forward in musical culture—a step toward the foundation of an institution which should endure and exemplify the esthetic, moral, and physical character of the people of America.

The expectations aroused by the announcement were woefully disappointed. There were nights of wondrous brilliancy and of extraordinary splendor in nearly every department. Some of the refulgence came from the new ambitions with which M. de Reszke and Mr. Seidl inspired the organization. The season had no prouder moments than those filled with the performances of "Tristan" and "Lohengrin" vouchsafed the subscribers to the regular subscription; but it had no deeper gloom than that which settled upon the subscribers to the special German season on most of the occasions set apart for them. The fate of "Fidelio" was utterly grievous; two representations of "Tristan" filled their souls with indignation instead of gratitude; there is no saintly intercession which could have won redemption for "Tannhäuser." The performances of "Tristan" and of the Italian "Lohengrin" at which Nordica, Brema, and the brothers de Reszke sang were brilliantly successful, but in each case the regular performance was made to precede that set apart for the German subscription. The circumstance would alone have sufficed to arouse suspicion that the management was at least willing to discriminate against the special Thursday nights, and the suspicion was wrought into conviction by the disparity between the performances of the two subscriptions. If it was the purpose of Abbey & Grau to put German opera on trial their method looked very unfair. "The drama for its own sake as an art work, and not for the sake of the singer" is a fundamental principle of German art, but it can only maintain its validity with the help of adequate performances. Saving the four singers who sang in Italian and French as well as German (Mme. Nordica, Miss Brema, and the brothers de Reszke), the German singers of 1895-96 were woefully inefficient, and the German season was an indubitable failure.

I shall append a list of performances of the operas presented in the seasons covered by this chapter and its predecessor, and its perusal will, I think, enforce even upon a careless reader the fact that, in spite of the shortcomings to which I have called attention, the administration of Abbey & Grau yet marked a gigantic step in the direction of dramatic sanity and sense over the lists which prevailed in the period when this story began. In the consulship of Mapleson the repertory might have been turned into verse quite as dramatic as most of that of the opera books. Thus:

"Favorita," "Puritani,"
"Lucia di Lammermoor,"
"Marta," "Linda di Chamouni,"
"La Traviata," "Trovatore";
"Il Barbiere di Siviglia,"
"Roberto il Diavolo,"
"Don Pasquale," "Rigoletto,"
"Faust," "Gli Ugonotti," "Un Ballo,"

and so on for quantity. Of the old hurdy-gurdy list "Favorita," "Traviata," "Trovatore," "Lucia," and "Rigoletto" were given, but unitedly they had only ten representations, and most of them were on Saturday nights, when popular prices prevailed. Even though Melba sang in "Lucia," it had to be consorted at the last with "Cavalleria," which Mme. Calvé made attractive. Against this fact we have the other that "Carmen" alone had a greater number of representations than the entire old-fashioned list, and that the operas which were most popular after it were "Tristan und Isolde," "Faust," and "Lohengrin."

Of the ten German performances three were devoted to "Tristan," two to "Tannhäuser," one to "Fidelio," two to "Lohengrin," and two to "Die Walküre." "Tristan," "Tannhäuser," and "Lohengrin" were in the repertory of the regular subscription season. Only two unfamiliar works were brought forward—Bizet's "Pêcheurs de Perles" (two acts only) and Massenet's "La Navarraise"; but there was an interesting revival of Boito's "Mefistofele" after a lapse of twelve years, and a more than interesting revival of "Tristan und Isolde," with Mmes. Nordica and Brema and the brothers de Reszke in the principal parts. Mme. Melba did not join the company until December 27th; she added Massenet's "Manon" to her repertory. Jean de Reszke increased the list of parts in which he was known by adding Tristan to it and the German Lohengrin. Mme. Nordica's new rôles were Isolde, Venus in "Tannhäuser," and Elsa in German. Miss Brema's operas were "Tristan," "Lohengrin," "Orfeo," "Aïda," and "Die Walküre," and, like Mme. Nordica, Mlle. Lola Beeth and Signor Kaschmann, she sang in German as well as Italian. "La Navarraise" was brought forward for Mme. Calvé on December 11, 1895; the two acts of "Les Pêcheurs de Perles" at a matinée on January 11, 1896.

Colonel Mapleson provided a prelude to the Metropolitan season of 1896-97 with a short season of Italian opera of the archaic sort at the Academy of Music. The doughty manager could no longer fly his old London colors, so he appeared as the sole director of "The New Imperial Opera Company." With two or three exceptions all his singers were strangers to the opera-goers of New York. Mme. Scalchi was again with him, and Signor de Anna; but the rest were newcomers. Among them were Mme. Hariclée-Darclée, Mme. Bonaplata-Bau, Susan Strong, and Mme. Giuseppina Huguet, sopranos; Mme. Parsi, Mlle. Ponzano, and Mme. Meysenheim, contraltos; Signori de Marchi, Randacio, Betti, Olivieri, and Durot, tenors; Signori Ughetto and Alberti, barytones, and Pinto, Terzi, Giordano, Borelli, and Dado, basses. The conductors, capable men both of them, were Signori Bimboni and Tango. Within a fortnight "Aïda," "Trovatore," "Traviata," "Les Huguenots," "Sonnambula," and "Faust" had been sung and a new work brought out. This was "Andrea Chenier," by Illica and Giordano, which had its first performance in America on November 13, 1896, the cast being as follows:

Andrea Chenier	Durot
Carlo Gerard	Ughetto
Maddalena di Coigny	Bonaplata-Bau
La Mulatta Bersi	Meysenheim
La Contessa di Coigny	Scalchi
Madelon	Parsi
Roucher	Dado
Il Romanziero	Alberti
Fouquier Tinville	—
Mathieu	Borelli
Un Incredibile | L'Abate, poeta |	Giordano
Schmidt, Carceriere a San Lazzaro	Terzi
Il Maestro di Casa	Olivieri
Dumas	Pinto

Tango conducted and the performance had a rude forcefulness quite in keeping with the character of the opera. Under better conditions "Andrea Chenier" would doubtless have held its own for a respectable space in the local repertory. But the seeds of dissolution were germinating in the company even before the performances began, and Colonel Mapleson did not dare to appear long in rivalry with the Metropolitan when it opened its doors on November 16th. In a week or so he went to Boston, where after one or two performances the orchestra went on strike and the Imperial Opera Company went to pieces. With it the last effort of the veteran manager. Mapleson had held out a promise of the likelihood that Giordano would come to New York to give personal superintendence to the production of his opera and carried his fiction to the extreme of telling a reporter of The Sun newspaper that the composer was in the city. Meeting the reporter in the Academy of Music, I expressed my doubt touching the correctness of his information, whereupon he pointed out the gentleman whom Colonel Mapleson had introduced to him as the composer. It was Giordano, the barytone! After its introduction to America "Andrea Chenier" disappeared for nearly a dozen years, when, on March 27, 1908, it had a single performance at the Manhattan Opera House, so that Mme. Eva Tetrazzini, the wife of Cleofonte Campanini, who had retired from the stage, might help at a gala representation in honor of her husband.

No season since the Metropolitan Opera House was opened was so full of vicissitudes as that of 1896-97. First came the death of Mme. Klafsky, who, under the reciprocal arrangement between Mr. Damrosch and Abbey & Grau, was to sing the chief Wagner rôles with Jean de Reszke. This happened in September, and was followed by the death of Mr. Abbey (nominally the leader of the managing directors, though from the beginning it was Mr. Grau who did the practical work of management), and of Mr. William Steinway, who had formulated and carried through the plan of reorganization which relieved the firm of Abbey, Schoeffel & Grau of its burden of indebtedness and transferred it to the shoulders of the Abbey, Schoeffel & Grau Company (Ltd.). Just before the season began Mme. Nordica, who had won her way to a high place in the favor of the public, and whose absence from the company's roster was widely and sincerely deplored, came forward with a story charging her failure to secure a reengagement to the intrigues of Mme. Melba and M. Jean de Reszke. So far as the gentleman was concerned the story seemed improbable on its face, and long before the season was over Mme. Nordica was willing to admit publicly that she had been misinformed as to the facts in the case. It remained, however, that Mme. Melba had reserved the exclusive right to herself to sing the rôle of Brünnhilde in Wagner's "Siegfried." It soon turned out that the failure to secure Mme. Nordica was to cost the management dear. Mme. Melba sang the part once, and so injured her voice that she had to retire for the season and cede the rôle to Mme. Litvinne (the Mlle. Litvinoff of Colonel Mapleson's company in 1885-86), who up to that time had not succeeded in convincing the public that she was equal to so great a responsibility, although she had been engaged to sing the part of

Isolde after Mme. Klafsky's death and the failure of negotiations between Mr. Grau and Mme. Nordica. The manager's judgment was never at fault in these negotiations; he wanted to secure the services of Mme. Nordica, for he well knew their value, but the unhappy contract with Melba stood in his way, and Mme. Nordica was beyond his reach when the failure of Melba's voice and her departure for France on January 23d left the company crippled. Happily the popularity which Mme. Calvé's impersonation of Marguerite in Gounod's "Faust" had found restored that perennial work to its old position as one of the principal magnets of the season. Mme. De Vere-Sapio was engaged to make possible the production of such operas as "Hamlet," "Le Nozze di Figaro," and Massenet's "Le Cid." Then there fell a double blow: Mme. Eames went into a surgeon's hands and Mozart's scintillant comedy had to be withdrawn. It was to have been given on February 10th. Flotow's "Martha" was substituted for it, and in the midst of the performance the representative of Tristan, M. Castelmary, fell on the stage, fatally stricken with heart disease.

It would be pleasant to say that the facts thus detailed exhaust the story of the institution's misfortunes; but they do not. I have already told of its financial outcome. Throughout the season a determined and wicked effort was made to injure the opera, and was helped along by columns of idle speculation and gossip in three or four newspapers. Without ground, so far as anybody could see, the notion was given publicity that there was grave doubt that opera would be given in the following year. The talk seemed wholly gratuitous, for if there were any signs of falling off in popular interest so far as the opera was concerned or in the confidence and satisfaction of the stockholders of the opera house company so far as Mr. Grau's administration was concerned, it escaped the notice of experienced and interested observers. The total attendance was larger than in the preceding season, and the interest displayed in the representations was fully as keen. But the newspaper gossips would have their way, and in the end turned out to be prophets, for there was no opera in 1897-98, for reasons which will have to be discussed in the next chapter.

The season began on November 16th. The regular subscription was for thirteen weeks, three nights a week and Saturday afternoons. Extra subscription performances were thirteen Saturday nights and three Wednesday afternoon representations at popular prices and an extra week—three nights and a matinée—at subscription prices. There were, therefore, in all, seventy-two performances, at which twenty-four different operas were brought forward, as shown in the table which is to follow. There was a less elaborate organization than in the preceding season, but the average merit of the performances was higher, there being no ill-equipped German contingent to spoil the record. There were, however, quite as many German performances without the special singers and the extra subscription. In place of the latter, an attempt was made to give extra Wednesday matinées, but the experiment was abandoned after three weeks.

The most sensational incident of the season was the collapse of Mme. Melba after her ill-advised effort to sing the music of Brünnhilde. To the loveliness of her devotion and the loftiness of her ambition honest tribute must be paid, but it must also be said that nature did not design her to be an interpreter of Wagner's tragic heroines. Her vocal and temperamental peculiarities put a bar to her singing the Brünnhilde music. It did not lie well in her voice, and she was not then, and is not now, of the heroic mould, and her experience should have taught her that her voice would not admit of the expansion necessary to fit her for that mould. That the music wearied her was painfully evident long before the end of the one scene in which Brünnhilde takes part in "Siegfried." Never did her voice have the lovely quality which had always characterized it in the music of Donizetti and Gounod. It lost in euphony in the broadly sustained and sweeping phrases of Wagner, and the difference in power and expressiveness between its higher and lower registers was made pitifully obvious. The music, moreover, exhausted her. She plunged into her apostrophe with most self-sacrificing vigor at the beginning of the scene, and was prodigal in the use of her voice in its early moments; but when the culmination of its passion was reached, in what would be called the stretto of the piece in the old nomenclature, she could not respond to its increased demands. It was an anti-climax. Wagner's music is like jealousy; it makes the meat it feeds on if one be but filled with its dramatic fervor. Recall what I have related of Mme. Lehmann's statement of how she was sustained by the emotional excitement which Wagner's dramas created in her, and how it made it easier for her to sing the music of Brünnhilde than that of Norma. But Mme. Lehmann was a woman of intense emotionality, and her voice was colored for tragedy and equal to its strain. It would be a happiness to say the same of Mme. Melba, but no judicious person would dream of saying it. "There is one glory of the sun, and another glory of the moon, and another glory of the stars; for one star differeth from another star in glory." Mme. Melba should have been content with her own particular glory.

Massenet's "Le Cid" was the only novelty of the season It was given on February 12, 1897, with the following distribution of parts:

Rodrigue (his original character) .... Jean de Reszke
Don Diégue (his original character) .... Édouard de Reszke
Le Roi .... Jean Lassalle
Le Conte de Gormas (his original character) .... Pol Plançon
St. Jacques |
L'Envoye Maure | .... Jacques Bars

Don Arras ………………………………….. Signor Corsi
Don Alonzo …………………………… Signor de Vaschetti
L'Infante …………………………….. Clementine de Vere
Chimène …………………………………….. Felia Litvinne

Conductor—Signor Mancinelli

The table of performances from 1893 to 1897 follows here:

PERFORMANCES IN REGULAR SUBSCRIPTION SEASONS

Operas 1893-94 1894-95 1895-96 1896-97

Opera	1893-94	1894-95	1895-96	1896-97
"Faust"	8	7	8	10
"Philémon et Baucis"	4	0	2	1
"Cavalleria Rusticana"	7	3	7	4
"Lohengrin"	5	5	6	6
"Lucia di Lammermoor"	2	3	3	2
"Hamlet"	1	0	2	1
"Roméo et Juliette"	5	4	4	5
"Orfeo"	1	0	1	0
"Pagliacci"	3	2	2	0
"Les Huguenots"	2	6	5	2
"Carmen"	12	7	11	7
"Don Giovanni"	1	3	0	3
"Rigoletto"	2	4	1	1
"Die Meistersinger"	3	0	1	3
"L'Amico Fritz"	2	0	0	0
"Semiramide"	3	1	0	0
"Tannhäuser"	2	0	3	3
"Le Nozze di Figaro"	3	0	0	0
"La Traviata"	1	1	2	3
"Guillaume Tell"	0	3	0	0
"Aïda"	0	3	4	3
"Il Trovatore"	0	3	2	2
"Otello"	0	4	0	0
"Mignon"	0	1	0	0
"Elaine" (Bemberg)	0	2	0	0
"Manon" (Massenet)	0	4	0	0
"Falstaff"	0	3	3	0
"Samson et Dalila"	0	1	0	0
"Tristan und Isolde"	0	0	6	2
"L'Africaine"	0	1	0	1
"La Favorita"	0	0	2	2
"La Navarraise"	0	0	4	0
"Fidelio"	0	1	0	0

"Die Walküre" 0 0 2 0
"Les Pêcheurs de Perles" 0 0 1 0
"Mefistofele" 0 0 2 4
"Martha" 0 0 0 2
"Siegfried" 0 0 0 6
* "Werther" 0 0 0 1
"Le Cid" 0 0 0 2

* "Werther" had a single performance in the supplemental season of 1893-94.

CHAPTER XIX
BEGINNING OF THE GRAU PERIOD

From 1896 to the end of the season 1902-03 Maurice Grau was in name as well as in fact the monarch of the operatic world of America. For a brief space he also extended his reign to Covent Garden, but the time was not ripe for that union of interests between London and New York which has so long seemed inevitable, and his foreign reign was short. So was his American dictatorship; but while it lasted it was probably the most brilliant operatic government that the world has ever known from a financial point of view, and its high lights artistically were luminous in the extreme. At the end of the period Mr. Grau had retired from operatic management forever, for though his desire to remain in active employment was intense, his mental powers unweakened, and his will strong, his health was hopelessly shattered, and before another lustrum had passed he had gone down to his death, his last thoughts longingly fixed on the institution which had brought him fame and fortune in abundant measure. For several years he had maintained a beautiful summer home at Croissy-Chatou, on the Seine, about ten miles from Paris. He died in the French capital on March 14, 1907, of a disease of the heart which had compelled his abandonment of active managerial life.

Mr. Grau was an Austrian by birth, his birthplace being Brünn; but he was brought to New York by his parents in 1854, when he was five years old, and all his education and business training was American. He passed through the classes of the city's public schools and was graduated from the Free Academy, now the College of the City of New York, in 1867. He then entered the Law School of Columbia College, and read law in the office of Morrison, Lauterbach & Spitgarn. His uncle, Jacob Grau, was an operatic and theatrical manager, and for him, as a boy, he sold librettos in his opera house. This opened the way into theatrical life, which proved to have such fascinations and hold such promises that he abandoned the law without having sought admission to the bar, and in 1872 also abandoned the service of his uncle and embarked on his career as manager. In association with Charles A. Chizzola, the joint capital amounting to $1,500, he engaged Aimée, a French opéra bouffe singer, who had made a hit two years before at the Grand Opera House, for a season of seven weeks. His first week, in Bridgeport, Conn., paid the expenses of the entire engagement. Aimée came to America again and again, and always under Mr. Grau's management. The same year he managed the American tours of Rubinstein and Henri Wieniawski, both of whom came to America with the financial backing of Messrs. Steinway & Sons. It was before the days of phenomenal honoraria. Rubinstein was content with $200 a concert, and in eight months his energetic young manager had cleared $60,000 on his engagement alone. The next year he organized the Clara Louise Kellogg Opera Company, continued his management of Mlle. Aimée, and brought to America the Italian tragedian, Tommaso Salvini. In 1874 he managed three opéra bouffe and operetta companies, besides Adelaide Ristori, and became lessee of the Lyceum Theater, in Fourteenth Street. There was a season of financial stress, and in 1875 he severed his connection with Chizzola, after another period of bad luck. In 1876 he gave concerts, directed by Offenbach, in the Madison Square Garden, which were a failure, but he recouped his losses from a forfeit of $20,000, which the Italian Rossi paid to him rather than give up a successful season in Paris. A highly successful tour of seventeen months in South America, Cuba, and Mexico with an opéra bouffe troupe, headed by the tenor Capoul, and Paola Marié continued his successes. In 1883 began his association with Messrs. Abbey and Schoeffel, whose experiences, together with his own, at the Metropolitan Opera House have repeatedly formed the subject of discussion in these chapters of operatic history.

The story of the management of the Metropolitan Opera House ended in Chapter XVII with an account of the disasters which overtook Abbey, Schoeffel, and Grau in 1897. Before the end of that season Mr. Grau announced, what had frequently been hinted at in the newspapers, that though he should obtain a lease of the opera house he would not give opera in 1897-98. The announcement had been received with incredulity, for though misfortune had overtaken the managers in Chicago and some of their other enterprises had been unfortunate, the New York season had turned out in all things successful. Besides, though, "Perjuria ridet amantum Jupiter," the public had long before learned to laugh at the oaths of managers. It turned out, however, that Mmes. Melba and Eames, who had become favorites of the stockholders, were not available for the next season, and the directors, who had learned to have confidence in Mr. Grau, were willing to let him make the experiment of a year of famine. As it turned out it cost them nothing except the performances, and Mr. Grau and the friends who had rallied around him very little money. The annual rental of $52,000 was made up to them by sub-rentals of the building to other managers, chiefly to Messrs. Ellis and Damrosch. Meanwhile the year of quiescence was put to a good purpose in strengthening the hold which Mr. Grau had resolved to obtain on opera in London as well as New York. Mr. Grau and his friends organized the Maurice Grau Opera Company and easily obtained a lease of the Metropolitan for three years and a release from the bankrupt corporation, Abbey, Schoeffel & Grau (Ltd.). On May 4th the old company accepted a report which recited the story of the season

1896-97, recommended that it go out of business, and released Messrs. Schoeffel and Grau from an obligation which they had entered into with the company not to engage in opera management. All that remained for it to do was to realize on the only valuable asset which it owned—the Tremont Theater, in Boston. This it soon did by selling the property to Mr. Schoeffel, who has managed it ever since.

The way now being open, Mr. Grau organized his new company, composed wholly of his friends. These were Edward Lauterbach, Charles Frazier, Robert Dunlap, Roland F. Knoedler, Henry Dazian, B. Franklin de Frece, F. W. Sanger, John W. Mackay, Sr., and Frederick Rullman. The capital stock, paid up, was $150,000, of which the Metropolitan Opera and Real Estate Company subscribed to $25,000. Mr. Grau was elected president and general director, Mr. Lauterbach vice-president, and Mr. Frazier treasurer. Mr. Sanger was made associate manager, with the specific duty of looking after the affairs of the house itself, and Mr. Ernest Goerlitz was appointed secretary.

There was no regular subscription at the opera house in the season of 1897-98, but the public were not without comfort. From January 17 to February 19, 1898, the Damrosch and Ellis company gave a series of performances which provided an excellent substitute. Opera-lovers were not even called on to forego the pleasure of hearing some of the singers whom they had come to consider essential to their happiness under the régime of Damrosch and Ellis's rivals. Mme. Melba was "not available" for Mr. Grau, but she was for Mr. Ellis, who was managing all her American business, and she headed the company. With her were Mme. Nordica and Mme. Gadski, and among old popular favorites were Emil Fischer and David Bispham. Other members of the company were Gisela Staudigl, who had been heard in the first German seasons; Mlle. Seygard, Mme. Brazzi, an American contralto with good presence, real warmth of feeling, and correct instincts; Miss Mattfeld, an extremely serviceable "juvenile," who remained such for years; Salignac and Rothmühl, tenors respectively for the Italian and German operas; Campanari, barytone; Ibos, a tenor, and Boudouresque, a bass whose name was picturesque. Melba added "Traviata" to her repertory at the opening performance, and later essayed "Aïda," only to prove, as she had done in the case of "Siegfried," that there are things in music which are unlike the kingdom of heaven in that they cannot be taken by violence. The repertory consisted of "La Traviata," "Tannhäuser" "Die Meistersinger," "Aïda," "Lohengrin," "Il Barbiere," "Faust," "Der Fliegende Holländer," "Die Walküre," "Siegfried," "Götterdämmerung," and "Les Huguenots."

Before the next regular season began under the new Grau administration Mr. Seidl, who would doubtless have continued in association with the institution with which he had long and efficiently been connected, died. The temporary suspension of the Metropolitan subscription season had forced him more actively than ever into the concert field. He had succeeded Mr. Theodore Thomas as conductor of the Philharmonic Society, and continued the popular triumphs of that organization. He had also organized a series of subscription orchestral concerts at the Hotel Astoria, and his friends were developing plans for a new endowed orchestra when he died, after an illness of only a few hours' duration, supposed to have been caused by ptomaine poisoning. This was on the night of March 28, 1898. His body was cremated after an imposing public funeral at the Metropolitan Opera House on March 31st, participated in by the Musical Mutual Protective Union, Männergesangverein Arion, the Philharmonic Society, German Liederkranz, the Rev. Merle St. Croix Wright, who delivered the memorial address, and Mr. H. E. Krehbiel, chairman of the committee of arrangements, who read a despatch received from Robert G. Ingersoll, who was absent from the city on a lecture trip. The pall-bearers were A. Schueler (who had been a classmate of the dead man at the Leipsic Conservatory); Oscar B. Weber, E. Francis Hyde (president of the Philharmonic Society); Henry Schmitt, Albert Stettheimer, Henry T. Finck (musical critic of The New York Evening Post); Walton H. Brown, Louis Josephtal, H. E. Krehbiel (chairman of the committee of arrangements and musical critic of The New York Tribune); Xavier Scharwenka, August Spanuth (musical critic of the New Yorker Staats-Zeitung); Albert Steinberg (sometime musical critic of The New York Herald); the Hon. Carl Schurz, Charles T. Barney, Rafael Joseffy, Julian Rix, James Speyer, Edgar J. Levey (musical, critic of The New York Commercial Advertiser); Dr. William H. Draper, Richard Watson Gilder, Paul Goepel, E. M. Burghard, Eugene Ysaye, Victor Herbert, George G. Haven, Zoltan Doeme, Edward A. MacDowell, and Carlos Hasselbrink.

Concerning Mr. Seidl's career I have already spoken at some length in these chapters; it will be long before those who knew him intimately will cease to talk about his personal characteristics, and to tell anecdotes which illustrate those characteristics. He was one of those strong personalities that give an interest to all manner of incidents, even the commonplace. Like Moltke, he could hold his tongue in seven languages; but it is a fact that all his friends must have observed that his taciturnity never made his company any the less entertaining. Moreover, when the mood was on him, he could talk by the hour, and then his reminiscences of the years spent in the household of Wagner or the story of his experiences while carrying the gospel of Wagner through Europe were full of fascination. But the talkative mood seldom came when a crowd was about him. He was indifferent to the many and fond of the few; so his circle of intimate friends never grew large in spite of the multitudes who sought his acquaintance, and though no combination of circumstances could disturb his self-possession he seemed to be most contented and comfortable when seated quietly with a single friend. Even under such circumstances he could sometimes sit for minutes at a time without speaking himself or expecting a word from his companion, yet never show a sign of weariness or ennui. In this particular he was something like Schumann, of whom it is related that once he spent an hour with a bright young woman to whom he was fondly attached without speaking a word. Knowing his peculiarities, she too remained silent, and was rewarded for her self-restraint when he departed by hearing him say that the hour had been one in which they had perfectly understood each other. Seidl's hero, Wagner, was the very opposite of Schumann in this particular, and there is a story which indicates that he must frequently have been amused at his pupil's reticence. Coming to a rehearsal once he found that Seidl had taken a cold which had robbed him completely of his voice, so that he could give no instructions to the musicians. Wagner laughed immoderately, and with mock seriousness upbraided him for his bad habit of talking too much, which had now brought him to the pass where he could not talk at all.

Seidl's epistolary habits were like his conversational—he wrote as little as he talked; but as the talking fit sometimes seized him, so did the writing fit. Then he could devote hours to a letter which had the proportions and sometimes the style of a formal essay. On such occasions he was so prone to drop into a pulpit manner that I once taxed him with it and asked an explanation. He paused for a moment and then smilingly made a sort of half-confession that he had once been destined for the priesthood. His Scriptural illustrations and "preachy" manner were relics which had clung to him from that early day. They were the only academic traces about him, however. It is doubtful if any of his friends ever heard him discuss a question in the theory or history of music. How far his exact knowledge in the art went may not be said; but one thing is certain—his practical knowledge embraced every measure of Wagner's works.

He seldom spoke of his conservatory days at Leipsic, and then generally in a spirit of amusement. Complimented once by me on the excellence of his pianoforte playing, he said: "Oh, I made quite a stir at a conservatory examination once with Mendelssohn's 'Rondo Capriccioso.' I was to be a pianist." That he could have been trained into a virtuoso of merit I can easily believe, for without paying much regard to the graces of pianoforte playing he yet had a remarkable command of those tone qualities which are so helpful in expressive playing. He was always eloquent at the pianoforte, especially when playing excerpts from the dramas of Wagner. Then his performances were peculiarly full and orchestral, a fact largely due to the circumstance that he never confined himself to pianoforte arrangements, but preferred to play from the orchestral score. That he appreciated the importance of giving consideration to the peculiarities of instrumental media he illustrated once when at a private rehearsal of music for one of my Wagnerian lectures, at which he had intended to play, but had been prevented by a sudden duty-call at the opera, he quickened the tempo considerably for the pianist beyond that heard at his own readings of the opera, and added in explanation: "Nie langweilig werden am Clavier!" ("One must never be tedious at the pianoforte!")

A few first representations of operas in this period outside of the Metropolitan Opera House call for brief mention, if not for the sake of the excellence of the productions, at least for the sake of completeness in the record. Thus on May 16, 1898, a company of Italian singers, some of whom had been singing in Mexico, some in South America, some in San Francisco—the sort of a gathering that, I think, I have described in these pages as New York's ordinary summer operatic flotsam and jetsam—gave in Wallack's Theater the first representation of Puccini's "La Bohème" which New Yorkers heard in their own city. The company was first announced as the Baggetto Grand Italian Opera Company, which was probably its official style in Mexico. In New York a hoary device of juggling with the name of Italy's chief opera house was resorted to, and it was called the Milan Royal Opera Company, of La Scala. Under either title the company proved itself capable of a deal of stressful and distressful singing, though a good impression was made by Giuseppe Agostini, a youthful tenor, and Luigi Francesconi, a barytone. "La Bohème" was performed on the opening night of the company's brief season (it made shipwreck according to rule within four or five days), with the following distribution of parts:

```
Mimi ........................ Linda Montanari
Musetta ..................... Cleopatra Vincini
Rodolfo ..................... Giuseppe Agostini
Marcello .................... Luigi Francesconi
Schaunard ................... Giovanni Scolari
Alcidero |
Benoit | ................... Antonio Fumagalli
Parpignol .................. Algernon Asplandi
```

Needless to say that scant justice was done to the play and score of "La Bohème" by the vagrant singers, and that the good opinion which the opera won later was shared by few among critics, lay and professional. After ten years of familiar acquaintance with the work, I like it better than I did at first, but it has not yet taken a deep and abiding place in my affections. I see in it, however, an earnest and ingenious effort to knit music, text, and action closer together than it was the wont of Italian composers to do before the advent of Wagner set Young Italy in a ferment. Music plays a very different rôle in it than it does in the operas of Donizetti, Bellini, and the earlier Verdi. It does not content itself with occasionally proclaiming the mood of a situation or the feelings of a conventional stage person. It attempts to supply life-blood for the entire drama; to flow through its veins without ceasing; to bear along on its surface all the whims, emotions, follies, and incidents of the story as fast as they appear; to body them forth as vividly as words and pantomime can; to color them, vitalize them, arouse echoes and reflections of them in the hearts of the hearers. But this it can do only in association with other elements of the drama, and when these are presented only in part, and then crudely and clumsily, it must fail of its purpose. And so it happens that Puccini's music discloses little of that brightness, vivacity, and piquancy which we are naturally led to expect from it by knowledge of Mürger's story, on which the opera is based, and acquaintance with the composer's earlier opera, "Manon Lescaut." One element the two works have in common: absence of the light touch of humor demanded by the early scenes in both dramas. However, this is a characteristic not of Puccini alone, but all the composers in the Young Italian School. They know no way to kill a gnat dancing in the sunlight except to blow it up with a broadside of trombones. Puccini's music in "La Bohème" also seems lacking in the element of characterization, an element which is much more essential in comedy music than in tragic. Whether they are celebrating the careless pleasures of a Bohemian carouse or proclaiming the agonies of a consuming passion, it is all one to his singers. So soon as they drop the intervallic palaver which points the way of the new style toward bald melodrama they soar off in a shrieking cantalena, buoyed up by the unison strings and imperiled by strident brass until there is no relief except exhaustion. Happy, careless music, such as Mozart or Rossini might have written for the comedy scenes in "La Bohème," there is next to none in Puccini's score, and seldom, indeed, does he let his measures play that palliative part which, as we know from Wagner's "Tristan" and Verdi's "Traviata,"—to cite extremes,—it is the function of music to perform when enlisted in the service of the drama of vice and phthisis.

On October 10, 1898, another band of strolling singers, which endured for a week at the Casino, also performed "La Bohème," and the Castle Square Opera Company of Henry W. Savage gave it in English at the American Theater on November 28th of the same year. It did not reach the Metropolitan Opera House until the season 1900-01.

Stockholders and subscribers of the Metropolitan Opera House having endured their year of privation, which, as we have seen, was not without its moments of refreshment, Mr. Grau opened the regular subscription season 1898-99 on November 29th. Its incidents of special interest were not many.

One was the return of Mme. Sembrich, who made what Mr. Sutherland Edwards called Rosina's "double entry" in Rossini's "Barber" on the second night of the season—November 31st. On the third night Mme. Melba, who sang by the courtesy of Mr. Ellis, appeared in "Roméo et Juliette." There were first appearances of several artists whose names became fixed in the prospectuses for some years to come: Mme. Ernestine Schumann-Heink as Ortrud in "Lohengrin" on January 9, 1899; Ernest Van Dyck as Tannhäuser on the opening night; Albert Saléza as Romeo on December 2, 1898; Suzanne Adams as Juliet on January 4, 1899; Anton Van Rooy as Wotan in "Die Walküre" on December 14, 1898. Mr. Franz Schalk, the conductor engaged for the German operas in place of Mr. Seidl, who had taken part with Mr. Grau in the summer season at Covent Garden and been engaged for the New York season that was to follow, introduced himself to New York on the same occasion.

Of acquaintances, more or less old, there were in the company besides Mmes. Sembrich, Eames, Lehmann, Nordica, and Mantelli, Miss Meisslinger, Miss Pevny, Frances Saville, Mr. Bispham, Mr. Dippel (who had been a member of the last German company in 1890-91), Pol Plançon, and Adolph Mühlmann. Newcomers besides those mentioned were Matilde Brugière, Herman Devries (son of Mme. Rosa Devries, a dramatic singer of renown half a century before), Henri Albers, barytone, and Lemprière Pringle, an English singer, who had worked himself up in the ranks of the Carl Rosa Opera Company. The two brothers, Jean and Édouard de Reszke, whom New York had come to look upon as indispensable to perfect enjoyment, were also members of the company. There were two cyclical performances of "The Ring of the Nibelung" to keep good Wagnerites in countenance, but Mr. Grau made his popular hit by a repetition of the device which had been successful before with "Faust"—he gave "Les Huguenots" with an "ideal cast." The device was simple, but it served. Meyerbeer's opera had been given three times, when on February 20th he announced it with Mme. Sembrich in the cast, and an all-'round advance on prices on the basis of $7, instead of $5, for orchestra chairs.

Only one novelty was produced in the season. This was Signor Mancinelli's "Ero e Leandro," which had its first American performance on March 10, 1899, with the composer in the conductor's chair. The principal singers were Mme. Eames (Hero), Saléza (Leander), and Plançon (Ariofarno). Mme. Schumann-Heink was set down to sing the prologue, but illness prevented at the first representation, and the music was sung by Mme. Mantelli. The opera had a pretty success and back of it was an interesting history. Boito wrote the libretto for himself, but put it aside when the subject of "Mefistofele" took possession of his mind. Two of the numbers, which he had already composed, found their way into the score of the later opera, one of them being the beautiful duet, "Lontano, lontano, lontano," in the classical scene. Boito turned the book over to Bottesini, who composed it, but failed to make a success of it. Signor Mancinelli then took the libretto in hand and, having a commission from the Norwich (England) festival of 1896 for a choral work, he composed it and handed it in to be sung as a cantata. It was sung at the festival. The next year it received its first stage performance at Madrid and by way of Turin and Venice reached Covent Garden, London, where it was produced on July 15, 1898.

What a simple tale it is that has so twined itself around the hearts of mankind that it has lived in classic story for ages and gotten into the folk-tales of more than one European people! Hero is a priestess of Aphrodite, who lives at Sestos, on the Thracian coast; Leander, a youth, whose home is at Abydos, on the Asiatic shore, beyond the Hellespont. The pair meet at a festival of Venus and Adonis and fall in love with each other at sight. The maiden's parents are unwilling that she shall cease her sacred functions to become a wife, and Leander swims the strait every night, while Hero holds a torch at the window to direct him to her side. One night there arises a tempest and Leander is drowned, and his body cast up at the foot of the tower. Then Hero throws herself upon the jagged rocks beside him, and the lovers are united in death.

"That tale is old, but love anew
May nerve young hearts to prove as true,"

sang Byron after he had put discrediting doubts to shame by swimming the Hellespont himself and catching an ague for his pains. A simple tale, yet I have included more than is ordinarily found in the recital in order to show how Boito utilized and added to it. A simple tale, but with what lovely fervor have the poets sung it over and over again! Byron could smile at his own Quixotic feat in the lines which he wrote six days after its accomplishment, but in "The Bride of Abydos" he did not attempt to conceal the affection which he felt for the tale, or his pride in the fact that Helle's buoyant wave had borne his limbs as well as Leander's; and who can without emotion call up Keats's picture of

"Young Leander, toiling to his death,"

pursing his weary lips for Hero's cheek and smiling against her smiles until he sinks, and

"Up bubbles all his amorous breath"?

Right nobly, too, did Schiller hymn the lovers and two centuries of opera-writers—Italian, French, German, English, and Polish—have sought to weave their pitiful story into lyric dramas.

Boito, as I have said, wrote the book of "Ero e Leandro" for himself, but eventually gave it to others. I can only speculate as to the cause of Boito's abandonment of his intellectual child. Probably he concluded that it lacked the dramatic elements which the composers of the last few decades, paying tribute, willingly or unwillingly, to Wagner's genius, have felt to be necessary to the success of a lyric drama. But dramatic action need not always be summed up in movement. Wagner's greatest tragedy has scarcely more external incident than "Ero e Leandro," and, indeed, is like this opera, in that the interest in each of its three acts centers in a meeting of the lovers and their publication of the play enacting on the stage of their hearts. But it takes music like Wagner's, music surcharged with passion, to body forth the growth of the dramatic personages and make us blind to paucity of incident. When that cannot be had, then pictures and functions of all kinds, solemn and festive, must be relied on to hold the interest. Boito built up such pictures and grouped such functions about his simple tale with a great deal of ingenuity. The eye is charmed at once with his classic landscapes in the first act—the cypresses, myrtles, and blooming oleanders, the temple portico, the statues and altar with its votive offerings, the kneeling chorus of priestesses and sailors, Hero with her ravishing robes (think of Mme. Eames in the part), the gallant Leander and the stately archon Ariofarno. It is the scene of the lovers' meeting at the festival, and to heighten its interest and provide something else than hymns and rites, Boito has turned Leander into a victor in the Aphrodisian games, both as swordsman and cytharist. Hero crowns him with laurel, and he sings two odes, which Boito cleverly borrows from Anacreon, the first without, the second with implied, but not expressed credit. The odes are the most familiar of Anacreon's odes, however, and no one could think of moral obliquity in connection with Boito's use of them. They are the address to the lyre which the poet wishes to attune to heroic measures, but which answers only in accents of love; and the tale of how the poet took Eros, shivering, out of the cold night and received a heart wound in return. Charmingly, indeed, do the odes fit into the dramatic scheme and offer two set pieces as a contrast to the solemn pronouncements of the archon and the excessive hymning of the chorus.

The development of the plot is now begun. Boito has created Ariofarno to fill the place of the wicked nun of the German folk-tales. He is obsessed with guilty love for Hero and seeks to divert her service from the celestial Venus to the earthly. She scorns his offers of love, and he leaves her with threats of vengeance. Filled with forebodings, she seeks an omen in the voice of a sea shell which had been placed on the altar of Aphrodite, the Sea-born. The words are charming, and the occasion prettily prepared for a vocal show piece. She invokes the shell as the cradle of Aphrodite, hears in its murmurs the song of the sea nymphs, the humming of bees amid the oleander's aeolian whispers, and the soft confessions of a mermaid. Then the sounds grow wild, and stimulate her fancy to a picture of rushing waters, flying foam, and wrathful surge—the vision which is realized in the last act. Here the suggestion for musical delineation is obvious, and Signor Mancinelli has utilized it in such a manner as to make his song (which, for reasons that I shall not pursue, awakened memories of the ballatella in "Pagliacci") the first really triumphant thing in the opera. The rest of the act is chiefly devoted to a love duet, at the close of which Hero, kneeling before the statue of the god, invokes Apollo to admonish her of her fate. Ariofarno, in concealment, answers for the god: "Death!"

In the second act, which plays in the part of the temple of Aphrodite devoted to the mysteries, Ariofarno carries out his plan of vengeance against Hero. Professing to have received an oracular command to that effect, he restores a service in an ancient town by the sea and to it consecrates Hero, who is powerless to resist his will. The duty of the priestess is to give warning of approaching storms, so that by priestly rites the angry waters may be placated. While pronouncing her sentence he, in an aside, offers to save her if she will accept his love. Again he is spurned, and when he utters the words which condemn her to the vigil Leander seeks to attack him. For this he is seized and banished to the Asian shore. Hero takes the oath, the dancers rush in and begin a bacchanalian, or Aphrodisian, orgy, while the chorus sings the "Io paean." Here Signor Mancinelli has really written with a pen of fire. The music is tumultuously exciting, though built on the learned forms, and there is the happiest union of purpose and achievement. In the last act, somewhat clumsily set and unnecessarily ambitious in its strivings for spectacular realism, the dénoument is reached. Songs of sailors come up from the sea; Hero sings her love and longing and lights her lover to his fate. Their love duet is interrupted by the bursting of the tempest, which had come upon them without being observed. The warning trumpet which she should have sounded is heard from the vaults below, and the chant of the approaching priests. Leander throws himself into the sea; the archon upbraids Hero for neglect of duty and discovers its cause. Her punishment, death, will be his vengeance, but the lifeless body of Leander is hurled upon the rocks, and comes into view when a thunderbolt tears away a portion of the tower wall. Hero sinks dead to the ground; the archon rages at the escape of his victim, and an invisible choir sings of a reunion of the lovers in death.

As a composer Signor Mancinelli is an eclectic. It would not be easy to specify any particular master as a model. He admires Wagner and has proper appreciation of the dramatic values, the continuity of idea, and the effect of development which flow from the recurrent use of significant phrases; but his manner is not at all that of the later Wagner whose influence, if found at all, must be sought in a few harmonic progressions and in a belief in the potency of orchestral color. Nearer to him than the master poet-musician are Verdi, Ponchielli, Boito, and the eager spirits of Young Italy. His music is as free as the later Verdi's from the shackles of set forms, but he is, nevertheless, at his best when the book permits an extended piece of lyric writing. This being so, it is disappointing that he has done so little that is good in the opening scene where the book invited him to consult the wants of the Norwich festival and to write in the cantata style. In the first act, however, there is little to praise outside of the settings of the two Anacreonic odes and the song to the shell. There is much striving, but a paucity of plastic ideas. What might have been an unconstrained lyrical outpouring, the prologue, mere thundering in the index, because of the composer's mistaken impression that it ought to be tragic, and in the "Ercles vein." When the rites begin and a swelling paean is expected, there is much making of musical faces, but no real beginning. Matters improve in the second act, where the part of Ariofarno becomes dramatically puissant. Here there are noble passages and the duet has moments of passionate intensity; but all these things pale their ineffectual fires before the "Io paean," which is as thrilling and well applied as anything that I can recall in the operas of the decade which preceded "Ero e Leandro."

CHAPTER XX
NEW SINGERS AND OPERAS

There now remained four years of Mr. Grau's administration at the Metropolitan Opera House. They were years of great activity, during which the fortunes of the manager and the institution rose steadily. Mr. Grau was no more of a sentimentalist in art than Mr. Abbey had been. He was quiet, undemonstrative, alert, and wholly willing to let the public dictate the course of the establishment. Outwardly he was always calm, urbane, neither communicative nor secretive. I sat behind him during all the years of his divided and undivided directorship, and never failed of a pleasant greeting, no matter what the expression of The Tribune had been on the morning of the day. He accepted congratulations with a "Thank you!" which had cordiality in its timbre, and let the subject fall at once. He met expressions of condolence in the same unperturbed and uneffusive manner. Only once in all the years during which we sat neighbors can I recall that he volunteered a remark indicative of either satisfaction or disappointment. It was on the night of the first performance of Reyer's "Salammbô," in the season 1900-01. He appeared in his place early and extended his gloved hand in his ordinary manner, but this time his eyes took a survey of the audience-room the while. Then, still half turned, he remarked without a touch of feeling in the tone of his voice: "Encouraging, isn't it? Some say the public want novelties." He had expended a large sum on the production, and the public had met him with half a house.

If the public cared little for new things, it may occasionally have disturbed the solitary musings of Mr. Grau, but it only emphasized his public exhibitions of willingness to give the people the old things which they liked. A strongly popular favorite had a safe hold on a long tenure of service under him. Changes there had to be from year to year, but so long as the public manifested a desire to listen to a high-class singer, and there were no untoward circumstances to interfere, that singer was re-engaged. Hence there came to be at the Metropolitan in the higher ranks something like the theatrical stock companies of an earlier generation. New singers there had to be, from time to time, but year after year (the serious interruption is not yet) the subscribers were assured before one season was ended that in the next they would still be privileged to hear Mmes. Sembrich, Eames, Nordica, Schumann-Heink, Ternina, Homer, and (until he retired from his active stage career) Jean de Reszke, and Messrs. Édouard de Reszke, Van Dyck, Dippel, Scotti, Plançon, Journet, Campanari, Mühlmann, Bispham, and Albert Reiss. The presence of these artists of the first rank naturally determined the character of the repertory, which was also cut to a pattern, since the public always wanted to hear the artists whom they admired in the rôles in which they were most admirable. The German Contingent made the Wagnerian list inevitable, just as Mme. Sembrich made inevitable the operas of the florid Italian school, and Mme. Eames the two favorite operas of Gounod. These circumstances simplify the presentation of the significant incidents of the remainder of this history. I have only to take account of the entrance of a few stars into the Metropolitan system, and the first production of a few operas—some of which came only speedily to depart, others of which have remained in the establishment's repertory.

First, then, as to the American débuts. Newcomers of the first rank there were none among the ladies in the season 1899-1900: the tenor, Alvarez, effected his entrance on the Metropolitan stage on the opening night of the season, December 18th, in Gounod's "Roméo et Juliette"; Signor Scotti, barytone, who has remained a prime favorite ever since, in "Don Giovanni," on December 27th; Fritz Friedrichs, whose success in New York was inconsiderable compared with that which he had won in Bayreuth in his famous character of Beckmesser in "Die Meistersinger," on January 24, 1900. The subscription season of fifteen weeks consisted, with all the extra performances, of 104 performances. It was full of disappointments because of the illness of singers, and many performances were slipshod because of evils that have remained with the institution, in spite of many protests on the part of press and public, and promises of reform on the part of the management. Several times the company was divided so that performances might be given simultaneously in New York and Philadelphia. Even when this was not done, the efficiency of the forces was sapped by wearisome midnight journeys to and from the latter city, which prevented adequate rehearsals. Nevertheless, there was a supplemental season of two weeks. Herr Hofrath Ernst von Schuch, director of the opera at Dresden, was a visitor, and conducted two performances of "Lohengrin" and four concerts. No new operas were produced.

Before the regular subscription season, 1900-01, the Metropolitan Opera House was the scene of an ambitious effort to habilitate opera in English, which was made by Henry W. Savage in co-operation with Maurice Grau. Mr. Savage had some years before established his Castle Square Opera Company, organized in Boston, in the American Theater. The repertory of the company was composed largely of operettas at first, but gradually operas of large dimensions and serious import were added. After the season 1899-1900 he entered into an arrangement with Grau to occupy the Metropolitan Opera House from October 1 to December 15, 1900, and under the title Metropolitan English Grand Opera Company the two managers issued a prospectus which contained the names of nearly all the singers then known favorably to the English opera stage in America. Many of them had also sung in the Carl Rosa Opera Company, of England, and there was a better command of routine in the organization than had been known in English performances thitherto. The repertory was quite as pretentious as that of the company of foreign artists regularly domiciled at the Metropolitan, save that it did not include the later dramas of Wagner. Instead, however, it comprised some light operas or operettas, and some specifically English works. The promises of the prospectus were fulfilled to the letter in respect both of singers and operas, and though the enterprise proved to be less successful than had been those of Mr. Savage in previous years (probably because of the air of aristocracy which it wore, without being able to assume the social importance which belonged only to the foreign exotic), it is deserving of extended record. Some of the names of the singers stand as prominently in the English record as in the American, and unexpected laurels have been wound round the brows of some of them in still more foreign fields. In the list were Ingeborg Ballstrom, Grace Van Studdiford, Fanchon Thompson, Rita Elandi, Mae Cressy, Grace Golden, Josephine Ludwig, Zélie de Lussan, Elsa Marny, Louise Meisslinger, Frieda Stender, Phoebe Strakosch, Minnie Tracey, Barron Berthald, F. J. Boyle, Philip Brozel, Forrest Carr, Lloyd d'Aubigne, Harry Davies, Harry Hamlin, Homer Lind, William Mertens, Chauncey Moore, Winifred Goff, William Paull, Lemprière Pringle, William Pruette, Francis Rogers, Joseph F. Sheehan, Leslie Walker, William F. Wegener, and Clarence Whitehill. The conductors were A. Seppilli and Richard Eckhold. The operas performed were "Faust," "Tannhäuser," "Mignon," "Carmen," "Trovatore," "Lohengrin," "The Bohemian Girl," "Traviata," "Romeo and Juliet," "Cavalleria Rusticana," "Pagliacci," "Martha," "The Mikado," and Goring Thomas's "Esmeralda." This last opera, a novelty in America, was brought forward on November 19, 1900, with the following distribution of parts: Esmeralda, Grace Golden; Phoebus, Philip Brozel; Claude Frollo, Lemprière Pringle; Quasimodo, William Paull; Fleur-de-Lys, Grace Van Studdiford; Marquis de Chereuse, Leslie Walker; Gringoire, Harry Davies; Clopin, F. J. Boyle.

Before taking up the history of the Metropolitan Opera House, record may be made of the production of another novelty earlier in the year, also by Mr. Savage's singers, but under the more democratic conditions which prevailed at the American Theater. This was Spinelli's "A basso Porto," which was given for the first time by the Castle Square Company on January 22, 1900.

Mr. Grau began the campaign of 1900-01 on the Pacific Coast, his first performance being in Los Angeles on November 9th. Thence he went to San Francisco, Denver, Kansas City, Lincoln, and Minneapolis, reaching New York in time to open the subscription season on December 18th. The season endured fifteen weeks, within which time eighty-two performances were given. It was an eventful period. No fewer than eight singers who achieved significance in the annals of the house effected their entrances on the New York stage. Mme. Louise Homer made her début in "Aïda" on December 22d; Mlle. Lucienne Bréval, in "Le Cid," on January 16th; Miss Marguarite Macintyre, in "Mefistofele," on January 14th; Fritzi Scheff, in "Fidelio," on December 29th; Charles Gilibert, on the opening night, in "Roméo et Juliette"; Imbart de la Tour, in "Aïda," on December 22d; Robert Blass, in "Tannhäuser," on December 24th; Marcel Journet, in "Aïda," on December 22d. The first of the operas given was "La Bohème," but, as I have already explained, it was no novelty in New York, having been performed by two Italian opera companies and in an English version three years before. Novelties in every sense were Puccini's "Tosca" and Reyer's "Salammbô." The former had its first representation (it was also its first representation in America) on February 4, 1901. Signor Mancinelli conducted, and the parts were distributed as follows: Floria Tosca, Ternina; Cavaradossi, Cremonini; Angelotti, Dufriche; Il Sacristano, Gilibert; Spoletta, Bars; Sciarrone, Viviani; Un Carceriere, Cernusco; Scarpia, Scotti.

The restraining influence of music has prevented the lyric drama from acquiring the variety and scope of subject material adopted by the spoken drama. For nearly two hundred years after its invention classic legend and ancient history provided the stories which the opera composer laid under tribute. Very properly dramatic song occupied itself at the outset with a celebration of that fabled singer at the sound of whose voice "rivers forgot to run and winds to blow." In the story of Orpheus and Eurydice, as told in what is set down in history as the first opera, music and love were mated; and they have not yet been divorced, though both have undergone many and great changes of character. Love—gentle, constant, chivalric, tried, and triumphant—has been hymned amid pictures suggested by a millennium of human happenings, and its expression has passed through all the phases that the development of the most direct vehicle of emotional utterance could place at its service—from the melodramatic strivings of the amateurs who stumbled upon opera in their effort to reanimate the Greek drama to the glowing scores of Richard Wagner, in which high art and profound science are joined in a product as worthy of admiration as any other product of the intellect fired by inspiration. In the progress from Peri to Wagner, however, despite many daring and dubious adventures in new territories, there has yet been an avoidance of material in itself ugly and repulsive. We have been asked to contemplate the libertinism of Don Juan, but at its worst it has served only as a foil to the virtue of his victims, which in the end emerged triumphant. We have seen exposed the monstrous double nature of Rigoletto, but only that the pathos of paternal love should thereby be thrown into brighter relief. We have seen convention sanctified by nature and approved by communal experience set at naught by Wagner's treatment of mythological tales of unspeakable antiquity, but only that the tragedy of human existence in its puissant types might be kept before the world's consciousness.

The relationship occupied by music to the drama, that is to the words, the pantomime, the pictures and the play, in "Tosca" is that which it occupies in melodrama—using the term in its original and correct sense—with the single difference that the dialogue which is illustrated and mildly expounded by the music, and which the instruments seek, more or less vainly, to accentuate, emphasize, and intensify, is not uttered in the speaking, but the singing voice. Even this difference, however, disappears at some of the climacteric moments, and the actors resort to the elocutionary devices which belong to the spoken drama, and, foregoing pitch and rhythm, shout or whisper or hiss out the words which tell of the feelings by which they are swayed. Thus the first principle of music, which is melody, in Wagner as much as it was in Cimarosa or Mozart, is sacrificed. Quite as significant as the degradation of music thus illustrated is the degradation of the drama which has brought it about. There has always been a restrictive and purifying potency in melody. It has that which has turned our souls to sympathy with the apotheosis of vice and pulmonary tuberculosis in Verdi's "Traviata," which has made the music of the second act and the finale of "Tristan und Isolde" the most powerful plea that can be made for Wagner's guilty lovers. Nowhere else is the ennobling and purifying capacity of music demonstrated as in the death song of Isolde. Without such palliation the vileness, the horror, the hideousness of a play like "Tosca" is more unpardonable in an operatic form than in the original. Its lust and cruelty are presented in their nakedness. There is little or no time to reflect upon the workings of perverted minds, to make psychological or physiological studies, to watch the accumulation of causes and their gradual development of effects, except in the moments, so plentiful in Puccini's operas, in which music becomes a hindrance and an impertinence. Dramatic action cannot be promoted by music. The province of the art is to develop and fix a mood or celebrate a deed. Tosca can sing of her love, her jealousy, her hate, her hope; she cannot sing her frantic efforts to escape the lustful arms of Scarpia; she cannot sing his murder (though she might have chanted its gory glory, if so she held it, after the fact); nor can she sing her own destruction. In fact, there is next to nothing in Sardou's drama fit for operatic song, either in the sense that prevailed at the time of Paisiello or prevails in the time of Wagner—which is now. In the opera a really fit incident for the lyric drama borrowed from Sardou is expanded adroitly into a scene which is both musically and dramatically effective. It is the scene in which the cantata is sung in the Queen's apartments while Scarpia is questioning Cavaradossi in his own. Here the set musical composition is a background for the dramatic dialogue. Parallel scenes provide most of the opportunities which Puccini has embraced for writing in what may be called a sustained effort outside of the scenes between Tosca and her lover in the first act. Thus the first finale has a pompous church office as its background, with tolling of bells, the booming of cannon, the pealing of a great organ, through all of which surges a stream of orchestral melody bearing the declamatory shrieks of Scarpia. All of this is purely irrelevant and external, and the device is cheap, but it serves. Similar in musical purpose, but at the opposite end of the color scheme, is the opening of the third act. The stage picture is one of great beauty. The foreground shows the platform of the Castle of St. Angelo. St. Peter's Cathedral and the Vatican are visible in the background. It is urban Rome alone that is visible, but there are sounds from the Campagna—the tinkling of sheep bells, the song of a shepherd lad mingling with a strangely languorous and fragmentary orchestral song. Then there arises from the distance the sound of church bells, large and small, while the orchestral song goes on. It is all mood-music, conceived with no necessary relationship to the drama, but providing an atmosphere which is really refreshing after the sup of horrors provided by the preceding act. Therefore, it must be accepted gratefully like the dance tune over which Scarpia and his associates declaim before the dreadful business of the second act begins, and the piteous appeal to the Virgin which Tosca makes before she conceives the idea of the butchery which she perpetrates a few minutes later.

And the melodramatic music upon which Sardou's play floats,—what is it like? Much of it like shreds and patches of many things with which the operatic stage has long been familiar. There are efforts at characterization by means of melodic, harmonic, and rhythmical symbols, of which the most striking, and least original, is a succession of chords which serves as an introduction to the first scene. This and much else came out of Wagner's workshop, and, like all else of the same origin in the score, is impotent because there is no trace of Wagner's logical mind, either in the choice of material or its development. Phrases of real pith and moment are mixed with phrases of indescribable balderdash, yet these phrases recur with painful reiteration and with all the color tints which Puccini is able to scrape from a marvelously varied and garish orchestral palette. The most remarkable feature, the feature which shows the composer's constructive talent in its brightest aspect, is the fluency of it all. Even when reduced to the extremity of a tremolo of empty fifths on the strings pianissimo, or a single sustained tone, Puccini still manages to cling to a thread of his melodramatic fabric and the mind does not quite let go of his musical intentions.

Reyer's "Salammbô" was brought forward for the first time on March 20, 1901, with the following cast: Salammbô, Lucienne Bréval; Taanach, Miss Carrie Bridewell; Matho, Albert Saléza; Shahabarim, Mr. Salignac; Narr-Havas, Mr. Journet; Spendius, Mr. Sizes; Giscon, Mr. Gilibert; Authorite, Mr. Dufriche; Hamilcar, Mr. Scotti. Signor Mancinelli conducted. The opera received a brilliant representation. Mr. Grau had piled up the stage adornments with a lavish hand, and, though it disappeared from the Metropolitan stage after two performances, material traces remained for years in the settings of other spectacular operas. The scenes were all reproductions of the Paris models and exquisitely painted; the costumes were gorgeous to a degree. Mlle. Bréval's beauty (Semitic, as became the character) shone radiant in the part of the heroine, and she sang and acted with an intensity that in its supreme moments was positively uplifting. Flaubert's brilliant novel supplied the material out of which "Salammbô" was constructed. The romance has a large historical incident for a background, namely, the suppression of a mutiny among the mercenaries of the Carthaginians in the first Punic war. Running through the gorgeous tissue which the French novelist wove about this incident is the thread of story which Camille du Locle drew out for Reyer's use—the story of the rape of the sacred veil of Tanit by the leader of the revolting mercenaries, his love for Salammbô, daughter of the Carthaginian general; her recovery of the veil, with its consequence of disaster to her lover, and the pitiful death of both at their own hands. The authors of the opera were adepts in the field of what might be called musical spectacle. M. du Locle had a hand in both of the operas written for Paris, "Les Vêpres Sicilienne," and "Don Carlos." Under the eyes of Verdi at Sant' Agata he wrote the prose scenario of "Aïda," which Ghislanzoni turned into Italian verse for the composer. If a prodigal and sumptuous heaping up of stage adornments could make the success of an opera, "Salammbô" would have been one of the greatest triumphs of the French lyric stage; but pompous pictures are not the be-all and end-all of opera, even in Paris, and the fortunate co-operation of du Locle and Verdi was not repeated in the collaboration of du Locle and Reyer.

There are, however, merits in "Salammbô" which entitle it to a better fate than befell it in New York. The people in the story have marked dramatic physiognomies; indeed, had M. Reyer's skill in characterization been half so great as M. Flaubert's, and M. du Locle's, there would have been much to praise in the work. The characters are admirably drawn, and show as much individuality in their intellectual and moral traits as they do in their physical—the crafty Greek, the treacherous Numidian, the energetic and manly Carthaginian, the storm-tossed heroine, and the lovelorn Lybian are good dramatic types, even if stamped with stage conventions. A genius in musical characterization, like Mozart, Wagner or Verdi, would have found means for making their utterances as picturesque as their presences; but this was beyond the powers of Reyer. His tastes are modern, his aims far above the frivolity which afflicts some of his colleagues, but his abilities do not keep pace with his ambition. His models are easily found; he clasps hands most warmly with Berlioz, and has some of the Frenchman's peculiarly Gallic reverence for Spontini and Gluck. There are indications in the score that "Les Troyens" occupied much of his attention while he was engaged upon it, and I fancy that that ambitiously planned, but star-crossed work, was also familiar to the librettist. This need not excite special wonder, for the association of ideas was close enough. The second part of Berlioz's tragedy is also Carthaginian, and ends with Dido's prophetic vision of the hero who should avenge her wrongs on Rome. That Reyer also venerates Wagner but shows itself more in the use of the German master's harmonic progressions than in the adoption of his methods. He adopts the device of reiterated phrases, but his purpose in doing so I could not discover. Two short melodies, which are the themes of his brief instrumental introduction, are brought forward again and again, but fail to disclose their relationship to any of the agencies or elements in the story, and without a sign of that organic development which is the distinguishing characteristic of Wagner's creative style. Reyer's orchestration is discreet and free from all taint of that instrumental Volapük which is so marked in the Young Italian school. His subject invites the use of Oriental intervals, and he employs them with the discretion which is noticeable in "Aïda," but not with Verdi's effectiveness. Some of his devices are admirable, others simply bizarre. As a whole the music is monotonous in character and color, but it is dignified and earnest, and for this it deserves praise.

Mme. Sembrich had absented herself from Mr. Grau's company in the season 1900-01 in order to make a tour of the country with a small opera company of her own; she returned to the Metropolitan fold in the next season, however, and has not been errant since. The newcomers in 1901-02 were de Marchi, the tenor, who sang first in "Aïda" on January 17, 1902; Albert Reiss, a German tenor and specialist in Wagner's Mime, and Tavecchia, bass. The last-named made no deep impression, and faded out of view, but Mr. Reiss has been a strong prop of the Wagnerian performances ever since, and has proved himself an exceedingly useful artist in many respects. Mr. Walter Damrosch joined Mr. Grau's forces as conductor of the German operas; with him were associated Signor Sepilli and M. Flon. The record of the subscription season embraced thirty-three subscription evenings, eleven subscription matinées, the same number of popular priced performances on Saturday nights, nine extra performances, including four afternoons devoted to "The Ring of the Nibelung," and a gala performance in honor of Prince Henry of Prussia. The additions to the institution's repertory consisted of "Messaline," by Isidore de Lara, and "Manru," by Ignace Jan Paderewski. Concerning these novelties I shall have a word to say presently; the importance of the German prince's visit, from a social point of view, asks that it receive precedence in the narrative of the season's doings. This right royal incident took place on the evening of February 25, 1902. The opera house never looked so beautiful before, nor has it looked so beautiful since, as when it was garbed to welcome the nation's guest, a brother of the German Emperor. The material most used in adorning the house was Southern smilax, which all but hid all that is ordinarily seen of the auditorium and the corridors. All the box and balcony fronts were covered with it, and strings of it hung at the sides of the proscenium opening from the top of the opening to the stage. These strips of green foliage were thickly studded with white and green electric lights. The same scheme was carried out above the stage opening, where long garlands of smilax, gleaming with tiny white and green lamps, were hung in festoons, while the apex was formed by a standard of American and German flags and shields. On the balcony and box fronts the screens of smilax were relieved with frequent bunches of azaleas and marguerites, and with stars of white lamps shining through the green. The royal box was formed by removing the partitions separating five boxes in the middle of the lower tier. The front was decorated with American beauty roses, in addition to the smilax. The interior was hung with crimson velvet, and across its front was a canopy of crimson velvet and white satin. Behind the royal box the corridor on which it opened was cut off from the other boxes by hangings of tapestry. One of the most beautiful effects of all was made by the ceiling, where the chandeliers shone through a network of strings of smilax and white and green electric lights radiating from the center like the strands of a cobweb. As may be guessed, the brilliancy of the audience was in harmony with that of the audience-room. The price of tickets for the stalls on the main floor was thirty dollars, and the chairs in the other parts of the room cost proportionately. Persons who could pay such sums to witness the function could also afford to dress well, and at no public affair in my time has New York seen such a display of gowns and jewels. The musical program was elaborate, but that was the least important feature of the evening. Mr. Grau had determined to disclose the entire strength of his company, and to that end, settling the order in some diplomatic manner, into the secret of which he let neither reporter nor public, he made a program according to which Mesdames Gadski and Schumann-Heink and Messrs. Dippel, Bispham, Mühlmann, and Édouard de Reszke were to perform the first act of "Lohengrin," Mesdames Calvé, Marilly, and Bridewell and Messrs. Alvarez, Declery, Gilibert, Reiss, and Scotti the second act of "Carmen"; Mesdames Eames and Homer and Messrs. Campanari, Journet, and De Marchi the third act of "Aïda," Mme. Ternina and Messrs. Van Dyck, Blass, Bars, Reiss, Mühlmann, Viviani, and Van Rooy the second act of "Tannhäuser," Mesdames Sembrich and Van Cauteren, and Messrs. Vanni, Bars, Dufriche, Gilibert, and Salignac the first act of "La Traviata," and Mlle. Bréval and Mr. Alvarez the first scene from the fourth act of "Le Cid." It was a generous rather than a dainty dish to set before a king's brother, but it served fully to disclose the wealth of resource in New York's chief operatic institution, and the performances took on a heightened brilliancy from the beautiful appearance of the audience-room, and the spirit of joyous excitement which animated the audience. Up to the last moment no one familiar with the interior workings of Mr. Grau's harmonious, yet unruly empire, felt certain that the program would be carried out as planned; and it was not. It was very late when the curtain of smilax and light fell on the act of "Tannhäuser," and, the prince having left the house long before, followed by a large portion of the audience, who had come to see royalty, not to hear regal singers, Mme. Sembrich put down her little foot and refused to sing. Otherwise everything went off according to program.

"Messaline" was produced at the Metropolitan Opera House on January 22, 1902. The list of those who took part in its performance reads thus:

Messaline .... Mme. Calvé
Tyndaris .... Miss Marilly
La Citharode .... Miss Van Cauteren
Tsilla .... Miss Juliette Roslyn
Leoconce .... Miss Helen Mapleson
Helion .... Mr. Alvarez
Myrtille |
Olympias | .... Mr. Journet
Myrrho .... Mr. Gilibert
Gallus .... Mr. Declery
Un Rameur de Galère .... Mr. Dufriche
Un Mime Alexandrin .... Mr. Viviani
Un Poète d'Atellanes .... Mr. Giaccone
Le Loeno .... Mr. Vanni
Un Marchand d'Eau .... Mr. Maestri
L'Edile .... Mr. Judels
Harés .... Mr. Scotti
         Conductor, M. Flon

When Mr. Grau produced "Salammbô" it was possible for the writers in the newspapers to give a detailed account of the purport and progress of the story, and also an account of its panoramic furniture without offending decency. This is scarcely possible in the present instance. "Salammbô" was written many years ago, before the conviction had dawned upon the minds of opera makers that thugs and thieves, punks and paillards, were proper persons to present as publishers of operatic themes. Since then there has grown up in Italy a notion that the mud of the slums is ennobling material for celebration by the most ethereal of the arts, and in France that lust and lubricity are lofty inspirations for dramatic song. Gautier's delectable account of one of Cleopatra's nights has furnished forth an opera book; the mysteries of Astarte have been hymned, and Phryne, Thaïs, and Messalina have been held up to the admiring views of the Parisians clothed in more or less gorgeous sound—and little else. There is no parallel between this movement on the part of opera and the contemporary tendency of the spoken drama. Those diligent regenerators of society, Ibsen, Pinero & Co., affect a moral purpose to conceal an obvious aim from the simpleminded; the French makers of opera are franker, for they seek to glorify impudicity in the persons of its greatest historical representatives by lavishing upon the subject the most gorgeous pictures, the most ingenious theatrical contrivances, and the most sensuous music at their command. "Messaline" is a case in point. This work has Armand Sylvestre and Eugène Morand, two brilliant Frenchmen in their way, for the authors of its book, and Isidore de Lara, at the time chief of the drawing-room musicians of London, as its composer. The story of the opera is a sort of variant of "Carmen" set in an antique key, its heroine being an historic Roman empress instead of a gipsy cigarette girl. But any one who shall take the trouble to glance at the sixth satire of Juvenal will recognize that all its motives were drawn from that source. The likeness to "Carmen" is accidental, after all, though Bizet's opera was not without influence upon the work of librettists and composer. Like Carmen, Messalina, merely to gratify her lust, draws an honest-minded and supposedly pure man into her toils, and then throws him over for the next man she meets who is handsomer and lustier. In Bizet's opera the men are the soldier Don José, and the bullfighter, Escamillo; in De Lara's Harés, a singer, and Helion, a gladiator. Both operas end with the arena as a background—the Plaza de Toros in Seville, on the one hand, the Roman Circus, on the other. But here the resemblances end unless we pursue the traces of Bizet's music into De Lara's score, and this I shall not do, out of respect for the most brilliant composer that France has produced since Berlioz. Echeon, the harper; Glaphyrus or Ambrosius, the flute players, who are castigated in Juvenal's diatribe against marriage, are the prototypes of Messaline's first victim, as also is Pollio, whom a lady of lofty rank so loved that she kept for her kisses the plectrum with which he had strummed his lyre. That lyre she had incrusted with jewels, and for the sake of him who twanged it she had not hesitated to veil her face before the altar of Janus, and speak the mystic formula after the officiating priest. ("What more could she do were her husband sick?" asks Juvenal; "what if the physicians had despaired of her infant son?") As for Helion, his prototype is the gladiator Sergius, save that we are permitted to find him comely to look upon, and not as one galled by his helmet, having a huge wen between his nostrils and "acrid rheum forever trickling from his eye."

So, too, in the exposition of Messalina's character the librettist, while constructing an entirely fanciful tale, and omitting all reference to the most notorious of her amours (the one which at the last wrung the decree of her death from the generally complacent Claudius), nevertheless managed to indicate Juvenal's description in the song which Harés sings against her, a recital by Myrrho, a scene in the slums, which she visits in disguise, and where she is rescued from a gang of roisterers by Helion, and in the scene of her wooing of the gladiator. (This scene, as it was played by Mme. Calvé, may not be pictured here.) A glimmer of palliation might be read out of a few passages in the book, and at the end there is an indication of something better than the groveling carnality of the woman whose name has been a byword for nineteen centuries in her offer of herself to Helion's sword, and her opening the door to the lurking assassin when the gladiator refuses to strike in obedience to his old vow to avenge the supposed death of his brother. But all of the stage Messalina's words and acts up to that time give the lie to the thought of her capability of feeling a single throb of pure sentiment. She is presented as all beast, and there is not one moment of cheer to relieve the horror of a play which shows how her lewdness compasses the death of two loving brothers, who, unknown to each other, were both her lovers. At the end the hand of Harés, stiffened in death, clings to her robe, and brings her face to face with that death which the veritable Messalina was too cowardly to give to herself when her own mother pleaded with her to do so at the fateful meeting in the garden of Lucullus.

But there is often palliation in music. To this fact I have called attention before. Music can chasten and ennoble; but not music like Mr. De Lara's, which, when it strives for anything, strives to give an added atmosphere to the incontinence portrayed by the stage pictures, and proclaimed in the text. It is not dangerous music, however, for it is impotent, with all its blatant pretense. The composer seeks to fill the opening scene with languor and lassitude; he fills it with ennui instead. If De Lara's music were a hymning of anything, I should say it was a hymning of sensuality in its lowest terms; but there are neither eloquent melodies nor moving harmonies in the score. De Lara is a feeble distemper painter. The current of his music never really flows; it moves sluggishly now and then, and eddies lazily about every petty incident. In the scene of debauchery in the second act, it waits for a xylophone to rattle an accompaniment to the dice; it holds its breath for a muted horn to obtrude its voice with an inane vulgarity which would be laughable were it not pitiful to hear it in a work which is admirable in its dramatic contrivance and scenic equipment.

Mr. Paderewski's opera, "Manru," had its first performance on February 14, 1902. Mr. Damrosch conducted. The composer, who had taken a hand in the preparations, listened to the representation from a box, and the list of performers was this:

Ulana	Mme. Sembrich
Hedwig	Mme. Homer
Asa	Miss Fritzi Scheff
Manru	Alexander van Bandrowski
Oros	Mr. Mühlmann
Jagu	Mr. Blass
Urok	Mr. Bispham

"Manru" had its original performance at the Court Opera in Dresden, on May 29, 1901. Before reaching New York it was given in Cracow, Lemberg, Zurich, and Cologne, and Mr. Bandrowski, whom Mr. Grau engaged to sing the titular part, had already sung it twenty times in Europe. Its production at the Metropolitan Opera House brought scenes of gladsome excitement. Hero worshipers had an opportunity to gratify their passion in connection with a man who had filled a larger place in the public eye for a decade than any of his colleagues the world over; students were privileged to study a first work by an eminent musician, whose laurels had been won in a very different field; curiosity lovers had their penchant gratified to the full. The popular interest in the affair was disclosed by the fact that never before in the season had the audience at the Metropolitan been so numerous or brilliant; naturally the presence of the admired composer whetted interest and heightened enthusiasm. Long before the evening was over Mr. Paderewski was drawn from his secluded place in a parterre box by the plaudits of the audience, and compelled to acknowledge hearty appreciation of his achievement along with the artists who had made it possible. Despite the flaws which were easily found in the work, "Manru," the performance showed, is a remarkable first opera. There will scarcely ever be a critic who will say of it as one of the composers now set down as a classic said of the first opera of a colleague, that first operas, like first litters of puppies, ought properly to be drowned. "Manru" has had its day, but it was brilliant while it lasted, and it is possible that now it is not dead, but only sleeping. The story, badly told in the libretto made after a Polish romance by a friend of the composer, Dr. Nossig, has the charm of novelty, and beneath it there lies a potent dramatic principle. But more than the story, more than the picturesque costumes and stage furniture, there is a fascination about the music which grew with each hearing. Many of its characteristic details are based upon national idioms, but on the whole Mr. Paderewski wrote like an eclectic. He paid his tribute to the tendency which Wagner made dominant (where is the composer of the last thirty years who has not?) and, indeed, has been somewhat too frank in his acknowledgment of his indebtedness to that master in falling into his manner, and utilizing his devices whenever (as in the second act) there is a parallelism in situation; but he has, nevertheless, maintained an individual lyricism which proclaims him an ingenuous musician of the kind that the art never needed so much as it needs it now. As a national colorist Mr. Paderewski put new things upon the operatic palette.

"Manru" is not an opera to be disposed of with a hurried ultimatum on either book or music. From several points of view it not only invites, it clamors for discussion. The book is awkwardly constructed, and its language is at times amazingly silly; yet the fundamental idea is kept before the mind persistently and alluringly by the devices of the composer. A Gipsy who forsakes his wife and child because he cannot resist the seductions of a maid of his own race would ordinarily be a contemptible character, and nothing more; but in this case, despite the want of dramatic and literary skill in the libretto, Manru is presented as a tragic type who goes to merited destruction, indeed, but doing so nevertheless creates the impression that he is less the victim of individual passion than of a fatality which is racial. I can easily fancy that the Polish novelist from whom the story was borrowed presented the psychological fact more eloquently than the librettist, but it is a question whether or not he did so more convincingly than Dr. Nossig plus Mr. Paderewski. Mr. Leland (after Mr. Borrow the closest of literary students of the Gipsies) has pictured for us the Romany's love for roaming, and our sympathy with his propensity. We look wistfully at the ships at sea, and wonder what quaint mysteries of life they hide; we watch the flight of birds and long to fly with them anywhere, over the world and into adventure. These emotions tell us how near we are to be affected or elected unto the Romany, who belong to out-of-doors and nature, like birds and bees. Centuries more than we think of have fashioned that disposition in the black-blooded people, and made it an irresistible impulse. Thus the poetical essence of Manru's character is accounted for, and the librettist has given it an expression which is not inept:

   With longings wild my soul is fill'd,
    Spring's voices shout within me;
   Each fiber in my soul is thrill'd
    With feelings that would win me.
   In bush and brake
    The buds awake,

Of nature's joy the woods partake,
And bear me helpless, spent, along
Where freedom lives far from the throng;
Thus pours the mountain torrent wild,
  That stubborn rocks would check;
Thus rolls the molten lava stream,
Dispersing havoc dire, supreme,
  Enfolding, whelming all in wreck!
Thus flies the pollen on the breeze
  To meet its floral love;
The song, outgushing from the soul,
  Thus seeks the starry vault above.
Is it a curse?
There is no other life for me.
'Tis written in the book of fate:
Thy race must ev'ry pledge abate
And wander, rove eternally!
  But why? and where?
I know it not,—
  I needs must fare!

But such a life is lawless, it creates infidelity, nourishes incontinence; its seeming freedom is but slavery to passion, and this, too, the poet proclaims in Manru's confession that faithfulness is impossible to one to whom each new beauty offers irresistible allurement, and whose heart must remain unstable as his habitation.

Into the music of Manru's songs, which tell of these things, Mr. Paderewski has poured such passionate emotional expression as makes them convincing, and he has done more. Music is the language of the emotions, and the Gipsies are an emotional folk. The people of Hungary have permitted the Gipsies to make their music for them so long, and have mixed the Romany and Magyar bloods so persistently, that in music Gipsy and Hungarian have become practically identical terms. It was a Hungarian gentleman who said: "When I hear the 'Rakoczy' I feel as if I must go to war to conquer the whole world. My fingers convulsively twitch to seize a pistol, a sword, or bludgeon, or whatever weapon may be at hand; I must clutch it, and march forward." It is because of this spirit, scarcely overstated in this story, that the Austrian Government, fearful of the influence of the "Rakoczy" during periods of political excitement, has several times prohibited its performance on public occasions, and confiscated the copies found in the music shops. Mr. Paderewski makes admirable use of this passion as a dramatic motive. When neither the pleadings of his tribal companions nor the seductive artifices of Asa suffice to break down

Manru's sense of duty to his wife and child, the catastrophe is wrought by the music of a gipsy fiddler.

As the subject of the opera has to do with the conflict between Christian and Pagan, Galician and Gipsy, so the music takes its color now from the folk-song and dance of Mr. Paderewski's own people, and anon from the Gipsies who frequent the mountainous scenes in which the opera plays. The use of an Oriental interval, beloved of Poles and Gipsies, characterizes the melos of the first act; the rhythm of a peasant dance inspires the ballet, which is not an idle divertissement, but an integral element of the play, and Gipsy fiddle and cimbalom lend color and character to the music which tempts Manru to forget his duty. The contest in Manru's soul has musical delineation in an extended orchestral introduction to the last act, in which Gipsy and Polish music are at war, while clouds and moon struggle for the mastery in the stage panorama.

The season 1902-03 may be said to have been eventful only in its tragic outcome, of which I have already spoken—Mr. Grau's physical collapse. There was a painful and most unexpected echo a few weeks after the doors of the opera house had been closed for the summer vacation in the death of Mr. Frank W. Sanger, who had been acting as associate manager with Mr. Grau, and who had been largely instrumental in persuading Mr. Grau to abandon work and seek health in France. The season covered seventeen weeks, and comprised sixty-eight subscription nights, seventeen subscription matinées, seventeen popular Saturday nights, and six extra performances—ninety-one performances in all. Promises of a serial performance of the chief works of Verdi and Mozart had to be abandoned, partly on account of the illness of Mme. Eames. Only one new opera was brought forward, and that under circumstances which reflected no credit on the institution or its management, the opera (Miss Ethel Smyth's "Der Wald") not being worth the labor, except, perhaps, because it was the work of a woman, and the circumstances that private influences, and not public service, had prompted the production being too obvious to invite confidence in the opera. Simply for the sake of the integrity of the record mention is made that the production took place on March 11, 1903, that Alfred Hertz conducted, and that Mme. Gadski, Mme. Reuss-Belce, Georg Anthes, Mr. Bispham, Mr. Blass, and Mr. Mühlmann were concerned in the performance. The newcomers in Mr. Grau's forces were Mme. Reuss-Belce, Georg Anthes, Emil Gerhäuser, Aloys Burgstaller, and the conductor of the German operas, Mr. Hertz, who, like Mr. Burgstaller, has remained ever since, and they were all active agents in promoting the sensational feature of the first season of the administration which succeeded Mr. Grau's. I have tabulated the performances which took place in the subscription seasons under Mr. Grau as follows:

THE GRAU PERIOD, 1898-1903

Operas 1898-1899 *1899-1900 1900-1901 1901-1902 1902-1903

"Tannhäuser," 6 5 4 2 4
"Il Barbiere" 4 4 0 0 3
"Roméo et Juliette" 6 5 4 3 2
"La Traviata" 2 2 0 1 4
"Die Walküre" 4 6 3 3 3
"Siegfried" 1 2 1 1 3
"Nozze di Figaro" 3 4 0 2 1
"Carmen" 2 11 0 7 3
"Lohengrin" 7 7 6 4 7
"Faust" 7 9 5 5 7
"Tristan und Isolde" 5 3 4 3 4
"Don Giovanni" 4 1 1 0 1
"Aïda" 3 5 3 5 7
"Les Huguenots" 4 2 3 3 3
"Das Rheingold" 1 2 1 1 2
"Götterdämmerung" 1 2 2 2 2
"Martha" 1 0 0 0 0
"L'Africaine" 1 1 1 0 0
"Rigoletto" 1 1 1 0 1
"Le Prophète" 2 2 0 0 1
+ "Ero e Leandro" 2 0 0 0 2
"Lucia di Lammermoor" 1 2 2 0 0
"Il Trovatore" 0 3 0 0 1
"Der Fliegende Holländer" .. 0 3 1 0 0
"Mignon" 0 1 0 0 0
"Don Pasquale" 0 3 0 1 1
"Cavalleria Rusticana" 0 6 3 4 1
"Pagliacci" 0 1 0 1 6
"Die Meistersinger" 0 4 2 1 2
"Die Lustigen Weiber" 0 1 0 0 0
"Fidelio" 0 1 1 0 0
"The Magic Flute" 0 5 0 3 2
"La Bohème" 0 0 5 0 3
"Mefistofele" 0 0 2 0 0
"Le Cid" 0 0 3 2 0
+ "Tosca" 0 0 3 3 4
+ "Salammbô" 0 0 2 0 0
"Fille du Régiment" 0 0 0 3 6
+ "Messaline" 0 0 0 3 0
"Otello" 0 0 0 3 3

\+ "Manru" 0 0 0 3 0
"Ernani" 0 0 0 0 3
"Un Ballo in Maschera" 0 0 0 0 1
\+ "Der Wald" 0 0 0 0 2

  * Performances in the supplementary season included.
\+ Novelties.

 Massenet's "Manon" had two performances with Saville and Van Dyck in the season 1898-'99; but both were outside the subscription.

CHAPTER XXI
HEINRICH CONRIED AND "PARSIFAL"

A prologue dealing with other things may with propriety accompany this chapter, which is concerned with the history of the Metropolitan Opera House under the administration of Mr. Heinrich Conried. It is called for by the visit which Pietro Mascagni made to the United States in the fall of 1902. Signor Mascagni came to America under a contract with Mittenthal Brothers, theatrical managers, whose activities had never appreciably touched the American metropolis nor the kind of entertainment which they sought to purvey. These things are mentioned thus early in the story so that light may be had from the beginning on the artistic side of the most sensational fiasco ever made by an artist of great distinction in the United States. The contract, which was negotiated by an agent of the Mittenthals in Italy, was for fifteen weeks, during which time Signor Mascagni obligated himself to produce and himself conduct not more than eight performances of opera or concerts a week. For his personal services he was to receive $60,000, in weekly payments of $4,000, with advances before leaving Italy and on arriving in New York. The contract called for performances of "Iris," "Cavalleria Rusticana," "Zanetto," and "Ratcliff" by a company of singers and instrumentalists to be approved by Signor Mascagni. The composer was hailed with gladness on his arrival by his countrymen, and his appearance and the three operas which were unknown to the American public were awaited with most amiable and eager curiosity. The first performance took place in the Metropolitan Opera House on October 8, 1902, and was devoted to "Zanetto" and "Cavalleria Rusticana," both conducted by the composer. There was a large audience and much noisy demonstration on the part of the Italian contingent, but the unfamiliar work proved disappointing and the performance of "Cavalleria" so rough that all the advantages which it derived from Mascagni's admirable conducting failed to atone for its crudities. There were three representations at the Metropolitan Opera House the first week, all devoted to the same works, and one at the Academy of Music in Brooklyn. Meanwhile promises of "Iris" and "Ratcliff" were held out, and work was done most energetically to prepare the former for performance. Rehearsals were held day and night and the Saturday evening performance abandoned to that end. "Ratcliff" was never reached, but "Iris" was given on October 16th with the following cast, which deserves to go on record since it was the first representation of the opera in the United States.

Iris	Marie Farneti
Osaka	Pietro Schiavazzi
Kyoto	Virgilio Bellatti
Il Cieco	Francesco Navarrini
Una Guecha	Dora de Fillippe
Un Mercianola	Pasquali Blasio
Un Cencianola	Bernardino Landino

I shall not tell the story of "Iris," which five years after was adopted into the repertory of the Metropolitan Opera House, it seemed for the purpose of giving Mme. Eames an opportunity to contend with Miss Geraldine Farrar in the field of Japanese opera; but the opera calls for some comment. Why "Iris"? It might be easier to answer the question if it were put in the negative: Why not "Iris"? The name is pretty. It suggests roseate skies, bows of promise, flowery fields, messages swiftly borne and full of portent. The name invites to music and to radiant raiment, and it serves its purpose. Mascagni and his librettist do not seem to have been able to find a term with which to define their creation. They call it simply "Iris"; not a "dramma per musica," as the Florentine inventors of the opera did their art-form; nor a "melodramma" nor a "tragedia per musica"; nor an "opera in musica," of which the conventional and generic "opera" is the abbreviation; nor even a "dramma lirico," which is the term chosen by Verdi for his "Falstaff" and Puccini for his "Manon Lescaut." In truth, "Iris" is none of these. It begins as an allegory, grows into a play, and ends again in allegory, beginning and end, indeed, being the same, poetically and musically. Signor Illica went to Sâr Peladan and d'Annunzio for his sources, but placed the scene of "Iris" in Japan, the land of flowers, and so achieved the privilege of making it a dalliance with pseudo-philosophic symbols and gorgeous garments. Now, symbolism is poor dramatic matter, but it can furnish forth moody food for music, and "Sky robes spun of Iris woof" appear still more radiant to the eye when the ear, too, is enlisted. Grossness and purulence stain the dramatic element in the piece, but when all is over pictures and music have done their work of mitigation, and out of the feculent mire there arises a picture of poetic beauty, a vision of suffering and triumphant innocency which pleads movingly for a pardoning embrace.

There are many effective bits of expressive writing in the score of "Iris," but most of them are fugitive and aim at coloring a word, a phrase, or at best a temporary situation. There is little flow of natural, fervent melody. What the composer accomplished with tune, characteristic but fluent, eloquent yet sustained, in "Cavalleria Rusticana," he tries to achieve in "Iris" with violent, disjointed shifting of keys and splashes of instrumental color. In this he is seldom successful, for he is not a master of orchestral writing, that technical facility which nearly all the young musicians have in the same degree that all pianists have finger technic. His orchestral stream is muddy; his effects generally crass and empty of euphony. He throws the din of outlandish instruments of percussion, a battery of gongs, big and little, drums and cymbals, into his score without achieving local color. Once only does he utilize it so as to catch the ears and stir the fancy of the listeners— in the beginning of the second act, where there is a murmur of real Japanese melody. As a rule, however, Signor Mascagni seems to have been careless in the matter of local color, properly so, perhaps, for, strictly speaking, local color in the lyric drama is for comedy with its petty limitations, not for tragedy with its appeal to large and universal passions. Yet it was in the lighter scenes, the scenes of comedy, like the marionette show; the scenes of mild pathos, like the monologues of Iris, in which the music helped Signorina Farneti, with her gentle face, mobile, expressive and more than comely, and her graceful, intelligent action, to present a really captivating figure of sweet innocence walking unscathed through searing fires of wickedness and vice, and the scenes of mere accessory decoration, like that of the laundresses, the mousmé in the first act, with its purling figure borrowed from "Les Huguenots" and its unnecessarily uncanny col legno effect conveyed from "L'Africaine," that the music seemed most effective. "Zanetto" is nothing more than an operatic sketch in one act. In its original shape, as it came from the pen of François Coppée, under the title "Le Passant," the story is a gracious and graceful idyl. A woman of the world, sated and weary with a life of amours, meets a young singer, feels the sensations of a pure love pulsing in her veins and sends him out of her presence uncontaminated. Here are poetry and beauty; but not matter for three-quarters of an hour of a rambling musical dialogue, such as the librettists and composer of "Cavalleria Rusticana" have strained and tortured it into. A drawing-room sketch of fifteen minutes' duration might have been tolerable. To add to the dulness of the piece, Mascagni, actuated by a conceit which would have been dainty and effective in the brief sketch hinted at, wrote the instrumental parts for strings, harp, and an extremely sparing use of the wood-wind choir and horn. Harmonies there are of the strenuous kind, but they are desiccated; not one juicy chord is heard from beginning to end, and the vitality of the listening ear is exhausted long before the long-drawn thing has come to an end.

Signor Mascagni entered upon his second week with disaster staring him in the face, and before it was over it was plain to everyone that the enterprise was doomed to monumental failure. The public after the first night became curiously apathetic. This apathy would have been justified had any considerable number of the city's habitual opera-patrons attended any of the performances. The welcome came from the Italians dwelling within the city's boundaries; the performances themselves could arouse no enthusiasm. The singers were on a level with the usual summer itinerants;

the orchestra, made up partly of inexperienced men from Italy and non-union players from other cities, was unpardonably wretched. It was foolishly reckless in the composer to think that with such material as he had raked together in his native land and recruited here he could produce four of his operas within a week of his arrival in America. He must have known how incapable, inexperienced, and unripe the foreign contingent of his orchestra was. The energy with which he threw himself into the task of trying to repair his blunders won the sympathy of the members of the critical guild, though it did not wholly atone for his conscious or unconscious misconception of American conditions. It was not pleasant to think that he had so poor an opinion of American knowledge and taste in music that before coming he thought that anything would be good enough for this country. His experience in Italy ought to have made him something of a student of musical affairs in other countries than his own, and he was unquestionably sincere in his hope that the American tour would win for him and his music the sympathetic appreciation which his countrymen had begun to withhold from him. Granting the sincerity of his desire to present himself fairly as a candidate for the good-will of the American people, it was inconceivable that he should have connived at or suffered such an inadequate preparation for the production of his works. Had he come to New York a month earlier than he did it would not have been a day too early.

After his New York fiasco Signor Mascagni went to Boston, where troubles continued to pile upon him till he was overwhelmed. He fell out with his managers, or they with him, and in a fortnight he was under arrest for breach of contract in failing to produce the four operas agreed upon. He retorted with a countersuit for damages and attached theatrical properties in Worcester which the Mittenthals said did not belong to them, but to their brother. The scandal grew until it threatened to become a subject of international diplomacy, but in the end compromises were made and the composer departed to his own country in bodily if not spiritual peace. One achievement remained: the Musical Protective Union of New York had asked the federal authorities to deport the Italian instrumentalists under the Alien Labor Contract Law, and the Treasury Department at Washington decided in its wisdom that no matter how poor a musician a musician might be, he was not a laboring man, but an artist, and not subject to the law. Exit Mascagni.

On February 14, 1903, the directors of the Metropolitan Opera and Real Estate Company by a vote of seven to six adopted a resolution directing the executive committee "to negotiate with Mr. Heinrich Conried regarding the Metropolitan Opera House, with power to conclude a lease in case satisfactory terms can be arranged." This was the outcome of a long struggle between Mr. Conried and Mr. Walter Damrosch, a few other candidates for the position of director of the institution making feeble and hopeless efforts to gain a position which all the world knew had, after many vicissitudes, brought fortune to Mr. Grau. The public seemed opera-mad and the element of uncertainty eliminated from the enterprise. Mr. Conried had been an actor in Austria, had come as such to New York, and worked himself up to the position of manager of a small German theater in Irving Place. He had also managed comic operetta companies, English and German, in the Casino and elsewhere, and acted as stage manager for other entrepreneurs. For a year or two his theater had enjoyed something of a vogue among native Americans with a knowledge of the German tongue, and Mr. Conried had fostered a belief in his high artistic purposes by presenting German plays at some of the universities. He became known outside the German circle by these means, and won a valuable championship in a considerable portion of the press. In the management of grand opera he had no experience, and no more knowledge than the ordinary theatrical man. But there was no doubt about his energy and business skill, though this latter quality was questioned in the end by such an administration as left his stockholders without returns, though the receipts of the institution were greater than they had ever been in history. He had no difficulty in organizing a company, which was called the Heinrich Conried Opera Company, on the lines laid down by Mr. Grau, and acquiring the property of the Maurice Grau Opera Company, which, having made large dividends for five years, sold to its successor at an extremely handsome figure. Mr. Conried began his administration with many protestations of artistic virtue and made a beginning which aroused high expectations. To these promises and their fulfillment I shall recur in a résumé of the lustrum during which Mr. Conried was operatic consul. Also I shall relate the story of the principal incidents of his consulship, but for much of the historical detail shall refer the reader to the table of performances covering the five years. The new operas produced within the period were but few. Some of them are scarcely worth noting even in a bald record of events; others have been so extensively discussed within so recent a period that they may be passed over without much ado here.

Mr. Conried succeeded to a machine in perfect working order, the goodwill of the public, agreements with nearly all the artists who were popular favorites, an obligation with the directors of the opera-house company to remodel the stage, and a contract with Enrico Caruso. Mr. Grau had also negotiated with Felix Mottl, had "signed" Miss Fremstad, and was holding Miss Farrar, in a sense his protégée, in reserve till she should "ripen" for America. The acquisition of Caruso was perhaps Mr. Conried's greatest asset financially, though it led to a reactionary policy touching the opera itself which, however pleasing to the boxholders, nevertheless cost the institution a loss of artistic prestige. I emphasize the fact that Mr. Conried acquired the contract with Signor Caruso from Mr. Grau because from that day to this careless newspaper writers, taking their cues from artful interviews put forth by Mr. Conried, have glorified the astuteness of the new manager in starting his enterprise with a discovery of the greatest tenor of his day. Many were the stories which were told, the most picturesque being that Mr. Conried, burdened with the responsibility of recruiting a company, had shrewdly gone among the humble Italians of New York and by questioning them had learned that the name of the greatest singer alive was Caruso. Confirmed in his decision by his bootblack, he had then gone to Europe and engaged the wonder. Caruso's reputation was made some years before he came to America, and Mr. Grau had negotiated with him at least a year before he got his signature on a contract for New York. Let the story stand as characteristic of many that enlivened the newspapers during the Conried period. A dozen of the singers who were continuously employed throughout the Conried period had already established themselves in public favor when his régime opened. They were Mme. Sembrich, Mme. Eames (who was absent during his first year), Mme. Homer, and Messrs. Burgstaller, Dippel, Reiss, Mühlmann, Scotti, Van Rooy, Blass, Journet, Plançon, and Rossi. To these Mr. Conried associated Caruso, Marion Weed, Olive Fremstad, Edyth Walker, Ernst Kraus (the tenor who had been a member of one of Mr. Damrosch's companies), Fran Naval, Giuseppe Campanari, Goritz, and a few people of minor importance. Miss Weed and Miss Fremstad and Messrs. Caruso and Goritz became fixtures in the institution; Miss Walker remained three years; Herr Kraus and Herr Naval only one season. The second season witnessed the accession of Bella Alten, Mme. Senger-Bettaque (who dated back to the German régime), Mme. Eames (returned), Signora De Macchi (an Italian singer whose failure was so emphatic that her activity ended almost as soon as it began), Mme. Melba (for one season), Mme. Nordica (for two seasons), Josephine Jacoby (for the rest of the term), and a couple more inconsequential fillers-in. The third year brought Signorina Boninsegna (who I believe had a single appearance), Lina Cavalieri (who endured to the end), Geraldine Farrar (still with the company and bearer of high hopes on the part of opera lovers for the future), Bessie Abott (a winsome singer of extremely light caliber), Marie Mattfeld (an acquaintance of the Damrosch days), Mme. Schumann-Heink (returned for a single season), Marie Rappold, Mme. Kirkby-Lunn, Carl Burrian, Soubeyran and Rousselière, tenors; Stracciari, barytone, and Chalmin and Navarini, basses. The list of German dramatic sopranos was augmented in the last year by Mme. Morena and Mme. Leffler-Burkhardt, the tenors by Bonci (who had been brought to America the year before as opposition to Caruso by Mr. Hammerstein), Riccardo Martin (an American), George Lucas; the basses by Theodore Chaliapine, a Russian, and a buffo, Barocchi. Among the engagements of the first season which gave rise to high hopes in serious and informed circles was that of Felix Mottl, as conductor of the German operas and Sunday night concerts (which it was announced were to be given a symphonic character and dignity), Anton Fuchs, of Munich, as stage manager, and Carl Lautenschläger, of the Prinz Regententheater, Munich, as stage mechanician, or technical director. These two men did notable work in "Parsifal," but in everything else found themselves so hampered by the prevailing conditions that after a year they retired to Germany, oppressed with a feeling something akin to humiliation. Likewise Herr Mottl, who made an effort in the line of symphony concerts on the first Sunday night of the season and then withdrew, to leave the field open to the old-fashioned popular operatic concert, which Mr. Conried commanded and the public unquestionably desired. His experiences in putting half-prepared operas on the stage also discouraged Herr Mottl, and he went through the season in a perfunctory manner and departed shaking the Metropolitan dust from his feet, and promptly installed his polished boots in the directorship of the Royal Court Theater at Munich.

The season opened on November 23, 1903, with "Rigoletto"; Mme. Sembrich reappeared as Gilda and Caruso effected his American début as the Duke. His success was instantaneous, though there was less enthusiasm expressed by far on that occasion than on his last appearance, five years later. In the interval admiration for a beautiful voice had grown into adoration of a singer—an adoration which even sustained him through a scandal which would have sent a man of equal eminence in any other profession into disgraceful retirement. The season compassed fifteen weeks, from November 23d to March 5th, within which period there were ninety-seven performances of twenty-seven works, counting in a ballet and a single scene from "Mefistofele," in which Mme. Calvé, who joined Mr. Conried's forces after the season was two-thirds over, and yet managed to give four performances of "Carmen," helped to improve a trifle the pitiful showing made by the French contingent in the list. The French element, which had become a brilliant factor in the Grau period, began to wane, and subsequently the German was eliminated as far as seemed practicable from the subscription seasons. The boxholders were exerting a reactionary influence, and Mr. Conried willingly yielded to them, since he could thus reserve certain sensational features for the extra nights at special prices and put money in his purse. This policy had a speedy and striking illustration in the production of Wagner's "Parsifal," which made Mr. Conried's first year memorable, or, as some thought, notorious. Certainly no theatrical incident before or since so set the world ringing as did the act which had been long in the mind of the new manager, and which was one of the first things which he announced his intention to do after he had secured the lease from the owners of the opera house. The announcement was first made unofficially in newspaper interviews, and confirmed in the official prospectus, which set down Christmas as the date of production. A protest—many protests, indeed—followed. Mme. Wagner's was accompanied with a threat of legal proceedings. The ground of her appeal to Mr. Conried was that to perform the drama which had been specifically reserved for performance in Bayreuth by the composer would be irreverent and illegal. To this Mr. Conried made answer that inasmuch as "Parsifal" was not protected by law in the United States his performance would not be illegal, and that it was more irreverent to Wagner to prevent the many Americans who could not go to Bayreuth from hearing the work than to make it possible for them to hear it in America. Proceedings for an injunction were begun in the federal courts, but after hearing the arguments of counsel Judge Lacombe decided, on November 24, 1903, that the writ of injunction prayed for should not issue. The decision naturally caused a great commotion, especially in Germany, where the newspapers and the composers, conductors, and others who were strongly affiliated with Bayreuth manifested a disposition to hold the American people as a whole responsible, not only for a desecration of something more than sacrosanct, but of robbery also. The mildest term applied to Mr. Conried's act, which I am far from defending, was that it was "legalized theft." It was not that, because in civilized lands thievery cannot be made lawful. It was simply an appropriation of property for which the law, owing to the absence of a convention touching copyright and performing rights between Germany and the United States at the time, provided neither hindrance nor punishment. Under circumstances not at all favorable to success, had success been attainable (there was always something more than a suspicion that the proceedings were fomented by enemies of Mr. Conried in New York), Mme. Wagner tried by legal process to prevent the rape of the work, but the courts were powerless to interfere. Having passed triumphantly through this ordeal, Mr. Conried found himself in the midst of another. A number of clergymen, some eminent in their calling and of unquestioned sincerity, others mere seekers after notoriety, attacked the work as sacrilegious. A petition was addressed to the Mayor of the city asking that the license of the Metropolitan Opera House be revoked so far as the production of "Parsifal" was concerned. The petition was not granted, but all the commotion, which lasted up to the day of the first performance, was, as the Germans say, but water for Conried's mill. He encouraged the controversy with all the art of an astute showman and secured for "Parsifal" such an advertisement as never opera or drama had in this world before.

 Mr. Conried had concluded at the outset of his enterprise that "Parsifal" was too great a money-maker to be included in the regular subscription list of the season. He followed his general prospectus with a special one, in which he announced five performances of Wagner's festival drama on special dates, under special conditions, and at special prices. The first was set down for December 24; the prices for the stalls on the main floor, the first balcony, and the boxes which were at his disposal were doubled (orchestra stalls, $10), but seats in the upper balcony and the topmost gallery were sold at the regular price. The first performance took place on December 24th, the cast being as follows:

Kundry	Milka Ternina
Parsifal	Alois Burgstaller
Amfortas	Anton Van Rooy
Gurnemanz	Robert Blass
Klingsor	Otto Görlitz
Titurel	Marcel Journet
First Esquire	Miss Moran
Second Esquire	Miss Braendle
Third Esquire	Albert Reiss
Fourth Esquire	Mr. Harden
First Knight	Mr. Bayer
Second Knight	Mr. Mühlmann
A Voice	Louise Homer

Anton Fuchs and Carl Lautenschläger were in charge of the stage; Mr. Hertz conducted. The first half of the season had been sacrificed to the production. As such things are done at Bayreuth and in the best theaters of Germany the preparations were inadequate, but the results achieved set many old visitors to the Wagnerian Mecca in amaze. So far as the mere spectacle was concerned Mr. Conried's production was an improvement on that of Bayreuth in most things except the light effects. All of Wagner's dramas show that the poet frequently dreamed of things which were beyond the capacity of the stage in his day—even the splendidly equipped stage of the Festspielhaus in Bayreuth. Later improvements in theatrical mechanics made their realization in more or less degree possible. The greatest advance disclosed by New York over Bayreuth was in the design and manipulation of the magical scenes of the second act. Such scenes as that between Parsifal and the Flower Maidens were doubtless in the imagination of Wagner, but he never saw their realization. Up to the time of which I am writing the Bayreuth pictures were exaggerated and garish. In New York every feature of the scene was beautiful in conception, harmonious in color, graceful in action, seductive as the composer intended it to be—as alluring to the eye as the music was fascinating to the ear. At a later performance Weingartner, conductor and composer, now director of the Royal Imperial Court Opera of Vienna, sat beside me. After the first act he spoke in terms generally complimentary about the performance, but criticized its spirit and execution in parts. When the scene of the magical garden was discovered and the floral maidens came rushing in he leaned forward in his chair, and when the pretty bustle reached its height he could wait no longer to give voice to his admiration. "Ah!" he exclaimed in a whisper, "there's atmosphere! There's fragrance and grace!" The music of the drama was familiar to New Yorkers from many concert performances. Once, indeed, there was a "Parsifal" festival in Brooklyn, under the direction of Mr. Seidl, in which all the music was sung by the best singers of the Metropolitan Opera House on a stage set to suggest the Temple of the Grail. Only the action and the pictures were new to the city's music lovers. Nevertheless the interest on the part of the public was stupendous. The first five representations were over on January 21st, but before then Mr. Conried had already announced five more, besides a special day performance on Washington's Birthday, February 22d. After the eleventh performance, on February 25th, Mr. Conried gave out the statement to the public press that the receipts had been $186,308; that is, an average of $16,937.17. But this was not the end. Under Mr. Grau the custom had grown up in the Metropolitan Opera House of a special performance, the proceeds of which were the personal perquisites of the director. In all the contracts between the director and his artists there was a clause which bound the latter to sing for nothing at one performance. Before his retirement Mr. Grau grew ashamed of appearing in the light of an eleemosynary beneficiary under such circumstances, and explained to the newspapers that the arrangement between himself and the singers was purely a business one. Nevertheless he continued to avail himself of the rich advantage which the arrangement brought him, and in the spring closed the supplementary season with a performance of an olla podrida character, in which all of the artists took part. Mr. Conried continued the custom throughout his administration, but varied the programme in his first year by giving a representation of "Parsifal" instead of the customary mixed pickles. The act was wholly commercial. That was made plain, even if anyone had been inclined to think otherwise, when subsequently he substituted an operetta, Strauss's "Fledermaus," for the religious play, and called on all of his artists who did not sing in it to sit at tables in the ball scene, give a concert, and participate in the dancing. A year later he gratified an equally lofty ambition by arranging a sumptuous performance of another operetta by the same composer, "Der Zigeunerbaron," and following it with a miscellaneous concert. That operetta was never repeated.

In the seasons 1904-05 and 1905-06 "Parsifal" was again reserved for special performance at double the ordinary prices of admission, and it was not until a year later that the patrons of the Metropolitan were permitted to hear it at the ordinary subscription rates. By that time it had taken its place with the Nibelung tragedy, having, in fact, a little less drawing power than the more popular dramas in the tetralogy. The reason was not far to seek. The craze created by the first year had led to all manner of shows, dramas, lectures with stereopticon pictures which were a degradation of the subject. Only one of the results possessed artistic dignity or virtue, and this justified the apprehension of the poet-composer touching what would happen if his unique work ever became a repertory piece. Mr. Savage in 1904-05 carried "Parsifal" throughout the length and breadth of the land in an English version, starting in Boston and giving representations night after night just before the Metropolitan season opened in the New York Theater. Nevertheless there were eight performances at the Metropolitan in that season and four in the season that followed. At regular rates in 1906-07 only two performances were possible. All of Mr. Conried's artistic energies in his second season were expended on the production of "Die Fledermaus," which he gave for his own benefit under the circumstances already referred to, on February 16th. The season lasted fifteen weeks, and consisted of ninety-five performances of thirty operas and two ballets, outside of the supplementary season, which, let me repeat, are not included in the statistics which I am giving. An incident of the second season was the collapse of the bridge which is part of the first scene of "Carmen," and the consequent injury of ten choristers. The accident happened on the night of January 7, 1905, while the performance was in progress. Fortunately nobody was killed.

CHAPTER XXII
END OF CONRIED'S ADMINISTRATION

A visit from Engelbert Humperdinck to attend the first German performance of his "Hänsel und Gretel" on November 25th, a strike of the chorus which lasted three days, a revival of Goldmark's "Königin von Saba" which had been the chief glory of the second German season twenty years before, and the squandering of thousands of dollars and so much time that nearly all of the operas in the repertory suffered for lack of rehearsals on a single production of Strauss's operetta "Der Zigeunerbaron," were the chief incidents of the season of 1905-06. That is to say, the chief local incidents. Out in San Francisco the company was overwhelmed by the catastrophe of the earthquake, which sent it back a physical and financial wreck. The calamity tested the fortitude and philosophy of Mr. Conried as well as the artists, but through the gloom there shone a cheering ray when Mme. Sembrich, herself one of the chief sufferers from the earthquake, postponed her return to her European home long enough to give a concert for the benefit of the minor members of the company, and distributed $7,691 to musicians who had lost their instruments and $2,435 to the chorus and technical staff.

The season of 1906-07 marked highwater in the artistic activities of Mr. Conried's institution. It was the year of "Salome" and the coming of Signor Puccini to give éclat to the production of his operas. Outside of "Salome" there was only one real novelty in the season's repertory, and that, "Fedora," might easily have been spared; but the current list of the house was augmented by no less than seven works, namely, "Fedora," "La Damnation de Faust," "Lakmé" (which had been absent from the list for many years), "L'Africaine," "Manon Lescaut," "Madama Butterfly," and "Salome." Berlioz's dramatic legend, "La Damnation," had been a popular concert piece ever since its first production by Dr. Leopold Damrosch at a concert of the Symphony Society more than twenty-five years before, and its novel features were those which grew out of the abortive efforts of Raoul Gunsbourg to turn it into a stage play.

In the presence of the composer, who was received with great acclaim by a gathering notable in numbers and appearance, and amid scenes of glad excitement which grew from act to act, Puccini's "Manon Lescaut" was performed for the first time at the Metropolitan Opera House on the evening of January 18, 1907. Signor Puccini reached the theater in the middle of the third act and, unnoticed by the audience, took a seat in the directors' box in the grand tier. After the first act the orchestra saluted him with a fanfare and the audience broke into applause which lasted so long that, finding it impossible to quiet it by rising and bowing his acknowledgments, he withdrew into the rear of the box out of sight so that the performance might go an. After the second act he sent the following statement in French to the representatives of the newspapers:

"I have always thought that an artist has something to learn at any age. It was with delight, therefore, that I accepted the invitation of the directors of the Metropolitan Opera House to come to this new world of which I saw a corner on my visit to Buenos Ayres and with which I was anxious to get better acquainted. What I have seen to-night has already proved to me that I did well to come here, and I consider myself happy to be able to say that I am among my friends, to whom I can speak in music with a certainty of being understood."

"Manon Lescaut" was not wholly new to the opera-goers of New York, for it had had one or two performances by a vagrant Italian company at Wallack's Theater in May, 1898; but to all intents and purposes it was a novelty, for the musical itinerants of nine years before were not equal to the task set by Puccini, and gave a perversion rather than a performance of the opera. Why it should have waited so long and for the stimulus of the coming of the composer before reaching the Metropolitan Opera House was not easily explained by those admirers of the composer who knew or felt that in spite of the high opinion in which. "La Bohème," "Tosca," and "Madama Butterfly" were held, "Manon Lescaut" is fresher, more spontaneous, more unaffected and passionate in its dramatic climaxes, as well as more ingratiatingly charming in its comedy element, than any of its successors from Puccini's pen. The voice of the composer rings unmistakably through its measures, but it is freer from the formularies which have since become stereotyped, and there are a greater number of echoes of the tunefulness which belongs to the older period between which and the present the opera marks a transition. Abbé Prévost's story, familiar to all readers of French romance, had served at least four opera composers before Signor Puccini. In 1830 Halévy brought forward a three-act ballet dealing with the story; Balfe wrote a French opera with the title in 1836, Auber another in 1856, and Massenet still another in 1884. Scribe was Auber's collaborator, and their opera, which like Puccini's ended with the scene of Manon's death in America, received a touch of local color from the employment of Negro dances and Créole songs. It would be interesting to see the old score now that the artistic value of the folk-songs of the Southern States as an incentive to a distinctive school of music has challenged critical attention and aroused controversy. Massenet's opera, which through the influence of Minnie Hauk was produced at the Academy of Music on December 23, 1885, dropped out of the local repertory until the restoration of the Italian régime as has been related elsewhere in this book. The opening and closing incidents in Massenet's opera are the same as are used by Puccini, though MM. Meilhac and Gille, the French librettists, did not think it necessary to carry the story across the ocean for the sake of Manon's death scene. In their book she succumbs to nothing that is obvious and dies in her lover's arms on the way to the ship at Havre which was to transport her to the penal colony at New Orleans. The third act of Puccini's opera plays at Havre, its contents being an effort to free Manon, the deportation of a shipload of female convicts, including Manon, and the embarkation of des Grieux in a menial capacity on the convict ship. Here the composer makes one of his most ambitious attempts at dramatic characterization: there is a roll-call and the woman go to the gang-plank in various moods, while the by-standers comment on their appearance and manner. The whole of the last act, which plays on a plateau near New Orleans, is given up to the lovers. Manon dies; des Grieux shrieks his despair and falls lifeless upon her body. Puccini has followed his confrères of the concentrated agony school in introducing an orchestral intermezzo. He does this between the second and third acts and gives a clue to its purposed emotional contents by providing it with a descriptive title, "Imprisonment. Journey to Havre," and quoting a passage from the Abbé Prévost's book in which des Grieux confesses the overpowering strength of his passion and determines to follow Manon wherever she may go, "even to the ends of the world." Here, at least, we recognize a sincere effort to make the interlude something more than a stop-gap or a device to make up for the paucity of sustained music in the course of the dramatic action.

"Madama Butterfly" in the original Italian had been anticipated by a long series of English performances by Mr. Savage's company at the Garden Theater, beginning on November 12th. This production is deserving of record. Walter Rothwell was the conductor, and the principal singers in the cast were Elza Szamosy, a Hungarian, as Cio-Cio-San; Harriet Behne as Suzuki, Joseph F. Sheehan as Pinkerton, and Winifred Goff as Sharpless. The opera reached the Metropolitan Opera House on February 11, 1907, when it was sung in the presence of the composer by the following cast:

Cio-Cio-San .... Geraldine Farrar
Suzuki .... Louise Homer
Pinkerton .... Caruso
Sharpless .... Scotti
Goro .... Reiss
   Conductor, Arturo Vigna

A great deal of the sympathetic interest which "Madama Butterfly" evoked on its first production and has held in steady augmentation ever since was due to the New York public's familiarity with the subject of the opera created by John Luther Long's story and Mr. Belasco's wonderfully pathetic drama upon which this much more pretentious edifice of Messrs. Illica, Giacosa, and Puccini is reared. To the popular interest in story and play Japan lent color in more respects than one, having at the time a powerful hold upon the popular imagination. We have had the Mikado's kingdom with its sunshine and flowers, its romantic chivalry, its geishas and continent and incontinent morals upon the stage before,—in the spoken drama, in comic operetta, in musical farce, and in serious musical drama. Messrs. Gilbert and Sullivan used its external motives for one of their finest satirical skits, an incomparable model in its way; but the parallel in serious opera was that created by Signor Illica, one of the librettists of "Madama Butterfly," and Signor Mascagni. The opera was "Iris," the production of which at the Metropolitan Opera House helped to emphasize the failure of the composer's American visit. "Iris" is a singular blending of allegory which had a merit quite admirable though ill-applied, and tragedy of the kind to which I have already several times referred in this book. In "Iris" as in "Madama Butterfly" we have Japanese music,—the twanging of samisens and the tinkling of gongs; but it was more coarsely applied, with more apparent and merely outward purpose, and it was only an accompaniment of a vision stained all over with purulence and grossness. "Madama Butterfly" tells a tale of wickedness contrasted with lovely devotion. Its carnality has an offset in a picture of love conjugal and love maternal, and its final appeal is one to infinite pity. And in this it is beautiful. Opera-goers are familiar with Signor Puccini's manner. "Tosca" and "La Bohème" speak out of many measures of his latest opera, but there is introduced in it a mixture of local color. Genuine Japanese tunes come to the surface of the instrumental flood at intervals and tunes which copy their characteristics of rhythm, melody, and color. As a rule this is a dangerous proceeding except in comedy which aims to chastise the foibles and follies of a people and a period. Nothing is more admirable, however, than Signor Puccini's use of it to heighten the dramatic climaxes; the merry tune with which Cio-Cio-San diverts her child in the second act and the use of a bald native tune thundered out fortissimo in naked unison with periodic punctuations of harmony at the close are striking cases in point. Nor should the local color in the delineation of the break of day in the beginning of the third act, and the charmingly felicitous use of mellifluous gongs in the marriage scene be overlooked. Always the effect is musical and dramatically helpful. As for the rest there are many moments of a strange charm in the score, music filled with a haunting tenderness and poetic loveliness, music in which there is a beautiful meeting of the external picture and the spiritual content of the scene. Notable among these moments is the scene in which Butterfly and her attendant scatter flowers throughout the room in expectation of

Pinkerton's return. Here melodies and harmonies are exhaled like the odors of the flowers.

Giordano's "Fedora," first performed on December 5, 1906, was given with this distribution of parts:

    Fedora .... Lina Cavalieri
   (Her first appearance.)
Olga .... Bella Alten
Dimitri .... Marie Mattfeld
Un piccolo Savojardo .... Josephine Jacoby
Loris Ipanow .... Enrico Caruso
De Siriex .... Antonio Scotti
Il Barone Rouvel |
Desiré | .... Mr. Paroli
Cirillo .... Mr. Bégué
Borow .... Mr. Mühlmann
Grech .... Mr. Dufriche
Boleslaw Lazinski .... Mr. Voghere
Lorek .... Mr. Navarini
    Conductor, Arturo Vigna

The opera is an attempt to put music to the familiar play by Sardou; an utterly futile attempt. A more sluggish and intolerable first act than the legal inquest it would be difficult to imagine. Fragments of inconsequential tunes float along on a turgid stream, above which the people of the play chatter and scream, becoming intelligible and interesting only when they lapse into ordinary speech. Ordinary speech, however, is the only kind of speech that an expeditious drama can tolerate, and it is not raised to a higher power by the blowing of brass or the beating of drums. The frankest confession of the futility of Giordano's effort to make a lyric drama out of "Fedora" is contained in the fact that only those moments in his score are musical in the accepted sense when the play stops, as in the case of the intermezzo which cuts the second act in two, or when the old operatic principles wake into life again, as in Loris's confession of love. Here, in the first instance, a mood receives musical delineation, and in the second a passion whose expression is naturally lyrical receives utterance. One device new to the operatic stage, in its externals at least, is ingeniously employed by the composer: the conversation in which Fedora extorts a confession from Loris is carried on while a pianist entertains a princess' guests with a solo upon his instrument. But the fact that singing tones, not spoken, are used adds nothing to the value of the scene.

On returning from Europe late in the summer of 1906 Mr. Conried announced his intention to produce Richard Strauss's "Salome," and his forces had no sooner been gathered together than Mr. Hertz began the laborious task of preparing the opera—if opera it can be called—for performance. There can scarcely be a doubt that Mr. Conried hoped for a sensational flurry like that which had accompanied the production of "Parsifal"; but, with an eye to the main chance, he confined his first official proclamation to a single performance, which, in connection with a concert by all his chief singers not concerned in the opera, was to be given for his annual benefit. Evidently he felt less sure about the outcome of this production than he had about that of "Parsifal," and was bound to reap all the benefits that could come from a powerful appeal to popular curiosity touching so notorious a work as Strauss's setting of Oscar Wilde's drama. The performance took place with many preliminary flourishes beyond the ordinary on January 22d. Two days before there was held a public rehearsal, which was attended by about a thousand persons who had received invitations, most of them being stockholders of the opera house, old subscribers, stockholders of Mr. Conried's company, writers for the newspapers, and friends of the artists and the management. The opera was given with the following cast:

```
Salome ................................. Miss Fremstad
Herodias ................................. Miss Weed
Herodias's Page ..................... Josephine Jacoby
Herod's Page ......................... Marie Mattfeld
Herod ................................. Carl Burrian
Jochanaan ............................ Anton Van Rooy
Narraboth ............................ Andreas Dippel
First Jew ............................. Mr. Reiss
Second Jew ........................... Mr. Bayer
Third Jew ............................. Mr. Paroli
Fourth Jew ........................... Mr. Bars
Fifth Jew ............................. Mr. Dufriche
First Nazarene ........................ Mr. Journet
Second Nazarene ...................... Mr. Stiner
First Soldier ......................... Mr. Mühlmann
Second Soldier ....................... Mr. Blass
A Cappadocian ........................ Mr. Lange
        Conductor, Alfred Hertz
```

Concerning the effect produced upon the public by the performance of the work I shall permit Mr. W. P. Eaton, then a reporter for The Tribune, to speak for me.

The concert was over a little after nine, and the real business of the evening began at a quarter to ten, when the lights went out, there was a sound from the orchestra pit, and the curtains parted on "Salome." The setting for "Salome" is an imaginative creation of the scene painter's art. The high steps to the palace door to the right, the cover of the cistern, backed by ironic roses in the center, and beyond the deep night sky and the moonlight on the distant roofs. Two cedars cut the sky, black and mournful. Against this background "Salome" moves like a tigress, the costumes of the court glow with a dun, barbaric splendor, and the red fire from the tripods streams silently up into the night till you fancy you can almost smell it. Here was atmosphere like Belasco's, and saturated with it the opera moved to its appointed end, sinister, compelling, disgusting.

What the opera is is told elsewhere. It remains to record that in the audience at this performance, as at the dress rehearsals on Sunday, the effect of horror was pronounced. Many voices were hushed as the crowd passed out into the night, many faces were white almost as those at the rail of a ship. Many women were silent, and men spoke as if a bad dream were on them. The preceding concert was forgotten; ordinary emotions following an opera were banished. The grip of a strange horror or disgust, was on the majority. It was significant that the usual applause was lacking. It was scattered and brief.

In this there is no hyperbole; it fails of a complete description only in neglecting to chronicle the fact that a large proportion of the audience left the audience-room at the beginning of the bestial apostrophe to the head of the Baptist. It was because of this pronounced rejection of the work by an audience which might have been considered elected to it in a peculiar manner that it was a sincere cause of regret that the action of the directors of the Metropolitan Opera and Real Estate Company caused a prohibition of further performances. It would have been better and conduced more to artistic righteousness if the public had been permitted to kill the work by refusing to witness it. In my opinion there is no doubt but that this would have been the result had Mr. Conried attempted to give performances either at extraordinary or ordinary prices. Immediately after his benefit performance he announced three representations outside of the subscription, the first of which was to take place on February 1st. Two days after the first performance, the directors of the opera house company held a meeting and adopted the following resolution, which was promptly communicated to Mr. Conried:

The directors of the Metropolitan Opera and Real Estate Company consider that the performance of "Salome" is objectionable and detrimental to the best interests of the Metropolitan Opera House. They therefore protest against any repetition of this opera.

Under the terms of the contract between the directors and Mr. Conried, such a protest was the equivalent of a command, disobedience of which would have worked a forfeiture of the lease. Mr. Conried parleyed, pleading his cause voluminously in the public prints, as well as before the directors, meanwhile keeping his announcement of the three performances before the people. But the sale of tickets amounted to next to nothing, and Mr. Conried yielded with as much grace as possible, when on January 30th the directors refused to modify their action, though they expressed a willingness to recoup Mr. Conried for some of his expenses in mounting the opera. The directors who took this action were J. P. Morgan, William K. Vanderbilt, G. G. Haven, Charles Lanier, George F. Baker, D. O. Mills, George Bowdoin, A. D. Juilliard, August Belmont, and H. McK. Twombly. Representatives of Mr. Conried's company who argued the case before the directors were Otto H. Kahn, Robert Goelet, James Speyer, H. R. Winthrop, and R. H. Cottenet. For some time Mr. Conried talked about performing the opera in another theater, and the directors of his company formally agreed that he might do so on his own responsibility; but nothing came of it. Mr. Conried had probably seen the handwriting on the wall of his box office. The next year there were more solemn proclamations to the effect that it would be performed outside of New York. Boston sent in a protest, and the flurry was over, except as it was kept up in silly and mendacious reports sent to the newspapers of Germany touching the influences that had worked for the prohibition. There never was a case which asked for less speculation. Decent men did not want to have their house polluted with the stench with which Oscar Wilde's play had filled the nostrils of humanity. Having the power to prevent the pollution they exercised it.

A reviewer ought to be equipped with a dual nature, both intellectually and morally, in order to pronounce fully and fairly upon the qualities of this drama by Oscar Wilde and Richard Strauss. He should be an embodied conscience stung into righteous fury by the moral stench exhaled by the decadent and pestiferous work, but, though it make him retch, he should be sufficiently judicial in his temperament calmly to look at the drama in all its aspects and determine whether or not as a whole it is an instructive note on the life and culture of the times and whether or not this exudation from the diseased and polluted will and imagination of the authors marks a real advance in artistic expression, irrespective of its contents or their fitness for dramatic representation. This is asking much of the harassed commentator on the things which the multitude of his readers receive as contributions to their diversion merely and permit to be crowded out of their minds by the next pleasant or unpleasant shock to their sensibilities. He has not the time, nor have his readers the patience, to enter upon a discussion of the questions of moral and esthetic principle which ought to pave the way for the investigation. If he can tell what the play is, what its musical investiture is like, wherein the combined elements have worked harmoniously and efficiently to an end which to their authors seemed artistic, and therefore justifiable, he will have done much. In the case before us even this much cannot be done until some notions which have long had validity are put aside. We are only concerned with "Salome" in its newest form,—that given it by the musical composer. If it shall ever win approbation here, as it seems to have done in several German cities, it will be because of the shape into which Richard Strauss has moulded it.

Several attempts had been made to habilitate Oscar Wilde's drama on the New York stage, and had failed. If the opera succeeds it will be because a larger public has discovered that the music which has been consorted with the old pictures, actions, and words has added to them an element either of charm or expressive potentiality hitherto felt to be lacking. Is that true? Has a rock of offense been removed? Has a mephitic odor been changed to a sweet savor by the subtle alchemy of the musical composer? Has a drama abhorrent, bestial, repellent, and loathsome been changed into a thing of delectability by the potent agency of music? It used to be said that things too silly to be spoken might be sung; is it also true that things too vile, too foul, too nauseating for contemplation may be seen, so they be insidiously and wickedly glorified by the musician's art? As a rule, plays have not been improved by being turned into operas. Always their dramatic movement has been interrupted, their emotional current clogged, their poetry emasculated by the transformation. Things are better now than they were in the long ago, when music took no part at all in dramatic action, but waited for a mood which it had power to publish and celebrate; but music has acquired its new power only by an abnegation of its better part, by assuming new functions, and asking a revaluation of its elements on a new esthetic basis. In "Salome" music is largely a decorative element, like the scene,—like the costumes. It creates atmosphere, like the affected stylism of much of Oscar Wilde's text, with its Oriental imagery borrowed from "The Song of Solomon," diluted and sophisticated; it gives emotional significance to situations, helping the facial play of Salome and her gestures to proclaim the workings of her mind, when speech has deserted her; it is at its best as the adjunct and inspiration of the lascivious dance. In the last two instances, however, it reverts to the purpose and also the manner (with a difference) which have always obtained, and becomes music in the purer sense. Then the would-be dramatist is swallowed up in the symphonist, and Strauss is again the master magician who can juggle with our senses and our reason and make his instrumental voices body forth "the forms of things unknown."

It would be wholly justifiable to characterize "Salome" as a symphonic poem for which the play supplies the program. The parallelism of which we hear between Strauss and Wagner exists only in part—only in the application of the principle of characterization by means of musical symbols or typical phrases. Otherwise the men's work on diametrically opposite lines. With all his musical affluence, Wagner aimed, at least, to make his orchestra only the bearer and servant of the dramatic word. Nothing can be plainer (it did not need that he should himself have confessed it) than that Strauss looks upon the words as necessary evils. His vocal parts are not song, except for brief, intensified spaces at long intervals. They are declamation. The song-voice is used, one is prone to think, only because by means of it the words can be made to be heard above the orchestra. Song, in the old acceptance of the word, implies beauty of tone and justness of intonation. It is amazing how indifferent the listener is to both vocal quality and intervallic accuracy in "Salome." Wilde's stylistic efforts are lost in the flood of instrumental sound; only the mood which they were designed to produce remains. Jochanaan sings phrases, which are frequently tuneful, and when they are not denunciatory are set in harmonies agreeable to the ear. But by reason of that fact Jochanaan comes perilously near being an old-fashioned operatic figure—an ascetic Marcel, with little else to differentiate him from his Meyerbeerian prototype than his "raiment of camel's hair and a leather's girdle about his loins," and an inflated phrase which must serve for the tunes sung by the rugged Huguenot soldier. Strauss characterizes by his vocal manner as well as by his themes and their instrumental treatment; but for his success he relies at least as much upon the performer as upon the musical text. A voice and style like Mr. Van Rooy's give an uplift, a prophetic breadth, dignity, and impressiveness to the utterances of Jochanaan which are paralleled only by the imposing instrumental apparatus employed in proclaiming the phrase invented to clothe his pronouncements. Six horns, used as Strauss knows how to use them, are a good substratum for the arch-colorist. The nervous staccato chatter of Herod is certainly characteristic of this neurasthenic. This specimen from the pathological museum of Messrs. Wilde and Strauss appears in a state which causes alarm lest his internal mechanism fly asunder and scatter his corporeal parts about the scene. The crepitating volubility with which Strauss endows him is a marvelously ingenious conceit; but it leans heavily for its effect, we fear, on the amazing skill of Mr. Burrian, not only in cackling out the words synchronously with the orchestral part, but in emotionally coloring them and blending them in a unity with his facial expression and his perturbed bodily movements. Salome sings, often in the explosive style of Wagner's Kundry, sometimes with something like fluent continuity, but from her song has been withheld all the symmetrical and graceful contours comprehended in the concept of melody. Hers are the superheated phrases invented to give expression to her passion, and out of them she must construct the vocal accompaniment to the instrumental song, which reaches its culmination in the scene which, instead of receiving a tonal beatification, as it does, ought to be relegated to the silence and darkness of the deepest dungeon of a madhouse or a hospital.

Here is a matter, of the profoundest esthetical and ethical significance, which might as well be disposed of now, so far as this discussion is concerned, regardless of the symmetrical continuity of the argument. There is a vast deal of ugly music in "Salome,"—music that offends the ear and rasps the nerves like fiddlestrings played on by a coarse file. In a criticism of Strauss's "Symphonia Domestica" I took occasion to point out that a large latitude must be allowed to the dramatic composer which must be denied to the symphonist. Consort a dramatic or even a lyric text with music and all manner of tonal devices may derive explanation, if not justification, from the words. But in purely instrumental music the arbitrary purposes of a composer cannot replace the significance which must lie in the music itself—that is in its emotional and esthetic content. It does not lie in intellectual content, for thought to become articulate demands speech. The champions of Richard Strauss have defended ugliness in his last symphony, the work which immediately preceded "Salome," and his symphonic poems on the score that music must be an expression of truth, and truth is not always beautiful. In a happier day than this it was believed that the true and the beautiful were bound together in angelic wedlock and that all art found its highest mission in giving them expression. But the drama has been led through devious paths into the charnel house, and in "Salome" we must needs listen to the echoes of its dazed and drunken footfalls. The maxim "Truth before convention" asserts its validity and demands recognition under the guise of "characteristic beauty." We may refuse to admit that ugliness is entitled to be raised to a valid principle in music dissociated from words or stage pictures, on the ground that thereby it contravenes and contradicts its own nature; but we may no longer do so when it surrenders its function as an expression of the beautiful and becomes merely an illustrative element, an aid to dramatic expression. What shall be said, then, when music adorns itself with its loveliest attributes and lends them to the apotheosis of that which is indescribably, yes, inconceivably, gross and abominable? Music cannot lie. Not even the genius of Richard Strauss can make it discriminate in its soaring ecstasy between a vile object and a good. There are three supremely beautiful musical moments in "Salome." Two of them are purely instrumental, though they illustrate dramatic incidents; the third is predominantly instrumental, though it has an accompaniment of word and action. The first is an intermezzo in which all action ceases except that which plays in the bestially perverted heart and mind of Salome. A baffled amorous hunger changes to a desire for revenge. The second is the music of the dance. The third is the marvelous finale in which an impulse which can only be conceived as rising from the uttermost pit of degradation is beatified. Crouching over the dissevered head of the prophet, Salome addresses it in terms of reproach, of grief, of endearment and longing, and finally kisses the bloody lips and presses her teeth into the gelid flesh. It is incredible that an artist should ever have conceived such a scene for public presentation. In all the centuries in which the story of the dance before Herod has fascinated sculptors, painters, and poets, in spite of the accretions of lustful incident upon the simple Biblical story, it remained for a poet of our day to conceive this horror and a musician of our day to put forth his highest powers in its celebration. There was a scene before the mental eye of Strauss as he wrote. It was that of Isolde singing out her life over the dead body of Tristan. In the music of that scene, I do not hesitate to say again, as I have said before, there lies the most powerful plea ever made for the guilty lovers. It is the choicest flower of Wagner's creative faculty, the culmination of his powers as a composer, and never before or since has the purifying and ennobling capacity of music been so convincingly demonstrated. Strauss has striven to outdo it, and there are those who think that in this episode he actually raised music to a higher power. He has not only gone with the dramatist and outraged every sacred instinct of humanity by calling the lust for flesh, alive or dead, love, but he has celebrated her ghoulish passion as if he would perforce make of her an object of that "redemption" of which, again following Wagner but along oblique paths, he prates so strangely in his opera of "Guntram."

It is obvious on a moment's reflection that, had Strauss desired, the play might easily have been modified so as to avoid this gruesome episode. A woman scorned, vengeful, and penitent would have furnished forth material enough for his finale and dismissed his audience with less disturbance of their moral and physical stomachs. But Strauss, to put it mildly, is a sensationalist despite his genius, and his business sense is large, as New Yorkers know ever since he wound up an artistic tour of America with a concert in a department store. When Nietszche was the talk of Germany we got "Also Sprach Zarathustra." Oscar Wilde's play, too unsavory for the France for which it was written, taboo in England because of its subject, has been joyously acclaimed in Germany, where there are many men who are theoretically licentious and practically uxorious; and Strauss was willing that his countrymen should sup to their full of delights and horrors.

To think back, under the impressions of the final scene, to the dance which precipitated the catastrophe is to bring up recollections of little else than the striking originality of its music, its piquancies of rhythm and orchestration, its artfully simulated Orientalism, and the thrilling effect produced by a recurrence to the "love music" ("Let me kiss thy mouth, Jochanaan,") at a moment before the frenetic close, when the representation of Salome (a professional dancer, Miss Froehlich, was deftly substituted for Miss Fremstad at the Metropolitan performance) approaches the cistern in which the white flesh, black hair, and red lips of her idolatry are immured, and casts wistful glances into its depths. Since the outcome was to be what it became it would have been folly in Mr. Conried's performance to attempt to disguise the true character of the "Dance of the Seven Veils." Miss Froeblich gave us quite unconcernedly a danse du ventre; not quite so pronounced as it has been seen in the Oriental quarters at our world's fairs, not quite so free of bodily covering as tradition would have justified. Yet it served to emphasize its purpose in the play. This dance in its original estate is a dramatic dance; it is, indeed, the frankest example of terpsichorean symbolism within the whole range of the pantomimic dance. The conditions under which Wilde and Strauss introduce it in their drama spare one all need of thought; there is sufficient commentary in the. doddering debility of the pleading Herod and the lustful attitude of his protruding eyes. There are fantastical persons who like to talk about religious symbolism in connection with this dance, and of forms of worship of vast antiquity. The dance is old. It was probably danced in Egypt before the Exodus; in Greece probably before Orpheus sang and

"Ilion, like a mist, rose into towers."

But it is not to be seriously thought that from those days to this there was ever any doubt as to its significance and its purpose, which is to pander to prurient appetites and arouse libidinous passions. Always, too, from those days to this, its performers have been the most abandoned of the courtesan class.

There is not a whiff of fresh and healthy air blowing through "Salome" except that which exhales from the cistern, the prison house of Jochanaan. Even the love of Narraboth, the young Syrian captain, for the princess is tainted by the jealous outbursts of Herodias's page. Salome is the unspeakable; Herodias, though divested of her most pronounced historical attributes (she adjures her daughter not to dance, though she gloats over the revenge which it brings to her), is a human hyena; Herod, a neurasthenic voluptuary. A group of Jews who are shown disputing in the manner of Baxter Street, though conveyed by Wilde from Flaubert's pages, are used by Strauss to provide a comic interlude. Years ago a musical humorist in Vienna caused much amusement by writing the words of a quarrel of Jewish pedlers under the voices of the fugue in Mozart's overture to "The Magic Flute." Three hundred years ago Orazio Vecchi composed a burlesque madrigal in the severe style of that day, in which he tried to depict the babel of sounds in a synagogue. Obviously the musical Jew is supposed to be allied to the stage Jew and to be fit food for the humorist. Strauss's music gives a new reading to Wilde; it is a caricature in which cacophony reigns supreme under the guise of polyphony. There are five of the Jews, and each is pregnantly set forth in the theme with which he maintains his contention.

This is but one of many instances of marvelous astuteness in the delineation and characteristic portions of the music. The quality which will he most promptly recognized by the public is its decorative and illustrative element. The orchestra paints incessantly; moods that are prevalent for a moment do not suffice the eager illustrator. The passing word seizes his fancy. Herod describes the jewels which he promises to give to Salome so she relieve him of his oath, and the music of the orchestra glints and glistens with a hundred prismatic tints. Salome wheedles the young Syrian to bring forth the prophet, and her cry, "Thou wilt do this thing for me," is carried to his love-mad brain by a voluptuous glissando of the harp which is as irresistible as her glance and smile. But the voluptuous music is no more striking than the tragic. Strauss strikes off the head of Jochanaan with more thunderous noise upon the kettle-drums than Wagner uses when Fafner pounds the life out of Fasolt with his gigantic stave; but there is nothing in all of Wagner's tragic pages to compare in tenseness of feeling with the moment of suspense while Salome is peering into the cistern and marveling that she hears no sound of a death struggle. At this moment there comes an uncanny sound from the orchestra that is positively blood-curdling. The multitude of instruments are silent—all but the string basses. Some of them maintain a tremolo on the deep E flat. Suddenly there comes a short, high B flat. Again and again with more rapid iteration. Such a voice was never heard in the orchestra before. What Strauss designed it to express does not matter. It accomplishes a fearful accentuation of the awful situation. Strauss got the hint from Berlioz, who never used the device (which he heard from a Piedmontese double-bass player), but recommended it to composers who wished to imitate in the orchestra "a loud female cry." Strauss in his score describes how the effect is to be produced and wants it to sound like a stertorous groan. It is produced by pinching the highest string of the double-bass at the proper node between the finger-board and the bridge and sounding it by a quick jerk of the bow. This is but one of a hundred new and strange devices with which the score of "Salome" has enriched instrumental music. The dance employs a vast apparatus, but the Oriental color impressed upon it at the outset by oboe and tambour remains as persistent as its rhythmical figure, which seems to have been invented to mark the sinuous flexure of the spine and the swaying of the hips of the dancer. Devices made familiar by the symphonic poems are introduced with increased effect, such as the muting of the entire army of brass instruments. Startling effects are obtained by a confusion of keys, confusion of rhythms, sudden contrasts from an overpowering tutti to the stridulous whirring of empty fifths on the violins, a trill on the flutes, or a dissonant mutter of the basses. The celesta, an instrument with keyboard and bell tone, contributes fascinating effects, and the xylophone is used;—utterances that are lascivious as well as others that are macabre. Dissonance runs riot and frequently carries the imagination away completely captive. The score is unquestionably the greatest triumph of reflection and ingenuity of contrivance that the literature of music can show. The invention that has been expended on the themes seems less admirable. Only the pompous proclamation of the theme which is dominant in Jochanaan's music saves it from being called commonplace. A flippant hunter of reminiscences might find its prototype in the "Lady Moon" chorus of Balfe's "Bohemian Girl." There is no greater originality in the theme which publishes Salome's amorousness for the white flesh of Jochanaan, which time and again shows its kinship to the andante melody in the first movement of Tschaikowsky's "Pathétique" symphony, but becomes more and more transfigured in its passionate loveliness when it aids the beatification of the more than ghoulish princess. There is no escape from the power of the music when it soars to grandiose heights in the duet between Salome 'and the prophet, the subsequent intermezzo and the wicked apotheosis. It overwhelms the senses and reduces the nervous system of the listeners to exhaustion.

The subscription season of 1906-07 at the Metropolitan Opera House began on November 26th and lasted seventeen weeks, compassing sixty-eight subscription performances of twenty-three operas and twenty-nine extra performances. Mr. Conried announced at the close of the supplementary season that his receipts had aggregated $1,005,770.20; but this sum doubtless included the receipts from the Boston season. The season 1907-08 began on November 18th and lasted twenty weeks. There were one hundred subscription performances (Thursday having been added to the subscription nights), twenty Saturday popular representations, and three special. Twenty-seven operas were in the list, but only one of them was new. This was Francesco Cilèa's "Adriana Lecouvreur," which was brought forward on the opening night of the season, and had one repetition afterward, notwithstanding that it had been incorporated in the repertory to give Signor Caruso an opportunity to appear in a new work together with Mme. Cavalieri. The cast was as follows:

Adriana Lecouvreur .... Lina Cavalieri
La Principessa .... Josephine Jacoby
Mlle. Jouvenot .... Marie Mattfeld
Mlle. Dangeville .... Mme. Girerd
Maurizio .... Enrico Caruso
L'Abate .... Georges Lucas
Michonnet .... Antonio Scotti
Il Principe .... Marcel Journet

Quinault .... Mr. Barocchi
Poisson .... Mr. Raimondi
Maggiordomo .... Mr. Navarini
      Conductor, Rudolfo Ferrari

    Cilèa has in this work attempted to put the familiar play of Scribe and Legouvé into music. Formerly, as we all know, composers used to try to make operas out of plays. The result is for the greater part a sort of spectacle recalling familiar things to the eye, accompanied by an undercurrent of music occasionally breaking into melody and buoying up long stretches of disjointed and fragmentary conversation, out of which, under the best of circumstances, it would be difficult to construct a drama and from which it is not possible to extract the pleasure which one can still find in the old-time style of entertainment derisively called a concert in costume. The manner of "Adriana Lecouvreur" is more or less that of Puccini, Giordano, and Spinelli—to mention the names that immediately preceded Cilèa's across the ocean—but it is only in the manner, not in the matter, except, as some disagreeable seekers after reminiscences will say, when that matter is borrowed. There is some graceful music in the score and some strains which simulate. passion; but to find in any of its parts the kind of music which vitalizes the word or heightens the dramatic situation is a hopeless task. It is melodramatic music, which becomes most fluent when there is least occasion for it, and which makes its best appeal when the heroine declaims above it in the speaking voice (as she does in the climax of the third act, when Adrienne recites a speech from Racine's "Phèdre" in order to accuse the Princess of adultery), when it inspires the heroine carefully and particularly to blow out every light in a large drawing-room, or when it accompanies a ballet which is neither a part of the play nor an incidental divertissement, but only a much-needed device to give the composer an opportunity for a few symmetrical pieces of music. Even here, however, this music must serve as a foil for the everlasting chit-chat of the people of the drama. A pitiful work it was with which to open a season. Mascagni's "Iris" was brought out on December 6th, and after it was all too late there was a carefully studied performance of "Don Giovanni" and a sumptuously, too sumptuously, mounted production of "Fidelio." These two works practically summed up the labors accomplished by Gustav Mahler, though he produced excellent representations (except scenically) of "Tristan" and "Die Walküre." Mr. Mahler, having laid down the directorship of the Court Opera at Vienna, was brought to New York by Mr. Conried, and his coming had raised high the expectations of the lovers of German opera. The record must also include the enlistment in the Metropolitan forces of Madame Berta Morena and Madame Leffler-Burckhardt, whose influence upon the season would have been much more marked had not Mr. Conried's policy of catering principally to the

Italianissimi prevented them from becoming as large factors as they deserved to be.

When Mr. Conried issued his prospectus for his fifth season it had already long been an open secret that some of the men whom he had invited to share the glories and the profits of his administration had decreed his downfall. During the fourth season he had been ill with sciatic neuritis, and there was no improvement in his physical condition when he entered upon his duties in 1907-08. His ability to attend to the arduous labors of the managing directorate was questioned. Worse than this, the air for months had been full of whispers of scandalous doings in the business department, and the chorus of dissatisfaction with the artistic results of his directorate, which had begun in the first season, had been swelling steadily. Two seasons before he had put forth a disingenuous apology for his administration, comparing the cost and difficulties of producing opera in the preceding season with the cost and difficulties under Mr. Grau. The matter was one which affected the stockholders of his company only so far as the finances were concerned; as to the difficulties, it was not easy to see how they could have been less formerly than now, when there was so much more money to spend, and so much more had been spent in improving the facilities for opera giving. The patrons of the establishment found large ground for complaint in contrasting the artistic achievements with the flamboyant promises which had been made when the new administration came in. Mr. Conried had told them that his first aim was to raise the standard of performance, and to this end he had banished all thought of profit from his mind. He was going to continue to employ the most refulgent "stars" in the world, but to abolish the "star" system. The season in Philadelphia was to be abandoned so that there might be more time for rehearsals, and less exhaustion of his artistic forces. Opera in English was to be added to opera in Italian, French, and German. As for the French and Italian works they were to be given as they had been under Mr. Grau, but the German was to be raised to a higher plane. Not one of these promises was redeemed. Italian operas were given great prominence over French, and the additions to the Italian list, which were really new, were of the poorest sort. Perfunctoriness, apathy, and ignorant stage management marked the German performances, which were all but eliminated from the subscription list. There were evidences of high striving at the outset in the engagement of Messrs. Mottl, Lautenschläger, and Fuchs, as I have already said, but the results were negligible because the men were unable to employ their capacities. There were sensational features, like the production of "Parsifal" and "Salome," but there were humiliating ones, like the prostitution of a great establishment for the performance of "Die Fledermaus" and "Der Zigeunerbaron" to deck out the Herr Direktor's benefits. The blight of commercialism had fallen on the institution. On

February 11, 1908, Mr. Conried resigned, and announcement was officially made of a reorganization of his company, and the engagement of Giulio Gatti-Casazza and Andreas Dippel as managers of the opera for the season 1908-09.

Following is a table of performances during the subscription seasons of Mr. Conried's administration:

THE CONRIED PERIOD: 1902-'08

Operas	1903-4	1904-5	1905-6	1906-7	1907-8
"Rigoletto"	5	2	5	2	4
"Die Walküre"	4	4	3	2	3
"La Bohème"	3	3	5	7	7
"Aïda"	6	5	4	6	5
"Tosca"	4	4	3	6	7
"Tannhäuser"	5	9	4	5	4
"Cavalleria Rusticana"	8	3	0	1	0
"Pagliacci"	5	3	3	4	4
"Lohengrin"	5	6	5	5	2
"La Traviata"	3	4	2	3	6
"Il Barbiere"	4	2	2	0	6
"Lucia di Lammermoor"	3	3	5	4	1
"Tristan und Isolde"	4	2	3	4	6
"The Magic Flute"	4	0	0	0	0
"Siegfried"	2	2	3	4	3
"L'Elisir d'Amore"	4	1	2	0	0
"Carmen"	4	4	2	1	0
"Coppélia" (ballet)	4	1	0	0	0
"La Dame Blanche" (Ger.)	1	0	0	0	0
"Faust"	4	4	5	4	6
"Mefistofele"	*2	0	0	0	7
"Roméo et Juliette"	2	4	0	5	0
"Nozze di Figaro"	1	2	0	0	0
+ "Parsifal"	11	8	4	2	0
"Fidelio"	1	1	0	0	3
"Das Rheingold"	1	2	2	1	0
"Götterdämmerung"	1	2	3	1	0
"La Gioconda"	0	4	4	0	0
"Die Meistersinger"	0	7	4	0	4
"Lucrezia Borgia"	0	1	0	0	0
"Don Pasquale"	0	2	2	1	0
"Die Puppenfee" (ballet)	0	1	0	0	0
"Les Huguenots"	0	4	0	0	0

"Un Ballo in Maschera" 0 2 0 0 0
+ "Die Fledermaus" 0 4 1 0 0
"Die Königin von Saba" 0 0 5 0 0
"Hänsel und Gretel" 0 0 11 8 5
"La Favorita" 0 0 4 0 0
"La Sonnambula" 0 0 2 0 0
"Il Trovatore" 0 0 4 0 6
"Don Giovanni" 0 0 2 0 4
"Martha" 0 0 4 3 3
"Der Zigeunerbaron" 0 0 1 0 0
+ "Fedora" 0 0 0 4 3
+ "La Damnation de Faust" ... 0 0 0 5 0
"Lakmé" 0 0 0 3 0
"L'Africaine" 0 0 0 2 0
"Manon Lescaut" 0 0 0 3 5
"Madama Butterfly" 0 0 0 5 6
+ "Salome" 0 0 0 1 0
+ "Adriana Lecouvreur" 0 0 0 0 2
"Der Fliegende Holländer" ... 0 0 0 0 4
"Iris" 0 0 0 0 5
"Mignon" 0 0 0 0 5

* One scene only. + Novelties.

CHAPTER XXIII
HAMMERSTEIN AND HIS OPERA HOUSE

Before the close of the season 1905-06 at the Metropolitan Opera House, Mr. Oscar Hammerstein, who was building a large theater in Thirty-fourth Street, between Eighth and Ninth avenues, announced that the building would be called the Manhattan Opera House, that it would be exclusively his property and under his management, and that it was to be devoted to grand opera.

It is no reflection on Mr. Hammerstein to say that many who have been prompt and generous in their recognition of his achievements since, looked upon his enterprise as quixotic, down to the very day of the opening of his house. True, he was known to be a manager of extraordinary resource and indomitable energy, but he had dallied more or less with the operatic bauble without disclosing any ambition to have his name written among the managerial wrecks which have been cast upon the shores of Italian Opera, from Handel's day to ours, It was easy to recall that the new opera house was not his first, but that he had built one in the same street, given it the same name thirteen years before, and begun a season of grand opera with an ambitious novelty, only to abandon the enterprise after a fortnight. He had even tried German opera with no less popular an artist than Mme. Lehmann in his earlier opera house in Harlem, and entered into rivalry with an established institution in 1891 for the production of "Cavalleria Rusticana," then the reigning sensation of the hour in Europe.

When the old Manhattan Opera House, so soon abandoned to the uses of vaudeville, opened its doors with Moszkowski's "Boabdil," on January 23, 1893, there was no rival operatic establishment in the city, for the interior of the Metropolitan had been destroyed by fire, and Abbey, Schoeffel & Grau were resting on their oars for a season while the question whether or not the home of the costly and fashionable entertainment should be restored was under discussion by its owners. Yet Mr. Hammerstein was discouraged by two weeks of failure. It was not strange that many observers refused to believe that he was of the stuff out of which opera managers are made. He did not seem illogical enough, though he showed some symptoms of having been bitten by the opera habit.

Neither was there much to encourage belief in his announcements in the manner in which he put them forth. He began early in the spring by saying that he had engaged Jean and Édouard de Reszke, and kept their names before the people almost up to the time of the opening. He went abroad to engage artists, and even after his return it looked as if it would be a physical impossibility to complete his theater in time for the date set for opening. In fact it was not completed, but when the season arrived he was ready to attempt all that he had said he would do, except keep some wild promises about singers; and when the season closed the fact that loomed largest in the retrospect was the undaunted manner in which he had carried on a difficult and dangerous enterprise, compelling a large element of the public to respect and admire him, and making it possible for him to lay out a second season on lines of real pith and moment, and carry an admirable enterprise to an admirable conclusion.

Mr. Hammerstein began his first season on December 3, 1906, and closed it on April 20, 1907. There were a few admirable artists in his company, but the majority were either inexperienced or of the conventional Italian type. His principal soprano leggiero was Mlle. Pinkert, a Polish singer of good routine and fine skill; his dramatic soprano, Mlle. Russ, whose knowledge of the conventions of the stage was complete, and expressive powers excellent, though they exerted little charm. He had a serviceable mezzo in Mme. De Cisneros (formerly a junior member of the Metropolitan Opera Company, under her maiden name, Broadfoot). Miss Donalda, a Canadian soprano of no little charm, helped to make the lyric operas agreeable. But the strength of the company lay in the male contingent—Bonci, the most famous of living tenors, after Caruso, whom Mr. Conried thought it wise to carry over to the Metropolitan Opera House, thus precipitating a controversy, which, as such things go, was of real assistance to the manager whom the rival sought to injure; Maurice Renaud, the most finished and versatile of French operatic artists, whom the foresight of Maurice Grau had retained for the Metropolitan, but whose contract Mr. Conried canceled at the cost of a penalty; M. Charles Dalmorès, a sterling dramatic tenor; M. Gilibert, a French baritone of refined qualities; Mme. Bressler-Gianoli, who, coming some years before in a peripatetic French company to the Casino, had stirred the enthusiasm of the critics with her truthful, powerful, and unconventional performance of Carmen; Ancona, a barytone who had been an admired member of the Metropolitan company, and a serviceable bass named Arimondi. Melba and Calvé came later in the season.

Exaggerated stories of Mr. Hammerstein's success followed the close of his season, and if all that Mr. Hammerstein himself said could have been accepted in its literalness the lesson of the season would have been that the people who live in New York and come to New York in the winter season were willing to spend, let me say, one and three-quarter millions of dollars every year for this one form of entertainment. It would appear, also, that fad and fashion were not the controlling impulse in this vast expenditure;

for the chief things which fad and fashion had to offer at the Metropolitan Opera House were noticeably absent from the Manhattan. On a score of occasions there were large gatherings representative of wealth and what is called society at the house in Thirty-fourth Street, but generally the audiences were distinct in their composition. It almost seemed as if Mr. Hammerstein had been correct in his deduction, that there were enough people in New York who wanted to go to the opera, but were excluded from the Metropolitan by the extent of the subscription, to support a second house. If this was so it marked a marvelous change from the time of the last operatic rivalry, which ruined both Mapleson and Abbey, and destroyed the prestige of the Academy of Music forever. Perhaps the city's growth in population and wealth furnished the explanation; I can scarcely believe from a study of the doings at the two houses that a growth in musical taste and culture was the determining factor. Twenty years ago such a list of operas as that presented by Mr. Hammerstein in his first season would have spelled ruin to any manager. Not even the prestige of Adelina Patti would have saved it. There was not a novelty in the list.

Many things contributed to the measure of success which Mr. Hammerstein won. There was a large fascination in the audacity of the undertaking, and its freedom from art-cant and affectation. Curiosity was irritated by the manager's daring, and admiration challenged by the manner in which he kept faith with the public. He seemed to be attempting the impossible, but he accomplished all that he said he would do. It is no secret—in fact, Mr. Hammerstein himself proclaimed it—that his artistic achievements were due in an overwhelming degree to the efficiency of Signor Cleofonte Campanini, his artistic director. But not to his efficiency alone—to his devotion and zeal also. Signor Campanini was not only the artistic director—he was also almost exclusively the conductor of the performances. His zeal fired all the forces employed at the opera house. A company gathered together from the ends of the earth succeeded in giving one hundred and thirteen performances of twenty-two operas, and making many of the performances of really remarkable excellence. The reason was obvious at nearly every presentation; from the principals down to the last person in the chorus and orchestra, every one had his heart in his work. Not only the desire to do their duty, but the pardonable ambition to do better than the rival establishment, inspired singers and players alike. It so happened that on one Saturday evening the same opera—Verdi's "Aïda"—was performed at both houses. A newspaper reporter carried the intelligence to the Manhattan Opera House that half the seats were empty at the Metropolitan, while the new house was crowded. The curtain was down at the time, and a score of the performers on the stage, headed by the conductor himself, at once formed a ring and danced a dance of triumph.

For musical effects, as well as some dramatic, there were distinct advantages with the new house. The disposition of the seats and stage brought the listeners and performers nearer together. The acoustical conditions at the Manhattan Opera House were admirable; there could be no such feeling of intimacy at the Metropolitan Opera House as existed here. The quality appealed to the music lover pure and simple, and him only, however, for in the things which make the opera a fashionable social diversion the new building was deficient and woefully inferior to the old.

The lovers of good singing were surprised by the excellence of Mr. Hammerstein's singers, especially the male contingent—a surprise which was heightened by the protestations, to which they had long been habituated, that there was no talent left in Europe comparable with that engaged at the Metropolitan. When in the face of such assertions the voices and the art of tenors like Bonci and Dalmores, and of barytones like Renaud and Ancona, were brought into notice their actual merit seemed doubled. The women singers of the first rank, save Mmes. Melba and Calvé, who appeared in what would have been called "star" engagements under the old theatrical stock régime, were in no way comparable with those of the Metropolitan Opera House, but those of the second rank were superior—a circumstance which was emphasized by the better ensemble performances, for which a discriminating public soon learned to thank Signor Campanini and the esprit de corps with which he inflamed the establishment's forces.

The opening of the season, on December 3 1906, had been proclaimed a week earlier, so as to make it synchronous with that of the Metropolitan Opera House; but Mr. Hammerstein's house was not ready, nor were his singers or stage fixtures. The fact looked ominous, and the enterprise took a lugubrious beginning a week later, when "I Puritani," which had been chosen as the opening opera because it was looked upon in Europe as affording to Signor Bonci his finest artistic opportunity, failed to arouse any public interest. It was an experience which Mr. Hammerstein was destined to have again and again with operas like "Dinorah," "Mignon," "Fra Diavolo," "Il Barbiere," and "Un Ballo in Maschera," for which the public seemed suddenly to have lost all liking, while still clinging to works of equal antiquatedness.

From the opening night to the closing the operas of the list were produced on the dates and in the succession indicated in the following table, which tells also the number of times each opera was performed. It must be stated, however, that there were a number of occasions in the course of the season when two operas or portions of several operas were performed on a single evening. This accounts for the large number of times that Mascagni's "Cavalleria" and Leoncavallo's "Pagliacci" were given, the latter being also helped in the record by the fact that it was twice bracketed with Massenet's "Navarraise."

Opera First performance Times

"I Puritani" ……………….. December 3 ………….. 2
"Rigoletto" ……………….. December 5 …………. 11
"Faust" …………………. December 7 ………….. 7
"Don Giovanni" …………… December 12 …………. 4
"Carmen" ………………… December 14 ……….. 19
"Aïda" …………………….. December 19 ……….. 12
"Lucia di Lammermoor" …….. December 21 …………. 6
"Il Trovatore" …………….. January 1 ………….. 6
"La Traviata" …………….. January 2 ………….. 3
"L'Elisir d'Amore" ……….. January 5 ………….. 3
"Gil Ugonotti" ……………. January 18 ………….. 5
"Il Barbiere di Siviglia" …. January 21 ………….. 2
"La Sonnambula" ………….. January 25 ………….. 3
"Pagliacci" ……………….. February 1 …………. 10
"Cavalleria Rusticana" ……. February 1 ………….. 8
"Mignon" …………………. February 7 ………….. 3
"Dinorah" ………………… February 20 ………….. 1
"Un Ballo in Maschera" ……. February 27 ………….. 2
"La Bohème" ……………… March 1 ……………. 4
"Fra Diavolo" ……………. March 8 ……………. 4
"Marta" ………………….. March 23 …………… 4
Manzoni Requiem (Good Fri.) .. March 29 …………… 1
"La Navarraise" ………….. April 10 ……………. 2

On three occasions the regular procedure was interrupted for the sake of matters of temporary and special interest. Thus, on March 2d, there was a miscellaneous bill, made up of an act of "Dinorah," one of "Faust," and all of "Cavalleria Rusticana"; on April 19th, the performance was little else than a concert, at which fragments of six operas, some of which were not in the repertory, were sung; while on Good Friday, Verdi's Requiem Mass, composed in honor of Manzoni, took the place of an opera, and was sung to popular prices, though it was on a regular opera night.

The subscription was so small that it seemed unnecessary to differentiate in the table between regular and extra performances. Of the latter there were twenty on Saturday nights, at popular prices, besides others given on holidays and for benefits. Though it is to be noted as a matter of history that the competition of the Manhattan Opera House did not appreciably affect the subscription of the Metropolitan, it is also to be noted that as a rule the attendance on the Saturday night popular performances was larger at the new house.

A few of the incidents of the season deserve to be passed in review. Of the singers whose presence in Mr. Hammerstein's company lent distinction to it, Signor Bonci appeared on the opening night in "I Puritani." The opera failed to awaken interest, but Bonci caught the popular fancy and held it to the end. Toward the close of February, however, it was announced that he had made a contract with Mr. Conried to sing at the Metropolitan Opera House the next season. Mr. Hammerstein first met the move of his rival by announcing the engagement of Signor Zenatello, but afterward began legal proceedings to prevent Signor Bonci from fulfilling his contract with the manager of the house in upper Broadway. M. Renaud, the great French barytone, effected his entrance in "Rigoletto," but he was not in his best voice and condition, and only later conquered recognition for his fine talents. The opera, however, took its place on the popular list, since it employed, at different times, the finest talent at the command of the management. The first large and complete triumph by an opera was won on December 14th, by "Carmen," in which Mme. Bressler-Gianoli appeared as the heroine. She enacted the part fifteen times before Mme. Calvé came to take back the territory which had so long belonged to her.

A second success followed hard on the heels of "Carmen." This was "Aïda," the triumph of which was one of ensemble, in which the chorus, under Signor Campanini, played no small part. Mme. Melba's coming, on January 2d, was the signal for the awakening of society's interest in Mr. Hammerstein's enterprise. She remained until March 25th, when she said farewell in a performance of Puccini's "Bohème," the production of which by Mr. Hammerstein in defiance of the rights of Mr. Conried (according to the allegations of the publishers, Ricordi) and the legal proceedings ending with the granting of an injunction against Mr. Hammerstein at the end of his season, was one of the diverting incidents of the merry operatic war. Mme. Melba sang three times in "La Traviata," five times in "Rigoletto," twice in "Lucia di Lammermoor," once in "Faust," and four times in "La Bohème."

The Bonci incident and the interest created in Mr. Hammerstein's enterprise by Mme. Melba's popularity stimulated interest in the offerings for a second season, which the manager answered by announcing the engagement, besides Zenatello and Sammarco, of Nordica and Schumann-Heink, and the re-engagement of Renaud, Bressler-Gianoli, Gilibert, and Dalmores. He also opened his subscription for the next season on March 19th, and announced the day after that he had received subscriptions amounting to $200,000, of which $110,000 had come from the four principal ticket speculators in the city. Mme. Calvé, who was engaged to give éclat to the conclusion of the season, effected her entrance on March 27th, and sang nine times—four in "Carmen," three in "Cavalleria Rusticana," and two in "La Navarraise."

CHAPTER XXIV
A BRILLIANT SEASON AT THE MANHATTAN

The prospectus which Mr. Hammerstein published for his second season was magnificently grandiloquent in its promises, but the season itself marvelous in its achievements. Eight operas "never produced in this city or country," "masterpieces of the most celebrated composers," which were his "sole property," were to be brought forward, in addition to many familiar works. He announced the engagement of "the greatest sopranos, mezzo sopranos, contraltos, barytones, and bassos of the operatic world." The eight new operas were to be Massenet's "Thaïs," Debussy's "Pelléas et Mélisande," Charpentier's "Louise," Breton's "Dolores," Massenet's "Jongleur de Notre Dame," Saint-Saëns's "Hélène," Offenbach's "Les Contes d'Hoffmann," and "an opera by our American composer, Victor Herbert." Offenbach's charming opera had been heard in New York before, from a French company managed by Maurice Grau, but it required a memory that compassed twenty-five years to recall that fact; so in respect of it Mr. Hammerstein's slip was venial at the worst. His list of the greatest singers in the world read as follows: Sopranos: Nellie Melba, Lillian Nordica, Mary Garden, Gianinna Russ, Camille Borello, Ludmilla Sigrist, Giuseppina Giaconia, Helen Koelling, Fanny Francisca, Mauricia Morichina, Jeanne Jomelli, Emma Trentini, and Alice Zeppilli; mezzo sopranos and contraltos: Ernestine Schumann-Heink, Bressler-Gianoli, Eleanore de Cisneros, J. Gerville-Reache, Emma Zaccaria, Gina Severina; tenors: Giovanni Zenatello, Amadeo Bassi, Charles Dalmorès, Jean Perier, Leone Cazauran, Carlo Albani, Emilio Venturini, Francesco Daddi; barytones: Maurice Renaud, Charles Gilibert, Mario Sammarco, Vincenzo Reschiglian, Mario Ancona, Hector Dufranne, Nicolo Fossetta; bassos: Adamo Didur, Victorio Arimondi, Luigi Mugnoz; basso buffo: Fernando Galetti-Gianoli. Cleofonte Campanini was again musical director.

These the magnificent promises. Had half of them been kept the fact would have amazed a public whom long experience had taught to put no more faith in the promises of impresarios than in those of princes. As a matter of fact, barring the extravagant attributes alleged to be due to the singers, the majority of whom were worse than mediocre, more than half were kept, and the deficiency more than counterbalanced by new elements which were introduced from time to time, as happy emergencies called for them. Chief of these was the engagement of Luisa Tetrazzini; of which more in its proper place. The official announcement was of subscription performances on Monday, Wednesday, and Friday evenings, and Saturday afternoons, for twenty weeks. Also there were to be twenty Saturday evenings at popular prices. Just before the opening of the season there was semi-official talk of popular performances also on Tuesday and Thursday evenings, which, had it been realized, would have kept the opera company as busy with a large repertory as the ordinary theatrical company with its single play running through a season. A beginning was made with the Thursday performances, but Mr. Hammerstein concluded after a short trial of the experiment, that the game was not worth the candle, and so abandoned it. Before the close of the season Mr. Hammerstein announced an extra week of five performances, which he invited his subscribers to enjoy without money and without price, on the ground that the exigencies of the season had compelled him to repeat operas on subscription nights. The season of twenty-one weeks, which began on November 4, 1907, and ended on March 28, 1908, was thus made to embrace 116 representations in all; that is to say, eighty subscription nights and matinées, twenty popular Saturday nights, five performances in the extra week, and eleven special afternoons and evenings. The discrepancy between these figures and the total of the last column in the appended table, showing the dates of first productions in the season, and the number of performances given to each opera, is accounted for by the fact that nine times in the course of the season the entertainment consisted of two operas, and once there was a bill of shreds and patches from various operas.

To complete the statistical record of the company's activity, it must be added that two performances were given in Philadelphia, and that there were eighteen concerts on Sunday nights, at the last few of which operas were given in concert form. Twice the opera house was kept closed on Sunday nights because of the enforcement of a rigid interpretation of the law prohibiting theatrical entertainments on Sunday.

A study of the list of performances shows that the 116 performances were distributed among twenty-three operas. Of these four had never been given in New York before (they were "Thaïs," "Louise," "Siberia," and "Pelléas et Mélisande"), three had been given in New York, but so long ago that they were to all intents and purposes novelties ("Les Contes d'Hoffmann," "Crispino e la Comare," and "Andrea Chenier"), and three, though familiar to the public, were new to the house ("La Gioconda," "La Damnation de Faust," and "Ernani"); the other thirteen were in the Manhattan repertory for the season of 1906-07.

Opera Composer First performance Times given

"La Gioconda," Ponchielli .... Nov. 4　4
"Carmen," Bizet .... Nov. 5　11
"La Damnation de Faust," Berlioz .... Nov. 6　3
"Trovatore," Verdi .... Nov. 9　5
"Aïda," Verdi .... Nov. 11　9
"Les Contes d'Hoffmann," Offenbach .... Nov. 15　11
"Thaïs," Massenet .... Nov. 24　7
"Faust," Gounod .... Nov. 28　4
* "La Navarraise," Massenet .... Dec. 9　5
* "Pagliacci," Leoncavallo .... Dec. 9　9
"Ernani," Verdi .... Dec. 11　1
"Rigoletto," Verdi .... Dec. 20　5
"Un Ballo in Maschera," Verdi .... Dec. 27　4
"Don Giovanni," Mozart .... Dec. 28　3
* "Cavalleria Rusticana," Mascagni .... Dec. 31　4
"Louise," Charpentier .... Jan. 3　11
"La Traviata," Verdi .... Jan. 15　5
"Lucia di Lammermoor," Donizetti .... Jan. 20　8
"Siberia," Giordano .... Feb. 5　3
"Pelléas et Mélisande," Debussy .... Feb. 19　7
"Dinorah," Meyerbeer .... Feb. 26　1
"Crispino e la Comare," Ricci brothers ... Mar. 6　3
"Andrea Chenier," Giordano .... Mar. 27　1

—
124

* Parts of double bills.

When Mr. Hammerstein issued his prospectus in the early autumn he promised to produce no less than eight operas which had never been performed in America. Managerial promises of this kind are generally made and accepted in a Pickwickian sense, but Mr. Hammerstein came nearer than is the custom to keeping his, though the season closed with his subscribers waiting for "Dolores," by Breton; "Le Jongleur de Notre Dame," by Massenet, and "Hélène," by Saint-Saëns. He also promised performances of three German operas ("Lohengrin," "Tannhäuser," and "Tristan und Isolde"), a new American opera in English, to be composed by Victor Herbert, and the following operas from the standard list, viz., "Le Prophète," Massenet's "Manon," "Roméo et Juliette," "Mefistofele," and "La Bohème." He had fought in the courts for the privilege of performing the last opera in the preceding season, but abandoned it without contention this season in the face of Mr. Conried's assertion that he had purchased the exclusive rights to all Italian performances of Puccini's operas in the United States. It is not likely that the statement about Mr. Herbert's opera was taken very seriously in any quarter; he is a prolific and marvelously ready writer of comic operetta scores, but it is not likely that he will ever attempt to find a suitable grand opera book and set it to music within six or eight months, while occupied, as he is, with a multitude of other enterprises. Mr. Hammerstein had promised in his prospectus that there would also be performances in German of "Lohengrin," "Tannhäuser," and "Tristan und Isolde." This part of the manager's scheme went by the board early in the season. It was contingent upon the presence in the company of singers familiar with the three works of Wagner. Of such there was only one when the season began, and she, Mme. Nordica, remained a member of Mr. Hammerstein's forces only six weeks, during much of which time she was idle. Mme. Schumann-Heink, though announced as a member of the company, interrupted her concert activity only long enough to sing once, and then she sang in an Italian opera ("Il Trovatore"), albeit she did her part in German.

Up to the coming of Signorina Tetrazzini Mr. Hammerstein pinned his faith on the interest which might be aroused in his French novelties. On the second subscription night he came forward with Berlioz's "Damnation de Faust," with which he had contemplated adorning his first season, and for which he had prepared the scenic outfit. The undramatic character of the transformed cantata had caused its failure at the Metropolitan Opera House in the season of 1906-07, and not even the fine performance of M. Renaud, whose impersonation of Mephistopheles is one of the noblest memories left by the season, the excellent singing of M. Dalmorès, and the beautiful pictures could save it. There was a long wait between the first and second representations, and after one more trial the work was abandoned. Meanwhile, however, Offenbach's "Contes d'Hoffmann," which had had a few performances at the Fifth Avenue Theater twenty-five years before, was brought forward. Again Messrs. Renaud and Dalmorès were admirably fitted with parts and scant justice done to the opera in the distribution of the women's rôles; but the charm of Offenbach's music overcame the defects of performance, and the opera achieved so pronounced a success that it could be given with profit eleven times before M. Renaud's departure from New York after the performance of February 4th.

The libretto of "Les Contes d'Hoffmann" proclaims a phase of French literary taste which made heroes two generations ago out of two foreign romancers,—the German E. T. A. Hoffmann and the American Edgar Allan Poe. Very much alike were these two men in some of their strongest characteristics. Both were possessed of genius of a high order; both led lives of dissipation, which wrecked them physically; both found their fantastic creations in the world of supernaturalism which imagination, stimulated by alcoholic indulgence, presented to them as realities. This is literally true, at least, of Hoffmann, who, coming home from his nightly carouses with the boon companions, whom he has celebrated in his "Serapion's Brüder" (the coterie somewhat vulgarly parodied in the beginning and end of Offenbach's opera), was wont to call for his wife to sit beside him through the remainder of the night to ward off the ghostly, ghastly, grisly creatures which his own perfervid imagination had conjured up. Sixty years ago France was full of admiration for the weird tales of Hoffmann, and in view of the singular vicissitudes of the fantastic romancer's life, some of them quite as startling as the adventures which he ascribed to his imaginary creatures, it was not at all strange that Barbier and Carré should have conceived the idea of making him the hero of a play dealing with incidents of his own invention. In 1851 they brought out their play in five acts at the Odéon. It did not endure long, but it made so deep an impression on the mind of Offenbach that when he was seized with the ambition to write a serious work, which he might leave to the world as a legacy, to prove that his ambitions went beyond the things with which he amused the careless folk of the Second Empire, he turned to the old play for his libretto.

In a way it was a happy choice. If an author was to be blended with his creations and utilized for operatic purposes, history might be searched in vain for a better subject than Hoffmann. He was jurist, court councillor, romancer, caricaturist, scene painter, theatrical manager, and musical composer. In several ways he is living in the musical annals to-day. His opera, "Undine," is forgotten, though it was highly praised by Carl Maria von Weber, who had not feared soundly to abuse Beethoven; but his literary creation, the Chapelmaster Kreissler, lives in Schumann's "Kreissleriana," and other conceits of his filtered through Jean Paul, in other compositions by the same master. His criticisms, though cast in fantastic form, opened the eyes of many to the beauties of Gluck, Mozart, and Beethoven. His admiration for Mozart went to such an extreme that he cast aside part of his baptismal name in order to substitute for it one of the given names of his hero—Amadeus. Of this admiration neither Offenbach nor his librettists were unaware, for when Hoffmann and Nicklausse come into the tavern where the roystering students greet them, in the prologue, they are still so full of the opera "Don Giovanni," to which they had just been listening, that Nicklausse quotes the words of Leporello's first song, and Offenbach reverently quotes the music.

Let no one think that the production of "Les Contes d'Hoffmann" was in any way analogous with the operetta performances with which Mr. Conried lowered the status of the Metropolitan Opera House when he performed "Die Fledermaus" and "Der Zigeunerbaron" at his benefits. No serious reader of mine will expect to see in this place dispraise of the genius of Johann Strauss; but the works mentioned are operettas in form and in spirit, while "Les Contes d'Hoffmann" was conceived in an entirely different vein, and shows the musician who composed it in a character that no one would dream was his who knew him only as the composer of the Bouffes Parisiens. It is a pathetic, but also lovely, document in proof of the fact that with all his frivolity he wanted to die at least in the odor of artistic sanctity. The piquant rhythms and prettily superficial melodies of his musical farces were a perfect reflex of the careless art-feeling of his day, just as the farces themselves were admirably adjusted to the taste of the boulevardiers who basked in the sunshine of Napoleon the Little, and laughed uproariously while their Emperor and their social institutions were being castigated by the cynical German Jew and his librettists. "He was the Beethoven of the sneer," said Émil Bergerat, when Offenbach died, and then with a fantastic pencil worthy of the caricaturist Hoffmann himself, he drew a dreadful picture of Offenbach and his times; of the mighty fiddler beating time upon the well-filled goatskin and sawing away across the strings, his mouth widened with a grin "like some drunken conception of Edgar Poe's, or some fantasy of Hoffmann, while the startled birds flew back to heaven, the moon split herself back to her ears, and the stars giggled behind their cloud-fans." The planetary system only revolved to frisky rhythms, and the earth herself, like a mad top, hummed comically about the horrified sun. En avant la musique! and the old edifice crumbled in dust around the musician. To Bergerat Offenbach was the great disillusioner of the age, the incarnation of what he conceived to be the spirit of the nineteenth century, a spirit that hated and contemned the past, mocked at the things which the simplicity of preceding centuries held sacred, threw ridicule upon social sentiments, rank, caste, ceremonialism, learning, and religion.

The composer of "Les Contes d'Hoffmann" is nothing of this. The opera was the child of his old age. He loved it, and labored over its score for years. It is full of lovely melody (the barcarolle of the second act will always exert a potent and lovely influence) fluent from beginning to end, and rich in dramatic characterization. No one is likely to listen to the trio at the culmination of the third act (that dealing with the fate of a singer's daughter) without realizing what a really admirable power of expression was that which Offenbach, for reasons explained by the spirit of the times and his own moral nature, chose to squander so many years on his opéras bouffes. Frequently the melodic line in the opera rises to admirable heights; always melody, harmony, and orchestration are refined, unless a burlesque effect is aimed at, as in the ballad of "Kleinzack," and Nicklausse's song of the doll. Offenbach's opera had its first performance on November 14, 1907, the cast being as follows:

Olympia	Zepilli
Giulietta	Jomelli
Antonia	Borello
Nicklausse	De Cisneros
A Voice	Giaconia
Hoffman	Dalmorès
Cornelius | Dappertutto | Dr. Miracle | Spalanzni | Grespel |	Renaud
	Gilibert
Lindorff | Schlemihl | Cochenille | Pitichinaccio |	Crabbe
	Daddi
Frantz	Gianoli-Galetti
Hermann	Reschiglian
Nathaniel	Venturini
Luther	Fossetta

Conductor, Cleofonte Campanini

On November 25, 1907, Mr. Hammerstein brought forward Massenet's "Thaïs," to signalize the first appearance in America of Miss Mary Garden. The opera was produced with the following cast:

Thaïs	Mary Garden
Crobyle	Trentini
Myrtale	Giaconia
Albine	Gerville-Reache
Athanaël	Renaud
Nicias	Cazouran
Palemon	Mugnoz
Un Serviteur	Reschiglian

Conductor, Campanini

With this work French opera won its second triumph. The charm of Miss Garden's personality was felt, but her singing compelled less tribute, and though the opera had seven representations before the departure of M. Renaud compelled its withdrawal, its success was due much more to him than to his fair companion. The Thaïs of MM. Gallet and Massenet is not the Thaïs of classical story, who induced Alexander to burn the palace of the Persian kings at Persepolis—"who like another Helen, fired another Troy"—but she is of her tribe. Also of the tribe of Phryne, Laïs, and Messalina, who live in history and in art because of their beauty and their pruriency, their loveliness and licentiousness. The operatic Thaïs is the invention of Anatole France, who borrowed her name for a courtesan of Alexandria some centuries after the historic woman lived. With the help of suggestions borrowed from the stories of innumerable saints who fled from the vicious world into the desert, and industriously cultivated sanctity and bodily filth, of converted trollops and holy Anthonys, he constructed a tale of how one of these desert saints, filled with ardor to save the soul of a cyprian who had the gay world of Alexandria at her feet, went to her, persuaded her to put her sinful life behind her, enter the retreat of a saintly sisterhood and die in grace, while he, falling at the last into the clutches of carnal lust, repented of his good deed and wrought his own damnation. Changing the name of the unfortunate zealot from Paphnuce to Athanaël, M. Louis Gallet made an opera-book out of France's story, and Massenet set it to music. It is a delectable story, but it fell into the hands of master craftsmen, and the admirers of "art for art's sake" and at any cost, have cause to rejoice at the treatment which it received. Glimpses into the life of the frowsy fraternity of cenobites, and fragments of their doleful canticles are not engaging in themselves, but they are fine foils to pictures of antique vice and the songs and dances of classic voluptuaries. There are splendid dramatic potentialities for those who like such things and those who find profit in exploiting in the juxtaposition cheek by jowl of saintliness and sin; of Christian hymning and harlotry; of virtue in a physical wrestle with vice, and coming out triumphant, but handing the palm over to the real victor at the end; in the picture of a monk sprinkling the couch of Venus with holy water, and decking his cowl with roses.

Also there was a large personal note in the original creation of "Thaïs," and there was a large personal note in its reproduction. It is not altogether a pleasant one for the lover of real art to listen to. Had there been no Sybil Sanderson, it is doubtful if Massenet would ever have been directed to the subject. True, he had shown a predilection for frail women as his heroines before, as witness Marie Magdalen, Eve, Herodias, and Manon Lescaut; but in the works which exploited these women the personal equation did not enter so far as the world knows or the printed page discloses. But when he wrote "Thaïs" it was neither histrionic nor musical art that be aimed primarily to exploit, but the physical charms of an individual. Something was needed for the jaded boulevardiers of Paris to leer at while they feebly clapped their hands and piped "Ah, charmante! Ravissante!" It may be that the fine command of Oriental color which is supposed to have affinity in the idioms of music with voluptuousness in all its forms, had something to do with the case, but the whole structure of the piece, superb as it is in its contrasting elements, and theatrically ingenious and effective, points nevertheless to the unfortunate Sanderson. And in the same way its Parisian revival points to Madame Cavalieri and Miss Garden, and its American production to the latter. For the sake of gifted singers and accomplished actors merely, the opera was not created, and will not be kept alive. It rests for its success on the kind of argument which Phryne, of classic story, presented to her austere judges.

The brilliancy of the play, its masterly handling of contrasts equally gratifying to the scenic artist, the actor, and the composer, challenged admiration and won it in large measure at the Manhattan performances. From the ordinary theatrical point of view it would not be easy to pick a quarrel with the drama. It would be almost churlish when there is so much to be grateful for, to pick flaws in M. Massenet's score. In the first place, compared with the vast volume of stuff poured forth by his younger colleagues of Italy, and even by some of his confrères of France, it makes appeal for approval by its evidences of consummate technical mastery. It never trickles; it never grows stagnant; it never gropes; it never fails for want of matter and manner in utterance. Its current is smooth and self-reliant. It carries action and scene buoyantly and unceasingly, even if it does not always expound them deeply or give them adequate external adornment. When it has no real warmth it simulates it admirably. Its texture is well-knit. There is purpose, not deep, not long-sustained, but, so far as it goes, logical, in the composer's application of the system of typical or representative phrases. There is, too, a measure of appositeness in the structure and character of his themes—the themes of asceticism, of Athanaël, of Thaïs. There is mastery of local color which makes the composer's use of Oriental tints as dramatically appropriate as it is engaging in all the scenes of ancient profligacy which fill the center of the artist's canvas.

M. Massenet's orchestra is an active agent in the development of the drama, and the episodes in which it becomes dominant are not pauses in the action created because of a felt need for something besides an undercurrent for the inane chatter of dialogue; instead they carry on the psychological action, the concealed drama which is playing on the stage of the hearts of the people concerned in the story. There is fitness in the interlude, in which Thaïs disposes herself to reproduce the pantomime of the loves of Aphrodite and Adonis, and a pretty touch of significance in the reminiscence of the music which had disturbed Athanaël's dream in the first act. There is more than mere musical charm in the intermezzo which follows the scene in which the monk wakes into life the conscience of the courtesan. She has defied him to the last, but the struggle in her soul has begun, and while he sleeps on the steps of her house the progress and outcome of the struggle are portrayed in the instrumental number which Massenet has called a "Religious Meditation." In itself it is not unlike scores of pieces similarly intituled, but it is made significant by its introduction of the theme of Thaïs in a chastened mood, in the garb of solemn gravity; and the melody of the violin solo, borne up by almost indefinable harmonies, and floated by harp arpeggios, recurs again before the death scene of Thaïs to delineate her ecstasy and Athanaël's despair. Though the intermezzo, thus admirably motived, marks the highest flight of Massenet's genius in this opera, there are many other pages in the score which might be chosen for praise. Enough that while the admirers of "Manon" and "Werther" are not likely to find the music of those operas equaled, they will yet find much to fascinate them in "Thaïs."

I have said, in effect, that the chief triumph in the performance of Massenet's opera was won by M. Renaud. Miss Garden had, indeed, established herself as a popular favorite, but it was not until the production of Charpentier's "Louise," on January 3, 1908, an opera with which her name was more intimately associated in popular report, that it could be said without qualification that French opera had won its battle. The principal parts in this opera were distributed amongst Mr. Hammerstein's singers thus:

> Louise .... Miss Mary Garden
> Julien .... M. Charles Dalmorès
> Mother of Louise .... Mme. Bressler-Gianoli
> Father of Louise .... M. Charles Gilibert
> Irma .... Mlle. Alice Zeppilli
> Camille .... Mlle. Morichini
> Gertrude .... Mlle. Giaconia
> Suzanne .... Mlle. Helene Koelling
> King of the Fools .... M. Venturini
> A Ragpicker .... M. Reschiglian
> A Junkman .... M. Mugnoz
> Elise |
> A Street Sweeper | .... Mlle. Severina
> A Street Arab .... Mlle. Trentini
> An Apprentice .... Mlle. Sigrist
>   Conductor, Campanini

"Louise" had made a great noise, both in a literal and figurative sense, during the greater part of the preceding eight years. It had made the rounds of the principal opera houses on the European continent, but most of the noise came from Paris, and among those who sat in Mr. Hammerstein's boxes and stalls on the occasion of its American production there were many who had already made the acquaintance of the work at the Opéra Comique, in the French capital. It is likely that their interest in the performance was mingled more or less with curious questionings touching the attitude which local opera-lovers would assume toward it. There is a vast difference in the mood in which Americans go to public entertainments in Paris and at home. In a sense, though not a large or dignified one, the tragic element in the story of Charpentier's opera is universal; but its representation is in every particular the most local and circumscribed of any opera ever written. I am not disposed to waste much time or space in a discussion of things to which the patrons of our playhouses have often exhibited a callous indifference. It is only to justify a hurried analysis of the artistic nature of the work that attention is called to some of its essential characteristics. "Louise" is not a French opera, though its score is French, its people speak French, and its music echoes French measures when it is original, and also when borrowed or imitated. "Louise" is Parisian in its gaiety, its passions, its vulgarity, and its artistic viciousness. If music could in itself give expression to ethical ideas, it would also be proper to say that this score is Parisian in its immorality. Coupled with its story, which glorifies the licentiousness of Paris and makes mock of virtue, the sanctity of the family tie, and the institutions upon which social stability and human welfare have ever rested and must forever rest, the music may also be set down as immoral. Certain it is that there is nothing in it that is spiritually uplifting, and as little that makes for gentleness and refinement of artistic taste. It is not French in the historic sense, because it rudely tramples upon all the esthetic principles for which the French composers, from Lully to the best of Charpentier's contemporaries have stood—elegance, grace, and beauty of expression.

It is, however, characteristic of the times—characteristic in subject and in utterance. To the intellectual and moral anarchism universally prevalent among the peoples of Western culture, which desires to have idealism outraged, sacred things ridiculed, high conceptions of beauty and duty dragged into the gutter, and ugliness, brutality, and bestiality placed upon a pedestal so long as a consuming thirst for things hot in the mouth may be slaked, it makes a strong appeal. To Mr. Hammerstein its success meant much. It was a reward for another exhibition of a bold and adventurous spirit; of his skill in gathering together a band of artists splendidly capable of presenting the works which he was trying to make the prop of a new lyric theater in the American metropolis; of a daringly enterprising purpose to make all the elements of his new productions harmonious and alluring—the stage pictures, the action, the singing, and the instrumental music. This achievement he accomplished when not only the large and striking features of the opera—its scenic outfit, its pictures of popular carousal on the heights of Montmartre, the roystering realism of the scene in a dressmakers' shop, the splendid acting of Miss Garden and Mme. Bressler-Gianoli, the fine singing of M. Dalmorès, and the more than superb acting and singing of M. Gilibert—found their complement in the finish of a hundred little details, insignificant in themselves, but singularly potent in helping to create the atmosphere without which "Louise" would be little better than Bowery melodrama,—a play that would be a hundred times more effective if its hero and heroine were represented as living in Williamsburg, swelling at the spectacle of the lights spanning the East River, and longing for the fleshpots of the so-called "Tenderloin District" in New York.

The story of "Louise," in brief, is that of a sewing-girl who lives with her parents on Montmartre, up to which, night after night, blink and beckon the lights of the gay city. An artist, who is her neighbor, wooes her and offers marriage, but her parents, a harsh, unsympathetic mother and a tender-hearted father, are rigid in their objections to him because of his insufficient means and loose character. Her lover lures her out of her workshop, and, after he has inculcated in her the doctrine of free love and free life, she leaves her parents to consort with him. The artist's jovial companions make her queen of a Montmartre festival for a purpose wholly extraneous to the story, but one that serves the composer, who is his own librettist, and in the midst of the merrymaking the mother appears and pleads with the girl to return to her home to comfort her dying father. Her lover permits her to do so on her promise to return to him. At home her father entreats her to give up her life of dishonor. She listens to him petulantly. The music of a fête in the city below, voices calling her from a distance, and the flashing lights in the great city below, throw her into a frantic ecstasy; she sings of her love and calls to her lover. The mother thinks her mad, but the father drives her out of the house, only to repent and call after her a moment later. But she is gone, and the drama ends with the father shaking his fist at the city, and shrieking at it his hatred and detestation.

The thoughts of opera-goers will naturally revert to "La Bohème"; but there are many points of difference between the story which Puccini's librettist pieced together out of Mürger's tales of bohemian life more than half a century ago, and this one of to-day. The differences are all in favor of the earlier opera. It was in a letter written by Lafcadio Hearn to me that he called attention to the fact that under the levity of Mürger's picturesque bohemianism there was apparent a serious philosophy, which had an elevating effect upon the characters of the romance. "They followed one principle faithfully,—so faithfully that only the strong survived the ordeal,—never to abandon the pursuit of an artistic vocation for any other occupation, however lucrative, not even when she remained apparently deaf and blind to her worshipers." There is very little in Puccini's opera to justify this observation, but the significant fact remains that throughout the dramatic development of the piece the bohemian artists and their careless companions grow in the sympathy of the audience. For one thing, there is no questioning their sincerity. For this there is only one parallel in Charpentier's opera. There is, in fact, only one really dramatic character in it. It is that of the father; in him there is honest, human feeling, a tenderness and love which yield only to a moment of passion when he is perplexed in the extreme and at a moment when the last drop of sympathy for Louise has oozed away. Her tender regard for her father is pathetic in the first act, where it is set against the foil of her mother's harshness. In the last act, however, she is petulant, irascible, and cold, until the moment of frenzy, when she surrenders to the call of Paris and her wretched passion. Julien is scantily and unconvincingly sketched. There is little indeed even to indicate sincerity in his love for Louise; at first, while she sings of the ecstasy of first love, he calmly reads a book; and when he responds, it is to invoke her to join him in a paean in praise, not of their love, but of Paris. Does she find him, when she rushes down the stairs, pursued by her father's broken-hearted calls? One can feel no certainty on the point. The last impression is only that she has gone to plunge into the flood of wickedness, never to be seen again.

It was said some years ago, when "Louise" was celebrating its first triumphs, that the opera was the first number of a projected trilogy, and that Charpentier would tell us the rest of the story of the sewing-girl in other operas. But the years have passed, the composer has grown rich and is giving no sign. Instead, there is an organized "Louise" propaganda in Paris. Funds are raised to send the working girls of the city to the opera in droves, there to hear the alluring call to harlotry, under the pretense that the agonies of the father will preach a moral lesson.

There are dramatic strength and homogeneity only in the first and last acts of the opera. The scenes between are shreds and patches, invented to give local color to the story. In the original form the picture of low life at dawn on Montmartre, in which charwomen, scavengers, ragpickers, street sweepers, milkwomen, policemen, and others figure, was enlivened by a mysterious personage called Le Noctambule, who proclaimed himself to be the soul of the city—the Pleasure of Paris. It was a part of the symbolism which we are asked also to find in the flitting visions of low life and the echoes of street cries in the music. But it was a note out of key, and Mr. Campanini eliminated it, with much else of the local color rubbish. And yet it is in the use of this local color that nearly all that is original and individual in the score consists. Until we reach the final scene of the father's wild anguish there is very little indeed that is striking in the music, except that which is built up out of the music of the street. We hear echoes of the declamatory style of the young Italian veritists in the dialogue, much that is more than suggestive of the mushy sentimentality of the worst of Gounod and Massenet in the moments when the music attempts the melodic vein, and no end of Wagnerian orchestration in the instrumental passages which link the scenes together. Some of this music is orchestrated with great beauty and discretion, like the preludes, but all that is conceived to accompany violent emotion is only fit to "tear a cat in" or to "make all split." The score, in fact, is chiefly a triumph of reflection, of ingenious workmanship, and there is scarcely a moment in the opera that takes strong hold of the fancy, for which the memory does not immediately supply a model, either dramatic or musical, or both. Wagner's marvelous close of the second act of "Die Meistersinger," with the night watchman walking through the quiet streets flooded with moonlight, singing his monotonous chant, is feebly mimicked at the close of the first scene of the second act of "Louise," when, all the characters of the play having disappeared, an Old Clothes Man comes down a staircase crying his dolorous (all the street cries are strangely melancholy) "Marchand d'habits! Avez-vous des habits a vendr'?" while from the distance arise the cries of the dealers in birdseed and artichokes. The spinning scene in "The Flying Dutchman," which reproduces a custom of vast antiquity, is replaced in "Louise" with a scene in the dressmaker's workshop, in which the chatter of the girls and the antics of the comédienne are borne up by the music of the orchestra, with the click-click of the sewing machines to make up for the melodious hum of Wagner's spinning wheels. Puccini's bohemians meet in front of the Café Momus, enlivened by the passing incidents of a popular fête; Charpentier's bohemians celebrate the crowning of the Muse of Montmartre with a carnival gathering and ballet. It is this fête, we fancy, which formed the nucleus around which Charpentier built his work. Twice before "Louise" was brought forward he had utilized the ideas of the popular festival at which a working girl was crowned and made the center of a procession of roysterers, and a musical score with themes taken from the noises of Paris. His "Couronnement de la Muse," composed for a Montmartre festival, was performed at Lille in 1898; from Rome he sent to Paris along with his picturesque orchestral piece, "Impressions d'Italie," a symphonic drama, "La Vie du Poète," for soli, chorus, and orchestra, in which he introduced "all the noises and echoes of a Montmartre festival, with its low dancing rooms, its drunken cornets, its hideous din of rattles, the wild laughter of bands of revelers, and the cries of hysterical women." But even here M. Charpentier is original in execution only, not in plan. There is scarcely a public library in the large cities of Europe and America which does not contain a copy of Georges Kastner's "Les Voix de Paris," with its supplement, "Cris de Paris," a "Symphonie humoristique," with its themes drawn from the cries of the peripatetic hucksters and street venders of the French Capital; and as if that were not enough, historic records and traditions trace the use of street cries as musical material back to the sixteenth century. There seems even to have been a possibility that a "Ballet des Cris de Paris" furnished forth an entertainment in which the Grand Monarch himself assisted, for the court of Louis XIV.

French opera had won its battle; but even now, the way was not wholly clear and open, for the successful operas were too few and their repetition caused some grumbling.

At this critical moment the star of Luisa Tetrazzini rose in London and threw its glare over all the operatic world. Two years before Mr. Conried had engaged the singer while she was in California, but had failed to bind the contract by depositing a guarantee with her banker. He failed, it is said, because when he wanted to complete the negotiations he could not find her. Mr. Hammerstein also negotiated with her for the season of 1906-07, so he said, but she proved elusive. Neither of the managers felt any loss at his failure to secure her. The London excitement may have set Mr. Conried to thinking; Mr. Hammerstein it stirred to action. On December 1st he announced that he had engaged her for the season of 1908-09, and hoped to have her for a few performances before the end of the season of 1907-08. A fortnight later he proclaimed that she would effect her New York entrance on January 15th, and that he had secured her for fifteen representations in the current season, with the privilege of adding to their number. Mr. Conried threatened proceedings by injunction, but his threats were brutum fulmen; she made her début on the specified date in "La Traviata," and when the season closed she had added seven performances (one in Philadelphia) to the fifteen originally contemplated. In New York she sang five times in "Traviata," eight times in "Lucia," once in "Dinorah," three times in "Rigoletto," three times in "Crispino e la Comare," and once in a "mixed bill." She was rapturously acclaimed by the public and a portion of the press. It is useless to discuss the phenomenon. The whims of the populace are as unquestioning and as irresponsible as the fury of the elements. That was seen in the Tetrazzini craze in New York and in London; it was seen again in the reception given to that musically and dramatically amorphous thing, "Pelléas et Mélisande." This was as completely bewildering to the admirers of the melodrama as to those who are blind and deaf to its attractions. It should have been more so, for it is more difficult to affect to enjoy "Pelléas et Mélisande" than to yield to the qualities which dazzle in the singing of Tetrazzini. Nevertheless, "Pelléas et Mélisande" had seven performances within five weeks.

Debussy's opera was performed for the first time on February 19, 1908, the parts being distributed as follows:

Arkël .... M. Arimondi
Pelléas .... M. Perier
Golaud .... M. Dufranne
Mélisande .... Miss Garden
Yniold .... Mlle. Sigrist
Geneviéve .... Mme. Gerville-Reache

Un Médecin .... M. Crabbe
    Conductor, Sig. Campanini

The production of "Pelléas et Mélisande" was the most venturesome experiment that Mr. Hammerstein had yet made and the one most difficult to explain on any ground save the belief that a French novelty, no matter what its character or its merits, would win profitable patronage in New York at the moment. There was nothing in the history of the work itself to inspire the confidence that it would make a potent appeal to the tastes of the opera-lovers of New York. Nowhere outside of Paris had it gained a foothold, and its success in Paris was like that which any esthetic cult or pose may secure if diligently and ingeniously exploited. Mr. Hammerstein knew this and he had seen the work at the Opéra Comique. It could not have escaped his discerning mind that only a small element in the population of even so cosmopolitan a city as New York could by any possibility possess the intellectual and esthetic qualifications necessary to enthusiastic appreciation of the qualities, not to say merits, of the work. These qualifications are quite as much negative as they are positive. It is not enough to the appreciation of "Pelléas et Mélisande" that the listener shall understand French. He must have a taste—and this must be an acquired one, since it cannot be born in him—for the French of M. Maeterlinck's infantile plays, "Pelléas et Mélisande" being on the border-line between the marionette drama and that designed for the consumption of mature minds. He must, moreover, have joined the inner brotherhood of symbol worshipers, and be able to discern how it is that the world-old story of the union of December and May, of blooming youth and crabbed age with its familiar (and, as some poets and romancers would have us believe, inevitable) consequences, can be enhanced by much chatter about crowns and rings dropped into wells, white-haired beggars lying in a cave, stagnant and mephitic pools, fluttering doves, departing ships, kings who lose their way while hunting and are dashed against trees at twelve o'clock, maids who know not whence they came or why they are weeping, and a whole phantasmagoria more, out of all proportion to the simple incidents of the tragedy itself.

This so far as the literary side of the matter is concerned. On the musical much more is demanded. He must recognize unrhythmical, uncadenced, disjointed, and ejaculatory prose dialogue, with scarcely a lyrical moment in it, as a fit vehicle for music. He must not only be willing to forego vocal melody, but even the semblance of melody also in the instrumental music upon which the dialogue floats; for everybody knows since the Wagnerian drama came into being that words which are in themselves incapable of melodious flow may be the cause of melody in the orchestral music which accompanies them. [There is here no allusion to tune in the conventional sense, tune made up of motive, phrase, period and section, but to a well modulated succession of musical intervals, expressing a feeling or illustrating a mood.] He who would enjoy the musical integument of this play must have cultivated a craving for dissonance in harmony and find relish in combinations of tones that sting and blister and pain and outrage the ear. He must have learned to contemn euphony and symmetry, with its benison of restfulness, and to delight in monotony of orchestral color, monotony of mood, monotony of dynamics, and monotony of harmonic device.

It is not at all likely that Mr. Hammerstein expected to find a sufficient number of opera-goers thus strangely constituted among the patrons of his establishment to justify him in the astonishing exhibition of enterprise or venturesomeness illustrated by the production of "Pelléas et Mélisande" with artists brought especially from Paris only because they had been concerned in the Parisian performances, with new scenery, and at the cost of much money and labor spent in the preparation. It is therefore safe to assume that he counted on the potent power of public curiosity touching a well-advertised thing. He had fared well with Mme. Tetrazzini in presenting operas which represent everything that "Pelléas et Mélisande" is not. In this he had much encouragement. He played boldly, and won.

"Pelléas et Mélisande" as it came from the hands of M. Maeterlinck, and in the only form which the author recognizes, had been presented in New York in an English version. What has been said above about the qualifications of him who would rise to an enjoyment of the music with which Debussy has consorted it ought to serve also to characterize that music. Nothing has been exaggerated, nothing set down in a spirit of illiberality. No student of music can be ignorant of the fact that the art, being a pure projection of the human will, is necessarily always in a state of flux, and in its nature, within the limitations that bound all the manifestations of beauty, lawless. M. Debussy might have proclaimed and illustrated that fact without in his capacity of a critical writer having sought to throw odium on dead masters who were better than he and living contemporaries who are at least older. The little Parisian community who pass the candied stick of mutual praise from mouth to mouth would nevertheless have given him their plaudits. In his proclamation of the principles of musical composition as applied to the drama he has proclaimed principles as old as opera. It needed no man who has outlived the diatonic scale to tell us that vocal music should be written in accordance with the rhythm and accents of the words, and that dramatic music should be an integral element of the drama, or, as he puts it, be "the atmosphere through which dramatic emotion radiates." The Florentine inventors of monody told us that, Gluck echoed them, Wagner re-enunciated the principle, and no modern composer has dreamed of denying its validity. The only question is whether or not such admirable results have been attained by M. Debussy; whether his music sweetens or intensifies or vitalizes the play. That question must be answered by the individual hearer. No one should be ashamed to proclaim his pleasure in four hours of uninterrupted, musically inflected speech over a substratum of shifting harmonies, each with its individual tang and instrumental color; but neither should anybody be afraid to say that nine-tenths of the music is a dreary monotony because of the absence of what to him stands for musical thought. Let him admit or deny, as he sees fit, that the principle of symphonic development is a proper concomitant of the musical drama, but let him also say whether or not what to some appears a flocculent, hazy web of dissonant sounds, now acrid, now bitter-sweet, maundering along from scene to scene, unrelieved by a single pregnant melodic phrase, stirs within him the emotions awakened by a union of melody, harmony, and rhythm, either in the old conception or the new. Debussy has had his fling at Wagner and his system of construction in the lyric drama; yet he adopts his system of musical symbols, It is almost a humiliation to say it. There is sea music and forest music in "Pelléas et Mélisande." What a flight of gibbering phantoms there would be if the fluttering of Tristan's pennants or the "hunt's up" of King Mark's horns could be heard even for a moment!

It would be difficult accurately and honestly to say what was the verdict of the audience touching the merit of the work; concerning the performance there was never a question. The first three acts were followed by a respectful patter of applause. When Mr. Campanini came into the orchestra to begin the fourth act he received an ovation which was both spontaneous and cordial. The dramatic climax, which is accompanied by superb music of its kind, is reached in the scene of Pelléas's killing at the end of the fourth act. This stirred up hearty enthusiasm, and after all the artists, Mr. Campanini, and the stage manager had shared in the expression of enthusiastic gratitude, Mr. Hammerstein was brought before the curtain. He made a brief speech, saying that by its appreciation of the opera, with its poetical beauty and musical grandeur, New York had set itself down as the most highly cultivated city in the world, and that for himself the only purpose he had had in producing it was to endear himself to the city's people! Would that one dared to exclaim: "O sancta simplicitas!"

Mr. Hammerstein did not perform all the novelties which he had promised in his prospectus, but to make good the loss he brought forward two operas, one a complete novelty, which he had not promised. This was Giordano's "Siberia." More surprising was the fact that only one day before the close of the season he produced the same composer's "Andrea Chenier" under circumstances which made the occasion a gala one for Signor

Cleofonte Campanini, the energetic and capable director who more than anyone else had made the marvelous achievements of the Manhattan company possible. The production of "Andrea Chenier" was not contemplated when Mr. Hammerstein came forth in the summer with his official announcement of the season; it had, however, been promised by Mr. Conried, who seems to have found that the production of two novelties of a vastly inferior kind taxed to the limit the resources of the proud establishment in Broadway. There it was permitted to slumber on with "Otello," "Der Freischütz," and "Das Nachtlager von Granada," whose titles graced Mr. Conried's prospectus. That circumstance may have had something to do with Mr. Hammerstein's resolve at the eleventh hour to add it to the list of five other new productions which he had already placed to his credit. If so, he gave no indication of the fact but permitted the announcement to go out that the performance was a compliment to Signor Campanini and his wife, who, as Signora Tetrazzini, had retired from the operatic stage after singing in the opera three years before. Incidentally the circumstance appealed to whatever feelings of gratitude the patrons of the Manhattan Opera House felt toward Signor Campanini and also to the popular curiosity to hear a sister of the Tetrazzini whose coming to the opera was the season's chief sensation.

The occasion was well calculated to set the beards of memory mongers to wagging. Those who could recall some of the minor incidents of a quarter-century earlier remembered that the indefatigable director of to-day was a modest maestro di cembalo at the Metropolitan in its first season, and on a few occasions when his famous brother Italo Campanini sang was permitted to try his "prentice hand" at conducting. Next they recalled that four years later, when that brother made an unlucky venture as impresario and sought to rouse the people of New York to enthusiasm with a production of Verdi's "Otello" it was Cleofonte Campanini who was the conductor of the company and Signorina Eva Tetrazzini who was the prima donna. The original American production of "Andrea Chenier" took place at the Academy of Music on November 13, 1896. At the revival on March 27, 1908, the parts were distributed as follows:

Maddalena de Coigny .... Mme. Tetrazzini-Campanini
Andrea Chenier .... Sig. Bassi
Carlo Gerard .... Sig. Sainmarco
Contessa de Coigny .... Sig'ra Giaconia
Bersi .... Sig'ra Seppilli
Madelon .... Mme. De Cisneros
Roucher .... Sig. Crabbe
Fouquier-Tinville .... Sig. Arimondi
A Story Writer |

Mathieu, a sansculotte |	Sig. Gianoli-Galetti
An Incroyable	Sig. Venturini
Abbé	Sig. Daddi
Schmidt, a jailor	Sig. Fossetta
Major Domo	Sig. Reschiglian
Dumas, president of the tribunal	Sig. Mugnoz

Conductor, Sig. Campanini

"Siberia" was performed on February 5, 1908, with the following cast:

Stephana	Sig'ra Agostinelli
La Fanciulla	Sig'ra Trentini
Nikona	Sig'ra Zaccaria
Vassili	Sig. Zenatello
Gleby	Sig. Sammarco
Walitzin	Sig. Crabbe
Alexis	Sig. Casauran
Ivan |	
The Sergeant |	Sig. Venturini
The Captain	Sig. Mugnoz
The Invalid	Sig. Gianoli-Galetti
Miskinsky	Sig. Reschiglian
L'Ispravnik |	
The Cossack |	
The Inspector |	Sig. Fossetta

Conductor, Sig. Campanini

Giordano's opera is an experiment along the lines faintly suggested by Mascagni in "Iris," but boldly and successfully drawn by Puccini in "Madama Butterfly" and Charpentier in "Louise." The Italian disciples of verismo are in full cry after nationalism and local color. A generation ago the scenes, the characters, and the subject of an opera were of no concern to the composer. His indifference to anachronism was like that of Shakespeare, whose stage-folk, whether supposed to be ancient Greeks, Romans, or Bretons, were all sixteenth-century Englishmen. When Verdi wrote his Egyptian opera he was content with a little splash of Orientalism which colors the chant of the priestess in the temple of Phtha; the rest of the music is Italian. So the Germans remained German in their music, and the Frenchmen continued to speak their own idioms, saving a few characteristic rhythms for the incidental ballet. Mascagni injected a little twanging of the Japanese samiesen into the music of "Iris" but let the effort to obtain local color stop there.

Nevertheless the hint was seized upon by both Giordano and Puccini, and apparently at about the same time. The former made an excursion into

Russia, the latter into Japan; Signor Illica acted as guide for both. The more daring of the two was Puccini, for Japan is musically sterile, while Russia has a wealth of characteristic folk-song unequaled by that of any other country on the face of the earth. Nevertheless there is nothing more admirable in the score of "Madama Butterfly" than the refined and ingenious skill with which the composer bent the square-toed rhythms and monotonous tunes of Japanese music to his purposes.

The dramatic structure of "Siberia" is not strong. Incidents of convict life in Siberia which have formed the staple of Russian fiction for so long are depended on to awaken interest and provide picturesque stage-furniture, while sympathy is asked for the heroine who obtains "redemption" by an honest love and a heroic sacrifice. Of course, that the requisite degree of piquancy may not be wanting, the martyr is a bawd who surrenders the luxuries of St. Petersburg provided by a princely lover, to endure the privations of the Siberian mines with that lover's successful rival. Only in the "redemption motive," so to speak, is there any likeness between the story of the opera and Tolstoi's "Resurrection," or the play based on that book which had been seen in New York five years before, though the two had been associated in the gossip of the theaters. There are three acts. The first, in which the young officer Vassili, with whom the heroine Stephana is in love, draws his sword against his superior officer, Prince Alexis, and thereby draws down on himself the sentence of banishment to the mines, plays in a palace in St. Petersburg, which the Prince had given to Stephana, who is his mistress. The second act discloses incidents in the journey of the convicts through Siberia, Vassili being joined at a station by Stephana, who has sacrificed her all to follow him into exile. In the third act phases of convict life and customs belonging to the Russian Easter festival are disclosed, and there is a resumption of the dramatic story which now hurries rapidly to its tragic conclusion. Gleby, the seducer of Stephana, is found among a gang of new arrivals at the mines, and the governor of the province, who had been among her old admirers, renews his protestations of devotion and promises her liberty and a life of pleasure. Him she repulses gently and proclaims the joy which Siberia has brought to her. Gleby also attempts to regain his old influence over her, but is cast aside with contumely. Thereupon he denounces her to the community. She and her lover determine to escape but are betrayed and the heroine is shot in her attempted flight. She dies "redeemed."

"Siberia" has no overture. In place of an instrumental introduction there is a chorus of mujiks, which, Russian in idea as well as in harmonization and manner of performance, introduces at once the most interesting as it is the most effective element in the score. Without this element the opera would be deplorably dull, so far as its music is concerned. Giordano's original melody is for the greater part commonplace and unexpressive. The dramatic scenes between the lovers in each of the acts are passionate only to ears accustomed or willing to find passion in strenuousness. Throughout Stephana and Vassili sing as the Irishman played the fiddle—by main strength. In the second act there is much more to warm the fancy and delight the ear. Here the lack of an opening overture is made good by an extended instrumental introduction of real beauty and power. In a way the music is both meteorological and psychological; it pictures the dreary waste of country; it seems to speak of the falling snow and biting frost; but it also gives voice to the heavy-heartedness which is the prevailing mood of the act. It introduces, too, as a thematic motive, the opening phrase of the Russian folk-song which the convicts sing as they enter. This melody is one of the gems of Russian folk-song so much admired by the composers of the Czar's empire that there are few of them who have not put it to artistic use. It is "Ay ouchnem," the song originally created for the bargemen of the Volga, who to its sighing and groaning measures, with broad straps across their breasts, towed heavy vessels against the current of the river. Now it is also used by workmen to assist them in the lifting and carrying of burdens. Giordano makes excellent use of it at the end as well as at the beginning of the act, though as a direct quotation, not for thematic treatment as Puccini uses the Japanese themes in his score. This is one of the characteristics of Giordano's opera and one which illustrates his inferiority as a musician to his more successful rival. In the second act a semi-chorus of women quote again from Russian folk-song by singing the melody of the air known to all musical folklorists by its German title, "Schöne Minka." In the third act there is a Russian Easter canticle which has little of the Russian character but makes an agreeable impression upon the popular ear by reason of its effective use of bell-chimes. There is another folk-melody in the opera which has gained publicity in a manner different from that which made "Ay ouchnem" and "Schöne Minka" widely known; it is the melody of the "Glory" song—"Slava"—which Beethoven used in the scherzo of one of his Rasoumowski Quartets.

The season was not without its humorous incidents. A quarrel of Messrs. Conried and Hammerstein over MM. Dalmorès and Gilibert, who were enticed away from their old allegiance by Mr. Conried but would not stay bought, was one of these. Another was a circular letter sent out by Mr. Hammerstein on December 23d, scolding his subscribers because they were not coming up to his help against the mighty. The letter caused much amused comment amongst the knowing, who asked themselves whether it was the scolding of the innocent or the coming of "Louise," Tetrazzini, and "Pelléas et Mélisande" which turned the tables in the favor of the manager. Mr. Hammerstein seemed to believe that the letter had been efficacious.

APPENDIX I
THREE SEASONS AT THE METROPOLITAN OPERA HOUSE

Season 1908-1909

The twenty-fourth regular subscription season of grand opera at the Metropolitan Opera House began on November 16th, 1908, and ended on April 10th, 1909. The subscription was for one hundred regular performances in twenty weeks, on Monday, Wednesday, Thursday, and Friday evenings, and Saturday afternoons. In their prospectus the directors, Messrs. Giulio Gatti-Casazza and Andreas Dippel, announced a change of plan in respect of the Saturday night performances which had been given for a number of years. Those at the reduced prices which had hitherto prevailed were to be limited to the first twelve and the last two weeks of the season; the others were to be at regular rates. From the end of February till April a series of special performances on Tuesday and Saturday nights was projected. Wagner's "Parsifal" was to be reserved for the customary holiday performances, and there were to be two performances of other works, the proceeds of which were to go into a pension and endowment fund, the establishment of which, it was hoped, would help to give greater permanency to the working forces of the institution. There was a promise of a large increase in the orchestra as well as the chorus, not only to give greater brilliancy to the local performances, but also to make possible a division of the company, with less injury than used to ensue, when it became necessary to give two performances on the same day—one in the Metropolitan Opera House and one in Philadelphia or Brooklyn as the case might be.

These plans were carried out practically to the letter, Mr. Gatti-Casazza reinforcing the Italian side of the house, and Mr. Dippel the German, with artists, scenery, and choristers, as each thought best, under the supervision of the Executive Committee of the Board of Directors of what became the Metropolitan Opera Company as soon as that style could be legally adopted. The management found it less easy to keep its word in reference to the repertory. Eight novelties were promised, viz.: D'Albert's "Tiefland," and Smetana's "The Bartered Bride" in German; Catalani's "La Wally," Puccini's "Le Villi," and Tschaikowsky's "Pique Dame" in Italian; Laparra's "Habanera" in French; Frederick Converse's "Pipe of Desire," and either Goldmark's "Cricket on the Hearth," or Humperdinck's "Königskinder" in English. Only the first four of these works was produced. A promise that three operas of first class importance—Massenet's "Manon," Mozart's "Nozze di Figaro," and Verdi's "Falstaff"—would be revived was brilliantly redeemed. To the subscription season of twenty weeks one week was added for Wagner's Nibelung drama and extra performances of "Aïda" and "Madama Butterfly," and Verdi's "Requiem," composed in honor of Manzoni, having been twice brilliantly performed in the series of Sunday night concerts which extended through the season, was repeated instead of an opera on the night of Good Friday. The extra performances, outside of those of the last week, were the holiday representations of "Parsifal" on Thanksgiving Day, New Year's Day, Lincoln's birthday, and Washington's birthday, and benefit performances for the French Hospital, the German Press Club, the Music School Settlement, and the Pension and Endowment Fund benefit. To the latter one of the Sunday night concerts was also devoted. At the operatic benefit performance, as also at a special representation at which Mme. Sembrich bade farewell to the operatic stage in America (on February 6th, 1909), the program was made up of excerpts from various operas—a fact which must be borne in mind (as must also the double bills at regular performances) when the following tabulated statement of the season's activities is studied. The table which now follows gives the list of all the operas performed in the order of their production and the number of representations given to each in the entire season of twenty-one weeks:

Opera	First performance	Times
"Aïda"	November 16	8
"Die Walküre"	November 18	5
"Madama Butterfly"	November 19	8
"La Traviata"	November 20	5
"Tosca"	November 21	6
"La Bohème"	November 21	7
"Tiefland"	November 23	4
"Parsifal"	November 26	5
"Rigoletto"	November 28	3
"Carmen"	December 3	6
"Faust"	December 5	7
"Götterdämmerung"	December 10	5
"Le Villi"	December 17	5
"Cavalleria Rusticana"	December 17	7
"Lucia di Lammermoor"	December 19	2
"Il Trovatore"	December 21	5
"Tristan und Isolde"	December 23	4
"L'Elisir d'Amore"	December 25	2
"Pagliacci"	December 26	5

"La Wally" .... January 6 4
"Le Nozze di Figaro" .... January 13 6
"Die Meistersinger" .... January 22 5
"Manon" .... February 3 6
"Tannhäuser" .... February 5 7
"The Bartered Bride" .... February 19 6
"Fidelio" .... February 20 1
"Falstaff" .... March 20 3
"Don Pasquale" .... March 24 1
"Il Barbiere di Siviglia" ...... March 25 2
"Siegfried" .... March 27 2
"Das Rheingold" .... April 5 1

SUMMARY

    Subscription weeks 20
Extra week 1
Regular performances (afternoons and evenings) 120
Special representations of the dramas in "Der Ring" 4
Special benefit and holiday performances 10
Italian operas in the repertory 17
German operas in the repertory 10
French operas in the repertory 3
Bohemian opera in the repertory 1
German representations 45
Italian representations 79
French representations 19
Oratorial performance on opera night 1
Double bills 11
Mixed bills 2
Novelties produced 4

    To arrive at the sum of the company's activities there must be added fifteen performances given in the new Academy of Music in the Borough of Brooklyn; twenty-four performances in the Academy of Music, Philadelphia; and four performances in the Lyric Theater, Baltimore. Brooklyn and Baltimore were privileged to hear "Hänsel und Gretel," which was denied to the Borough of Manhattan.

    There was an unusual number of artists new to New York in the company. With Giulio Gatti-Casazza, the Italian General Manager, came Arturo Toscanini, who, though an Italian, chose Wagner's "Götterdämmerung" as the opera in which to make a striking demonstration of his extraordinary abilities as a conductor. It was he, too, who prepared the revival of "Falstaff" and the production of the two Italian novelties, "Le Villi" and "La Wally." His assistant in the Italian department was Signor Spetrino, to whom was intrusted the Italian and French operas of lighter caliber. Of the two German conductors, Mr. Mahler and Mr. Hertz, neither was a newcomer. The former brought about the revival of "Le Nozze di Figaro" and the production of "The Bartered Bride," two of the most signal successes of the season. Mr. Hertz placed "Tiefland" on the stage and added to his long Wagnerian record the first performance heard in America of an unabridged "Meistersinger." Singers new to the Metropolitan Opera House Company were Miss Emmy Destinn (whose engagement had been effected by Mr. Conried some two years before), Mmes. Alda, Gay, Di Pasquali, L'Huillier, Ranzenberg, and Flahaut; and Messrs. Amato (an admirable barytone), Grassi, Didur (a bass who had sung in previous seasons in Mr. Hammerstein's company), Hinckley, Feinhals, Schmedes, Jörn, and Quarti.

A painful and pitiful incident of the season was the vocal shipwreck suffered by Signor Caruso. After the first week of March he was unable to sing because of an affection of his vocal organs. At the last matinée of the subscription season and again on the following Wednesday evening, he made ill-advised efforts to resume his duties, but the consequences were distressful to the connoisseurs and seemed so threatening to his physician that it was deemed advisable to relieve him of his obligation to go West with the company.

Season 1909-1910

This, the twenty-fifth subscription season at the Metropolitan Opera House, began on November 15th, 1909, and ended on April 2nd, 1910, and thus endured twenty weeks. But the twenty weeks of the local subscription by no means summed up the activities of the Metropolitan company; there was a subscription series of twenty representations in the Borough of Brooklyn, a subscription series of two representations each week during the continuance of the Metropolitan season at the New Theater in the Borough of Manhattan, many special performances, and subscription representations in Philadelphia and Baltimore which, though they did not belong to the local record must still be mentioned because of the influence which they exerted on the local performances. The first performance of the company took place in Brooklyn on November 8th, and before the season opened at the official home of the company representations had also been given in the distant cities mentioned which heard twenty performances each. There were also eleven performances in Boston, five in January and six in the last week of March. After all this there still remained before the company a Western tour and a visit to Atlanta, Ga. The season began with a proclamation of harmonious cooperation between the General Manager, Signor Gatti-Casazza, and the Administrative Manager, Mr. Dippel, and ended with what amounted to the dismissal of the latter, who solaced himself by accepting the directorship of the Chicago-Philadelphia Opera Company, which was called into existence after the principal financial backers of the Metropolitan Opera House had retired Mr. Hammerstein from the field by the purchase of the opera house which he had built in Philadelphia and paid him for abandoning grand opera at the Manhattan Opera House in New York, which had been the Metropolitan's rival for four years. The season of operas of a lighter character than those given at the Metropolitan Opera House which was undertaken at the New Theater, a beautiful playhouse built for high purposes by a body of gentlemen most of whom were interested in the larger institution, proved to be a disastrous failure for reasons which are not to be discussed here, but which were not wholly disconnected with the causes which, a year later, led to the abandonment of the New Theater to the same uses to which the other playhouses of the city are put.

The local season can be most clearly and succinctly set forth in tabular form, it being premised that apparent discrepancies between the number of meetings and the number of performances are to be explained by the fact that frequently two, and sometimes three, works were brought forward on one evening or afternoon. These double and triple bills came to be very numerous in the last month, when it was found that the Russian dancers, Mme. Pavlowa and M. Mordkin, exerted a greater attractive power than any opera or combination of singers:

SUBSCRIPTION SEASON AT THE METROPOLITAN

Opera First performance Times given

"La Gioconda" …………….. November 15 ……… 5
"Otello" …………………. November 17 ……… 6
"La Traviata" …………….. November 18 ……… 3
"Madama Butterfly" ………… November 19 ……… 6
"Lohengrin" ……………….. November 20 ……… 6
"La Bohème" ……………….. November 20 ……… 6
"Tosca" ………………….. November 22 ……… 6
* "Cavalleria Rusticana" …… November 24 ……… 7
* "Pagliacci" …………….. November 24 ……… 7
"Il Trovatore" ……………. November 25 ……… 6
"Tristan und Isolde" ………. November 27 ……… 5
"Aïda" …………………… December 3 ………. 6
"Tannhäuser" ………………. December 4 ………. 4
"Manon" …………………… December 6 ………. 3
"Siegfried" ……………….. December 16 ……… 2
"Orfeo ed Eurydice" ……….. December 23 ……… 5

"The Bartered Bride" .... December 24 1
"Faust" .... December 25 5
"Rigoletto" .... December 25 2
"Die Walküre" .... January 8 3
"Il Barbiere di Siviglia" ..... January 15 3
"Germania" .... January 22 5
"L'Elisir d'Amore" .... January 27 1
* "Hänsel und Gretel" .... January 29 1
"Don Pasquale" .... February 2 2
"Stradella" .... February 3 2
"Fra Diavolo" .... February 6 3
"Falstaff" .... February 16 2
"Das Rheingold" .... February 24 1
"Werther" .... February 28 2
* "Coppélia" (ballet) .... February 28 4
"Götterdämmerung" .... March 4 1
"Pique Dame" .... March 5 4
"Der Freischütz" .... March 11 2
* "The Pipe of Desire" .... March 18 2
"Die Meistersinger" .... March 26 2
* "Hungary" (ballet) .... March 31 2
"La Sonnambula" .... April 2 1

* Performed only in double bills.

SUMMARY

Weeks in the season 20
Subscription performances 120
Number of operas produced 36
German operas 11
Bohemian opera 1
Russian opera 1
English opera 1
Italian operas 18
French operas 4
German performances 34
French performances 13
Italian performances 79
English performances 2
Double bills (including ballets and divertissements) 23
Number of ballets 2
Performances of complete ballets 6

EXTRA REPRESENTATIONS AT THE METROPOLITAN OPERA HOUSE

"Parsifal," Thanksgiving matinée, November 25.
"Hänsel und Gretel," special matinées, December 21 and 28.
"La Bohème," benefit of Italian charities, January 4.
"Manon," benefit of French charities, January 18.
"Das Rheingold," serial matinées of "Der Ring," January 24.
"Die Walküre," serial matinées of "Der Ring," January 27.
"Siegfried," serial matinées of "Der Ring," January 28.
"Götterdämmerung," serial matinées of "Der Ring," February 1.
"Stradella," benefit of German Press Club, February 15.
"Vienna Waltzes," ballet, benefit of German Press Club, February 15.
"Parsifal," special matinée on Washington's birthday, February 22.
"La Gioconda," benefit of Italian charities, February 22.
Mixed bill, benefit of Opera House Pension Fund, March 1
"Aïda" and ballet divertissement, benefit of the Legal Aid Society, March 15.
"Hänsel und Gretel" and "Coppélia," ballet, special matinée, March 15.
"Parsifal," Good Friday matinée, March 25.

SUMMARY

Total number of extra performances 16
German operas 7
German representations 11
French opera 1
French representation 1
Italian operas 3
Italian representations 3
Miscellaneous program 1
Double bills (operas, ballets, and divertissements) 5

PERFORMANCES AT THE NEW THEATER

Opera First performance Times

"Werther" .... November 16 4
"The Bartered Bride" .... November 17 2
"Il Barbiere di Siviglia" .... November 25 3
"Czar und Zimmermann" .... November 30 4
* "Il Maestro di Capella" .... December 9 3
"Cavalleria Rusticana" .... December 9 3
"La Fille de Madame Angot" .... December 14 4
"Don Pasquale" .... December 23 3
* "Le Histoire de Pierrot" (pantomime) ... December 28 4

* "Pagliacci" .... January 6 2
"Fra Diavolo" .... January 11 2
"Manon" .... February 3 1
"L'Elisir d'Amore" .... February 4 1
"L'Attaque du Moulin" .... February 8 4
"La Bohème" .... February 17 2
"Stradella" .... February 22 1
"Madama Butterfly" .... March 4 1
"Tosca" .... March 22 1
"La Sonnambula" .... March 23 1
* "The Awakening of Woman" (ballet) ...... March 31 1
* "The Pipe of Desire" .... March 31 1
* "Hungary" (ballet) .... March 31 1
* "Coppélia" (ballet) .... April 1 1

* In double bills only.

SUMMARY

Number of performances 40
Number of operas produced 19
German operas 2
Bohemian opera 1
English opera 1
Italian operas 9
French operas 6
German representations 7
French representations 15
Italian representations 20
English representation 1
Double bills (including ballets and divertissements) .. 15
Pantomime 1
Ballets 3

THE BROOKLYN SEASON

Opera Date of Performance

"Manon" .... November 8
"Tannhäuser" .... November 15
"Madama Butterfly" .... November 22
"Tosca" .... November 29
"Lohengrin" .... December 6
"Martha" .... December 13
"Il Trovatore" .... December 20
"Il Maestro di Capella" and "Pagliacci" .... January 3

"Aïda" .... January 17
"Faust" .... January 27
"Fra Diavolo" .... January 31
"Stradella" and divertissement .... February 7
"L'Attaque du Moulin" .... February 13
"La Bohème" .... February 21
"Otello" .... February 28
"La Gioconda" .... March 7
"Il Barbiere" and divertissement .... March 14
"Rigoletto" .... March 21
"Der Freischütz" .... March 29
"Madama Butterfly" and "Hungary" (ballet) ...... April 4

There was an extra performance of "Hänsel und Gretel," and ballet divertissement on Christmas day. New York was never before in its history so overburdened with opera. The following table offers an analytical summary of the entire season:

Subscription performances 160
Total performances 197
Operas produced 41
German operas produced 13
Italian operas produced 18
French operas produced 7
Bohemian opera produced 1
Russian opera produced 1
English opera produced 1
German representations 56
Italian representations 115
French representations 23
Double bills (including ballets and divertissements) 48
Performances of complete ballets 12

"The Awakening of Woman" and "Hungary" have been treated as ballets in this record simply for the sake of convenience. They were, in fact, a testimonium paupertatis to the feature which had aroused the greatest interest during the dying weeks of the season. The public wanted to see the two Russians dance; the management cared so little for artistic integrity that it did not trouble itself to keep its promises even as to the ballet. "Vienna Waltzes," which had figured in the prospectus, was performed but once, and then only because it was demanded by the German Press Club for its annual benefit. "Die Puppenfee," "Sylvia," "Les Sylphides," and "Chopin," though on the program, were not given, short divertissements after long operas being made to take their place. Operatic novelties promised but not given were: Leo Blech's "Versiegelt," Goetzl's "Les Précieuses Ridicules,"

Goldmark's "Cricket on the Hearth," Humperdinck's "Königskinder," Laparra's "La Habanera," Lehar's "Amour des Tziganes," Leroux's "Le Chemineau," Maillart's "Les Dragons des Villars," Offenbach's "Les Contes d'Hoffmann," Rossini's "Il Signor Bruschino," Suppé's "Schöne Galatea," and Wolf-Ferrari's "Le Donne Curiose." The works which had a first production in New York were Franchetti's "Germania;" Tschaikowsky's "Pique Dame," Converse's "Pipe of Desire," and Bruneau's "L'Attaque du Moulin." In familiar operas the public was permitted to see new impersonations of Elsa, Floria Tosca, and Santuzza by Mme. Fremstad, and of Floria Tosca by Miss Farrar. Notable achievements from an artistic point of view were the representations of "Tristan und Isolde" and "Die Meistersinger," under the direction of Signor Toscanini, and "Pique Dame," under Herr Mahler.

SEASON 1910-1911

The twenty-sixth season at the Metropolitan began on November 14th, and ended on April 15th, thus embracing twenty-two weeks. When the public was invited to subscribe for the season in the summer, performances were promised in French, Italian, German, and English. In the preceding two years there had been talk of producing Goldmark's "Heimchen am Heerd" ("The Cricket on the Hearth") and Humperdinck's "Königskinder" in English, and so there was again this; but on his return from Europe in the fall Signor Gatti put a quietus on it immediately by proclaiming that the project was impracticable. Nevertheless, in midseason he announced an opera in English by an American composer (Arthur Nevin's "Twilight"), and withdrew it, although the public had been told to expect it. Meanwhile a somewhat singular combination of circumstances led to a partial fulfilment of the promise in the prospectus. Mr. Dippel, who had undertaken the management of the Chicago Opera Company (renamed the Philadelphia-Chicago Company after the Chicago season was over and that in Philadelphia begun), had carried with him from New York the purpose to give opera in the vernacular. He was encouraged in this by Mr. Clarence Mackay and Mr. Otto Kahn, the chief backers of the Chicago institution, but the Chicago season was not long enough to enable him to bring it to fruition. For his second season at the Manhattan Opera House, Mr. Hammerstein had promised to produce an English opera "by our American composer, Victor Herbert" (see p. 372). This opera, entitled "Natoma," had been offered to Signor Gatti-Casazza, and an act of it tried with orchestra on the stage of the Metropolitan; but the director did not care to produce it. It was then offered to Mr. Dippel, who accepted it, and produced it first in Philadelphia and then at the Metropolitan Opera House in New York, where the Philadelphia-Chicago company gave a subscription series of French operas on Tuesdays from January to April. To this incident there is a pendant of more serious purport. The Directors of the Metropolitan Opera Company had met what seemed to them a challenge on the part of Mr. Hammerstein by offering a prize of $10,000 for the best opera in English by a native-born American composer. The time allowed for the competition was two years and the last day for the reception of scores September 15th, 1910. On May 2nd the jury of award, composed of Alfred Hertz, Walter Damrosch, George W. Chadwick, and Charles Martin Loeffler, announced that the successful opera was a three-act musical tragedy entitled "Mona," of which the words were written by Brian Hooker, the music by Professor Horatio Parker of Yale University.

The change of plan occasioned by the abandonment of the representations at the New Theater and in Baltimore, the latter city being left to the ministrations of Mr. Dippel's organization, brought with it a large reduction of the Metropolitan forces, but the smaller company nevertheless gave eight performances in Philadelphia and fourteen in Brooklyn besides those called for by the subscription and special representations in New York. Support on occasions had been promised by the affiliated companies in Chicago and Boston, but the little that was offered was not very graciously received by the New York public. Mme. Melba sang once in "Rigoletto," and once again in "Traviata," one of the two performances being in the regular subscription list. Then she was announced as ill, and departed for England. Mlle. Lipowska sang a few times, as also did Signor Constantino (who had been a member of Mr. Hammerstein's company and was now the principal tenor in Boston), but the public was indifferent to these performances of the old Verdi operas.

Interesting incidents were the visits of Signor Puccini and Herr Humperdinck to superintend the rehearsals and witness the first performances on any stage of their operas, "La Fanciulla del West" and "Königskinder," the latter of which was sung in the original German instead of the promised English. For the Italian opera the management had arranged two special performances at double prices; these were popular failures in spite of the interest excited by Mr. David Belasco's play "The Girl of the Golden West," on which the opera was based. The presence of the Russian dancers, who had won much favor in the preceding season, was particularly fortunate in the closing weeks of the season, when another failure of Signor Caruso's voice threatened disaster. Mme. Pavlowa and her companion, M. Mordkin, supported by a very mediocre troupe of dancers, had discovered themselves to their admirers before the opera season opened. They then took part in the Metropolitan entertainments until the end of the first week of January. Thereupon they departed, but came back very opportunely for the second fortnight of March.

The rest of the story may be read out of the following table and remarks. There were twenty-two weeks of opera with subscription performances on Monday, Wednesday, Thursday, and Friday evenings, and Saturday afternoons. At these performances operas were given as follows:

REGULAR METROPOLITAN SUBSCRIPTION PERFORMANCES

Opera	First Performance	Times
"Armide"	November 14	3
"Tannhäuser"	November 16	5
"Aïda"	November 17	6
"Die Walküre"	November 18	4
"Madama Butterfly"	November 19	5
"La Bohème"	November 21	5
"La Gioconda"	November 23	6
"Rigoletto"	November 24	3
"Cavalleria Rusticana" (double bill)	November 25	5
"Pagliacci" (double bill)	November 25	7
"Lohengrin"	November 28	5
"Il Trovatore"	December 1	5
"Faust"	December 10	4
"Orfeo ed Eurydice"	December 10	5
"La Fanciulla del West"	December 26	7
"Königskinder"	December 28	7
"Tristan und Isolde"	January 4	4
"Roméo et Juliette"	January 13	2
"Siegfried"	January 14	1
"Die Meistersinger"	January 20	4
"Germania"	February 1	2
"La Traviata"	February 2	2
"Tosca"	February 8	5
"Die Verkaufte Braut"	February 15	4
"Otello"	February 27	5
"Ariane et Barbe-Bleue"	March 29	4
"Hänsel und Gretel" (double bill)	April 6	2

There were ten Saturday evening subscriptions at regular prices at which the following operas were given, viz.: "Cavalleria Rusticana" and "Pagliacci," "Madama Butterfly," "Il Trovatore," "Parsifal," "Lohengrin," "Thaïs" (Chicago Opera Company), "Aïda," "Königskinder," "Tannhäuser," and "Tosca." There were holiday, benefit, and special performances as follows:

EXTRA PERFORMANCES

Opera First Performance Times

"Parsifal" .... November 24 3
"La Traviata" .... November 29 1
"La Fanciulla del West" .... December 10 2
"Cavalleria" and ballet .... December 24 1
"Hänsel und Gretel" .... December 26 4
"Königskinder" .... December 31 3
"Aïda" .... January 7 1
"Rigoletto" .... January 14 1
"Roméo et Juliette" .... January 21 1
"Die Meistersinger" .... January 28 1
"Das Rheingold" .... February 2 1
"Madama Butterfly" .... February 4 2
"Die Walküre" .... February 9 1
"Siegfried" .... February 13 1
"Götterdämmerung" .... February 22 1
"La Bohème" and ballet .... March 30 1
Mixed bill .... April 6 1

Twenty-six representations; sixteen operas.

There was also an extra subscription season by the Chicago Opera Company, which made a showing as follows:

SUBSCRIPTION SEASON OF THE PHILADELPHIA-CHICAGO COMPANY

Opera First Performance Times

"Thaïs" .... January 24 1
"Louise" .... January 31 2
"Pelléas et Mélisande" .... February 7 1
"Les Contes d'Hoffmann" .... February 14 1
"Carmen" .... February 21 1
"Natoma" (once in double bill) .... February 28 3
"Il Segreto di Susanna" (in double bill) .... March 14 2
"Le Jongleur de Notre Dame" (in double bill) ... March 14 1
"Quo Vadis" .... April 4 1

Eleven evenings, one extra, nine operas, three double bills.

METROPOLITAN PERFORMANCES IN BROOKLYN

Opera First Performance Times

"Il Trovatore" .... November 19 1
"Orfeo ed Eurydice" .... November 26 1

"Tannhäuser" .... December 3 …….. 1
"Cavalleria" (double bill) .... January 3 ……… 1
"Pagliacci" (double bill) ………….. January 3 ……… 1
"Lohengrin" ……………………….. January 17 …….. 1
"Königskinder" ……………………. January 24 …….. 1
"La Bohème" ……………………… January 31 …….. 1
"Rigoletto" ………………………… February 7 …….. 1
"Madama Butterfly" …………….. February 21 ……. 1
"Tosca" …………………………….. February 28 ……. 1
"Aïda" ……………………………… March 7 ……….. 1
"Otello" ……………………………. March 14 ………. 1
"La Fanciulla del West" …………… March 18 ………. 1
"Parsifal" ………………………….. March 21 ………. 1

Fourteen representations, fifteen operas, one double bill.

The novelties produced in the season were Gluck's "Armide," Puccini's "La Fanciulla del West," Humperdinck's "Königskinder," Dukas's "Ariane et Barbe-Bleue," Herbert's "Natoma," Wolf-Ferrari's "Il Segreto di Susanna," and Nouguet's "Quo Vadis."

APPENDIX II
TWO SEASONS AT THE MANHATTAN OPERA HOUSE

The third season of opera under the sole direction of Mr. Oscar Hammerstein at the Manhattan Opera House, New York, began on November 9th, 1908, and lasted twenty weeks until March 27th, 1909. During this period there were five regular performances each week. Had there been no deviation from the rule there would have been one hundred representations, but advantage was taken of occasions which seemed auspicious to give extra performances, and therefore there were also representations on Thanksgiving Day, New Year's Day, Washington's birthday, and to signalize by special attention (and, incidentally, special prices) the coming of Richard Strauss's delectable "Salome." So there were added four performances to the weekly five originally set down for Monday, Wednesday, Friday and Saturday evenings, and Saturday afternoons.

In his prospectus, issued in the summer, Mr. Hammerstein specifically promised to produce "Samson et Dalila," by Saint-Saëns, "Salome," by Richard Strauss, "Le Jongleur de Notre Dame" and "Grisélidis," by Massenet, and "Princesse d'Auberge," by Jan Blockx. He brought forward all of these except "Grisélidis." In the list of operas which he was less specifically bound to perform were Massenet's "Manon," Bizet's "Les Pécheurs des Perles," Verdi's "Falstaff," Bréton's "Dolores," Giordano's "Andrea Chenier" and "Siberia," Puccini's "Madama Butterfly," Donizetti's "Linda di Chamounix," Verdi's "Un Ballo in Maschera" and "Ernani," all of which fell by the board. The chief features of interest in the season were the productions of the novelties, "Salome," "Le Jongleur de Notre Dame" (with Mary Garden in the part of the Juggler, which was written for a man), and "Princesse d'Auberge," and the series of performances headed by Mme. Melba, who opened the sixth week of the season on December 14th in "La Bohème," and concluded her engagement on January 11th in "Rigoletto." Her performances were confined to these two operas and "Otello." For the rest let the following table speak:

Opera First performance Times

"Tosca" ………………….. November 9 ………… 5
"Thaïs" ………………….. November 11 ………. 7
"Samson et Dalila" ………… November 13 ………. 6

"Il Barbiere di Siviglia" ..... November 14 3
"Lucia di Lammermoor" .... November 18 7
"Gli Ugonotti" .... November 20 2
"Carmen" .... November 26 2
"Le Jongleur de Notre Dame" ... November 27 7
"Cavalleria Rusticana" .... December 4 5
"Pagliacci" .... December 4 5
"Rigoletto" .... December 5 5
"Traviata" .... December 12 5
"La Bohème" .... December 14 5
"Les Contes d'Hoffmann" .... December 16 7
"Otello" .... December 25 6
"Pelléas et Mélisande" .... January 6 4
"Crispino e la Comare" .... January 9 3
"Salome" .... January 28 10
"Aïda" .... February 10 2
"La Sonnambula" .... February 13 3
"Louise" .... February 19 5
"I Puritani" .... February 26 2
"Il Trovatore" .... March 1 1
"Princesse d'Auberge" .... March 10 3
"La Navarraise" .... March 20 1

Total number of performances, 111; number of representations, 104; total number of operas, 25; operas composed in Italian, 14; in French, 9; in German, 1; in Flemish, 1; Italian representations, 59; French, 52. The difference between the number of representations and the total of performances of the different operas is due to the fact that on seven occasions two operas were given on the same afternoon or evening.

SEASON 1909-1910

Before beginning his fourth season Mr. Hammerstein opened his house for a season of "educational" opera, as he called it at first, which began on August 30th, 1909, and lasted until October 30th, 1909. In this preliminary season Mr. Hammerstein not only made trial of a considerable number of singers, some of whom remained with him throughout the regular season, but also experimented with operas, some of which went over into the subscription repertory with no considerable change either in casts or settings, while others, notably "La Juive" and "Le Prophète," might well have done so. In them also some singers of notable excellence were heard, like Zerola, the tenor; William Beck, the barytone, and Marguerite Sylva, but after the regular season got under way they were heard from chiefly in the newspapers in connection with the disaffections and disagreements which were almost incessant.

In the season proper Mr. Hammerstein tried to give opéra comique, as he politely called it, though it was largely opéra bouffe, and when the experiment proved a failure he courageously abandoned it. The proceeding has its parallel in the so-called "lyric" opera conducted by the Metropolitan management of the New Theater. After pondering the matter for a space, Mr. Hammerstein substituted opera at popular prices on Saturday evenings for the opéra bouffe, with a result of which we are not in a position to speak.

The promises of an impresario, whether made positively, like "The following operas will be performed," or vaguely, like "The repertory will be selected from the following lists"—an old and favorite device—are always accepted by the public in a Pickwickian sense. Mr. Hammerstein did not disturb the precedents in this respect, but he came creditably near to keeping his definite promises. He said that "Hérodiade," "Elektra," "Grisélidis," and "Sapho" would be among his novelties, and they were. He said that "Cendrillon," "Feuersnoth," "The Violin Maker of Cremona," and Victor Herbert's "Natoma" would also be given—and they were not. Of old works the only ones promised in the list of grand operas and not given were "Crispino e la Comare," "Siberia," "Lohengrin," "I Puritani," "Meistersinger," and "Le Prophète." Most of them were easily spared, especially the two Wagnerian operas, the futility of which in French must have been obvious after Mr. Hammerstein had admitted the failure of his French singers to grasp the spirit of "Tannhäuser."

Here is the tabular record:

Opera First performance Times

Opera	First performance	Times
"Hérodiade"	November 8	6
"Traviata"	November 10	4
"Aïda"	November 12	3
"Thaïs"	November 13	6
"Cavalleria Rusticana"	November 13	4
"Pagliacci"	November 13	8
"Lucia di Lammermoor"	November 16	7
"La Fille de Madame Angot"	November 16	2
"Sapho"	November 17	3
"La Fille du Régiment"	November 22	4
"Mascotte"	November 23	1
"Carmen"	November 25	6
"Tosca"	November 26	3
"Les Dragons des Villars"	November 27	2
"Le Jongleur de Notre Dame"	December 4	5
"Les Cloches de Corneville"	December 4	3

Opera	Date	Performances
"Faust"	December 8	3
"Tannhäuser"	December 10	3
"Les Contes d'Hoffmann"	December 25	8
"Trovatore"	January 8	2
"La Bohème"	January 14	5
"Grisélidis"	January 19	4
"Samson et Dalila"	January 28	2
"Elektra"	February 1	7
"Rigoletto"	February 11	4
"Louise"	February 23	2
"La Navarraise"	February 28	2
"Salome"	March 5	4
"Pelléas et Mélisande"	March 11	3
"Lakmé"	March 21	1
Mixed bill	March 25	1

After the conclusion of the season Mr. Hammerstein sold his Philadelphia Opera House, which had been opened a week after the performances began in New York, to a company of gentlemen largely interested in the Metropolitan, and entered into an obligation with them not to give grand opera in New York City for ten years. It seems appropriate, therefore, to print the following tabular record of his performances during his four years' management of the Manhattan Opera House:

Operas	1906-1907	1907-1908	1908-1909	1909-1910
"Aïda"	12	9	2	3
"Andrea Chenier"	0	1	0	0
"Ballo in Maschera"	2	4	0	0
"Barbiere di Siviglia"	2	0	3	0
"Bohème"	4	0	5	5
"Cavalleria"	8	4	3	4
"Carmen"	19	11	2	6
"Contes d'Hoffmann"	0	11	7	8
"Cloches de Corneville"	0	0	0	3
"Crispino e la Comare"	0	3	3	0
"Damnation de Faust"	0	3	0	0
"Dinorah"	1	1	0	0
"Don Giovanni"	4	3	0	0
"Dragons des Villars"	0	0	0	2
"Elektra"	0	0	0	7
"Elisir d'Amore"	3	0	0	0
"Ernani"	0	1	0	0
"Faust"	7	4	0	3
"Fille de Mme. Angot"	0	0	0	2

"Fille du Régiment" 0 0 0 2
"Fra Diavolo" 4 0 0 0
"Gioconda" 0 4 0 0
"Grisélidis" 0 0 0 4
"Héodiade" 0 0 0 6
"Huguenots" 5 0 2 0
"Jongleur de Notre Dame" 0 0 7 5
"Lakmé" 0 0 0 1
"Louise" 0 11 5 2
"Lucia di Lammermoor" 6 8 7 7
"Martha" 4 0 0 0
"Mascotte" 0 0 0 1
"Mignon" 3 0 0 0
"Navarraise" 2 5 1 2
"Otello" 0 0 6 0
"Pagliacci" 10 9 5 8
"Pelléas et Mélisande" 0 7 4 3
"Princesse d'Auberge" 0 0 3 0
"Puritani" 2 0 2 0
"Rigoletto" 11 5 5 4
"Salome" 0 0 10 4
"Samson et Dalila" 0 0 6 2
"Siberia" 0 3 0 0
"Sapho" 0 0 0 3
"Sonnambula" 3 0 3 0
"Tannhäuser" 0 0 0 3
"Thaïs" 0 7 7 6
"Traviata" 3 5 5 4
"Tosca" 0 0 5 3
"Trovatore" 6 5 1 2

Milton Keynes UK
Ingram Content Group UK Ltd.
UKHW020625050324
438776UK00006B/1060